Ruffo: My Parabola

Ruffo: My Parabola

(La Mia Parabola)

THE AUTOBIOGRAPHY OF TITTA RUFFO

translated by
Connie Mandracchia DeCaro

with additional material translated by
Nathalie Hester, Andrea Stabile, George Nyklicek

epilogue and chronology by
Ruffo Titta, Jr.

notes by
Ruffo Titta, Jr., and Giorgio Gualerzi

discography by
William R. Moran

compact disc prepared by
Syd Gray

GREAT VOICES
series edited by
Andrew Farkas

BASKERVILLE
PUBLISHERS, INC.

Baskerville Publishers, Inc.
7616 LBJ Freeway, Suite 220, Dallas, TX 75251-1008

Library of Congress Cataloging-in-Publication Data

Ruffo, Titta, 1877-1953.
   [Mia parabola, English]
   Ruffo, my parabola : the autobiography of Titta Ruffo = La mia
parabola / translated by Connie Mandracchia DeCaro ; with
additional material translated by Nathalie Hester, Andrea Stabile,
George Nyklicek ; epilogue and chronology by Ruffo Titta, Jr. ;
notes by Ruffo Titta, Jr., and Giorgio Gualerzi ; discography by
William R. Moran ; compact disc prepared by Syd Gray.
      p. cm. -- (Great voices)
   Includes bibliographical references, discography, and index.
   ISBN 1-880909-39-1 (alk. paper)
   1. Ruffo, Titta, 1877-1953. 2. Baritones (Singers)--Biography.
I. Title. II. Series.
ML420.R893A3 1995
782. 1'092--dc20
   [B]   95-33721
                                              MN

Manufactured in the United States of America
First Printing, 1995

List of Selections on CD

1. Dunque io son (1907)—*Barbiere* (Rossini)
with Maria Galvany
2. Pari siamo (1920)—*Rigoletto* (Verdi)
3. Deh non parlare (1911)*—*Rigoletto* (Verdi)
with Giuseppina Finzi-Magrini
4. Lassù in ciel (1908)—*Rigoletto* (Verdi)
with Graziella Pareto
5. Deh vieni alla finestra (1912)—*Don Giovanni* (Mozart)
6. Eri tu (1915)—*Ballo in maschera* (Verdi)
7. Prologo (1912)—*Pagliacci* (Leoncavallo)
8. O Pescator (1912)—*Gioconda* (Ponchielli)
9. Credo in un dio crudel (1914)—*Otello* (Verdi)
10. Era la notte (1920)—*Otello* (Verdi)
11. Sì, pel ciel (1914)—*Otello* (Verdi)
with Enrico Caruso
12. Aman lassù le stelle (1914)—*Cristoforo Colombo* (Franchetti)
13. Sei vendicata assai (1914)—*Dinorah* (Meyerbeer)
14. Tremin gl'insani (1915) —*Nabucco* (Verdi)
15. Già, mi dicon venal (1915)—*Tosca* (Puccini)
16. Adamastor (1920)—*Africaine* (Meyerbeer)
17. Brindisi (1920)—*Hamlet* (Thomas)
18. Demon's aria (1922)—*Demon* (Rubinstein) in Russian
19. Per me giunto (1905)—*Don Carlo* (Verdi)

*Date provided by Syd Gray, producer of the CD,
which is not reflected in the discography.*

Contents

Editor's Preface

BASKERVILLE PUBLISHERS is pleased to introduce its series of opera biographies entitled *Great Voices*. The objective of the series is to enable the interested reader to become familiar with the life and career of those opera singers whose vocal endowments and artistry made opera grand.

Greatness is a value judgment, not measurable in absolutes. Applied to singers, it can only denote a relative standing, the regard in which an artist is held by the public. With this understanding, as the series title implies, we will try to select those opera singers whose career, success, renown, and critical acclaim suggest that they command a high and lasting esteem by a large majority of international audiences.

As a matter of editorial policy, we will try to balance the biographical and autobiographical writings of living artists with those of the past. It is, in part, our ambition to reacquaint readers and listeners with the celebrated models of yesteryear who have served as paragons to emulate. Therefore, the supporting documentation of each biography will vary from subject to subject according to the time available to gain historical perspective and generate critical literature.

Among the recording artists of the opera world there is none who would better qualify for inclusion among truly great voices than Titta Ruffo. For those who heard him in person and even for those familiar only with his recordings, his was and remains *the* baritone voice—brilliant, immensely powerful, and produced with natural ease, like a force of nature. By sheer determination, he raised himself from an uneducated ironworker without any schooling to a polished artist and respected gentleman of the world. His rise was meteoric, with a glorious peak and a sudden decline, tracing the geometric pattern of a parabola, the very word Titta Ruffo himself chose as the title of his memoirs. He penned it in a single summer, without the aid or interference of editors. Ever since its publication in 1937, it has been regarded as the best autobiographical effort by an Italian singer.

It is, therefore, with great pride that Baskerville Publishers launches its *Great Voices* series with the first English language edition of Titta Ruffo's autobiography, *My Parabola*. Our aim is to rekindle interest in this unique artist who deserves to be known and heard by each successive generation of music lovers. We are confident that readers and listeners will approve of our inaugural choice.

Andrew Farkas
Series Editor

CHAPTER 1

The First Steps

I WAS BORN IN PISA on June 9th, 1877, to a family of artisans.[1] My father, Oreste Titta, worked with wrought iron.
Strong, healthy, intelligent, his medium build topped by a thick,
curly head of black hair, with a wide forehead tanned by the
fire from the forge, he looked like a picture of one of the classical Romans. He was habitually called Mastro Titta, for in
his field he was a distinct personality. He was well thought of,
and even though he had only a rudimentary education, he spoke
with a certain eloquence and distinction which was in contrast to his physical appearance. In certain moments his voice
had a soft, almost feminine quality of great dignity; at other
times, instead, he seemed another person and his voice acquired a rough and vehement character which inspired fear.
Indeed, from my earliest days, I had more of a feeling of fearful respect for him than one of affection.

My mother was an extremely sensitive woman with regular features and a rather pale complexion, almost diaphanous;
her clear eyes were very large and of a deep green color. Her
ingenuity was almost juvenile, and her sense of morality quite
severe. There was a look in her eyes at times which I have
never encountered elsewhere. Perhaps I was precocious, but
even as a small child it seemed to me that she was not in harmony with my father, and I wondered how she could have

married him. The family consisted of my brother Ettore, two years older than I, and two sisters, Fosca and Nella. In time there were two others, Settima and Velia.[2]

The first in our family to be christened "Ruffo" was our hunting dog; the second a singer—myself! The third was a doctor of economic and commercial sciences (he is my son) and the fourth—still in God's mind.[3] My father from his youth simply loved hunting, and on holidays went with a congenial group to a preserve near Torre del Lago. One day he received as a gift two handsome puppies, which the group decided to christen: one as "Pellicione," the other as "Ruffo." My father gave the first to a good friend and kept the other for himself. The two dogs were splendid, especially Ruffo, who showed exceptional qualities. He was most handsome—all black, with light spots of white; his ears were unusually long and his beautiful eyes held an expression that was almost human. My father took a great liking to him, almost as if he were a personal friend. Unfortunately, during one of these hunting parties poor Ruffo was shot in the head accidentally and, after a week of suffering, died. His loss affected my father most deeply. He wasn't able to be at peace about it.

My mother, at that time, was carrying me, and when I was born my father wanted to christen me with the name of his most faithful deceased dog. In spite of Mother's opposition— she found this unfair and absurd—Father's will overcame all. I was christened "Ruffo," followed by a middle name— Cafiero.[4] From the day I was born Mother never called me anything but Cafiero, and it was not until much later that I found out it was not my actual name. Like a grown-up, then, I entered the world known as Ruffo Titta. The dear dog's name brought me good luck; later, when I began to acquire a bit of fame, I thought the name would sound better inverted, so reversing my first and last names I became, and am, Titta Ruffo.[5] When my son was born, with my wife's agreement, we decided to give him the same name. I hope that he too will continue this tradition and thereby give me the satisfaction, if the succession is never interrupted, of passing into immortality.

My father was foreman at the German-owned foundry

"Bederlunger" in the Piazza St. Antonio. He had been itching for a long time to leave Pisa for a larger and more important city where he might open his own foundry and fully develop his talents and new ideas. I can state with certainty that he was greatly talented, especially in wrought-iron work, and some of the pieces still in existence today are highly regarded, both in Italy and abroad, as exceptional works of art in this field.[6] If in time I succeeded in making something beautiful myself through proficiency in this noble art, I owe it to his training and example.

Of my life in Pisa, or what is the same thing, of my infancy, I recall very little. However, I believe two incidents are worthy of mention. Both occurred when I was about six years old and both are concerned with a little girl named Gemmina.

Here is the first:

We were living in a working-class suburb on Carraia Street[7] on the second floor of a rather squalid and dismal house, known as the Casone apartments. In the stairwell voices seemed to be magnified, as with an amplifier. With a child's impressionable mind I found something devilish in this, a bogeyman trick. One day I was sitting under the big table and Mother was standing by the window. I suddenly began to whimper without apparent reason and couldn't seem to stop. Mother asked me very gently, several times, to hush, but I increased the dosage (she could put up with a lot from me) until she decided to pick me up and hold me in her arms by the window. Some large baskets of fresh cherries had been conveyed to the front of a fruit stand below—the first cherries of the season. Knowing how greedy I was for them, she said, "See those lovely cherries? If you'll be a good boy and stop crying, I'll buy some for you!" Instantly, as if my voice had been stopped by pushing an electric button, I stopped bellowing. While avidly eyeing the baskets of red cherries, my eye fell on little Gemmina.

She was a lovely blonde child of whom I was very fond— my chosen companion in children's games. I was wearing for the first time that day a brand new smock of blue with white stripes, and there were two large pockets in front. My mother had made it herself. Eager to be seen by Gemmina in my new outfit I begged Mama to let me go down to play with her. Given permission, I was down the stairs and out in the street in the blink of an eye, but to my consternation Gemmina was no longer there. I crossed the street and planted myself in front of the baskets of cherries. An evil genius put an idea in my head. The fruitseller was now inside the shop and couldn't see me. I raised my eyes to the window where Mama had been standing moments ago, but since the blinds were closed I imagined she was inside tending to her housework. In a moment I filled first one and then the other pocket of my smock with cherries, crossed the street and reentered our building.

I took my first mouthful hidden behind the door, then kept eating as bit by bit I climbed the stairs. Suddenly from the apartment landing I heard a man's footsteps and a rough, bellowing voice calling out. *Laudomiaaa!* I trembled with fear. I imagined it the voice of some ogre who was coming after me to denounce my misdeed. Conscience was already punishing me! I stopped eating the cherries and hurried into our flat, as our door was still open. I ran on tiptoe to conceal myself in Mama's room, and had just hidden behind the linen chest when she pounced on me with fiery eyes. She had seen everything from behind the blinds. Her voice shaking, she asked what I was hiding in my pockets.

I was lost, and did not know how to answer. To save myself I made up the story then and there that the fruit vendor had given me the cherries as a present.

More furious than ever at my lie, Mother did not let me finish my story, and tried to pull my hands out of my pockets. She did not succeed, however, and I clutched the remaining cherries in my fist so firmly that they were reduced to a pulp. Red stains appeared on my smock, droplets as of blood spotted the floor. Mother suddenly grabbed me by the arm and dragged me downstairs as if I were a toy—I went from the second floor to the street without my feet touching the ground. Highly agitated she asked the vendor if I had been given a present of cherries, and when she received a negative answer, Mother gave me such a lesson, such punishment as she looked me in the eye, that I would never forget it in a million years.

For several days after the deed, I remember, my black and blue spots were hurting, and my hands were swollen and sore. This, I believe, was the first and last time that Mother ever hit me.

I can't describe my spirits during the days that followed. I did not want to eat, and if Mother had not come looking for me at dinnertime I would have died of starvation; such was the extent to which I was ashamed to look her in the face and to see her at all. My brother and sisters had been told not to speak to me. I did not go out at all, and remained crouched behind the linen chest where Mama had caught me with the theft in my pockets. It seemed to me that everyone knew of my guilt and I did not want to be pointed out as a thief. I visibly deteriorated more and more. Finally Mama, taking a serious view of my condition, decided to forgive me. She came behind the armoire one day, took me by the arm, and gently asked, "You won't do that again?"

I almost fainted, as I had begun to feel that her abandonment of me, were it to continue, would result in my death. I threw my arms around her neck, like a shipwrecked sailor come to safety, crying silently and begging her pardon. She was more moved than I was. She caressed me so much that I felt myself returning to life. From this time forth the thought of taking something that did not belong to me, even the suggestion of such a thought, never came to mind.

And here is the second memory:

One day my brother, returning from school, brought in a silver box which he had found on the slope of the Ponte Nuovo where it enters the via Carraia, near a pile of sand from the Arno which was to be strewn on the street next Sunday when the cortege of the Garibaldisti and his Republican cohorts was supposed to pass through the suburbs. Mother thought that some foreigner might have lost the box—many came to see the beautiful sights in Pisa—when it slipped soundlessly into the sand. She kept it for several days, while carefully scanning the Lost and Found column in the newspaper. Finally, since no one had come forward to claim it, she took it to a silversmith for an evaluation. He told her it was an antique of some value, and that he could offer her 60 lire for it. This small sum, considering the time and our circumstances, was not to be sneered at, and Mama accepted.

My mother thought, with this money, she would offer me and my brother a surprise. We both had expressed a desire to wear sailor's suits, with long pants. So, on the next Sunday (Garibaldi Day) while the via Carraia was full of fluttering banners, and the band was playing the Garibaldi anthem and that of Mameli, the tailor brought the two suits which he had made up and we put them on quite delightedly. I felt like Napoleon himself when I put on that sailor's suit with bell-bottoms, and the beret with the inscription "Italian Merchant Marine." Mother decided that we should go down to Misocchè's[8] for pastries and *acqua dolce*, which was really nothing but plain tap-water with a few drops of anice. We asked her to let us leave right away and wait for her in the street—and in a flash we were downstairs!

Below, who did I see at her door but Gemmina, and my vanity impelled me to rush across the street, leaving my brother behind, and proudly show her my new sailor suit.

"Oh, how nice you look!" she exclaimed right away. And just as quick I told her that when I grew up I was going to be a real sailor. Meanwhile, taking her by the hand, I proposed that we play in the sand. There were two piles near the sidewalk, and we played, as children do, by making little mountains and hills. All of a sudden, withdrawing my hands, I had the surprise, alas, to see them soiled with a material that my nose could readily identify. Instinctively I began to wipe my hands on my sailor's blouse... Well, you can imagine how I decorated it.

Gemmina, disconcerted, stood well away, holding her little nose between thumb and forefinger, unable to keep from expressing vocally what her nose had discovered.

"Now what are you going to do? Your clothes are all stained and soiled!"

With my hands in the air I recrossed the street to join my brother, who was waiting at the door. I shed floods of tears, showing him what had happened. Just at that moment, Mama arrived. Poor dear, to see me in such a state! I could only stammer, "Mother, it wasn't my fault—it was in the sand! Gemma saw it!"

In desperation Mother called a neighbor who sometimes helped her with housework and turned me over to her. The lady rushed me into our house, addressing some choice words to me in the meantime, then tore off my blouse and plunged my hands into boiling water. As if warm water would not do to clean them! Then, still scolding me for being a bad boy, she dressed me in my white-striped smock, shut me up in the house and left.

I stayed the whole time behind the usual armoire where the linens were kept, where Mama found me upon her return, mortified in a different way this time, but in my childish consciousness or unconsciousness, no less mortified than when she'd seen the red cherries in my pocket.

In the meantime, in fulfillment of a long-held desire, my father had obtained a position as foreman in Rome at Signor Riccioni's ironworks, and had left at once for the capital. About a month later we joined him there.

My first ride on a railroad train was for me a very high adventure. It seemed I was going to the North Pole. As soon as I got on the train—naturally, in third class—I rushed over to the window and watched everything that went by, wide-eyed with the most vivid amazement. I was chiefly struck by the solitude and squalor of the Maremma region. The towns there, whose names I did not know, seemed like something out of a fairy tale.

We made Rome in the evening and took lodgings in a small hotel in the via Principessa Margherita, now Principe di Piedmonte,[9] near the station. I believe it was called the "Stella d'Italia." The owner, who was also the porter, led us to the rooms already reserved for us by Father, telling us that he was at our service for whatever we needed. Bidding us good night, he left singing, "O Caroli, you of the dark eyes,/You're probably beautiful, but not for me." This is the first melody which ever entered my head, and one I never forgot.

We opened our shabby suitcases and took out the things

we needed to clean up. Mama stood by the window watching the coming and going of the trains, whose monotonous whistles induced a profound melancholy. Her eyes were full of tears. I crept close to her without saying a single word. In my silence she sensed the participation of my heart.

My father arrived later. He had finished his day of work and was badly concealing his worries. After several weeks we moved to an apartment on the first floor of a house at number 48, via Castelfidardo. Our few possessions had already arrived from Pisa, and we settled in, remaining there for a period of several years. In the evening, as we sat around the table eating our usual vegetable soup and potatoes, I heard my parents' conversation with great interest. Mother often poured forth her homesickness for Pisa. Daddy, on the other hand, went on about our intolerable economic conditions.

This move to Rome had, indeed, caused him much sacrifice. My brother Ettore was sent to elementary school while I remained at home to help Mother in any way I could. I was a sort of miniature domestic; I was anxious to make myself useful even in the most humble service, but I was very unhappy with this kind of life.

One day, going out for bread to a bakery not far from home I wandered a little farther than usual and at some point I heard the blows of hammer on anvil. I was standing before an ironworker's shop. In order to go inside I had to go down a dozen stairs. I halted at the threshold and felt heroic for a moment. Then I took my courage in both hands and went down into a sort of cellar, asking for the proprietor.

A man with a pleasant look on his face said, "I am the owner. What do you want?"

I told him I was looking for work, as I needed to help my family. The man, and a few nearby workers, seeing what a boy I was, began to laugh. I didn't lose heart and said I would work the bellows and do anything else that I was physically able, at my age, to do.

The proprietor reflected a moment, then addressed himself to his most senior worker, exclaiming: "Strange! This little fellow trying to help his family... OK, I'll take you on. Come on Monday. But I warn you, for now I cannot pay you more than 50 centesimi [one-half lira] a day."

I accepted with many thanks and left them, bounding up the stairs. I was radiant with joy! This was the first important step, the first success of my life.

Mama, however, took another view of it, saying I was crazy, and that she would never give me permission, small as I was, to work in such a dangerous place, where I might be exposed to bad words and reprehensible habits.

Crying, I insisted it was beyond me to continue with the housework and spend the rest of the time doing nothing. I assured her that the boss was a good man and had already hired me for 50 centesimi a day, or 3 lire weekly—which I would give to her to help buy salt, sugar, oil and other things we needed.

Mother, touched by my feelings, finished by being practically dragged by me to the smithy to talk to the boss. Very kindly and gently he told Mother that he would take care of me as if I were his own son, and that he had taken me on because my firm decision to help my family had won him over.

Next Monday I appeared in the shop promptly at the appointed hour, and thus my life of work was begun. For a whole week we said nothing to my father. When I came home I had time to clean my hands and face before he arrived. At the end of the week, when I brought Mama my earnings, she hastened to tell him the news. He limited himself to saying contentedly, "Very good! He will be a good craftsman, and later I will take him on in my shop." I wanted him to meet my boss, his colleague, and good feelings developed between the two. Thus, with the express consent of my father, my position was regularized. Mother was not entirely happy about the situation, above all because she saw me in a position inferior to that of my older brother, who was the apple of Father's eye and, who, because he had to attend school, dressed differently than I.

Ettore resembled Mother. He was handsome, blonde and distinguished. Where he was concerned I never experienced any feeling of envy or jealousy; on the contrary, I felt protective of him, and I would have suffered had I seen him in my circumstances. We slept in the same room, which contained two iron beds, a washstand, also of iron, the clothes-rack nailed to the wall, a table of unfinished wood, and two straw-stuffed chairs—this was our Salon Louis XVI! The dining room doubled as our living room and as study for my brother. It was furnished with a square wooden table with carved legs, four chairs like the above, and a clock on the wall that sounded out of tune. On another wall was a picture of Garibaldi, and an oleograph representing a scene from *Il trovatore*, showing Azucena asleep in the jail cell with Manrico, who is embracing the dying Leonora; in shadow at the door was the grim figure of the Count di Luna. So much for our art gallery. Sometimes my brother had schoolmates over, and as my face was covered with soot from the shop and I was dressed in work clothes, I avoided meeting them. I did not wish them to see the contrast between these two brothers.

I had a deep love for Mother. I lived for her and through her, always intent on sparing her the slightest upset. She overwhelmed me with caresses, especially when I came back from the shop. I felt that my affection was deeply reciprocated. On Sundays when my two sisters went out with my brother or my father, Mother preferred to stay at home, and I almost always stayed with her, in spite of her insistence that I go out too for a little diversion. Together at the window we would watch people pass. Sometimes I would nap in her lap, as if I were still a baby. This was for me the most coveted and sweetest reward. How great is maternal instinct! Perhaps she already felt that I would be the material and moral support of her future existence. Still, my early childhood was rather sad. Painful things happened within the four walls of our household, partly due to financial conditions, but above all because of growing discord between Father and Mother. She was always the victim. Poor Mama! I saw her weeping often.

After a year had passed I followed my father to his own foundry, which he owned and managed after Riccioni's death. The shop was part of an orphanage where trades and skills were taught to hundreds of children. My father had fifteen boys under his tutelage who were being trained in the ironworker's trade by him and other workers in the market-place. I spent about six years in the shop, from about the time I was nine to fifteen years of age. It would be too hard for me to narrate my life experience during this period. Father, taking advantage of my serious character and precocity—I already seemed a man—entrusted me with the major responsibilities of the shop. I could not stand his authoritarian (rather, I should say despotic) temperament, so that there were frequent unpleasant disputes between us, if not downright quarrels. I hid everything from Mother because she would have suffered immensely, but there was growing in me a desire to abandon him.

As if this were not enough, I had to fight with fifteen apprentices—who, almost without exception, besides being orphans, were dangerous juvenile offenders, violent and ill-mannered. I was always embroiled with them, and very often fists flew. I was not going to let them take over and often had to defend myself physically.

My nature was becoming increasingly embittered; I became sad, neurasthenic, and drew more and more into myself. My soul became poisoned, my face had assumed a sullen, one might say tragic, expression. Sometimes, crying bitterly, I would recount to Mama all the unjustified scoldings I had received from Father, without satisfaction and scarcely any remuneration of any kind. In fact, I hardly got a whole lira per week. I confided to her that I was longing to run away, and if I hadn't done so yet, it was so as not to be apart from her. She, dear soul, begged me to have patience, and did everything to dissuade me from my plans.

My lack of education worried me. When I saw my brother's books, of which I could grasp nothing at all, the future looked chaotic to me. I could not resign myself to the idea of having to lead such a miserable life—to grow old while hammering iron in a shop, breathing in an atmosphere in which my spirit always risked becoming more brutalized or being drowned. I spent a good deal of time in this anguished state which gave me no peace. The rebellion could not be put off much longer; the inevitable would happen.

One day my father came into the shop, and for some trifling reason I no longer remember, addressed rebukes to me—which seemed unjust—in front of the other workers. I, who had not been afraid of him for some time (he knew it, and this was the basis of a deep resentment) was on this day as impulsive as he, and hurled forth everything that had been weighing on me inside. The workers, who had never seen me in such an excited state, remained speechless. My father himself also remained surprised by my unsuspected audacity. I had scarcely finished my outburst when Father said, "Enough! I don't want to see you again! You are now grown up, so go out and earn your living. Get out!... And never set foot in this place again!"

I replied insolently, "I am very happy to get out of this hell. And be assured you'll never see me again!"

In an excess of rage at these words he grabbed what was on a nearby bench and made as if to hurl it at me.

Bewildered and upset beyond words, I hurried home to Mother. It seemed I was going mad, yet I felt that something most important would happen in my life. I was now free of the things I detested: free, master of my own will.

Mother, seeing me in this state, knew intuitively that I had had a big struggle with my father. I related all to her, and she, most concerned, reproved me severely for having shown him a lack of respect. Sensing me resolute about leaving Rome the very next day, she began to cry. Poor Mama! I remember her as if she were before me today: wrinkles on her forehead, eyes full of the quiet tears which would not stop flowing. With what sad words she revealed her fear of another and perhaps worse altercation when my father came home that evening!

I assured her that nothing would happen, and above all that I would be doing nothing wrong by leaving; that I wouldn't give her the slightest regret, and that all the money I might have the good fortune to earn, I would scrupulously put aside for her. She ought never to weep over my absence—there was already in my voice a sure sense of my future good fortune.

She embraced me fervently, crying, "But where shall you go, my son?"

I couldn't answer. I didn't know. But my plans, for all the buffeting, remained the same.

How to describe my state of mind on the evening of my departure—or, shall I say, my flight? Besides my other feelings, the doubts I felt about the Unknown, the fear of loneliness, of the perils I would encounter—there was plenty to cause a sleepless night. I did not expect much from mankind as I already knew through a certain experience of life that the majority of people aren't often inclined to help their neighbor, and the very ones who profess themselves Christians frequently manifest the most barren egotism.

My brother came to bed and lay down beside me, and not knowing what had happened, bid me the usual good night, thinking me asleep. However, I was wide awake, thinking over what I should do on the morrow. With dawn's first rays of light I looked at my sleeping brother's face, noting his wavy blond hair, the aristocratic expression. I felt the need to look at myself in the mirror. At the sight of my very different face, additionally deteriorated by all I had been through, I threw myself on the bed and wept. Recovering somewhat, I dressed myself, trying not to make noise, but the splash of water in the basin woke my brother, who asked me with some astonishment why I was going to the shop so early. I asked him to get up and go himself to open up, as I was leaving and would not be coming back home.

He didn't believe me and, convinced I was joking, rolled over in bed and murmured *"Bon voyage!"*

CHAPTER 2

Away from Home

I SLIPPED OUT OF THE HOUSE on tiptoe, closing the door behind me very carefully. When I was out in the street I took one last look at the window of Mother's room and slowly walked away, my thoughts returning to her. The sun had not yet risen, and the fresh air, which I gulped in deeply, my mouth open and my eyes half-closed, reinvigorated me. It was a clear April morning as I made my way to the Piazza Termini. I continued on through the Principessa Margherita Avenue and, passing in front of the little hotel "Stella d'Italia," I remembered the family's arrival eight years before and mentally repeated the song which the hotelkeeper had sung *sotto voce*: "O Caroli" and the rest. At the end of the avenue I turned toward the Piazza Emanuele and arrived at the Porta San Giovanni.

When I was in the open Roman countryside the sun had begun to warm the air. I took off my cap and walked bareheaded. I walked and walked without feeling a bit tired. Everything I saw along the way excited my imagination: the wagoneers loaded with wine from the Castelli region, with their Pomeranians as traveling companions; the flocks of sheep bleating with their white voices and their clear, innocent eyes; the enormous ruins of the old Roman aqueducts. I kept on walking without any aim or plan, my head full of fancies.

Anyway, what do plans mean in the life of a man? His destiny is in him: in his mentality, in his will, in his rectitude and decency. So it is in the majority of cases, I say. Whatever the case I was afraid of nothing by this time. It appeared I had solved the problem of life without too much difficulty, and I was not deceiving myself. Sometime later I arrived at Frascati. On the long slope before arriving in the town I met a milk-maid carrying two pails of milk, one each at the end of a wooden bar on her shoulders. I begged her to please give me a little, explaining that I had left home very early and had been walking for some time. The good woman set the pails down on the ground and gave me a good helping from the dipper. While I avidly gulped down the milk, she kept looking at me and then asked me whence I had come and where I was going. I answered that I had come from home and was going to Naples on foot. Shaking her head in compassion, she exclaimed, "Poor boy! That is such a long way!" I thanked her and resumed my journey.

As I arrived in Frascati, whence one could perceive the panorama of Rome in the distance, I felt my heart soften and the vision of mother came back to mind. I kept on and about two p.m. arrived at the Lake Castel Gandolfo. I asked a pass-erby where I could find the villa of the sculptor Monteverde,[10] whose cook was an old friend of the family, and had left some days previously for Gandolfo, where the sculptor usually went in the spring. Thus destiny had led me where I might meet an outstanding person of extreme friendliness and one of the few real Christians I have known: Francesco Forti, a native of Bagni di Lucca, whose goodness of heart and generosity were worthy of heaven. I hurried to find him, and he received me with the most cordial good nature.

I told him my story, and why I was there. I told him I would push on to Albano, where I was counting on spending the night, and from there would continue on in time to Naples. There, I said—and in fact by now it was my intention—I would ship out on a merchant vessel.

He was stunned by this information and advised me to return home, but seeing my determination could not be altered, he refreshed me, without my asking, with an ample meal—fresh bread, meat and wine—and also offered me some money. I refused the latter, however, telling him I had enough in my pockets, and after thanking him affectionately, shook hands with him and resumed my journey.

I arrived at Albano toward 7 p.m. in the evening,[11] and when I arrived at the outskirts of the town, turned left. After one hundred or so meters I found myself in front of the shop of a wheelwright (*carraio*), or in the Roman dialect, *facocchio*. Outside the shop were large hoops of iron, big blocks of wood, old oil presses which were no longer usable, broken wheels and so forth. I guessed that work wouldn't be lacking.

A young workman who was wearing a long, leather apron, called out in his rural accent, "Mastro Peppe, there's a boy here to see you!"

I explained my situation and my desire in a few words to the owner, saying I wanted to work, but he discouraged me immediately, telling me gruffly that he had no need of a helper. I did not consider my cause lost, and retorted that by taking me on he risked no capital, as I would be satisfied to receive only my living expenses—that is to say, about 50 centesimi per day—and in sum, if he didn't think I was worth this small sum by the end of the week, he could dismiss me, having spent only three lire.

My reasoning made him reflect. Naturally he wanted to know who I was and whence I had come. I made him understand that my father was an outstanding wrought-iron artist, that I had grown up in his shop in Rome, but on account of a family dispute I had left to be on my own.

My logic and sincerity persuaded him. He told me to be at the shop at 7 a.m. the next day. I answered that if necessary I could come earlier than that. "Good," he answered. "I'm always here."

I set off for the center of the town, following the main street. I stopped momentarily for a rest at the Ariccia bridge, where my attention was drawn to some ruins in the form of two enormous cones on the right bank below the bridge, next to a little cemetery. I asked a passerby what these ruins were and he answered that they were the tombs of Rome's legendary Horatii and Alba's Curiatii.

I remembered that one evening at the shop these Horatii and Curiatii leapt out of a discussion as six warriors (three brothers each) who passed into immortality for having decided among themselves to wage a long and cruel war between Rome and Alba: all of which kindled my imagination.

Dark was coming on so I walked to the center of town and went into a shop with my last remaining money, 25 centesimi. I bought 10 cm worth of bread, 10 cm worth of cheese, and with the remaining 5 centesimi a large flask of wine in a nearby inn. The wine was so good and heady that it made me a little tipsy. In this happy state of what might be called mixed blessedness I went back to the Ariccia bridge.

It was night by now and I felt tired and sleepy. I walked down a little path like an automaton to reach the base of the tomb. There, amidst the croaking of frogs, the distant barking of dogs and the *grégré* of the crickets I fell asleep, dreaming that Mother rocked me on her lap, caressing my forehead.

I awoke in the depths of the night, the cold interfering with my sleep. The deathly silence and a pale ray of moonlight which appeared and disappeared among the clouds seemed to animate that white marble of the nearby tombs. All of this filled my soul with a sense of death. My head filled with fancies and I was lulled again into dreaming. Half asleep I saw myself as an Ancient Roman, already a man, with a gladiator's chest, magnificent shoes ornamented with a golden boss, a splendid sculpted helmet, a shield and dagger with chiseled allegoric battle scenes, a rich purple mantle...

I awoke to the singing of distant roosters. Reality was quite different. Muscular stiffness and the sharper cold had provoked in me a convulsive yawning and a case of hiccups which accompanied me as far as Mastro Peppe's shop. I was there at six and while awaiting him dozed off seated on the entrance to the shop. When he came he was shocked to find me already there, and asked me in what inn I had spent the night. He could hardly believe the truth, and had compassion for me.

When the shop was open I went to work with zeal. I cleaned

the benches, arranged the iron, swept the floors, cleared away half of the wood shavings which had accumulated everywhere, lined up the different bars of iron, broke up coal for the forge, and afterward was quite satisfied.

When the workmen entered (there were seven of them) they appeared to be surprised at the changed aspect of the shop. Mastro Peppe, who had been watching me in silence, smoking his pipe, came over to me when I had finished my work. Putting his hand on my shoulder, he exclaimed, "You're a fine boy!" He then asked me whether I had eaten breakfast.

I told him that I seldom ate breakfast, and moreover, even if I had wanted to, I wouldn't have been able, because I had not a penny in my pocket. On this pretext I asked him for a regular advance as soon as I'd finished a half day's work because, otherwise, I wouldn't have money for food. He was most kind, and answered that he had decided to pay me one lira per day for the first week, and at noontime advanced me one lira. In some few hours I'd succeeded in winning the respect and the trust of the boss, and the friendship of all the workmen. I truly felt proud.

This first day at work was of great importance to me, as I was convinced that I was a better workman than any of the others; in addition to the many mistakes I saw them making, I noted that jobs that ought to be done in a few hours ate up the entire day. At noontime, when they all went out to dine until two p.m., I remained in the shop, and with my one-lira advance, had some bread, local cheese and good wine brought in. I ate seated on a block of wood near the door, thinking over the events which had caused such a big change in my life. Mother's image was stronger and more indelibly etched on my mind than any other. I felt that she was near to protect me, advise me and bless me. So many thoughts in those hours of solitude and repose in the desolate silence of that enormous shop! I wondered how long I would spend together with this new group, who generally seemed to be hard, uncouth rustics without initiative or aspiration.

Mastro Peppe returned first and asked me how much I had spent on lunch. I told him only 25 centesimi, so that the balance would take care of my dinner and the night's lodging. He was quite sensitive, somewhat paternal. Before the others returned from work he took me to a modest house nearby and introduced me to an elderly lady, who he told me was step-mother to Righetto, his youngest apprentice. He spoke very highly of me, explained my circumstances to her and charged her with arranging for me to sleep well there that very night. The lady agreed, saying she would have a room prepared as well as she could, a tiny room near her stepson's. A price of 30 centesimi per night was agreed upon. When we got back to the shop Peppe told Righetto that I'd taken a room in his house. The youngster slapped me on the back in friendship and ca-maraderie. All this gave a great lift to my depressed spirits, and I kept on working till evening with more confidence.

At day's end, somewhat tired, I went to eat in an inn nearby, on the main street of the town. The owner was called Sor Giuliano. He was a most affable old man, who quickly took a liking to me, so much so that for only 40 centesimi he filled my stomach most satisfactorily, and also offered me a large glass of wine, which played the same trick on me as the wine I had drunk the night before.

Arriving home to go to bed, what was my unpleasant sur-prise but to see that Righetto's stepmother had prepared a straw mattress for me, on the ground, in one corner of a dark room where she kept corn and potatoes, and on the wall strings of garlic which looked like prehistoric plaits of hair. There was neither a blanket nor a washbasin in this dismal hole, not fit for a dog.

Choking down the sense of humiliation I felt growing in me, I reflected to myself that Righetto's stepmother had cer-tainly never been a mother. Still, with that spirit of adaptation to circumstances which was always with me, I went to sleep peacefully, warmed by my vision of Mother, who was cover-ing me with my old woolen blanket and tucking me in bed.

I continued for several weeks in this monotonous, sad way of life and gradually began to get along well with my fellow workers. I never gave up my habit of eating lunch alone in the shop. After gulping down my usual meal with a little bread and some other small morsel, I would set to work on various little jobs quite different from those done in a simple wheelwright's shop. I made small implements that were useful or necessary to me, steel graving-tools of various sizes, hammers to work iron like those I had made use of in my father's shop, etc. Modesty aside, in a few years I had become a pretty good artisan, and for my age (I was not yet fifteen) I had already made some rather important pieces. Thus, having the necessary tools, in my spare time—always the midday hours of repose—I could make interesting and pretty things. Since the boss had observed this serious side of my character, he entrusted me with a key to the shop, and this profited me and gave me great joy, as I could come in at five-thirty or six o'clock and work all alone until seven.

After a time I proudly presented Mastro Peppe with a beautiful rose, complete with buds and foliage—not one bought from the florist, or one plucked from a garden, but one drawn in wrought iron by the blows of a hammer. In this artistic trifle I had poured all my skill and pride, and it turned out to be a little masterpiece. As the workers entered the shop one morning I surprised the boss, asking him to accept the gift in recognition of the kindness he had shown me. He stood there stunned. He could hardly believe I had been the creator. He showed the other workers who, astonished themselves, regarded me with disbelief. It seemed impossible to them that such a perfect gem could have been fashioned by a child like me.

I gained a certain popularity in the neighborhood thanks to my creation, especially at Sor Giuliano's inn. His fondness for me grew with every passing day. When I went to him for supper he greeted me affectionately, continually praising me to the habitués as a fine young boy, serious, well-mannered, and a true artist. He insisted that I would become a great man. These panegyrics and prophecies didn't go to my head. I pushed on with ordinary life, never looking for other distractions. I wrote several letters to my mother, though I was careful not to give her a precise address for fear she might come and take me home. I wrote her that I was working, that I was saving my money exclusively for her, and that one of these days I would bring it to her. So she shouldn't worry. On my part, I had no news of the family.

One Sunday I asked and obtained permission from the boss to stay in the shop since I wanted to make him another complimentary art object. This time I moved from the plant to the animal realm and fashioned a "tarantula," which was what we called the salamander. I worked on the little beast for some hours, spending most of the time chiseling out its eyes and its little claws. When it was finished, to make it appear real I smeared it with green soap. Then I climbed a ladder and attached it to the ceiling. From a distance it really looked like a living tarantula.

The next morning, when work was already intense in the shop, I pointed out the reptile to my mates. At this they abruptly stopped working, alarmed by the animal, saying it was most poisonous. Suddenly they were throwing hammers, stones and pieces of iron at the ceiling, but the animal did not move. Finally Remo, the senior worker, got hold of a long iron bar, trailed it along the ceiling and the tarantula came loose and fell on an anvil. I can't describe the uproar which broke out when the tarantula, striking the anvil, produced a metallic sound. Yes, it was so perfect that even when I picked it up and showed it to them, they still weren't sure whether it was real or not.

When I had washed and polished my salamander they couldn't stop admiring it. Everyone wanted it for himself. They only quieted down when I told them that I had made it as a gift for Mastro Peppe to use as a paperweight. I put it on his table, and when he returned I gave it to him. He was so pleased by this proof of my gratitude that the following week he raised my salary. Meanwhile, the fame of my new work and of the trick I had played on the workmen spread around the town, and my popularity increased.

One Sunday the workmen took me to an inn where a bocce ball game was going on under a large pergola. They introduced me to everyone as "the Master." I laughed, happy with my popularity. However, I protested that I was no artist, just an artisan of wrought-iron work and they should call me Ruffo.

They all vied to offer me wine, which, however, I refused or accepted in great moderation, alleging reasons of health.

I became thereafter a "regular" at this inn. As for those pleasures I might call aesthetic, I had to curtail them almost entirely because in imitating me the other workmen were losing too much time at their regular jobs. The last thing I made as a gift for Sor Giuliano, the innkeeper, was a good luck charm in the form of a cornucopia. He attached it to the door of the inn, and my homage to him reinforced his goodwill and esteem for me.

After three months my salary was raised to three lire a day. I was able to save two, keeping only one for all my needs, including that of education, the lack of which was goading me more and more. One day I bought a copy of *The Count of Monte Cristo* by Dumas. This book exerted quite an influence on my mind, and excited my lively imagination. It was an old secondhand book, abundantly illustrated, and that which struck me especially were the vignettes and pictures with pertinent captions, which made me dream for the first time of strange characters. I went through the book avidly and fell in love with the characters one after the other. This book became my inseparable companion. How it delighted me, made me shudder, cry and daydream!

Most sympathetic of all the various characters was Edmond Dantes: I pictured him in my imagination and I envied him, wanted to *be* him. And the Abbé Faria—what a marvelous apostolic man. How much heart and what angelic resignation in that tremendous prison of the Chateau d'If! I still recall today the emotions this book roused in me and can say that it constituted the first stimulus toward my development of a modest literary culture.

From then on I began to read more and write more fluently and correctly, or should I say, less incorrectly. All the passion which I had dedicated before to my works of art was transfused to literature. My ordinary life continued to flow on as usual between the shop and Sor Giuliano's inn, which I visited ever more frequently. I was now taking my noontime meals there as well, which gave him much pleasure. For only a few soldi more I could eat more healthily and my strength profited by it. After meals I would stay awhile to talk with the old man of many things. I would describe the characters in the books I was reading. However, he wasn't much interested in them. His favorite discourse concerned the memory of his wife, who had died of consumption in the flower of her youth. He kept a photograph of her in the bench drawer, amongst many dirty, dog-eared papers and sometimes, while telling me of her beauty and gentleness, tears would come into his eyes. I tried to cheer him up and we always ended by drinking half a glass of the best. I had finally become accustomed to the good wine of Castello. I felt that a glass with my meals was good for my health and put me in a contented frame of mind, unusual for my temperament, which was inclined to melancholy.

Sor Giuliano, who knew that I often went to the bocce ball inn, was somewhat jealous of my patronizing the place, and advised me to be careful, as the place was frequented by low company, dangerous to a serious-minded boy like me. I paid no attention. Next to the inn was a wheat field, and I, during bocce games that held little interest for me, preferred to lie in the field watching the limpid blue sky—such an azure that it could only have been painted by God. I stayed there for hours in contemplation of the infinite, and my imagination abandoned itself to exaltations which stole me away I don't know how many times from everyday realities. While in this blessed state between joy and melancholy, when the sun set, the thought of my mother far away would take over and tears would streak across my face.

My reading of novels and my great desire to live in the open with full freedom, as did some of the characters I read about, was beginning to make me hate the shop and my work, which interfered with my cherished dreams. In the evening, strolling around, I looked at everything through different eyes. My powers of observation had become acute and were getting more and more so every day. I often passed by the Ariccia bridge, and the sight of the mausoleum with its two cones where I had passed my first night, awakened in me a sense of wonder. It seemed to me that I had already come a long way in life and made great progress.

With some of my savings and the help of Sor Giuliano I went to a tailor friend of his and had him make me a good black suit, for which, if I recall rightly, I spent less than 50 lire. I also bought two shirts and accessories, so I could dress decently, if modestly. Besides this, I bought a nice warm woolen blanket for my poor bed. I felt that I was bettering myself in every way from day to day, and that the time would come when I would achieve something unusual. My outstanding traits, strengthened a good deal at this time, were my frugal and prudent spirit, and my desire to be distinguished. This last was almost exaggerated. I wanted to be different from other boys of my station. I liked to dress with a certain elegance. I had a weakness for a white shirt with a flowing black tie. I couldn't stand pants with baggy knees, and couldn't go to bed at night without being sure that I'd put my pants away so carefully that I'd find them in the morning looking as if they'd been ironed. This last habit has served me faithfully and it seems to me that it was a sign, slender though it might have been, of that internal aesthetic sense that directed and ruled my whole life. When I first put on that nice black suit, linen shirt, flowing tie, soft black hat and black oxfords I really felt proud, and had only one wish: that Mother could see me.

It happened that one Sunday I suddenly felt an overpowering impulse to return to Rome. Combined with homesickness for Mother and my brother and sisters was an inner longing to show Father that I could live independently of him. However, this impulse soon left me. I realized that it would have been a mistake. I did not have enough money set aside for Mother, and perhaps I would be unable to tear myself away. I satisfied myself with having some photographs made of me in my genteel new attire, and sent one of them to Mother. The photo turned out well—I gained from it. I am not physically goodlooking, but I did look so in the photo, and in my new outfit I looked serious and dignified, which was my ambition.

When Sor Giuliano saw me so elegantly dressed he was

much impressed, and invited me to dinner, during which he admired me affectionately, as if I were one of his own. Dear old man, whose bones already long since have become dust, how many events both happy and sad have befallen me since those days. The little boy whom you befriended long ago in Albano did, as you prophesied, in a few years become a world-wide celebrity; but if ever there is any correspondence of feelings and thoughts between the living and the dead, know that I have never forgotten you. In my heart you are still alive. I still see you behind the counter of the inn, with the portrait of your lost life-mate in your hands, wiping away a tear with the edge of your apron, and suddenly, hearing my words of comfort, raising your honest face to me, between laughter and tears, as if to thank me.

Luck was always with me.

One morning while the shop was busy a two-wheeled cart pulled by a white horse and driven by a man in his forties who impressed me immediately pulled up at the door of the shop. Robust physically, merry and frank in appearance, with a green velvet coat and black leather boots covered with dust, with small moustaches and a Spanish-style beard, he appeared to be a handsome, dashing and eccentric country farmer—and in fact he was.

He got out of the cart and asked for Mastro Peppe. Mastro Peppe greeted him like an old acquaintance, shouting from the back of the shop, "Oh, dear Mr. Romolo, how are you? It's been months since we have seen you."

Mastro Peppe shook hands effusively and asked the reason of his welcome visit. The other, indicating the bottom of a broken oil-press, asked if it could be repaired. The broken base of the press was very heavy and it took three workers to get it down. A discussion began among them on the possibility or lack of it that it could be put in order. After discussing it a bit the boss and his workers finished by declaring that there was nothing for it but to send it to a foundry.

Vexed by this report the farmer took off his hat and passed a hand over his forehead, which was bathed in sweat. "Damn!" he said. "I didn't need this."

I, who had heard everything, but said nothing until then, intervened and, having observed the enormous cast-iron support closely, I affirmed that it would surely be possible to repair, except that here we lacked the tool required to do so. This tool was the *cricche* (a certain wrench) which could be purchased in Rome. The farmer looked at me a little astonished, asking me explanations of the way I would go about making the repair.

It would take too long to describe how, in about a week of hard work, with the help of the wrench and of three workers, I was able to make the oil-press as good as new. This success brought about a certain antagonism between me and the other workers, especially the more senior. They had suddenly found themselves in an obviously inferior position. They saw in me someone who would in time supplant them all and from that day forth they were no longer so affable toward me. Even Mastro Peppe became a little distant. He who had recently extolled my exceptional qualities to the farmer—praising the works of art I'd created and given to him, my seriousness, my precocious good judgment—now appeared almost sorry that he had.

Sor Romolo, who had had his eyes on me from the first moment, had been coming to the shop almost every day during the work on the press. When he saw the work finished he was so happy with it that, besides paying Mastro Peppe the agreed price, he wanted to make me a present of 25 lire. I didn't want to accept it because I'd already been paid by my boss. The farmer, astonished by my refusal, begged the *padrone* to persuade me, saying that I merited it. Mastro Peppe, though reluctantly, induced me to take the money. Thanking him, I let the farmer know that, should he need some other work done, I was free on Sunday and would take care of it for the same amount that Mastro Peppe paid me on other days. That was what the farmer wanted to hear.

I didn't immediately take into account the fact that my proposal amounted to a false step that put me in competition with the boss's interests—but he didn't hesitate to make me aware of it. From that day I was no longer in anyone's good graces. Jealousy and rancor oozed from all the faces. Certainly I wasn't a timid or cowardly sort. I'd already been trained in fighting after the manner of the boys in my father's shop, threatening and bullying. Surely I wouldn't lack the courage to defend myself if need be, all the more if I were subjected to an unjust remark. If I had already rebelled against my father, how much more vehement would be a revolt against a stranger? I preferred diplomacy to violent reactions, but with these people it took more than diplomacy to prevail. The only course left me was a change of air. Therefore, when I saw that my position was untenable, one Saturday evening while we were being paid I surprised everyone by announcing to Mastro Peppe in a loud voice that I wouldn't be back next Monday. I had the strength to thank everyone for all the kindness that they had already shown me, but also to add that from certain details and from certain expressions from someone I was aware that I had come to be disliked, and I didn't intend to remain any longer in paradise to spite the saints: I was therefore resigning. Finally I shook hands with everyone, asking them not to think ill of me, and if I had been lacking in something, not to wish me ill because of it. I said goodbye to Mastro Peppe in my most courteous manner and thanked him for the hospitality granted me in his shop. Then I went out, heading straight for Sor Giuliano.

That evening the dear old man was waiting for me with more impatience than usual. He had prepared lamb with olives, a dish he cooked perfectly. I thought a lot about the strangeness of human nature. The conduct of all the workers on the eve of my goodbye would merit a page by itself. Men who had almost come to hate me showed clearly by their faces how sorry they were for the injustice done me, and some even expressed the desire to have me back, not just remorse. Everyone had shaken my hand without offering a word. All this was going through my mind in Sor Giuliano's inn.

As I entered the inn he exclaimed, "I made a lamb that will make you remember me for a long time."

When I told him that I had left the shop for good, he dropped the ladle he had been holding into the cooking pot and remained pensive for some minutes. I could see by his expression that he knew I would leave Albano, and he would lose me. Seeing his dejection I patted him on the shoulder and told him to cheer up, it wasn't an occasion to be gloomy, nothing had happened.

"Well, dear boy," he responded at length, "you'll be going away now, who knows where, and you'll never come back here. For that I am sad. Tell me all about it."

When he learned everything in detail there was an outburst of indignation.

"If one of them comes into my inn he had better watch out. I'll give him a piece of my mind!"

In the meantime he would certainly have gone at all costs to speak to Mastro Peppe if I hadn't expressly prohibited it. Hearing that I would be leaving for Naples in a few days, he advised me to go see Sor Romolo, who had been so kind to me. When asked if he might accompany me there he couldn't believe his ears.

At home I found Righetto in the kitchen, quite upset by what had happened. He was a rough sort of fellow, and during the time I'd stayed with him we had never become familiar. Yet this evening I became aware that there was more of timidity than hardness in his character. He told me how, after I had left the shop, a tumultuous discussion had broken out among the workers. Each wanted to blame the other, and even Mastro Peppe bawled out the senior worker. I must admit that Righetto's story gave me much pleasure, and I was pleased with myself for having been able to leave the situation with dignity, leaving everybody with regrets rather than rancor.

The next day, at noon, in the company of Sor Giuliano, I set out toward the farmhouse of Sor Romolo.

CHAPTER 3

At the Farmhouse "Del Riposo"

W E ARRIVED, OUT OF BREATH, about two-thirty in the afternoon, at a farmhouse about halfway between Marino and Genzano. We entered where it was written, if I remember correctly, *Fattoria del Riposo,* and underneath in large letters, *Sor Romolo.* Following a long avenue of cypresses and Roman pine trees, we reached open ground in the middle of a large vineyard. Dogs began to bark, and numbers of chickens of every color ran away flapping their wings at our approach. The ruckus brought forth the owners. At the nearest door a woman of mature age appeared, dressed in black muslin and wearing white stockings, who asked, in a country accent, what we wanted.

Sor Giuliano addressed her by name. "Why, Sora Rosa, don't you know Giuliano the widower anymore?"

Sora Rosa, putting her hand up on her forehead to shield her eyes, recognized him, and was happy to see him. Informed that I was the object of the visit, she invited us in, saying her husband had gone to the *grotte,*[12] but would be back shortly. The lady, as the reader will have surmised, was the wife of Sor Romolo. She offered us some sweet wine. While she spoke her eyes were always upon me, full of curiosity and attraction. Naturally, I had put on the black suit, the white shirt and flowing tie. When she heard that I was the boy who had done the emergency job so efficiently, she seemed startled, as if she found herself in front of a great personage. She said she knew all about me from her husband, who often spoke of me. Sor Giuliano did not tire of singing my praises now, stronger than ever—the usual praise of my seriousness, my good heart, my intelligence and education. And I, embarassed, thanked him tirelessly.

The good lady, the classical type of the farmer's wife, brought out some pizza with prosciutto, peaches and figs, in addition to the wine. She was falling all over herself to show me her happiness to see me in her home. At one point she remarked regretfully: "It's too bad he is working at Mastro Peppe's, or my husband would be glad to have him work here at our farm."

The look on my old friend's face at these words! He jumped to his feet, exclaiming, "My dear Sora Rosa, the Lord sent me here. This boy is free and I would be happy if you employed him! Just last night he quit at Mastro Peppe's!"

The good lady, overjoyed, explained that for some time now her husband had been determined to go to Albano and ask Mastro Peppe to release me to do needed work at his farm.

So, you see, Fate was always good to me, and I had a fine new position without a single day of unemployment.

When the farmer arrived, his rejoicing was hard to describe; I thought he was about to hug me. Told what had happened he finally shouted: "You did well to quit them!"

And his wife added, "What good fortune! It was the will of God to send this boy. Just looking at him is a pleasure."

Sor Giuliano was mad with delight, too. I already felt at home. They kept us there for supper with them, and then the farmer accompanied us in his cart as far as the Ariccia bridge. We agreed that the following day I would move to the farm where there was much work awaiting me, and settle in. Both Sor Giuliano and I were very happy that my new situation might give us the opportunity to see each other often.

The next morning, when about noontime I arrived at the farm, both husband and wife were awaiting me. I brought with me, in a large suitcase which I had purchased second hand some time before, the few clothes I had and my books. I was now dressed in blue fatigues with pants to match. Sora Rosa, happy to see me again, took me right away to see the little room she had prepared for me. It was the simplest room, but very neat and furnished with all the necessities—modest and clean. Back downstairs I saw the dining room table already set, and immediately realized that in this house a good table was not the ultimate in life.

After a copious lunch—during which, in spite of Sora Rosa's urging, I drank no wine, as I wanted to keep my head clear for the work ahead—the farmer took me to a sort of cellar where he showed me three old oil-presses. Left unused there for a long time, all covered with cobwebs and rust, they seemed unserviceable by now. Would it be possible to put them in running condition?

First of all I had them carried out onto the threshing floor by some of his peasants so that I could make a more thorough inspection and decide what was to be done. In the sunlight they looked more dilapidated than ever, but I thought they could be repaired, and set to work on them at once.

After fifteen days and much sweat—dirtying quite a few shirts—the three presses were completely restored: cleaned, polished, and put in perfect condition, all with the least expense, because, except for fuel oil, petrol, sandpaper, and two files for putting the main screws in order, I managed to spend less than fifty lire, while the presses were now worth several thousands. The farmer rejoiced, particularly because he hadn't been wrong in his estimate of my ability, but also because of the speed of the repair. At the end of the week he paid me the same sum I had been receiving at Mastro Peppe's, but with the addition of room and board, not to mention the good wine, which was never lacking, and was for me, as it would have been for anybody, the best treat of all. This way I could save all my pay. I was blessed.

On Sunday I asked permission to go visit Sor Giuliano, which he gave me at once—offering, furthermore, to come in the evening with his cart to pick me up. I had a very happy Sunday, eating with my old friend, spending an hour at the bocce inn, where I saw several of my former workmates, who were quite pleasant. Nor did I omit going to greet Mastro Peppe. That evening, toward seven, the farmer came with his wife, right on time to take me back.

I should say here that Sor Romolo and Sora Rosa had no children, and in a short time became unbelievably affectionate, especially the lady, feeling that her life had been enhanced by the presence of one who was, in her words, a *fine, good boy*, in the household—one who in addition was very useful to their interests. At the end of the week, when they saw that the work was far along and knew that another week would be enough to finish I noticed a marked displeasure on their faces. They loved each other a lot, these two; they were two souls born to stay together, and the only shadow in their married life came from the lack of children. This regret made the knowledge that I was about to leave all the more sad for them. Without wishing to I often heard their conversation from my room. They vied with each other to find some way to keep me from leaving, or at least to delay my departure as much as possible.

When the presses were finished and delivered, each in its proper place, ready for use, Sor Romolo, in addition to my second week's pay, offered me fifty lire. I refused it, saying that he and his wife had been almost too good to me, and that I had saved my entire earnings. The way they had treated me, and the pleasure of their company, and the sharing of meals with them really had meant more to me than any sum of money. When I informed them that, if there was no other work to be done, I would be leaving, Sora Rosa, although there *was* no other work to be done, pretended not to understand, and insisted she needed me still retained me for another week with the greatest pleasure. Nor was my pleasure, naturally, any less.

For the third week, in order to do something useful, I went on my own initiative to Albano, where I bought brushes, varnish, and other such things. I revarnished all the doors of the house, whitewashed the farmhouse office, improved the appearance of the writing desk (unfinished wood and quite unattractive), put brass handles on the doors and drawers. I did countless other little things which I won't mention. After one week the house certainly looked much different.

To work this way, earn money this way, and save it—this was a joy for me as well as a satisfaction for my employers. And their satisfaction was such that for the fourth week I was served first at table, in spite of my protests. In short, during the brief period of my stay, the couple had become as fond of me as if I were their own son. Indeed, when I spoke of my mother (which was quite often) Sor Rosa gave evidence of a feeling of jealousy and said that my mother was more fortunate than she, as she had children in the house to brighten her life.

On Thursday of my fourth week Sor Romolo took me to a shoemaker in Genzano and had him measure my feet. I asked him his purpose, and was told, "You'll see at the right moment."

The next Monday, the day that I should have left, there was the shoemaker with a beautiful pair of riding boots that reached almost to my thigh, like the ones Sor Romolo wore when he went hunting. When I put them on I was stunned. I protested, saying I did not merit so much, but they would be a keepsake, and besides, just the thing for going to Naples on foot, which was my plan.

"What? Naples and Palermo?" the farmer interrupted, directing a smile at his wife. "You are going to stay here as long as you like. We will go hunting together and you will keep the farm in order."

You can imagine with what joy I heard the news. I could no longer contain myself.

I embraced Sora Rosa (her husband intimidated me a bit) and thanked her and her husband, too, for their kindness. The dear woman's eyes were bathed in tears.

"My son," she said, "where do you want to go to be better off than you are here? We love you, and by now we are used to seeing you here; you're like a son. If you leave us, there will be nothing here for us but weariness and sadness. Can't you see that Romolo can't do without you?"

That day at mealtime we were happier than usual. We talked until late and, upon bidding me goodnight, Sor Romolo told me that tomorrow we would lunch with a farmer friend, tenant of one of the estates of Prince Torlonia. He would always take me with him, since I had become, no longer his dependent, but his inseparable friend.

He found me a good gun and taught me how to use it. We often went hunting. Yet I disliked shooting birds. Once I was pressed to shoot at one which was flying close by me and I hit it. It was a little blackcap, and I had shot it between the eyes. I held it in my hand for a few minutes and felt such a feeling of sadness and regret that I was never capable of firing a shot from that day on.

I remonstrated with Sor Romolo, saying that it was cruelty to shoot at these little creatures. However, he was so used to hunting by now that it had no effect on him; on the contrary, it often happened that the more he killed, the happier he was about it. On the hunting trips which followed I always accompanied him, but while he was minding the birds, I read my books.

The months passed, save for the inevitable moments of filial nostalgia, like an enchantment. I felt myself surrounded by tenderness and consideration, and to be worthy of it, when there was nothing to do, I invented work. I also had, or took, time to give my fancies free rein. I always got up early, while the old folks were still asleep, opened the window and breathed deeply of the balsamic morning air, happily letting the fresh breeze caress my face and ruffle my hair, watching the sun rise and gradually inundate the immense Roman plain with its divine light. The song of the rooster, so startling when one is alone and in silence, speaks with one's own soul, makes itself felt, varying with its harsh happiness the soft sweetness of the birds', that in their idiom, unknown to us, seems to rise in competition to the highest peaks of feeling, and vie to celebrate the glory of creation. I would half-close my eyes in ecstasy—mother would come to me in my imagination, speaking to me, gently complaining about my long absence, and an overpowering desire to see her prevailed at once over all my other emotions. I wished I had wings sometimes to fly to Rome, reach the old house, penetrate my mother's room where she was sleeping; to alight on her bed at the head; to caress her until she might wake up and open her eyes and see me happy. Sometimes I stood in the meadow near the threshing floor with a book, immersed in reading, or watching the overarching clouds changing from moment to moment, steering themselves to I knew not what destination. I forgot the time. In this ecstasy I was called back to reality by the voice of Sora Rosa telling me that the *caffelatte* was ready.

One afternoon Righetto, all out of breath, arrived at the farm. He had been sent by Sor Giuliano to tell me that my father was waiting for me at the inn. This unexpected news nailed me to the door. At once my mind went back to our bitter quarrel, but without even a shadow of resentment; no more rage, no more pride, rather an indescribable emotion of affection. His coming to look for me made me feel how much I really loved him in the depths of my soul, and in spite of the differences and disputes we had had in the past, I did not now know, or didn't wish to see in him, any but the best qualities.

I ran straight to the *grotte* to tell Sor Romolo the news. The farmer was strongly affected by this unexpected turn of events, and curiosity to know my father induced him to drive me to Albano in the cart. Sora Rosa, who was in the kitchen preparing our dinner, took the news as if it had to do with a disaster, and in a voice full of emotion said to me, "I urge you to return with Sor Romolo. Tell your father that you are in good hands, are well treated, and that you have nothing to fear."

I reassured her, jumped on the cart with Sor Romolo and Righetto, and we drove off. The farmer, very agitated, whipped the mare and we arrived in Albano much faster than usual. When we were almost there I told Sor Romolo to stop and to wait until I came out to call him. Regardless how I would be welcomed by Father, I would have been very unhappy if the farmer had to witness a nasty argument that could have arisen between us.

My heart was beating tumultuously as I stepped down into the inn. I caught sight of my father sitting where I usually sat, talking with the old man, a liter of wine half-empty in front of

them. I went bravely over and addressed him in a humble tone
of voice. He immediately understood by my approach that
this was no time to scold me. In the end, what had I done
wrong? As a matter of fact, I had only carried out the wish he
himself had expressed that I go out into the world and earn
my own living. Sor Giuliano had surely already told my father
how, in this time away from home, I had become so well regarded in general, how good the farmer couple had been to
me, and of all that had happened, because I found father quite
conciliatory. The expression on his face was more of regret
than wrath.

I was the first to speak. I told him I was very happy to see
him and thanked him for coming. I asked him to pardon me
for not having written, but explained that I had not done so
because I was afraid he was still angry with me. Finally I asked
how Mother was.

He listened in silence, but finally decided to speak. He did
not reprove me for having run away, but for my behavior towards her. He told me that since I had left, Mother was very
upset, hardly sleeping at night, and not a day passed in which
she did not weep for me. The news she received from me she
did not think true. She always imagined me to be in danger, so
that she lived in a perpetual state of anguish—and he had therefore decided to come find me.

In spite of all my efforts, on hearing this I could not hold
back my emotion and burst into sobs. I began to weep softly,
tears that choked me. I wanted to run out then and there,
rejoin Mama as soon as possible, to reassure her that what I
had written her was pure truth, and to give her as proof the
fruit of all my economies. After having told Father how good
Sor Romolo had been to me, I told him that he had brought
me to Albano in his cart and was waiting outside to meet him.

Father immediately told me to call him in. When the two
men stood face to face they shook hands with great emotion.

Sor Romolo, whom my father did not fail to thank most
gratefully for his kindness to me, sang my praises no less generously than had Sor Giuliano, and told my father all the rea-

sons why he and Sora Rosa had become as fond of me as a son, without trying to hide the fact that separation from me would cause them a grave sadness.

With all these exaltations it now seemed to me that they were actually appropriating affections that didn't belong to them. I had a legitimate mother and father, who had given me life and intelligence and energy to go alone on life's road. Although I felt a debt of gratitude toward everyone, how could I cut my soul loose from the bonds of Nature? My father was my father, and in spite of his character, I wouldn't have changed him for any other. And least of all now that I found him meek enough with me and preoccupied with poor Mama.

Still, when he told the farmer that he would take me back to Rome this very evening, I flatly refused. I told Father that there was no reason for worry, and that I could never readapt to life in a shop, that there was nothing more wonderful in the whole world than true freedom of action. Whenever a man had the desire to work and the will to get somewhere, all doors would open. I explained that I did not wish to disobey him, only pleaded with him to let me find my own way in life. He had seen what I had been doing, and my present condition, and thus could reassure Mother and calm her fears.

My firm resolution brought great joy to both Sor Romolo and Sor Giuliano, while it left my father perplexed. He had to understand that he had created a gap between us, and it wouldn't be possible to continue to live together. Still he kept insisting that I return, imploring me to think of Mother, my brother and my sisters. All this was surely worth my serious reflection, if not worth leaving for. My decision, then, was to remain, though I assured my father that I would return to Rome as soon as possible, and begged him to embrace Mother and comfort her.

We accompanied Father to the station. He climbed in the train with a slow and tired step and we separated without a word. My heart was beating wildly. I wanted to jump on board, embrace him and leave with him. With great difficulty I restrained the impulse. When the train was in motion my father waved at the farmer for the last time, and looked at me with such a sad, disillusioned expression in his eyes that I have it with me still, imprinted on my soul.

No sooner had the train left than I could bear no more and wept bitter tears. Sor Romolo urged me to calm myself as we got back into the cart, and we both returned to the farm quite silent, exchanging only a rare word.

Sora Rosa was waiting for us, ran to meet us, and seeing me so hurt embraced me like a mother. Dinner was ready, but I hadn't the strength to touch food. Sor Romolo told his wife everything that had happened in the meeting, stressing particularly the feeling of empathy my father had inspired in him. And he was right. In fact, in his best moments, especially when he was sad and thoughtful, my father radiated around him an irresistible force of attraction. I—I don't know whether in large or small part—have inherited it, and owe to the privilege of Nature much of the courage with which I have confronted the problems of life, and the fortune I have met with in the world.

Sora Rosa continued to caress my head, saying, "Dear boy, don't be this way! Look— you're in good hands. Go see your mother and then come back to us!"

I thanked her, and as I usually did now before going to bed, gave her a good night kiss as a sign of gratitude, on one cheek. This night, however, I had a hard time falling asleep. I saw my father arriving in Rome and telling Mother all that had happened, I saw her anxiety and that of my brother and sisters at the telling, and it seemed to me that I was being cruel to the whole family. After floundering a long time among so many phantoms, in which the doleful image of my mother predominated, I dropped into a profound sleep.

About a week later I received a letter from my brother, begging me to return home, since Mother had fallen ill and was calling for me continually. Though I thought this sickness might be more fictional than real, I packed my suitcase and left the next day. To give the impression that I would return I left the blanket I had bought for my pallet at Righetto's stepmother's in Albano, and the blue fatigues I used at the farm, and those handsome boots I had received. I also left one of the portraits of me in my handsome black outfit, and wrote on it, "To Mama Rosa, your affectionate and grateful son, Ruffo."

She held it tight in her hand and exclaimed, "Alas! Nothing of you remains to me but this, and it's much too little for all the sadness I feel. God bless you and help you always!"

Sora Rosa embraced me and fled sobbing into her room. The farmer, who was waiting with the cart to take me to the station, was also much upset. Along the way he told me, "I would rather restore that oil-press a thousand times than suffer what I'm going to with Rosa because of your leaving. I confess I would have preferred you were a bastard; at least you would remain with us for good."

I looked at the man with his little Spanish beard and red eyes, who was irritably whipping his horse at the moment, and I pardoned all his simplicity—that is to say, the egotism of his affection, the roughness of his sentiments and the crudeness of his language.

Today I understand and justify the impressions of my childhood, as I realize I had inherited from my father a certain forceful character, but until a certain age what prevailed in me was the ingenuity, gentleness, and affability of my mother, gifts which quickly earned me the good will of all. In addition she aided my spiritual growth. My every act and deed, though in no sense feminine, was governed by an uncommon self-possession and graciousness. Precocious experience of life, the spirit of initiative, courage in my undertakings—all contributed to forming a character and a manner that was more or less impressive at times. I felt these talents in me, and without abusing them, knew how to make the best use of them. And as for the consciousness of this personality of mine that went forth every day more fully developed and integrated, I had a great faith in myself and in the future.

We arrived at the station a few minutes before the train was due to depart, and Sor Romolo gave me many words of encouragement and advice. Above all he advised me to return soon, and then confessed, reproaching himself for having done so, that he had been imprudent enough to write a letter to Morriggia's shop, of which I had spoken often, and thus my father had come to know that I was being sheltered at his farm. The truth was, my father had been searching for me, but without success. Perhaps without realizing it Sor Romolo loved to blame himself, it was almost a comfort. He was really desperate, seeing me leave. He embraced me and clapped me forcefully on the back. "God be with you!" he said. Those were his last words. The train began to move, and from then on I never saw him again, nor Sora Rosa.

CHAPTER 4

Home Again

THE FAMILY WAS NOW LIVING on via Vicenza close to the station, and in order to calm down a bit, when I reached home I stopped a bit at the door for a few moments. My inner commotion quieted somewhat as I walked slowly up the stairs. Manzoni was right—what a mixed-up thing is the human heart. Notwithstanding the intense desire to embrace Mother again, I was regretting my return; I was already resolving to convince her of the need to leave again after a few days.

As I knocked on the door my heart was beating as violently as the door-knocker. I had a presentiment that Mother would open the door. Sure enough, I heard excited steps and her voice crying, "It's Ruffo! It's Ruffo!" [Apparently she refers to him as Ruffo sometimes, though he is always Cafiero when she speaks to him. *Tr.*]

Strange telepathy. I believe firmly in this phenomenon, because I have experimented with it with myself and others so many times. The most persuasive example was when I was about to drown. On Sundays I usually went to a gymnasium with one of my workmates. One day it was unusually warm and we decided to go swimming in the Tevere, and unwittingly picked one of the most dangerous spots, a beach called l'Albero Bello.[13] Though not a good swimmer, as soon as we got there, with youthful energy, I jumped into the water. I was quickly overwhelmed by the whirlpool currents which carried me out to the middle of the river, where the most violent current pulled me under several times. My companion, seeing my peril, hurled himself into the river to try to save me. I grabbed hold of him with the desperation of those who are about to drown. All at once we were both upside down in the depths and lost consciousness. I regained consciousness on the riverbank after protracted artificial respiration. Unfortunately my generous friend paid with his life for his heroism. All this happened toward four in the afternoon. At just that time, I learned when I was taken home, my father had awakened from his customary afternoon nap in great agitation, asking my mother where I was, because in a dream he had just seen me drown.

When I was in Mother's arms at last and felt her breath lightly touching my face, and her hands in my hair caressing me, and her tears bathing my face, I understood how much she had suffered during the long months of my absence. She seemed to have wasted away and had some white threads in her dark hair. She told me that she was positive I would arrive before noon, as the previous night she had dreamed of me, and saw me exactly as I was now before her: robust, healthy, and handsome in my black outfit. She felt reborn in the joy of seeing her dearest son again. She used the expression *most dear* because in reality she had a certain predilection for me, due to the fact that, in comparison to the other children I was, so to speak, the Cinderella of the house.

When the first emotion was past I hastened to turn over to Mother all that I had saved, experiencing in this act the greatest satisfaction. The sum amounted to something over five hundred lire, a considerable sum for that time; besides, I had all my other things. The suitcase was full of clothes. Nothing was lacking, I could consider myself outfitted like a modest gentleman.

She did not want to accept this money, earned by the sweat of my brow. I begged her to accept it as the only recompense I was able to offer for all her sufferings and assured her that whenever I left home again, it would only be to earn something for her. Finally my insistence prevailed, and she took the money, putting it into a little box as if it were a great treasure. Every time she mentioned this little hoard it was "Ruffo's money."

When we all found ourselves seated at table it was a moment of indescribable intimacy. Even Father was more gentle, though I sensed that some resentment still remained at the bottom of his heart. After lunch he hurried back to the shop. I spent the whole afternoon recounting in the smallest detail what I had done at Albano during my absence. I remember not only my Mother's absorption, but that of my brother and sisters. After my story they looked upon me as if I had returned from the North Pole.

I found quite a few changes in the house. There was now a piano, rented by my brother for ten lire per month. With yellowed keys and a sound of times gone by, lacking in vibrancy, it was really a relic. Fortunately Garibaldi, under whom the piano had been placed, was only paper. In my months of absence my brother, besides studying design at the Accademia di S. Luca, had also taken up music in order to learn flute and piano and was attending the Accademia di Santa Cecilia as well. My father had a certain weakness for him and approved his aspirations.

So it was that I found in my family an atmosphere more in keeping with my future destiny. While I spoke to my brother about future travels all over the world, dreams of independence, economies, and so on, he continued to talk about music: harmony, counterpoint—things of which I was ignorant, which didn't interest me at all. My culture in this regard consisted in my knowing (and I boasted of it) that Verdi was the composer of *Il trovatore*. My brother, besides Verdi, spoke of Donizetti and Bellini as if they were personal friends of his and proclaimed them two geniuses. He passed whole hours running his hands up and down the length of his decrepit keyboard. I heard what he was doing but did not listen to it.

I was drawn instead to the portrait of Garibaldi with his beautiful head of blond hair and his Nazarene beard. It seemed to me that with his magnetic eyes he was asking where I had

been until now. I had a different view of him now than before
I left home because, from my reading, I'd come to know of his
life as a seaman and hero. Even so I had found a striking similarity between him and Jesus. It seemed that if Jesus had worn
a cloak similar to Garibaldi's, they could have been taken for
brothers! I admired both of them immensely and wanted to be
like them.

I stayed home for some time, idling the days away. I no
longer had the desire or will to return to my father's shop, no
longer loved the art of wrought-iron work, and knew I could
not adapt to life in a forge, nor on the other hand did this life
of a parasite suit my temperament. After having worked so
long out in the open air the thought of being confined in a
shop with that gang of young, ignorant ruffians who had poisoned my youth seemed a step downwards—from liberty to
slavery. I felt melancholy and considered myself a ruined man.
Undoubtedly the books I had hungrily acquired had influenced
my new state of mind. I felt myself to be half vagabond, half
artist, something of a sailor like Edmond Dantes, something
of an adventurer like Garibaldi in his youth, discontented with
the present and longing for I don't know what in the future.

In the meantime, should I return to the *Fattoria del Riposo*?
This idea too had no attraction for me. Soon friction again
arose between myself and Father, who wanted to know what I
might decide, and I felt he had bitter arguments with Mama
on the subject. The situation was growing ever more insufferable.

Finally for the sake of peace in the family and chiefly to
avoid my mother's displeasure, I agreed, though reluctantly,
to return to the shop. The workers greeted me joyfully. Cataldi,
who had taken my place when I left, was most glad to see me.
The orphan apprentices, even more numerous and perverse
than before, showed no such pleasure in my return. I passed
several weeks in the shop without the slightest enthusiasm. I
often thought of my life in the country and wrote two affectionate letters to Sor Romolo and Sora Rosa, who answered
that they were awaiting my return from one moment to the
next.

The new musical atmosphere being created in our houses by my brother finally influenced my spirit, too. In the evening after work I began to listen with great interest—listen, not just hear—when my brother played the flute. One time I found him intently studying the serenade from *Cavalleria rusticana*, an opera then in vogue, the theme of which could be heard repeated everywhere.

While he played I read the text:

> *O Lola, ch'ai di latti la cammisa*
> *si bianca e russa comu la cirasa*
> *quannu t'affacci fai la vucca a risa,*
> *biatu pi lu primu cu ti vasa!*

I repeated these lines often in my mind.

One evening my brother surprised me by inviting me to go with him to the Teatro Costanzi, where *Cavalleria* was being given. The protagonists were the creators of the roles: Gemma Bellincioni and Roberto Stagno. I had never heard an opera in my life. We could only find a place to sit in the last row of the gallery, which was packed. Lots of people were standing behind us, pushing against our shoulders. The atmosphere was suffocating, but when the orchestra played the first chords of the Prelude, that divine melody, and suddenly at the raising of the curtain the tenor's voice began to intone behind the set: "*O Lola, ch'ai di latti la cammisa,*" I remained ecstatic with my attention turned to the footlights. When the serenade ended the audience burst into deafening applause, crying "*Bis! Bis!*" but fortunately the orchestra did not interrupt the flow of the wonderful music which was sending us out of this world.

In the middle of the performance, after the narrative to Mamma Lucia, the duet of Stagno and Bellincioni so vibrant with truth and passion, made me bite my lips. At the sobs especially, and then in the pleading of Santuzza with Turiddu, Bellincioni moved me to tears. When Turiddu, amidst complete silence, cries out "*Dell'ira tuo no mi curo,*" and Santuzza, in a jealous rage, responds "*A te la mala Pasqua, spergiuro!*" the tragic pathos filled me from head to foot, and although not knowing the rest of the opera, I anticipated that the terrible curse would have its sinister effect on Turiddu. At the end of the opera I asked myself where I was, when a woman behind the scenes shrieked *"They have killed our Turiddu,"* I felt as if I had received a tremendous blow on the head. Behind the scene I saw Turiddu lying in a pool of blood, and Alfio fleeing through the country.

The artists were called out again and again and the enthusiasm was such that it quite resembled collective insanity.[14] I did not applaud or utter one syllable, nor decide to leave my seat. I looked at my brother in silence, unable to speak. As we walked home very slowly I was still mute and amazed, while my brother was praising Mascagni as the world's greatest genius—greater than Verdi, Rossini, Beethoven or Wagner.

It was a moonlit night, a little cold, but most agreeable. As soon as we got home I begged my brother to play the serenade for me on his flute, which he refused to do because of the lateness of the hour. Finally he yielded to my insistence, took up his flute and began to play.

Totally unconscious of what I was doing I was taken by an access of enthusiasm to sing and sing, following the flute, and I arrived finally at the end of the serenade with a tenor voice of such beauty and spontaneity that, when it was over, we were looking at each other in surprise. He could not explain where the voice had come from and, picking up his flute with trembling hands, exclaimed: "This is a miracle! Let's start over and see if you can still sing."

We opened the window and moonlight flooded the room. We saw people standing at their windows in the surrounding houses. My voice had been heard in the silent night, and they were apparently waiting for more.

Mother got out of bed and came into our room, asking, "Who was singing in that voice?"

My brother, pointing at me where I stood pale with emotion, said, "It was Ruffo!"

I hurried to sing some more, and towards the end of the serenade, though I forgot the words, I came out with the notes and my voice this time was even more beautiful and free. At the end I heard applause coming from the houses nearby and also someone calling "*Bravo!*"

That was my first success as a singer! A new light appeared among us, as if some rare microbe, or to put it better, a celestial spirit, had entered into my blood and brain, and I already saw myself onstage in the presence of a crowd. I would have liked to continue singing, but it was too late by now. Mother asked me if I felt tired and I told her I could have kept going all night, putting out notes even higher. It seemed to me that the voice gushed out without the slightest effort, natural, limpid and powerful.[15]

After this my mind was on fire with new images. I had glimpses of a destiny that was radically changed. No more shop! No more farm! Something other than hammer and engraving tool! Something besides salamanders or roses in wrought iron, masterpieces though they might be! In my voice I had found a vein of gold of which nothing or no one, except Death itself, could deprive me. A new horizon, immense and boundless, had opened for me.

That night we all went to bed very late and I couldn't get to sleep. The fear came upon me that the revelation of my voice had been nothing but a trick of Nature, and that on the morrow, without the moonlight and the warmth of enthusiasm excited by the fever of theatrical performance, I would no longer be able to sing.

Right after I got to the shop in the morning I told Cataldi what had happened. He wanted to hear me immediately. My fear was repudiated! I put forth some powerful sounds which seemed even more beautiful in the cavernous shop. My joy could not be described! I would have embraced the whole world. I lighted the fire under the forge but my heart was not in it. There beside the flashes and shrieks of the forge I heard and saw nothing but the stage at the Costanzi, with Turiddu and Santuzza, or, what is the same thing, with Stagno and Bellincioni and their superhuman singing.

Resignedly I continued my work at the shop, secure in my determination that someday I would fly away. No longer was

I for leaving from Naples on a merchant ship, or staying with the good farmer and Sor Rosa. I would launch myself in the theater. This dream remained fixed in my head by now, it possessed me internally. Meanwhile, I could not stay on here. Those damned boys thought up something new every day. I no longer had the strength to stand them or the courage to defy them. A blow-up was inevitable sometime.

One morning, when the regular workers were making an outside installation, four of them, egged on by the biggest rascal, started betting on who was able to break, with a sole hammer-blow on a steel chisel—break in half, I'm saying—the handles of the new files for which father had just made me responsible. Those files cost one lira each, and they had already broken three of them, though the handles were made of very hard wood. Seeing what was going on, I went decisively over to the wrongdoers, menacing them with a hammer, and told them to make an end of their savage game or I was going to hit someone without a by-your-leave.

We began to brawl. As they were four, they tore the hammer from my hand. I was overwhelmed and struck on the mouth with great force by one of the madmen's fists. My gums were bleeding. At this moment my father entered the shop screaming and separated us. Seeing the blood flowing from my mouth he became furious.

Then, through tears not of sadness but of rage, I told him the reason for the fight and saw the passion blind his eyes. Wasting no time he set about beating the stuffing out of the boys—he had plenty of strength—calling them cowardly bastards, who weren't ashamed to go four on one. Not content to have given them a sound thrashing, he threatened to report them to the director of the orphanage. Had he done so, the punishment would have been severe, but the blows they had been given were sufficient. Some were missing teeth, for my father, when he thrashed someone, did the job well.

A heavy silence descended on the shop after the turmoil. I continued to wash my mouth with cold water, but the bleeding from my gums would not stop. Exasperated I told my father that I was tired of fighting this rabble, and warned that sooner or later something more serious was bound to occur. I then turned to the bunch of ruffians, my eyes still dark with rage, and challenged them, affirming that I wasn't afraid of them; that one by one I would face them all, including the strongest, who had struck me on the mouth; that I would be avenged if there was a scar from that blow. All of them should be on guard. My father, well aware of my character, saw a serious threat in my words and then urged me to stop.

Evening came, and at the sound of the whistle, according to regulations, the orphans changed and left for evening school. About an hour later one of the boys came running, having slipped out of school, to warn me that tomorrow I shouldn't go to work, because some of the angriest boys were planning to disfigure me.

I answered, "All right! We'll see!"

With this thorn in my side I closed the shop and went home. I told Father not to say anything to Mother about the occurrences of the afternoon. When we got home my wound had begun to heal. I told Mother I had accidentally hurt myself with a bar of iron. I ate very little and hurried off to bed, but had no success getting off to sleep with all the fury in me. I didn't know what to do on the morrow. Not return to the shop? That would humiliate me. Confront my adversaries— or better, my enemies—again? Against hoodlums of that sort I wouldn't be able to defend myself without being armed. But armed with what? The very idea was repugnant to me. Finally, tired and half-asleep, I outlined a plan.

I arose earlier than usual and felt a delicious shudder run through me as I left the house. I passed the Piazza d'Estero and at a kiosk where coffee and liquor were sold I felt the need of a brandy. I ordered nothing less than a glass and swallowed it in one gulp. It warmed both my stomach and my head. I immediately gulped down another in the same way. My eyes began to shine and my vision became foggy.

When I got to the shop, I took an iron bar of about two centimeters thickness, and cut off a piece about a meter long. Very calmly—I don't know where the idea came from—I fashioned a sort of grip handle for it so that it could neither slip out of my hand nor be wrested from it. When it was finished, in case I was obliged to use the end of my terrible weapon, I sharpened it to a fine point, so that it became a sort of lance. This done, I sat down between calm and exaltation to await the arrival of the ruffians.

The regular workers were away on an outside job this morning also. There was no one in the shop but Tarabo, a man about forty who stammered so badly that on some days he could not utter a single word, only incomprehensible sounds. He was one of those unfortunates who are born retarded, who grow physically but not mentally, and remain all their lives in a state more animal than human. On his face was the authentic expression of the idiot.

The clock in the courtyard struck eight and the whistle sounded for the boys to come to work. My fearful hour was at hand. When the fifteen junior wolves put on their work clothes and poured into the shop I felt the blood rush to my head and my heart beat violently. I was torn by two feelings: fear, not slight, of facing them—and the overpowering desire to protect my face from the planned disfigurement. I conquered the desire to go further, whatever might follow. I had already considered that one day I would be going on the stage before the public. I needed to save myself from disfigurement at all costs. I called to mind the faces of Fanfulla and of Fieramosca,[16] which I knew for having read their story on my Sundays off. With these images in mind I awaited what might come in the corner by the forge with my implement hidden in the ashes.

The boys had hardly started to work when the oldest, who had faced the brunt of my father's attack, took one of the ordinary file handles, and readied the chisel to cut it in half.

I told him immediately to drop it, or it would cost him dear. The words had hardly left my mouth when, with a sudden leap, he rushed over to me and smacked me on the left cheek with such force that for a few moments I was not myself. I was insensitive to my surroundings. My ears began to buzz. I had the impression that he had ruptured the eardrum and I would never again be able to hear musical sounds. I leaned on the forge, holding one hand on my cheek, which seemed to be bleeding.

Poor Tarabo was waving his hands frantically, bellowing, bleating—inconceivable sounds. He had wanted to come to my rescue and had moved to intervene, but did not have time, as one of the four, the toughest one, had laid hands on him and thrown him to the floor.

There was a momentary silence as the dizziness left me. I managed to get my hand onto the grip of my lance without being seen and turned to the one who had dealt me the blow, who was standing triumphant only a few meters away, and called him a bastard, along with the other four, inviting him, if he dared, to repeat his cowardly act.

I do not know how to tone down what happened next. I shall never forget it because there are episodes in life that only happen once: I remember that, gripping the lance with the certainty that no one would be able to wrest it from me, as the wretch approached to strike me a second time, I didn't give him time. In a flash I pulled my weapon from the ashes and brought it down on his head with such force that he fell like a corpse at my feet in a puddle of blood.

Tarabo was torn between fear and joy at seeing this bully put out of action. He let out an inhuman howl, then burst into hysterical laughter, like the poor dimwitted soul he was, thus mixing the tragic and the grotesque.

The worst among the other boys, seeing that I was ready for them all, massed a fanatical attack on me like so many devils, but I gave none of them respite, nor did I count the number of blows. In a short time I was master of the battle-field. When I could observe the effects of my beating, I noted that I had hit the mark on every single one of them, some on the shoulders, some on the arms, some on the legs. In short, nearly all of them emerged bruised to such a degree that even one who was not disposed to have pity might have been caused to feel it for them.

So as not to drag out this incredible story, I will simply say that Tarabo's howls had caused a number of workmen from other departments to gather at the door of the shop, and the rumor of what happened spread rapidly while the wounded were being taken off to the hospital. Many prefects were pouring into our work place and the director of the orphanage also came. I stood my ground fearlessly, my weapon in my hand, and would not let anyone come near me. I was still beside myself.

When I saw those whom I had wounded in the head being carried out my inner feelings were indescribable. In my mind's eye pictures passed of my mother, my family, Sor Giuliano, Sor Romolo and Sora Rosa, who thought me such a good boy and who loved me so much. I felt my strength slipping away...

At this point my father came in, having already been given an exaggerated account of everything. His face was quite pale, almost deathly, as if all the blood had left his veins. As he came near to me he whispered in a voice broken by sobs: "I told you so!" He was probably preoccupied and sad at the thought of the probable consequences. The incident, in fact, was not confined to the orphanage, but bruited around the vicinity. Indeed, one of the newspapers took it up and related it in such a manner that I was almost put in a heroic light for having stood off such a gang at my age, alone.

Exasperated and still beside myself I told the people standing around me all the iniquities and infamies I had been subjected to in this near prison. My statements began to cause concern: some of the most interested tried to shush me because quite a few among them would be compromised and a real scandal would follow.

I was taken home and when Mama was told what had happened, she aged visibly by ten years in that one moment. I saw her cry a lot then. Calm returned only when we were informed that the wound I had inflicted on my luckless first assailant had not been fatal.

As a consequence of this ugly turn of events, many changes were made at the orphanage. A strict investigation was ordered and the outrages, the bullying, the tyranny of these young ruffians, which had been increasing because of the lack of supervision and discipline, was stopped once and for all. My father was obliged to leave the shop. He took his equipment to a shop in via Ludovisi, where he remained many years. I opened, for myself, a small, separate shop in the same district. He sent me jobs, and so began the routine of our new life.

A few weeks later, towards the end of October, when the most seriously wounded of my adversaries had fully recovered, the workers of the School of Arts and Crafts threw a party for me at the Faccia Fresca Inn, near the Porta San Giovanni, and as a sign of their admiration for my prowess and of satisfaction for the lesson I had inflicted on my enemies, they carried me aloft in triumph. Thus was closed an episode in my life which brought me more sorrow than joy, and made me weep many times along with Mama. As for my father, notwithstanding the upset which forced him to move his business, he never reproached me in the least. The consequences of my act could have been much more serious, but Destiny wanted to help me.

During this period the work I did was only on a small scale, and with the expenses connected with starting my new business, I was often constrained, in order to keep pushing ahead, to search for a few lire. The failure of Moroni, the big contractors, had been felt in Rome and some thousands of workers remained unemployed.[17] Father sent me two of these workman, Giovanni and Pietro, with whom I shared work harmoniously. After several weeks, however, I found I was running at a loss, and they had to content themselves with a salary for only a half-week's work. I had lost my tranquility again. Fortunately, I knew the two sons of a contractor, a certain Bellatalla, who had been keeping busy with work on the iron bridge in front of the military college, which he had just finished building at about that time. I decided to go and find one of them in the shipyard.

I told him my problem—he already knew that I had opened a shop on my own account—and asked him if he or his father might have the means to procure me something to do which would help me to pay my workers. He assured me that he would come to call on me, which he did a few days later. He saw my workers on the job, observing my little shop with obvious satisfaction, and proposed that I accept in association with him a contract for the demolition of a certain Velletri agricultural enterprise. The part we would be concerned with was the dismantling of two enormous boilers, weighing several tons. The iron recovered was destined for a Roman smelter. According to his calculations the work we could accomplish together would require about two months and few tools of the trade. Though the job didn't look too easy to me, I accepted his offer at once.

A week later we were both on the site with all our equipment: huge sledgehammers and chisels, pliers... In three weeks time we had already removed all the bolts and taken apart one of the boilers. Actually, a very exhausting labor: we needed to be inside the boiler for entire days. We were toiling by the light of oil or acetylene lamps, our ears stuffed with wads of cotton, to save our eardrums from the reverberations, hour after hour, of the hammers. One held the pincers and the chisel while the other wielded the sledgehammer, up and down, blow by blow. Two or three blows sufficed to knock off the bolts, and then with a punch we were able to get the internal rivets out of the way without difficulty.

The whole job took two months, as my partner had estimated, and we divided the take of 1,500 lire. Thus was I able to pay the rent of my workshop and the wages of my workers, who, in their turn, during my absence, had carried out other jobs. I gave the remainder to Mama to help her muddle through at least the worst eventualities. So as not to leave out any of the important particulars of my semi-savage life—nothing, whether it be happy or sad—it seems right to add that these two months of labor brutalized me a little.

To save money the two of us slept, while we could endure it, on two straw mats inside the boiler we were working on. In the morning we went to wash in a stream a little way off, and in the evening we took a bath in the same place. Our appetites—need I say it?—were formidable. My partner, Pilade Bellatalla (for such was his name) was good company for me, as I was for him. He was a terrific comrade, about one year

older than I, with an easygoing, fair and balanced temperament. I respected and liked him tremendously. He had learned
from early childhood "how salty bread coming from others
can be."[18] He had had an even tougher time of it than I, since
he hadn't the good fortune to possess my temperament and
character, thanks to which everyone became attached to me,
making coexistence quite easy.

And what about my voice? Naturally nothing was said of
it, except to regret its disappearance. The smoke of the lamps
had produced a hoarseness and loss of voice so acute that I
struggled even to get out the least sound.

Back in the house after two months of absence my brother
immediately tried to get me to sing again, but it was impossible. At the shop work was always scarce, so to make both
ends meet in the least disagreeable way we set ourselves to
making little iron objects: candelabra, door-knockers, orna-
mental flowers and paperweights. I had them displayed in a
case by the door of my shop, and now and then they were sold
at bargain prices.

Then mother became ill with anemia and for several weeks
we were very anxious about her health. By good fortune she
was cured by a kindly doctor who, knowing our straitened
circumstances, took his profession as a healer very much to
heart. It isn't true, as popularly supposed, that doctors taken
together are people without a heart. There are among them
some true apostles, with profoundly generous spirits, worthy
of the highest gratitude and reverence.

CHAPTER 5

My First Love

I T WAS JUNE 9, 1895;[19] I was eighteen years of age, tending
to my duties at the shop, weaving fancies about my future.
I had just finished a beautiful wrought-iron lamp in the style
of the Cinquecento quite like the one in the Strozzi Palace in
Florence, except for the smaller dimensions. I'd been working
on and off on it for two months. I'd wanted to finish it on this
day, because I would be paid for it on delivery and I'd already
counted on spending the money as soon as I received it on a
beautiful black Venetian shawl, embroidered with flowers, with
long fringes, which I'd acquired the week before as a gift for
Mother to mark my eighteenth birthday.

At noon I received the agreed amount upon delivery of the
lamp and ran immediately to claim the shawl from the woman
who had sold it to me. She lived on the third floor above my
shop. One day, with just such a beautiful black shawl on her
shoulders, she had stopped to look at the pieces I had on display. I went up to her and asked if she wanted to buy something. She replied that she had stopped here on other occasions
but could never bring herself to buy anything because she was
a widow, poor and alone. I proposed to her that she should
pick out the work that pleased her the most, and let me have
her shawl in exchange for it. She thanked me but told me that
it was a keepsake to remind her of her dead husband, the only

object of a certain value remaining to her that, for some time now, she had been trying to sell. I asked what she would want for it. She wavered: a nice young girl living on the mezzanine had offered her 100 lire some time ago, which she had refused, since she had not been in dire necessity at the time. Now she would give it up for 90, all the more since she had acceded to the young girl's offer some time later, but by then the girl hadn't the money to pay for it, and had never since come to ask for it again.

I accepted her terms—I already saw the shawl on my mother's shoulders—and asked her to set it aside for me for one week. She consented, and thus it was that on this day, with part of the proceeds from my sale of the lamp, I was able to conclude the deal. I remember the sad expression of the poor woman when she counted the 90 lire on the table in her little sitting room. She couldn't bring herself to give me the shawl, seeming almost sorry to have sold it to me. It seemed as though she'd been obliged to tear a relic off her back, the last sacred relic of her life as a married woman. She caused me to feel so much pity that I advised her to think about it longer, and out of kindness and for no other reason offered her ten lire more than we had already agreed. Then, thanking me, she made up her mind...

On the way downstairs, on the mezzanine, I met a young woman of singular beauty. Seeing the shawl that I had on my arm she stopped for a moment and, touching the long fringes of it, asked me if I had bought it from the woman on the third floor. Right away I assumed that this was precisely the young woman of whom the widow had spoken. She asked me, perhaps a little indiscreetly, how much I had paid. I lied a bit in reply, saying that it had cost me more than one hundred lire. She remained vexed and explained how she had wanted to have it some time ago, but owing to unforeseen circumstances, couldn't come up with the money.

I will not try to conceal the fact that I was going out of my mind at the sight of this beautiful woman. She had big, black eyes; pale skin with a rosy complexion; a small mouth; perfectly white teeth; rosy lips, rather sensual; abundant black tresses in a roll at the nape of her neck, and a figure at once slender and ample. But why list all these details which tell the reader next to nothing? Perhaps the reader could picture her better if I say she resembled *la Fornarina* of Raphael. I stood frozen in front of her. Trying to get a conversation going I told her that today was my birthday, my eighteenth birthday, and the shawl was a gift to my mother to help her to celebrate, since she had expressed the desire to have one like it. I described the virtues of my mother, the affection that she had for me, and so many other things that certainly couldn't have been interesting to her. I did note that she was listening to me with pleasure.

Soon the conversation threatened to become compromising. Tenants coming downstairs had noticed us and she became embarrassed. But where to find the strength to end our conversation? I was in ecstasy as I stood before this angel, and in this ecstasy I had the courage to whisper: "How beautiful you are! I would never leave here! Pardon my audacity, but it's the truth: these are the first words of love I've ever addressed to a woman."

Courage, I called it, but that's not the right word, since this declaration required no strength at all. The words came from me with a frankness and facility that astonished me. Then there was a brief moment of silence. She was looking at me in such a way that she could not have been indifferent. In this hesitation, or in the few moments before, another bug had bitten me—the music microbe had been killed or at least dampened by the boilers of Velletri—and a terrible, adoring passion had sprung up in me and instantly become mysteriously huge: love.

With trembling hands and a face gone pale I remained some instants longer without speaking. Then holding out the shawl, I begged her to accept it.

"Thank you," she replied suavely, "but I can't accept it for two reasons: in the first place, because it is for your mother; then, second, because I am married, and when my husband returns I would be unable to explain how I came by it."

I moved on then, making my excuses for having detained

her too long. In taking my leave I told her my name; she, however, remained silent about hers. Still, I understood that the
voice of my heart had not left her unfeeling. Returning to the
shop, I gave the workmen their orders and advised that I would
be returning to the shop later than usual. Then I headed home.

We were now living on the via Nomentana, in a house
near the Mezzo Miglio called the Breccia Palace: so named,
surely, because on the façade were terra-cotta bas reliefs representing elite army units in combat-ready position, with bayo-
nets on their gun barrels, calling to mind, of course, the famous
breach of the Porta Pia. We lived on the uppermost of the five
floors, and on the south was a large terrace which Mother and
my sisters had beautified with roses and carnations, and which
dominated the Sabine hills and the Castelli romani.

I reached home breathless, my heart beating loudly. Nella,
who had come to open, appeared amazed to have seen me
return at such an unaccustomed hour. She remained more than
amazed when, having asked what I was hiding under my shirt,
I brought forth and fully unrolled it to show it to her. I told her
under my breath to stop crying out in astonishment, for this
was a surprise I was going to make Mother on my birthday.
Together we ran into the kitchen where mother was preparing
our evening meal, and I threw the beautiful gift over her shoulders. She embraced me, radiant with delight and with gratitude for my having thought to satisfy the wish she'd expressed
so long ago. It was easy to guess the questions that followed.
When she'd learned the story, she was saddened to think of
the poor woman who'd given up the shawl.

Naturally I refrained from telling of the encounter on the
stairs with the woman, and the rest. I felt shame and remorse
that the vehemence of my emotion, excited by her beauty, had
pushed me to offer to the woman the gift that had been for my
mother, and I would have wished to confess my weakness, or
should I call it my guilt, but since the deed hadn't actually
been done, I preferred to keep silent on that point, nor did I
need to say why. Sad humanity! There is no sentiment, however noble and sacred, that cannot be obscured or led astray
or destroyed once the passion of love has taken over.

I stayed at home till four o'clock. I helped Mother to cut flowers on the terrace, talking of so many things, but especially of my uncertain future. Then I finally went back to the shop, where I stayed until evening. When evening came we waited for Father until nine o'clock. Seeing that he was late once again we sat down to dinner. I was so full of emotion that I had even lost my appetite thanks to the face that was fixed in my mind. Mother was angry, though she tried to dissimulate it, not to see my father put in an appearance on such an occasion. I was given two presents then, wrapped in green tissue paper and tied with a red ribbon. In one package was the gift of my brother and sisters: two black, flowing ties. In the other package was my mother's gift, the *Cuore* of De Amicis, that she herself had given me a few years before, of which I had been inexpressibly fond; only this time it was bound in red Moroccan leather with gilded inscriptions.

We began to eat as the moon began to shine, and in spite of Father's absence, we had an enjoyable time together. The evening was capped off most pleasantly with the welcome surprise visit of Francesco Forti, my friend from Castel Gandolfo, who brought a bottle of sparkling wine. In addition some lady friends of the family came with a magnificent bunch of roses which were offered to me among kind words of felicitation.

Though it was after midnight before I went to bed, I couldn't sleep. I got up and returned to the terrace, half naked and barefoot. The moon was already high, grown smaller and more distant, flooding all creation with its melancholy light. There wasn't the hint of a breeze. Silence everywhere. Before this enchanting immensity I stood in contemplation I don't know how long and always, everywhere, in earth, in heaven, there she was. The cold of the night brought me back to reality. I went back to my room and this time was not slow in going to sleep, always, it goes without saying, with the same vision in my mind and the hope in my heart that the time might fly until we should meet again. Two days passed without my being able to see her again. I couldn't keep working; I couldn't keep living.

The third day the postman stopped for a while near the door of my shop with various letters to be distributed in the house. I came forward and offered him two lire if he would do me the great kindness of telling me the name of the young woman on the mezzanine floor. Without refusing the money, he began to laugh, making fun of me. That was forbidden fruit, he told me, and nothing could be done about it. Many, many others besides myself had tried to get close to her, and none had ever succeeded. She always stayed shut up in the house with her paralyzed mother... He briefly told me the whole story. Her name was Armida. She was the wife of a man much older than she. He had been arrested for political reasons after only two months of marriage, and condemned to two years, of which a year and half had already been served in the prison at Viterbo. He was a violent, jealous, robust man. I thanked him and went back inside my shop.

I was now feeling guilty that I had requested the woman's name of the mailman, feeling that I might have compromised her. In addition to my feelings of love, hearing her sad story had mixed in a profound feeling of pity. That evening at closing time, to my most delighted surprise, I saw her watching me from behind the glass of her window. I signalled her to open it, and came closer, begging her pardon if I was permitting myself to importune her, but I felt that I had to speak to her. I invited her to come out and go for a walk with me outside the city walls, where, since it was getting dark, no one would be able to see us.

At length she came out. She told me to talk very quietly; she whispered that she could not listen to me, that she would be compromised; besides, she could not go out because of her mother.

I insisted with such fervor, telling her that I would go and wait for her behind the wall of Porta Salaria, and finally, after much wavering, she agreed to come. I set off for the agreed place of meeting. After about a quarter of an hour, in the near dark, I saw her approaching. Is it necessary to say that my heart was no longer in my chest? I poured forth expressions of gratitude, my mother's joy at receiving the beautiful shawl, the moments I'd spent on the terrace with her image always before me. She listened to me preoccupied, often turning around out of fear that someone had followed her and might be able to recognize her.

We were proceeding toward the country, near the Policlinico,[20] an area that wasn't much frequented. Pretty soon we were in complete darkness. She had on a light dress of blue silk and a modest summer shawl. I understood then why she had wanted the Venetian shawl and was more appreciative of the generosity of soul she had shown in not having accepted it from me. I admired her beautiful black tresses, fastened behind her neck, and her most beautiful eyes, shining in the darkness like two stars. I searched for the most suitable words to convey my feelings to her. I took her little hand and pressed it against my cheek and kissed it and without further ado, as if it had been decided a long time ago, I began to address her with the familiar *tu*.

"How beautiful you are! God was good to permit me the joy of knowing you, looking in your eyes, kissing your little hand. I seem to be in a beautiful dream, from which I hope never to waken!"

When I repeated that this was the first time I had ever been alone with a woman, and that these were my first words of love, she could hardly believe me.

With these and other similar discourses not difficult to imagine, the time flew quickly. She asked me to go back home: her mother was home alone waiting for her return, and she could put it off no longer.

I had timidly kissed her hand; before separating I had the courage to ask her to let me kiss her on the face. Smiling at my shyness and inexperience, and without demonstrating the least unwillingness, she gave me her cheek. She didn't return my kiss but she caressed me with a look whose tenderness was every bit equal to it, saying that I had caused her to feel something she'd never experienced before, and she feared she would suffer greatly for it. With these words we parted. I followed her with my gaze, until her beautiful figure had vanished in the shadows of the night.

For all that I tried to save time by walking briskly back to the house, I arrived much later than usual. Mama, who was awaiting me anxiously on the terrace, spared me no reproof. My dinner was still on the table but I could eat nothing. I couldn't make up my mind whether or not to tell my mother what had happened. She was scrutinizing me in the meantime. She wanted to know where I'd been till such an hour; I didn't have the courage to lie to her. She remained thoughtful and limited herself to saying that it was absurd for a boy my age to already be involved with something like love.

"Dear Mama," I told her, "when the heart is touched with this fire, no advice is any good. It's only a few days since I met her, but already my life is completely full of her. If you knew her you would understand my passion."

She wanted to know who she was, this *donna fatale*, and where I had met her. I had never been able to have secrets from my mother. I would have felt that I was deceiving myself. I therefore decided to tell her the whole story with all the ins and outs, from the beginning. At the end my mother's facial expression had substantially changed. She reproved me acidly for having harbored such a feeling for a married woman, who had a husband in prison, and she absolutely forbade me ever to see her again. Otherwise she would go in person to the lady and there would be a scandal.

"All relationships outside the law and morality," she concluded with a severe accent that was aimed beyond me, "are destined to end sadly."

Seeing mother so dismayed, I could not succeed, that night, in getting to sleep. The trembling flame of the candle seemed to be trying to tell me something. I stared at it for a long time. For a long time I reflected on my mother's words, on the danger I would be facing, of all that I would surely suffer from the inevitable renunciation of Armida when her husband was released from prison. With fancy animating all that had transpired and all that was about to come, it seemed to me that I was already living the adventurous life of the characters in my novels.

In the morning, entering my shop, I looked up at her window; I saw her in my imagination in bed with loosened hair, I could almost feel her breath and the beating of her heart. My drama of love had begun and I was already enveloped in flames. No force could have made me take one step backward, and to legitimize my absurd passion I wanted to convince myself that all of this had been written prior to my birth, that destiny had sent her to me. Striking a heroic pose, I now felt I was ready to defy all the consequences, including the wrath of the returned prisoner.

I continued to work mechanically, without getting anything done. At the slightest sound I ran outside the door, hoping to see her in the window. But, seeing that Giovanni and Pietro were mindful of my actions, I struggled to get control of myself.

After lunch, eaten as usual in the shop, while the workers were gone, I was left alone for around two hours. I went back more times to look up at her window, but in vain. Seeing the futility of my hope I threw myself, as was my habit, into reading. I had begun the drama, *La morte civile* of Giacometti;[21] I'd reached the meeting in the abbey between the abbot, Buvo, and Corrado. Each page became more interesting. Corrado had just entered. His narration of his flight from the penal colony after thirteen years of forced labor, burned me like a fever. Naturally, I recalled to my mind the husband of the woman I loved; I imagined how he must have been made to suffer, to have to leave his young bride all alone (she was as beautiful as Rosalia) and with what anxiety he longed for his freedom. I pictured him vigorous and violent like Corrado; capable of killing me with one knife thrust the way Corrado killed Alonzo. I saw myself on the floor at the entrance of the shop in a large pool of blood. In sum, my life already seemed to involve a great tragedy, all because I'd spoken on two occasions to a woman. When the workers reentered the shop they found my attention riveted to the last part of the book. Pietro shook me, telling me it was time to change my occupation.

I went back to work with the vision of Armida never leaving me. In the evening we always returned to our meeting place near the Policlinico because it was close to home, yet safe. Our reciprocal passion grew more and more. She had married without love. Her mother, who remained a widow, infirm for some time, afraid of leaving her daughter alone without support, had given Armida to the first one who came along, and mindlessly, for her mother's peace of mind, Armida had consented.

Also for her, then, first love was now awakening. In her sentiment was something of brotherliness and motherliness together, and in my feeling something of the mystical. Surely neither of us was lacking a desire for complete union. But for the present there was only what is called a *pious desire,* platonically contained.

The hour of a perfect union arrived—how to deny it?— even for the two of us. How and where and when, and with what obstacles overcome and the help we had in doing so, through what precise circumstances, all this should be material for another work, and I look forward to it. But this aura of romanticism that always accompanies, or at least used to accompany, every first love, never left us, not even then; not even, I say, when the ideal and poetic was undermined by that which is vulgarly called, and often is, prose of the worst sort. No, this passion of ours, even during, even after the supreme fulfillment, always had something spiritual about it, and, let it be said, something eternal, through which, forgetting her actual condition, it seemed to me that God—if I may be pardoned the audacity—had blessed her. But there was one person, just one, who thought quite differently, and it is easy to guess who that was.

My mother, after having tried in vain every possible way to induce me to spontaneously sever this relationship, resolved to resort to, as it is said, strong-arm tactics, and by her good grace she managed to succeed. First, cleverly disguising her plan, she showed herself ready to get to know the woman of my dreams. Because it seemed like the right thing to me, I acceded in her wish. However, when Armida learned of it, she received the news in any way but favorably. Nevertheless the meeting was arranged in the shop (which, as I have indicated, adjoined her house). When she found herself face to face with my mother at the door of her house, she felt uneasy; then much more so when Mother asked if she might meet her in her own house, because she also wanted to know her mother. The request was made with such courtesy—one of my mother's outstanding qualities—that Armida, no less ingenuous and inexperienced than I was, consented. Thus the ruin of all our happiness.

I never did learn what happened in this three-way discussion, but from that day I never saw Armida again. I went a number of times to knock on her door, but no one answered. I cried, I despaired, I became crazy. Loving mother most tenderly as I did, I nevertheless reached the point, in paroxysms of grief, of accusing her of cruelty: it had been inhuman to tear apart two souls possessed by such a great love. I repeatedly told her that, having no reason to live without Armida, I wanted to die.

Poor Mama! With what goodness, with what kindness, with what wise abnegation she gradually calmed the tempest in me and showed me the injustice of my resentment, and the abyss—besides the moral degradation—into which I would have been precipitated if I hadn't pulled back in time!

But it took much doing. I saw her everywhere. I could no longer sleep. Everything was empty inside and outside me. My voice had almost disappeared. The idea of singing had been completely eclipsed. On the other hand, my father, who wasn't aware of anything that had been going on, was always on my back, reproving me for the lack of interest that I had been displaying in my everyday work. My mother, however, was always there, vigilant and loving, exhorting me to be calm, assuring me that my voice would come back, swearing that Nature would not have betrayed me. My brother, for his part, was aware of everything and sympathized fully with me. He thought to distract me by introducing me to a young lady who was his piano pupil.

One day in fact I let myself be persuaded to accompany him to the lesson and was thus presented to her and her family. The young woman was most beautiful, with big eyes and black hair, a beautiful mouth, and a delicious soprano voice. Also when, some time later, my brother went into the army, I kept on frequenting the young woman's house, and naturally a certain feeling grew between us. And the feeling would perhaps have become love. With time, however, I noticed with surprise that her hair had changed color, and from black had been transformed to golden blonde. In spite of how strong my attraction to her had been, it was overcome by this metamorphosis. I found myself, almost without being aware of it, visiting less and less, until I stopped altogether. Later she married a man who had, obviously, a liking for blondes. So it is, sometimes, that a woman who through silly vanity alters even just the color of her hair, alters her appearance and changes, without knowing it, her destiny.

CHAPTER 6

A New Revelation

TWO MONTHS PASSED in some tranquility. One evening close to Christmas[22] my father came to the house all enthusiastic. The music bug—or if you wish, devil or angel—had gone to work on him also. At one of the cafes in the Piazza dell'Esedra he had heard a young man with a marvelous voice sing several pieces, a young man who had come to Rome with the hope of studying the baritone repertoire. He was so excited that he wanted my brother to hear him, with the eventual aim of seeking admission for him at the Conservatory of Santa Cecilia, and he had, also for that reason, invited him to pass Christmas Eve with us. This future singer was Oreste Benedetti.[23]

On the whole he looked like an Indian. Actually, he too was from Pisa and spoke a pure Tuscan. Tall, thin, with a very dark complexion and rather sparse and shiny black hair that adhered to his head, he had beautiful, big eyes of an indefinite color, an even mouth, big, white teeth, and a winning smile. The first impression he made, in spite of his somewhat uneasy manner, was most favorable, and we soon took a great liking to him. My brother asked him some questions and he began to tell us how he had discovered he had a voice.

He was working in a brick factory in Pisa.[24] One day while he was pouring cold water on his chest to counter the excessive heat of the kiln he began to sing a popular song. His fellow workers, hearing his beautiful voice, advised him that he would be better off singing on the street than broiling himself there. My brother, seated at the piano, invited him to sing something. He didn't have to beg. Such was the power of this voice that the little room rang with it and the windowpanes were vibrating noticeably. Quite a phenomenon. It wasn't merely a matter of power. My brother, having opened the score of *La favorita*, which Benedetti said he knew, accompanied him in the first *romanza*, "*Vien, Leonora, a' piedi tuoi...*" He interpreted it with such subtlety and musical taste that we all immediately realized the reason for Father's enthusiasm.

We all sat at table happy to have him with us. I was lost in thought, convinced that my tenor voice in comparison with his was next to nothing, and my heart was full of the most bitter regret. Yet my enthusiasm for him was no less ardent than my father's. I would have heard him sing, again and again, endlessly. By now, in spite of the fact that I felt so inconsequential when compared to Benedetti, the passion to sing had become gigantic in me, a second nature.

Christmas Eve passed in an atmosphere that was essentially musical. After dinner friends of my father came over, invited expressly by him to make Benedetti's acquaintance, and Benedetti spontaneously offered to sing pieces from *Belisario* and *L'africaine*. The room boomed with notes that were echoing formidably in the distance. In the street people were applauding. The guests were as enthusiastic as we. Mother, looking at me, intuited the joy and suffering alternating on my face. I envied Benedetti's voice so much, I would have liked to steal it. His manly temperament grew more lovable thanks to his affability and his rudimentary youthful simplicity.

My father, after conferring with Mother, offered him our hospitality in spite of our limited means, saying: "Dear Benedetti, we're happy to share our modest meals with you; what suffices for nine will do for ten. My two sons, Ettore and Ruffo, sleep in two separate beds in a big room; I can add a third; and, if they don't have a problem with that, as of tomorrow you could come to stay with us. You would complete your studies here in Rome; with my friends we would find you a good maestro. This way the whole world will someday admire your voice, and I could hold myself in some small way responsible.

Benedetti was astonished. With tears in his eyes he thanked us, and on the morrow he came to stay with us, where he remained for about a year.

He was taken under the artistic tutelage of the Roman maestro Caio Andreoli,[25] who was very knowledgeable of opera and its traditions and had no great difficulty placing his voice, as he already had an exceptional natural placement. In a very short time Benedetti was able to study operatic scores with extraordinary results. He learned by memory *Il trovatore, Ruy Blas, Ballo in maschera, Aida, Rigoletto* and other operas of the standard repertory. Our affection for him was always more fervent, as was our admiration. Returning home from work was special for me. Every day that magic voice penetrated deeper into the innermost fibers of my being.

It was a divine voice. I don't remember its equal in the world. Above all in the phrase from *Belisario*: "*Ah, se potessi piangere, di duol non piangerei...*"[26] He came up with notes that had a softness and color so noble, so aristocratic that I was mesmerized. I followed him mentally and sometimes also imitated his pose of body and all his movements. In this way many melodies became part of me, and I took them with me to the shop, and repeated them inside me many times while I worked mechanically. I couldn't wait to return to the house to hear them again from his golden voice. I considered myself defeated. I never spoke to my brother or my mother about my tenor voice, still entombed. I didn't want the slightest mention made for fear of exacerbating my wound. But, just as "the tongue continually touches the aching tooth," the subject was always hammering in my brain.

"You see," I told Mother to comfort her, "this just isn't my destiny. Even if I still had it, what would my little voice be in comparison to his? A little stream compared to an ocean."

She readily replied: "Even the slightest stream of pure water, persisting with logical good sense, can become a vein of precious gold."

I always ended with a sigh and, caressing her, concluded that it would be better not to think about it further, instead of saddening ourselves with vain dreams. However, in the depths of her soul she had faith that one day my voice would return.

One thing is certain in spite of my doleful lamentations during Benedetti's stay with us: I was aware of great changes in myself. I grew in stature, in robustness, in willpower, in ambition, in mental serenity, my entire being was absorbed, fixed and centered on one thought only: the stage. I fought against destiny; I hoped against hope. I read some book or other again and on Sunday I went to the theater, whether to see a play or an opera. Maestro Andreoli, who was one of the directors of the Quirino,[27] gave free tickets to our guest, and in this way we were able to go with him to hear, among others, *Faust* with the bass, Lucenti, who had the most beautiful voice and made a magnificent Mephistopheles, and the *Forza del destino* with the tenor, Cartica,[28] another admirable voice that rose with surprising facility to the very highest notes.

Benedetti was now ready to be judged by the public. My father was awaiting the best occasion for his debut. Andreoli on his part had begun to inform the impresarios that he had a truly outstanding pupil, and promised them to let them hear him as soon as possible. Meanwhile, working in the shop I was still humming Benedetti's repertory, trying to imitate every note, every accent, every shading. By now I knew practically the entire *Belisario*. Now and again I'd look for my tenor voice, which had been gone for some time, but I felt more in tune with the baritone voice. I was used to the superhuman voice of Benedetti, and next to his no tenor's voice seemed strong enough to raise itself in the world.

One day it happened that after work, while I was washing up with Pietro at the fountain in the shop, I tried to describe the voice of Benedetti and, to give him an idea of it, tried to sing the phrase of *Belisario*:

Sognai... fra... genti barbare...
Terribile un Guerriero...
Che minacciava... i cardini
Crollar... del greco Impero.

While I was clowning around trying to imitate Benedetti's vocal power there really erupted from my lungs a voice so powerful, massive, enormous that Pietro was transfixed. How could something so prodigious have issued from a kid like me? I continued to sing, seeking to heighten and enlarge the sounds, using what is called in theatrical terms the *voce di bocca*, and finally succeeding in exaggerating the already incredible amplitude of the notes. I was in another world! I dried my hands and face in a hurry, closed the shop, and went home. Inside I looked for Mother with my heart in my mouth.

"Mother," I shouted, "I have a baritone voice! I tried it just now in the shop! Pietro was struck dumb by it. Now I can't sing, though—I'm tired. Anyway, I'd be too ashamed in front of Benedetti. But later you'll hear."

My brother thought that I was joking because I was laughing convulsively. After I regained my composure, I took the score of *Belisario*, made my brother find the page of the famous phrase; I asked Benedetti and my mother to sit down for a moment, and began to sing. When I had finished the phrase, they were looking at each other with amazement. Benedetti—who during the solemnity of my *mise en scène*, had asked, laughing, "What the devil are you going to do?"—exclaimed, "By God, what a voice! Where did it come from? Tomorrow I'm taking you to Andreoli."

I told him that in all this time I'd done nothing more than study and imitate him, and that in the long workdays, while staring at the fire in the forge to see when the iron was white hot, I had often repeated by memory the melodies I'd been hearing in past months.

My mother was radiant with joy. The faith that my voice would return, which had always been alive in her, now received its reward. By nature I had a great ear and a perfect grasp of music which permitted me to fix in my head with ease a great number of melodies, as if I had studied them from the scores.

The next day Benedetti and my brother and I went to Andreoli.

After hearing me the maestro told Benedetti: "This is a voice which will be the rival of yours in a few years." Clapping me on the back he asked how old I was. At the time I was just a little over eighteen.

"All right then," he added, "if you will have patience— because now you're too young for the power of voice that you have—you can aspire to a great career. There are exceptional elements in your voice as there are in Benedetti's."

I told him of the disappearance of my tenor voice, and expressed the fear that the same thing might happen with the baritone voice I had now.

He reassured me that the cavities where the voice gained resonance were now completely developed, and I should relax about this, because my present baritone voice would never abandon me. He recommended that I live a healthy life, that I not smoke, that I not go to bed late, and above all that I refrain from singing for another year.

I thanked Andreoli for his advice, which I promised to scrupulously obey, and went right home to tell everything to Mother. Kissing me she said, "Now, then, it's up to you to keep that voice."

As for Father it was decided, with Benedetti's agreement, to tell him nothing of what had happened. The contagion of opera which had been introduced by my brother had spread rapidly and become even more invasive with the presence of Benedetti. Without being fully aware of it we had given our minds to it quite a bit and then more than quite a bit, until my father had been distracted from his routine. Already upset with me because of my indifference about going to work at the shop, woe to me if he knew of my audition with Andreoli and the idea, which had been reinforced, of making a singer out of me! He would certainly have been up in arms, as in fact he was later when I began my musical studies. With the certainty in my heart that my voice would still be there, with newly revived hope, with the experience of so many things—I remembered the physical debility caused by my relationship with Armida, which served as a lesson on how to preserve myself during my career—I set to work from that day forth with greater energy. I kept secret my intimate aspirations, but demonstrated to Father by my actions that I was of good will. In turn, Father showed himself more calm and conciliatory.

After about a year of studies Benedetti debuted at the Quirino in *Trovatore*, as Count di Luna,[29] a part that perfectly suited his at once powerful and melodious voice. His success was tumultuous, and he was spoken of as a revelation. Toto Cotogni[30] swore he had never heard a voice so beautiful and predicted a glorious career. The judgment of such a great artist quickly made the rounds in all the agencies in Milan.

I was never absent, I never missed even one evening of the performances of *Trovatore*. For me it was a superhuman enchantment and a continuous lesson. Above all I loved the recitative and aria in the second act. Benedetti ended the recitative, *"Leonora è mia!"* with a sustained G-natural of the purest timbre imaginable; then he started the *romanza* chiseling the words with a *mezza voce* of such a delicious finesse that he was obliged to repeat it every night amid roars of acclamation. It goes without saying that he was exultant, and that I was rejoicing along with him. It seemed somehow that his triumph belonged to me.

My love for him was no less than my admiration. I was in and out of his dressing room, helping him to change his costumes. We went home together. My father, who was pleased to have brought such a unique and rare voice to public attention was worried that Benedetti would ruin himself by smoking too much—he always had a lit *toscano* cigar in his mouth—began making severe but just observations to him. The maestro repeated the same warnings, but Benedetti listened to none of them. He insisted that he wouldn't have been able to sing at all without his cigars, and owed to them his ability to sing piano. How many artists have been ruined by this mania!

When the performances at the Quirinal were finished he was engaged again in Rome for *Ernani* at the Teatro Manzoni.[31] He signed the new contract without saying anything to my father, who was justifiably resentful. Aside from the wrong to my father, it was a serious mistake. The guilt for it resided with Maestro Andreoli, who attempted to justify the action by saying that it was necessary to make his pupil known in another opera of his repertory.

Now Benedetti was bowing in the part of Carlo V. The part was perfectly suited to his voice. For the rest of it, however, he wasn't Carlo V but merely Benedetti dressed in a dark costume of the Cinquecento style, with no knowledge whatever of the character, without authority, without majesty. It was a step backward, as he himself was quickly made aware. I suffered from it more than he did. After the event Andreoli began to fall in my estimation, since he had induced his pupil to take the engagement to satisfy the greed of certain impresarios who were friends of his, and to expedite the appearance of another of his pupils in the part of Elvira.[32] Benedetti, to recover, began to study new operas—among them I remember *Torquato Tasso*[33] of Donizetti and *I pagliacci* of Leoncavallo. In the famous prologue of this last he emitted stupendous sounds, which I sought and was able, several years later, to reproduce with the same power.

A year after Benedetti's departure I had wanted Maestro Andreoli to hear my voice, but since he was away I was able to arrange for myself, with the help of my brother's knowledgeable friends, to be admitted to an audition at the Conservatory of Santa Cecilia, with the idea of studying singing there one of these days. It was more dream than idea, and the hard struggle to earn a living always held me back more and more from achieving it, all the more because the voice was something unstable that came and went, and this beautiful muse, when I was seeking her out, didn't always obey me in a docile way. The hardships of my family, the want even of sufficient food sometimes (and other circumstances I haven't mentioned) constrained me to look in a practical way at the bitter realities of things. True, my brother persisted sometimes in making me do vocal exercises, but since it did not seem to me that I possessed a voice as magnificent as the one of a year before, I was losing confidence in myself. However, when it was decided that I was to be admitted to the requested audition I applied myself with the full strength of my will to train my voice every day, and quickly obtained rewarding results. My mother was always there to comfort me, assuring me that the admission examination would go well, and that I would be accepted. After about two months of study, I presented myself with my brother at the famous Conservatory of Santa Cecilia.

This was the first time that I had ever crossed the threshold of a school. I can't tell you how nervous I was. We entered a huge room on the ground floor. There were other aspirants to be heard. When would my turn come? My brother's harmony teacher, Alfredo Palombi,[34] one of the most capable musicians of the school, tried to assure in a polite way that I would be called among the first. I was called, in fact, second. I had brought an aria from *Dinorah* of Meyerbeer to sing for my first offering—later I will tell you why. When I found myself in front of all these old professors I felt my strength dwindling, but, from the moment the maestro played the first chord on the piano I felt myself being entirely separated from my personality so that all at once, as if by means of a magical effect, I had assumed another, ready to sing with the complete confidence. After the recitative, which I delivered with a calm and passionate accents, I began the aria, *"Sei vendicata assai,"* emitting the clearest possible tone and sustaining all the G-flats with surprising facility. All the professors were making signs of approbation amongst themselves. I had won the day: I felt it, I saw it! At the end of the aria I hastened to offer the maestro my second piece, but they wouldn't let me continue and said right out that I had already demonstrated vocal qualities sufficient to secure admission.

I was in the clouds. I left the semblance of a stage I was on, saying thank you to my examiners with an obsequiousness which my joy was exaggerating. My brother and I embraced each other, and after thanking Maestro Palombi, we ran home.

Now I shall tell you how it was that I brought the aria from *Dinorah* with me.

At that time I was executing numerous little jobs for the palace of Prince Caetani, among them, the repair of a music stand which was decorated with a lyre. When I was bringing it back finished I had to pass through a big salon in the style of Louis XVI, where there was a grand piano. I stayed there several minutes alone while I was waiting and lots of images passed through my mind. I imagined myself being received in these luxurious surroundings, not as a common ironworker, but as a lyric artist, with my music in my hand, going right to the piano to sing and be applauded. While I was thus absorbed in my fancies, a liveried servant came to tell me to come back tomorrow for further orders.

That night I dreamed, and not with open eyes this time, that in that superb room a great concert was being given. I was present; the grand piano was open. Standing erect behind the piano there was a most handsome Moor in evening clothes, and hundreds of people were milling around, filling up the room at the pleasure of a great lady with a white wig and a splendid pearl necklace that reached almost to her waist. The Moor began to sing in a baritone voice that called to mind Benedetti's and even resembled my own somewhat. It was an aria, the one from *Dinorah*, which he performed stupendously. At the end noisy applause broke out, and at this point I awoke. Under the influence of this strange dream I decided to take this very same selection to the audition with me, and in singing it, to try to imitate the art of the brilliant Moor.[35]

My admission to Santa Cecilia was received with great joy by my family, especially by my mother, who—I like to repeat it—had always had faith in my career. Not so with my father. It seemed to him that we had all lost our minds, and his customary quarrels with my mother were reignited. Though I promised that I merely intended to make trial efforts, and would only be absent from my duties at the shop two hours at a time, three times a week, he understood perfectly that after such a success these were just so many words, and that the music mania had me in its grip just as surely as it had my brother, and that we would end by being alienated from him. He was even angry at himself before it was over, and cursed the day he had met Benedetti.

At the conservatory three classes for male voices were conducted by Professors Ugolini and Persichini.[36] I was assigned to the latter, and for the first months I was there as a mere auditor. Lessons began at 9:30 a.m., and Persichini always arrived on time. He was a fine-looking man of about sixty-five: tall, wavy white hair parted very carefully in the center of his head; large white moustaches which he curled continually, and a goatee à la Napoleon III. He customarily wore a black vest and jacket, striped pants, ironed to resemble razor blades before him; he wore shoes, also black, of course, whose squeaking always announced his arrival some time in advance. For the rest, he was the prototype of the nineteenth-century gentleman. His pupils were very obsequious to him. When he entered the classroom, all of them rose to their feet, someone took his gloves, and someone else his silk hat, another his cane. Then he rang his little bell for coffee. He sipped it very quietly while looking at himself indulgently in the mirror. Finally he brought forth a white handkerchief, dried his mouth with great delicacy, dividing his moustaches to do so, and replaced it with great elegance in his breast pocket, so that only a perfect triangle was showing. The whole ceremonial preparation took twenty minutes. Finally he sat down to the piano, pulling diligently on his pants to conserve the crease, played a dozen or so scales to warm up his fingers and called his first pupil.

If I remember correctly Persichini's class was then composed of seven pupils: three tenors and four baritones. With the lessons beginning at around ten and ending at noon, it often happened that there was hardly time for each pupil to study more than a quarter of an hour. The pupil who got the most attention from the maestro was Giuseppe de Luca,[37] who, already five years ahead in his studies, was now rehearsing the operas.

Sometimes De Luca's lesson lasted three-quarters of an hour, so that for all the rest there was barely ten minutes to do some *vocalises,* and sometimes it was so annoying to be there so many hours without doing anything that I began to yawn and sometimes even to fall asleep. Moreover, the shop was feeling my absence, and from my father there were continual recriminations. When he went to the shop and almost never found me at my post, often in order to be at the Conservatory, I did not have to put up with mere annoyance, but rage and fury over the waste of my time. In addition, I was not one of Maestro Persichini's favorite pupils, and on the rare times that he deigned—I've told how I was admitted as an auditor only for the first months—to have me vocalize for him, he found my voice sluggish, and predicted that I would never be able to sing as a baritone. When I reflected that, according to the regulations, I was facing six years there in that "purgatory" rather than in the conservatory, I was mortified. No, it wouldn't be possible to tolerate such a parasitic life, or submit to such a torture for so much more time.

When I began my regular lessons, doing my *vocalises* for a quarter of an hour every morning, the maestro insisted that my voice was that of a bass, and sought to train it as such. In his stubborn fixation he was soon wanting to teach me the aria of Zaccaria in *Nabucco*, a piece which I didn't like at all. So I felt the first stirrings of dissension between us. Besides, my economic condition was steadily becoming more unsettling. At times I didn't even have the means to pay the modest monthly fee. As an actual student I stayed there for about seven months, but I didn't even take the exam for the second course of lessons.

I studied a little solfeggio and, with Maestro Lucidi,[38] a little piano, but my hands were so stiff that one fine day he sent me home, asking me not to come back, that it would be a waste of my time. He was quite right, but the regulations required that pupils of singing know how to play the piano, and no one imagined that, after my singing lesson, a hammer and a file were awaiting me. Maestro Lucidi, though an eminent pianist, had little knowledge of people and was completely lacking in tact. He treated me as a poor wretch, and finished by making a report to the director's office—then occupied by Marchetti[39]—describing me as "absolutely refractory" in music.

On the other hand I demonstrated special aptitudes and made noteworthy progress in the recitation classes. The maestro of recitation was the celebrated Virginia Marini.[40] She was then fifty-five years old, but she didn't look it. She was a most attractive woman, with lively and luminous eyes, full of intelligence. She was affable with everyone, and patient enough with the students, without in any way diminishing the respect and deference that her fame as a great artist and her imperious personality inspired. I went to her lessons three times a week. She had me read passages from *Francesca da Rimini* and *Cavalleria rusticana*, and, finally, for the first public examination she entrusted me with the part of Loustalot[41] in *Linda di Chamounix*.

I put as much feeling as I could into this part. After Linda is cursed in the house in Paris, I added something of my own that no one had taught me, which elicited lengthy praise from the maestra. I recall that she said to the Count of San Martino[42] that I had something exceptional in my temperament, and would succeed as a real actor. For this I was encouraged to keep going to the Liceo for a few months more; otherwise, between the adverse judgment of Maestro Lucidi regarding the piano and the standstill I'd reached with Persichini regarding my singing ability, I would have left a lot sooner.

One fine day the inevitable blow-up between me and the latter came to pass. I was becoming ever more intolerant of his lessons, and finally had to tell him what I really thought. I told him frankly that his school wasn't adapted to all voices, and that he had not understood my voice at all. I reproached him for all the time I had wasted on his method and even hazarded some other unfavorable comments of a personal nature.

Persichini became a monster of rage. He called me every name in the book, the least harsh of which were, as I remember it, "ignoramus," "scoundrel," "misfit," "wrecker of musical culture," and so on. He enjoined me to leave his class. To his furious outburst I replied with great calm: I knew I was ignorant, and between me, the ignoramus, and him, the expert, there could never be any agreement. I took from his piano my Concone *vocalises*[43] and my hat, saluted my schoolmates, who pitied me for throwing away my position, and so, with a bit of scandal attached, I finished my course of study at the Conservatorio. On the way down the stairs I met the bursar, who tried to extract from me some twenty lire which he claimed I owed the school. I promised to bring it to him, but I didn't have it, and I never did bring it to him thereafter—the only wrong for which I had to reproach myself.

When my brother learned from Palombi, the harmony teacher I've already mentioned, that I had abandoned the school, he was desperate. Mother was inconsolable, especially because of the bit of scandal I had provoked. I explained that, with everything else aside, given the perpetual friction with my father because of singing, it was impossible that I would persist in frequenting the Liceo for many years to come. And so the clouds began to build up again on my horizon.

I spent several months feeling the effects of discontinuing my singing. I had turned nineteen years of age and it seemed to me, without exaggeration, that I had turned fifty. What path to take? By now I saw all the roads closed except that which led to the shop, but even there in the soot of the forge there was no escape because my business was going to the dogs. I had been steering between high and low perils without going under; now it appeared that I was ready to sink. My mother's sufferings for this catastrophic life of mine were indescribable. My brother continued to scold me for having left the conservatory the way I had. I wailed and I trembled. Only by working to earn my bread was I able to avoid going to hell. I was in this state of mind when, with the aid of Bellatalla's son, who had brought me some work for which he advanced some hundreds of lire, I could reopen a little shop in via Napoli in front of the American church. I called back one of my workers, Pietro Cardolini, a man of heart and conscience, and we managed fairly well for a while. My father, whom I saw rarely, was somewhat appeased when he found out about the new shop. Thus I found a little calm and with Pietro's help could dedicate myself for several hours each day to work on my voice. In the depths of my soul I didn't want to give Persichini the last word.

The baritone Sparapani[44] was mentioned to me as a good singing teacher, a man who was in his time a celebrated artist. Now retired from the stage, he had opened a school in Rome.

One morning I decided to let him hear me. I formed a high impression of him. A mature man, with dyed beard and moustache, eyeglasses on his nose, he looked to be about sixty years old. He was an outstanding pianist and accompanied his pupils himself. I briefly recounted my sad history as a student and my resolve to continue. After having listened to me sympathetically, he sat down at the piano and, when he had heard my voice, marveled that Persichini could have judged me a bass. He affirmed on the contrary that it was the purest baritone, and he asserted also, as had Andreoli, that with serious study I could have an important career. I told him of my financial situation, which did not permit me to pay for lessons. He responded that he lived from his teaching work, and could arrange three hours for me each week, but to take me on for nothing would be absolutely impossible for him. I settled with him for three hours a week at the minimum price of fifty lire per month, and I went my way planning to advance him, on a future date, the first fifty lire that I would have the good fortune to earn. My brother and my mother were overjoyed by the happy result of my latest audition.

But how to put together the necessary fifty lire? To scrape it up as fast as possible I worked without any time off with dear Pietro. The old adage *"volere è potere"* (if you want to, you can) was right this time. Getting our wrought-iron products ready and selling them at very moderate prices, after a week I had the means to advance the fifty lire to my new maestro and begin my lessons.

Right away I made considerable progress. One hour with Sparapani was worth more than a month with Persichini. In the second month I advanced him twenty-five lire, promising to bring the rest when I had finished the first six lessons. I was able to do so and thus completed my second month of study.

By the third I was flat broke. Reluctantly Sparapani continued to keep me for another month without being paid, but finally, in spite of my progress, he declared that he would have to suspend the lessons. And here I was once again having to stop my lessons out of hard necessity. What to do? At home we fought for our daily bread without knowing which way to turn, as they say.

As it happened for some time now my father had been receiving from an American millionaire, Mr. Christy, the commission from a grand barred gate he had made. A large sum was involved in this work and my father assigned me and Pietro to do the most difficult part. I had been working on the job with more or less eagerness and diligence, as when I had been drowning with passion for Armida, but now I redoubled my efforts, fueled by my despair. This piece was destined to close a 15th century portico at the entrance of a splendid castle which Mr. Christy was having built near Philadelphia, spending his patrimony lavishly. I would have to be a consummate stylist to describe it properly. I will only say that the work was executed with a style so exquisite and harmonious that all together, though it was made of iron, it seemed to be the finest lace, and many artists—sculptors, painters and engravers—friends of my father, came to admire it and compliment us for it.

The barred gate was almost finished when Mr. Christy came to Rome to see it. He was enthusiastic about it, and knowing that the most difficult part, which he had most admired, had been my work, he couldn't believe it, and squeezing my hand with enough power to do me some damage, he told me: "Braffo, piccolo Cellini!"

I can't have done discussing this work without mentioning my brother's role in its success, since he had furnished me with patterns for the eight panels of sheet iron which were to overhang the base. Without doubt this was the strongest work which I ever executed prior to embarking on my career of lyric artist. The price paid—and from the price one can guess its value—was 14,000 lire, an extraordinary sum for the time.[45]

Now I must make it known, going back a little, that my father had already gone and spent an advance of 9,000 lire of this payment. I was resentful, since the most conspicuous part of the gate had been the work of Pietro and me. Quite upset I told him that in two months I would certainly have finished the chiseling of the eight panels of sheet iron, but with the understanding that he would reserve me enough to enable me to acquire two suits and a heavy overcoat, as well as a small sum which would be enough for me to go to Milan, where I had the intention of beginning my career as a singer.

My father, most indignant, called me a fool. According to him it would be a lot easier to become famous with a chisel than with a voice. He didn't have any belief whatever in my success in such a career.

When the gate was finished and I had received the rest of the agreed sum, my father, perhaps because his conscience was bothering him, reluctantly gave me what I might need to go to Milan. I closed the shop for the last time, and at the end of October 1897, with a third-class ticket and three hundred lire in my pocket, the fruit of two years of patient work, I left for the capital of Lombardy.

CHAPTER 7

The Difficult Threshold

I ARRIVED IN MILAN in the evening and put up at a small inn near the station, and on the morrow, with a letter of introduction that I had obtained in Rome, I went to see Lelio Casini.[46] Casini, like Benedetti, was a native of Pisa and spoke the pure Tuscan. He was a fine figure of a man: tall, with gray hair, beard and moustache à la Carlo V—in this he much resembled Persichini—with a fine file of white teeth a bit stained with nicotine, because he was a relentless smoker; a very attractive smile; in all and everything agreeable. After he had read the letter he presented me to his wife, an accomplished pianist, asking her to accompany me since he wanted to hear my voice right away. I sang two arias. Casini was enthusiastic, and though informed by the letter that I had no means at my disposal, he very generously offered to give me lessons. It goes without saying that I accepted, touched. We arranged a schedule on the spot.

On the piano were many photographs of artists, among which I noticed Angelo Masini, the great tenor,[47] with the dedication: "To the elite singer, Lelio Casini, with admiration." The brief dedication was exactly right. He was truly a singer of extraordinary worth: a classical singer. He had a full, sweet voice with such a softness that it sounded like a cello. This was especially true of his middle voice. I noted that when he was emitting the highest sounds he leaned back on his heels, making a slight exertion.

The lady, a pure Florentine type, was quite a bit younger than her husband. Tall, slender, stately, with a full head of the blonde hair associated with Titian, her mouth was a bit large, her teeth the whitest; she too spoke pure Tuscan; she was elegantly dressed, but without ostentation, and had a simple character but full of dignity. When she disliked something she didn't know how to hide it. After my first lessons they had agreed—the signora had pointed it out as soon as I had sung the two arias mentioned above—that my voice was similar to, but better than, Benedetti's. Their evaluation at once revived in me all my dormant hopes, but the comparison was too flattering, and a sense of modesty and justice would not permit me to consider Benedetti's voice inferior to mine. I said with modest frankness that any interest my singing could boast of I owed to the good luck of having closely followed Benedetti's studies during his long stay with us in our house in Rome.

Maestro Casini and his wife quickly grew quite fond of me. However, one month later I had the bad luck to become ill, and for the following reason. Right after my arrival in Milan I had rented a room in the via Ansperto,[48] near the Teatro Dal Verme. I refer to it as a room, but it was in reality an inside room, sunless and stuffy. For fifteen lire per month, which was the amount of the rent, there was nothing better to be had in Milan. I didn't trouble to apprise myself of exactly what noxious effect the room was having on my health, since very shortly afterward I fell ill with bronchitis. In addition Casini had accepted a contract and would be absent from Milan for some time. I went through some sad enough days now, and my savings were almost used up.

Before leaving, by good fortune, Casini had introduced me to Luigi Mennini, the proprietor of a restaurant in via Santa Margherita near the Teatro alla Scala. It was a restaurant frequented by theater people: singers, impresarios, conductors, ballerinas, mimes.[49] The clientele, instead of calling him by name, Signor Luigi or Signor Mennini, had invented a nickname for him and called him "Barba," because he had a white beard. He was no less than seventy years old, and had shaved his head bald, but his skin was always fresh-looking, a rosy bronze. He resembled one of the biblical figures of Titian or Veronese. Always smiling, always in good humor. He and his old wife Teresina and his numerous children, all of whom worked there with him, took a liking to me right away and called me "Sciur Titta." The good Teresa would sometimes sit down near me and, noticing my dark mood, would do her best to calm and encourage me, predicting that my career would begin soon, and auspiciously. Barba was the benefactor of artists down on their luck, and in his accounts one could read the names of artists who owed him money—who, later, had attained riches and glory. When Casini returned to Milan I wanted to continue my lessons, but the annoying bronchitis that I had contracted in my hole on via Ansperto prevented me.

I was becoming worried, since time was passing and I wasn't getting anywhere. It wasn't a rare evening when I found myself crying alone in my cold room. Perhaps because of the medicines of all kinds I had been swallowing, I'd given myself a bad stomach. I hadn't completely lost my appetite but I was getting thinner. The Christmas Eve of that year was for me the ultimate misery. Such was the degree of misery to which I had been reduced by this miserable life, even thoughts of suicide came to mind.

As a distraction I spent hours and hours in the Galleria di Milano, that unique destination and refuge of all artists, from the most illustrious to the most obscure. I was ignored by all and full of despair. Several times I began listening to the conversation of the artists gathered in every corner, boasting of their voices and the relative success they had had. What an impression all the *divi* made on me then, covered with their furs and jewels, already well along in their careers, gesturing and bawling with a glorious air as if they held the world in their hands. Some others, singing sotto voce, were explaining to their adoring audiences the places where their performances had roused the greatest applause. I returned home with a heavy, heavy heart and tears in my soul.[50]

But I was looking for a way to react. I went to Barba's

cafe, where they scolded me for not having come by for so long. I told them that I had other engagements, but in reality I had been reduced to dining and supping in my room alone... with bread and cheese. Teresina implored me to accept no more dinner invitations, and told me that my absence had upset them, and they had worried that I had contracted a malady more serious than bronchitis. When I had finished my dinner that evening which, in order to elude my endless sadness, was less humble than usual, costing me my last lire, the Mennini family wanted me at their table. All were happy to have me with them, and so, in the general cheerfulness, I was a little more myself.

My mind flew to Rome, to my home, to my mother, to whom I had written two days before a letter full of lies and hopes. Certain sorrows are so intimate that we cannot share them with others. These sorrows are those that strengthen our character, so that, with the passing years, we inure ourselves to a practical philosophy, one less utopian and abstract, and are able to bear the tribulations of our lives with more serenity.

Sainted mother of mine! If I had known what a hard battle I would have to fight to win a sprig of laurel and a little wealth, I might perhaps have done without the choice of this path. All is ephemeral here below, and when the end comes an impartial shadow presses upon us and covers all glory in darkness.

I left the Mennini family late that evening. It was intensely cold and the fog was so thick one could hardly see anything a few yards ahead. The city was wrapped in a deathlike silence. Nothing could be heard but the *tan tan* of the tram. This sound, continuous and monotonous, traversed the dense fog and entered my brain. The frost and freezing damp of the night burdened my lungs, overworked from my bronchitis; I was breathing with difficulty. My overcoat was much too light for the severe Milanese weather. The cold penetrated my bones. And naturally, the more winter advanced, the more I felt the lack of a fur or a heavy overcoat. I followed the streetcar tracks and soon arrived at the Teatro Dal Verme, near my rooming house, numb with cold. I found my way upstairs by lighting a match, then another. Putting the key in the lock I heard animated voices inside. In fact the landlady was entertaining a family from the second floor and a party was under way.

I had hardly entered my squalid room when the landlady appeared, inviting me to have a drink in company. Her guests were a lady and her two children, a son and a daughter. I no longer remember her name, but I remember theirs. The young man, about 25, was blond, with blue eyes, strongly built, who spoke a pure Milanese dialect, and was called (in the manner of Manzoni) Adelchi. The young woman was a girl of about twenty, called Edgarda, and very attractive: tall, slender, with a cute nose turned up a bit, a fine, small face, blonde hair, a small waist. At first sight she seemed rather thin, but observing her closely I realized that she was, as they say, falsely thin. The defect of a pug nose was an advantage in her case, conferring a pleasingly naughty air. She became seductively more attractive thanks to the dialect which she too was using. From the way they greeted me I understood that they had wanted to meet me.

I sat with them at table and we ate and drank until the wee hours. I told them something about myself, of my hopes for a debut before too long, of the torment I had endured for a month now because of my accursed bronchitis. I should not have mentioned it! Everyone wanted to do something for me. From that moment they didn't leave me alone. Their elderly mother suggested massaging my chest. Adelchi would take me to his friend who was a doctor. Edgarda wanted to go immediately upstairs to get certain pills which she guaranteed would cure me. They were bitter as poison, but I did feel a perceptible improvement after a few days.

As she was giving me the box of pills, Edgarda whispered softly so as not to let the landlady hear: "Take care! Other lodgers have fallen sick in your room, because it's so damp and has a thin external wall that faces the courtyard." This was evidently the cause of my stubborn bronchitis. In leaving, Edgarda made me promise to visit them soon, and the mother said that she was ready, any time I wished, to give me a massage with some special ointment.

The next day I got up late. I didn't eat all day and after

reading the instructions on the box, took about ten or so of the pills during the day. I drank warm milk kindly offered me by the landlady. I went out briefly toward evening for a short walk, and returned home. As I was putting my key into the lock I heard the door open on the floor above.

It was Edgarda with a candle in her hand, asking me to come upstairs because her mother wanted to speak to me. I consented. Adelchi hadn't yet returned home. They told me that they never went to bed before midnight and would be delighted if I were to join them occasionally. They advised me to change my quarters right away if I wanted to free myself of further health problems. I noticed that their rooms were much warmer than mine. There was always a fire in the little stove, while in my room there was never a fire burning.

They gave me small bundles of firewood to light before going to bed that night. The warmth helped me to fall asleep easily. These kind people, who knew me only a short time, were so good in their concern for me, especially Edgarda, of course, whose attentiveness infused me with great courage and the will to get well at any cost.

The flame which the affection of a loving woman can rouse and nourish in a man's heart is enough to transform the darkest, most desperate ideas into luminous hope. So it was that without a cent in my pocket, and insecure about tomorrow, I could go to sleep all the same almost happy, thinking that, upon awakening, some saint would have helped me.

I woke after a long sleep. The fire had gone out but the room was still warm. I got up in haste, feeling hunger pangs; it was thirty-six hours since I had last eaten anything.

I stepped out into the street. The day was less foggy than usual and now and then a few rays of sunshine filtered through. After wandering around a bit, I came to the Piazza del Duomo and went into the cathedral. The veiled light coming through the ancient stained glass windows and the mystic silence of the place enabled me to concentrate my thoughts. I dreamed of ways to solve my present situation because I knew I could not go on much longer without food—every hour that passed increased the potency of my hunger pangs.

When I left the Duomo I went towards the Galleria, and at the corner of the Via San Raffaele I passed close to the Fiaschetteria Toscana. It was close to noon and from within came the aroma of sauces, veal stews, roasting chickens, and my mouth began to water—I just couldn't stand it. Still I continued to stroll around in the Galleria until about two, trying to regain control of myself but finally the old adage, "Hunger brings the wolf from out of the woods," was again proven to be true in my case. Though reluctantly, I headed for Barba's trattoria.

Given the somewhat late hour the place was almost empty. That day Barba wasn't there, nor was his wife. I sat down at a table in the back and waited, unable to decide whether or not to call the waiter. Finally the usual old waiter, who was called Piedoni, brought me the list of dishes and invited me to choose. I didn't have the courage to do it, because it seemed I was committing a theft. I did have the courage, or perhaps I should say the heroism, to say that I wasn't hungry; he should only bring me a glass of port and some biscuits; I would eat more that evening when I got back my appetite. After drinking the little glass and finishing the biscuits—there were ten or so and I didn't leave a crumb—I pretended to have forgotten my money at home, and told Piedoni to add it to my bill that evening. He made no objection.

What I had put in my stomach had—would you believe it?—perked me up somewhat and I felt strong enough to last till tomorrow. I spent the rest of the afternoon at home. I happily noticed that the landlady had continued to keep my fire lit. I threw myself on the bed and began to read. I knew that Edgarda, employed in a spinning mill outside the Magenta Gate, would get home from work about seven. About seven, in fact, I heard her ascend the stairs, and I went quickly to her door. I told her the pills had made me better.

Happy, she exclaimed: "I knew it! I'm so glad! Come up to Mother's!" Taking me by the hand she pulled me forthwith to her apartment. I spent the evening with her and her mother, and they pressed me to stay for dinner. It was more stupid than wise to refuse their food, but I had the courage—which, yes, I would call heroism—to do it. I sat with them as they ate without too much suffering. The presence of Edgarda was my food. Without being in love, the friendship of this most likable girl gave me spirit. I began to sing something *piano*; my voice was getting back its resonance; the two women who were blissfully listening exclaimed often: "How well he sings! What a beautiful voice he has!"

Adelchi was in Switzerland on his company's orders and was going to be away for several days. Therefore I remained to keep them company till nearly midnight. Edgarda, accompanying me to the door, gave me another box of pills that she had bought for me, in order for me to continue with my cure. Moved by so much attention, I expressed my emotion by kissing the hand that held the little box, saying that I would never forget her kindness, and that someday, when I would be singing in Milan, I would invite her and her mother to the theater.

The next day I got up early. My stomach was no longer bearing up. My eyes had begun to get cloudy. I asked the landlady for a glass of milk, and she brought it to me herself, asking me if I was pleased to have found my room warm. It seems that, moved by remorse not to have warned me that the room was damp, she was now trying to make up for it.

I left around eleven, again headed for the cathedral, but I didn't experience the same admiration as I had the first day. The beautiful windows—it was cloudy this day—without the vivid reflection of the sun, burdened me with a sense of cold and melancholy. These windows which, animated by sunlight, had been a revelation of the most superb enchantment of art, without it seemed dead. Even the aura of mysticism that was in the air the day before, had vanished. I went forth from the spot disillusioned at having had my first impression cancelled by my last. I wandered about aimlessly for two hours more till my legs told me they no longer had the strength to carry me.

After having reflected at length, my fast—to put it in a somewhat Dantesque fashion—was more powerful than heroism. I headed for Barba's trattoria. I sat at one of the tables that had already been set. Piedoni gave me a menu full of good things. I ordered without reticence and after an hour my physical appearance and humor had changed. I drank almost half a flask of wine and ate heartily for three. As I finished the long meal, crowning it with an excellent coffee and a glass of Three Star brandy, I was overcome by sleep and napped with my elbows upon the table.

There was no one in the trattoria when Piedoni woke me to give me the bill. Scratching my head, I asked him what time Barba would be in, as I had something important to discuss with him. The waiter probably understood what important affair was now in question as, smiling mischievously, he said: "If you have the patience to wait, Barba will be here very soon."

In fact the kind old gentleman came in shortly afterwards, and surprised at seeing me still there at that hour, sat down beside me with the usual affable and smiling air. I had the bill for my meal in hand while I told him my state, promising that I would pay it with the first money I had.

Barba was used to such cases as mine and attached no importance to them. On the contrary, he assured me that his door was always open for me.

Need I say that I was moved when I thanked him? I had scarcely left the cafe before everything that I had eaten had been digested. I felt like a lion. Moreover, the tablets Edgarda had given me had worked a miracle—my bronchitis was dried up, I wasn't coughing any more but breathing easily and freely. I would have been able to sing at the top of my voice.

When I came home to my room I found it nice and warm. The last coals were still glowing in the fireplace. I sped off immediately to thank the landlady, but couldn't find her. I imagined that she had gone up to see Edgarda's mother. I opened the window a bit to air out the room, and then tried out the voice. Since I found it responsive to my will I began to sing out, emitting some very fine notes! Just then the landlady entered, all aglow, saying I could be heard all over the house and that all the roomers were listening.

The bells chimed six o'clock and I was impatiently awaiting Edgarda's arrival to run and greet her. As soon as I heard her enter I went up the stairs like a bolt of lightning, but I hadn't rung the bell before she opened the door, exclaiming,

"What a pity I was not in while you were singing! Mother told me your voice is just beautiful!"

I was so happy I could have hugged her, but limited myself to grasping her two hands and thanking her for the second box of tablets, and repeated that they had effected a wonderful cure.

In a gesture of gratitude (without having been asked to do so) I began to sing in full voice an aria from *Rigoletto* ("*Miei Signori, perdono, pietade...*").[51] As I reached the end without the least effort, her mother exclaimed in Milanese dialect, "What a bold one you are! You sound like Tamagno!"[52]

Edgarda was no longer in her skin, and her eyes clearly betrayed the same desire I had had a little earlier at the door; I believe she didn't act on it out of regard for her mother. Moreover, in those days, to express certain sentiments in that way was detrimental to the reputation of a young girl!

I slept happily the whole night. In the morning I wrote my mother a long letter, and though I had no money for the stamp, I put it in my pocket all the same, hoping to send it in some way or another. I headed directly for the Galleria, where I ran into the Roman baritone Oreste Mieli, who was in Milano without a contract.[53] Just to earn something he had been charged with finding good new voices for the newly-formed Columbia Records company. He suggested I make some records, as it would serve to publicize me a little, and give me a chance to hear my own voice reproduced.

I consented immediately, but only on condition that I be paid a little money. Mieli didn't waste time. Leaving me in the lurch he said, "Wait here. I'll be back in a quarter of an hour and we'll arrange something."

In fact he returned in twenty minutes, panting, and invited me to go with him, explaining on the way that before speaking of money, it was necessary to hear my voice. He convinced me by mentioning that many established artists had begun by singing without a fee.

I was frank and told him that I had not a penny in my pocket, not even enough to buy a stamp for the letter to my mother, which I showed him.

Without realizing it we had reached a first floor on a side street of the Corso, and entered a sort of dark office where I was introduced to the manager. After a long preparation, including several scales with piano, there I was standing before a long sort of iron funnel. I had my voice recorded several times. I saw that it was not an easy thing to do as I had to continue singing for around two hours. "We're dealing with finding the right sound of your voice," a technician told me, so in all I sang seven or eight pieces.

When we had finished I was quite tired, and asked for something in compensation.[54]

After a long discussion with Mieli I, who ten years later signed a contract with the Gramaphone Company and the Victor Talking Machine Company for an outstanding sum, had to content myself with twenty lire.

This was the first money I had made by singing. Naturally, my first thought once I had the money in my pocket was to run to Barba and, while telling him about my good luck, pay my bill, which amounted to seven lire.

He accepted only after I had insisted, but he only did so by making me promise that money or no money I would come to his trattoria regularly for my meals, whether at noon or in the evening, and he told old Piedoni, the waiter who had served me, to always reserve for me a little table by the window looking out on the Piazza Santa Margherita.

I was about to refuse his generous offer, when Teresina added her urgings. May God bless you, dear old lady, wherever you may be! She took my head between her wrinkled hands and kissed me as as a mother would, saying, "Sciur Titta, if you do not come here every day for lunch and dinner, you will make me and my husband very unhappy."

Before leaving the restaurant I gave a nice tip to Piedoni who, seeing me so lively, said, "Things are going well for you, Sciur Titta!"

I opened the letter to Mother and added the news about my records. I passed several happy days in the glow of my first success while awaiting Casini's return. Meanwhile I continued to vocalize alone, happy that my voice had reacquired its former fullness and richness.

I went to give my best wishes to Edgarda and her mother on New Year's eve. Since her brother was still in Switzerland, and she had asked and obtained her mother's consent, she asked me to accompany her to the traditional fair at the Porta Magenta. Which of us two was the happier? We left about nine o'clock and as soon as we were in the street Edgarda hooked her arm around mine and we walked along like two newly-weds.

Around the Porta Magenta there were carrousels and music of all kinds. From the doors of their tents hawkers were inviting the crowds to come in, announcing with deafening cries superb fireworks, lady cannonballs, bearded women, dog-faced men, Indian fakirs, marvelous tightrope walkers, and a thousand other wonders more or less amazing.

The two of us strolled around in the hubbub till nearly midnight, carried off like steam by sentimental intoxication. I took the liberty of offering her exotic American peanuts, candied prunes on toothpicks, and a sweet drink. We were happy, not so much for what we were seeing and hearing, but for the youthful spirits which made us think that we were in the best of possible worlds.

Yet, as the hours passed and we were more engulfed in the merrymaking and she was pressing ever more closely to me, as if she never would have to leave me, I didn't fail to reflect a little. Without looking her in the face, without doing anything wrong or saying a word, I was observing her, I was hearing her, and I was reproaching myself for having accompanied her and to have found myself alone with her. I was afraid; I felt that I had committed a base action. In my heart I reproved her mother for allowing her to come with me. I didn't know how to behave.

But occasionally in the crowd I passed an arm around her waist and then she, giving me a look that seemed to say, "How that pleases me," pressed herself so hard against me she could have been trying to become a part of me. I regretted then to have let myself go so far.

When, leaving the hubbub, we found ourselves back in the

sudden darkness of the street, far from the dazzling acetylene lights and from the noise of the tents and the tumult of the crowd under the faint gaslights of old Milan, we were overcome by a sense of melancholy and walked a long time without saying a word. Now and again she sighed, and finally she broke the silence: "What a shame we have to go home!"

I felt that a word, a signal, an allusion would have been enough to kindle in her a great fire and bind me to her forever. It was for me to give the signal, but I refrained from doing so. The powerful desire to embrace her was vanquished by my caution. I answered her disappointment by saying that it was already too late, and that we were being imprudent to stay out till such an hour. As we moved on I told her that, to my great displeasure, I had to leave the house on via Ansperto because I had no more money to pay the rent. I assured her, however, that the separation from her would never make me forget the courtesy I'd received, and that her sweet company had embellished an otherwise quite sad period of my life.

Tears came to her eyes. Wasn't this more than enough to understand her feeling about me? The impetus of the sensual and the sentimental lacked little to overcome me, but I resisted.

I would not know how to say truly whether my restraint was inspired by a sort of egoism that is often called prudence, but is fear, or from a genuine sense of rectitude and protection. I cared for Edgarda very much, but how could I, in my condition, open my heart to her, permit myself to think of corresponding with her? When a man knows that he is not able to marry a woman, he commits a crime if he seeks to take her, to disturb her life, to stain her soul. If I had abandoned myself to the impetus of the sensual and sentimental I would probably have brought about her ruin, and with hers, mine. I resisted then, and I have never regretted it.

It was almost one o'clock when we returned. Via Ansperto was deserted. In the darkness a black cat passed close to us and slipped in the outside gate. I'd forgotten the matches. There was nothing to do but climb the stairs in darkness. The eyes of the cat in the darkness seemed like two fiery coals. We stopped to wait on the ground floor. She was alarmed by the phosphorescent eyes of the animal, which seemed to be watching us. She started to tremble and put her head on my chest, putting my arm around her neck and murmuring, "I'm so afraid!"

I caressed her face like a sister's. She took my hand and kissed it a few times, saying, "I'm fond of you! You're so good! I like you so much!"

It appeared that this was the moment to open up to her without reticence and I made her understand that her feeling for me was painful to me. I urged her to forget me. I still had to make my way in life and she should have understood that. I added that she should be going away with a smile on her lips and not a tear in her eyes, and I invited her to go up, because without taking any notice of it the time was passing. I can't deny that I hadn't felt an overwhelming desire to hold her in my arms and carry her into my room, but I was able to contain myself.

On the second flight of stairs the eyes of the cat were watching us with a dreadful fixity. Was there inside it some soul watching us through its strange eyes? I called to mind at that moment her brother, Adelchi, who had wished to help me cure my bronchitis by taking me to his doctor friend.

Having reached the door to her house, trembling, I took in my hands the small face of this dear young girl and said, "My good friend... Perhaps this will be the first and the last time... I will remember this evening for the rest of my life..."

Covering her mouth with mine we remained for a moment in paradise!

With the door open I bade her farewell with the following wish: "God protect you always!"

The cat had vanished. I went back down the stairs, had difficulty getting the key in the lock, entered my room, felt about for some matches and lit a candle. "Human vanity," I observed to the mirror. I was distraught. I couldn't get to sleep without difficulty. The image of Edgarda stood firmly before me. To placate my vehement emotions I talked things over in my own mind, wanting to convince myself that the most beautiful part of love was renunciation.

CHAPTER 8

My Career Begins

NEW YEAR'S DAY, 1898, signalled the beginning of my career in the lyric theater. I was twenty years old. I awoke about ten to a silent Milan. So as not to impose on the generosity of the Mennini family I usually only went there in the evening, limiting myself to one meal per day, but on this morning they had invited me to the midday meal, and insisted I not fail to come, because there was a surprise in store for me.

My first impulse as I started to leave the house was to see Edgarda, but since Adelchi was returning today from Switzerland, I headed for the Duomo without delay. I stayed an hour at the Galleria. The records I had cut had turned out magnificently and had achieved a certain popularity for me, as several people congratulated me for my success.

About 12:30 I entered Barba's trattoria, and he, with a certain mysterious air, invited me straight up to the first floor, to a nicely furnished little room. "Here is the surprise," he said. "From tomorrow you will sleep here until you leave Milan to make your debut."

Was I dreaming or wide awake? I have always firmly believed that human affairs are governed by a provident Law of Compensation. Now, I thought, my father's kindness to Benedetti, providing for him like a child, was being reciprocated in the same way for my benefit by the Mennini family.

This year a new life opened for me. Much moved I embraced Barba and told him simply, without an excess of sentiment, that what he was doing for me would remain written on my heart for as long as I lived. We had a drink in honor of my forthcoming debut, and I promised that I would bring all my things over in the morning.

When I left I went directly to pay my respects to Edgarda and her family and also to the landlady. Edgarda was sad. Her expression as she looked at me was indescribable. Happy as the mother and brother had been to see me, when they understood that I would be leaving tomorrow, they became gloomy. Edgarda fled to her room, not returning until later, her eyes red from weeping. We started playing cards. The landlady, after a short time, took her leave. Adelchi had to absent himself. Edgarda's mother excused herself to take a nap. Apparently this was a sort of harmless plot to enable me to propose marriage, but by now the critical moment was past.

Left alone we were able, fortunately, to converse with ease and hurt each other less. I told her that I felt her sadness deeply. I told her to be wise and keep her good memories of me without embittering her young life. I explained that certain feelings of affection and esteem were more enduring than many a love. I told her that I would never forget her and—was I convinced at this moment, or lying out of pity?—that I would never marry, as an artist belongs to his art and his public, and must therefore remain free. I repeated that it would be dishonest on my part to make promises I could not keep. Leaving her I asked her to call me *tu*, as she would a brother. I swore that the bonds of pure friendship between us would never be broken. Edgarda thanked me, touched by my fine words, which expressed a feeling which she reciprocated with the same tenderness.

When I settled into my new quarters at the Mennini's my life changed completely. Casini had returned, as I said, and I was thus able to take my lessons regularly with most profitable results, the bronchitis having disappeared some time ago and my voice become more reliable. I worked on *Faust, Nabucco, Lucia, Ernani* and *Traviata,* and on various chamber music. Casini for his part was rehearsing some operas with Maestro Fornari,[55] his wife accompanying him on the piano. I particularly remember *Tannhäuser*, which he sang marvelously. His voice, though clearly baritone, had a touch of bass. In *Tannhäuser* his Bard's Song and the Evening Star were a delight to hear. He had such exquisite pianos, inflections, and irresistible tone-colorings, besides exceptionally fine low notes of organ-like sonority. Just to listen to him was for me a lesson in bel canto; though I must confess that I never succeeded, with all my talent, in equalling his remarkable finesse. Singing, Casini was transfigured—a sculptor of the exquisite. Less successful in producing true high tones well—the heroic tones not in his usual register—he would turn to me and sigh, "Oh, Ruffo! If only I had your F-natural—for the roles I have undertaken that would be enough to enable me to sing for many more years."

Sometimes, when I took my lesson after eating, we went out together, and almost always went to visit friends of his who were theatrical agents. I remember D'Ormeville especially, who was very kind to everyone, though a little professorial in conversation—he was a good poet and writer.[56] There was a certain Tresolini, with his forest of white hair that made him resemble De Amicis.[57] There was Viviani, then editor of the *Rivista Teatrale Melodrammatica*. He had been a baritone and never lost his love of singing, practically a mania—sometimes he screamed out tones so strident and off-pitch that you had to shut your ears.[58] There was Count Brogli, who had a habit of immersing his index finger in the river of his immense beard as if he were exploring a secret treasure that bestowed eloquence, meanwhile conversing in measured tones. And now and then I was mentally cutting his beard while looking in vain for the reason he received us with such haughtiness.[59]

It was this group which was to give me an audition shortly, Casini having presented me to them as a student of great promise.

After a month and a half of daily, patient studies, I was confident that I could make a successful debut, and I longed to make it soon. Casini on the contrary wanted me to continue my studies for some time longer, but it was not possible for me to do so. Mother had written me that conditions at home were insufferable since I had left. My father had frequent fits of rage, blaming her for having encouraged me to take a false path, while the whole family resented the continuous discord. In addition the situation was aggravated by the absence of my brother, who was doing his military service.

One morning I made a clean breast of the situation to Casini, declaring my urgent need to debut at the earliest possible moment—otherwise I would have to look for a job in Milan or return home. I confessed that since my departure from Rome my father had not written me a single word, and I needed to overcome his contempt and also his skepticism about the career I had chosen. The first auditions for the theatrical agents would be around the end of February, and every one of them would be a battle I would have to win.

With a pounding heart and a fear of failure I appeared at the agencies. With the cold of that winter, caused by the Milanese fog, my voice wasn't always as ready as a barrel-organ. However, I made the rounds and had all the agents hear me. By good luck every one of them along the way was full of admiration for my voice. Therefore when an impresario was arriving the agents would send for me and try to arrange a contract. However, the impresarios, although forming a "magnificent impression" after hearing me, would add that they were sorry that I hadn't debuted yet. They were hesitant to sign a beginner. I was on tenterhooks the whole time. I unbosomed myself to Barba.

The kind old man told me not to be in such a hurry. "You'll see, it will be easier than you think. Your voice leaves nothing to doubt." He added, "You're scarcely twenty years old—still a boy—so take it easy. I have never been mistaken in my judgment. I have navigated these waters for many years, and when Barba judges, he judges well."

I continued to frequent the Galleria, where some of those who had heard me audition had been talking about me, referring to me as one of the new hopes of the opera. Then one day they introduced me to counselor Molco,[60] then legal representative of the celebrated baritone Giuseppe Pacini. Pacini was one of the finest singers to come from Florence, in fact the finest baritone of the time, and he was then singing at the Lirico in Milan. Molco, after hearing the good things that had been said about my voice, looked at me incredulously and said in a joking manner, "Young man, if you really want to hear a great voice, go to the Lirico tonight."

I told him I greatly admired baritones, and if I had the means I would certainly go. He then kindly offered me a ticket.

I do not remember exactly what Pacini sang that night— *Sansone e Dalila,* I think—I only remember that the power and beauty of his voice carried me to heaven. To me it seemed like the voice of an Archangel. On comparing him with Benedetti at the latter's Rome debut, I couldn't have said who deserved the laurels.[61]

One morning I was called to an audition by the Agenzia Argenti, where I was presented to the impresario Bolcioni, who (like Viviani) had been a baritone.[62] By great good luck, that morning my voice was in exceptionally good form. Bolcioni was already negotiating to sign the baritones Giani and Arcangeli, considered two of the best voices at that time,[63] but after I had sung two numbers from my repertoire, he broke off negotiations. He told Argenti that I had a voice of the Old School and that I could consider myself signed, but first he wished to hear me in a theater, to see whether my voice, which sounded tremendous in a small room, would be the same in a large theater. He paid me many compliments and told me to study the part of the Herald in *Lohengrin,* and he would hear me again in a few days.

I learned that he was seeking the personnel to round out a company which was to present a season in the coming spring at the Costanzi in Rome, and he needed a baritone for the role of the Herald.

I cannot describe the emotion I felt when I learned that I was to make my debut in my home town. I couldn't sleep. I confided in Barba, told him all about my hopes and doubts that this wonderful dream would come true. The good Barba knew Bolcioni very well, and told him not to let me slip away, as one day or another some other impresario would be sure to grab me.

One of the regulars at Mennini's trattoria was the Spanish tenor Emanuele Izquierdo,[64] who had heard much about me and my voice, and he asked me whether I would mind having an audition tomorrow at the Teatro Alhambra,[65] where there would be literally hundreds of singers of every type to be heard by the impresario Cavallaro, who came to Rome every year to form companies for the opera houses of Sicily and Calabria. Naturally, I accepted and we agreed to meet tomorrow at the theater. Izquierdo had already been signed by Cavallaro.

I immediately told Casini, inviting him to the audition, but he unfortunately could not accompany me. Then I went to the Agenzia Argenti to inform Bolcioni.

The next day Izquierdo introduced me to Cavallaro, saying "This is the baritone I was telling you about."

Cavallaro looked me over from head to foot, then said, "He's too much of a kid and too green for me, but nevertheless I will hear him for a possible engagement next year."

Cavallaro looked like a Saracen, but was a pure Sicilian. He was an attractive type, tall, with gray hair and turned-up whiskers after the fashion of that time, with a dimple in the middle of his chin. He was most intelligent about voices and theatrical matters, and had all the requisite qualities of a top-flight impresario, but by choice limited his activities to Sicily and Calabria.

The Alhambra was already full, as Izquierdo had told me it would be, of singers of every range of voice and of both sexes, resembling a theatrical rally. Cavallaro had already heard many of them that morning. With him was another Sicilian impresario, Mastrojeni, from Messina, a more aristocratic type than Cavallaro, but less competent in the field.[66] After a few minutes I was asked to go onstage.

The very thought of undergoing an examination in front of all those singers made me freeze. If I cut a bad figure it would immediately be broadcast throughout the theatrical Olympus, and I would be through before I started. However, I bucked up and boldly sang the aria from *Ballo in maschera*.

When I had finished, Cavallaro turned smiling to Mastrojeni and exclaimed, "*Minchia!*[67] What a voice that boy has! What's his name?" Izquierdo hurried to answer, "Ruffo Titta," to which Cavallaro replied, "I don't like it. It's not artistic. We'll change it."

I felt that he was pleased with everything else. Security had replaced the doubt in me. At the end of the aria all present had applauded me noisily. I asked Cavallaro to let me sing, for my own pleasure, the *Dinorah* aria. He did, and as I had foreseen, it was decisive in my success. Cavallaro, pulling his whiskers from low to high between his thumb and index finger, a habit with him when on the verge of pronouncing judgment, exclaimed, "At last! After so many years I have found the voice I've been looking for." He had me come down from the stage and sit next to him.

Bolcioni, who hadn't failed to make the audition for fear of losing his Herald, called me aside to tell me that my contract was ready and he would expect me at the Argenti Agency at 5:00 p.m. to sign it.

Cavallaro asked me if Bolcioni were my agent, and I answered with a small lie. "I have already signed a contract with him for my debut in Rome," thereby raising my commercial value in Cavallaro's eyes.

In this audition my destiny had been decided, as that same evening I not only signed Bolcioni's contract for Rome, but another with Cavallaro for the term of one year, binding me to him from October 1898 until September 1899. Bolcioni's contract for my first season of two months stipulated a fee of 300 lire. After subtracting the agent's commission, my pay was 3½ lire per day. Cavallaro, on the other hand, after deducting his commission, was to pay me 9½ lire per day for a year.[68] Thus, in only one day, I had succeeded in winning great acclaim in the theatrical world.

All the auditioners then flocked to the Galleria, saying wonderful things about my voice. Casini, although he would have preferred that I continue my studies with him, heard the news with much pleasure. When I arrived at Barba's, he already knew the whole story, including the terms of my contracts. The good Teresa, as a sign of homage and joy at my success, had had my little room decked out with flowers. She embraced me happily and told me, "Dear Titta, I'm as happy for you as I would be for my own son." I borrowed ten lire from her and ran, full of happiness and pride, to the telegraph office to pass on the news to Mother. That same night I wrote two letters—one to my mother, telling her in minute detail the story of the contracts and expressing my happiness to be able to embrace her soon as a contracted lyric artist for the Costanzi in Rome. The other letter was to my brother in the armed forces.

The next day I did not fail to visit Edgarda and her mother, who received the news of my coming debut with all possible joy. I stayed a while with them, and upon leaving told them I would soon depart for Rome. Edgarda accompanied me to the street. Squeezing my hand, pale as could be, she whispered sadly, "If you think of me sometimes, it would mean a lot to me." In that moment—incredible but true—the same cat that we had seen coming back from the fair was slipping under the outside gate. She was revisited by the terror of that night. I drove it away and from that night I never saw poor Edgarda again.

Sometimes, again evoking my tormented past like a motion picture, I recall the gentle figure of the young Milanese girl that I had loved in my troubled twenties, and I am profoundly moved, asking myself, "What was her fate? Is she still alive, or has she passed on? Was she consoled or desolate?" But I go no further than to ask my questions. I like to see her again within myself as I left her then with her fine-featured face, with her slender waist, her fresh Milanese accent, and with her slightly turned-up nose which conferred upon her a pleasingly naughty air.

I studied without respite right up to the day of my departure for Rome and then took leave of the Casinis, assuring them of all my gratitude. They were so used to seeing me every day that my departure made them very sad.

CHAPTER 9

From Rome to Leghorn and Pisa

I HAD THE GOOD FORTUNE to enter the operatic world honorably. I was able to make my debut in the ranking theater of the Eternal City in a part (the Herald) which suited me perfectly, and in the company of a group of singers who were already celebrated. I remember each and every one of them even today, and would be able to do a portrait of each of them. I do not wish to draw this out, however, and will only cite their names.

The conductor was Mingardi, the Lohengrin was the great Spanish tenor Francisco Vignas, who sang the part most admirably. The Elsa was the soprano, De Benedetto; Ortrud was the celebrated Armanda degli Abbati; Telramund, the baritone, Gnaccarini and the King was the bass, Spangher.[69]

Among them I was the last wheel on the cart, so to speak. By the end of the very first rehearsals, I realized the difficulties, huge in scope, of crystallizing an opera performance. I took pains to blend into the ensemble, although I had studied the music thoroughly. From the very first my voice impressed all by its power and musicality. It triumphed most by perfectly intoning the famous calls which are the most difficult part of the role, as I was completely exposed then—that is, without any instrumental accompaniment.

Things did not always go smoothly, though. During one

rehearsal, I remember, Maestro Mingardi, who was a nervous type, found nothing in my voice to reprove, except that at one point, because I had entered too quickly, in the middle of orchestral chords and warriors, I had lost my bearings. In the presence of the chorus and the orchestra he exclaimed, "What are you doing there, so stiff? If you are going to be an artist, then I will become Pope!" I felt the blood freeze in my veins. I asked his pardon, but he couldn't even hear my voice well, because, unlike my singing voice, I spoke with a light tenor timbre, almost a young boy's. I went home somewhat dejected.

The hours before the coming performance were excruciating for me. I felt I was going to the gallows. When necessary, Mother quietly came in and out of my room, where I had shut myself up again so that no one could see me. She exhorted me to be calm, saying that I was certain of success. Being quite religious, Mother lit a candle to the Madonna, that she might protect me. I longed for evening to arrive to be rid of this incubus that oppressed me. And my father? I never saw him. After all our controversies, the baptism by fire was about to take place. This caused contradictory feelings in me. My brother, who would have made me quite comfortable, was in north Italy in the army and no one would give him leave so that he could be present at my debut.

One hour before leaving for the theater I recalled the *Cavalleria* I had heard with him a few years before, and this made me all the more nervous. I wished I had never heard of such a thing as a stage. I would rather have gone back to Sor Romolo's farm or to Sor Peppe's inn, even to the shop on Via Ludovisi. But I was already chained. That Sphinx, Art, which had taken hold of me and pointed me to the stage, now seemed to be asking me with a cynical grin: "Well, wasn't this your dream? Get going, coward!" The reaction came which roused me from the nightmare. I picked up my makeup box, embraced Mother, who seemed more dead than alive, and said, "Goodbye, Mother, I'm going. God be with me!"

When I was made up and costumed as the Herald, I felt that the beard was troublesome, as it seemed to impede full emission of my voice. I continued to try my mouth, opening and closing it many times and articulating the words. I paced up and down on the stage impatiently, longing to get started, until finally I heard the orchestra begin. The stage manager handed me my lance and pressed an electric bell to signal the beginning of the performance.

I was already standing in the middle of the stage. There was a deathly silence. The curtains opened. I was immediately dazzled by the footlights, so I concentrated on a spot which would not hurt my eyes—which was, to be exact, on the prompter's box—from which I heard, "*Sta' tranquillo; in bocca al lupo*." ["In the mouth of the wolf," a traditional Italian send-off, similar to "Break a leg!" in English. *Tr.*]

Instead of a wolf's mouth I seemed to be facing a hydra-headed monster with innumerable open mouths, ready to devour me. However, when I delivered my opening phrase (which lay in the best part of my voice), "Hear ye! Counts and princes of Brabant," my voice gushed out—flexible, secure, powerful—and I felt myself reborn.[70] Then came the calls: "Who then shall champion the cause of Elsa of Brabant, let him step forward!" and the audience broke into applause. My mother's faith had been vindicated.

When the opera was over all the artists came to congratulate me. Vignas, the hero of the evening, told me, "I've never heard a baritone voice like yours. If you study and learn to conserve it, you have great glory ahead of you."

Mother and my sisters Fosca and Nella witnessed my successful debut from the first row of the gallery, and Mother was so overcome with emotion that she felt ill. When the curtains parted she had almost fainted and only after the ovation did she feel reassured. Father had attended as well, watching from the standee section on the main floor with a group of his friends.

We all met at the house. My encounter with Mother was indescribable, and we were locked in each other's arms for minutes. My poor mother! It is a shame that you were permitted to see only the beginning of my career!

After five performances the part of Telramund, sung by Gnaccarini, was taken over by Benedetti, and thus after two years we found ourselves together on the stage of the Costanzi, and also for some evenings at my house, with the most intense mutual delight.[71] He was thunderstruck to see me so secure and at ease in front of an audience, and praised my voice.

I sang fourteen performances of *Lohengrin* at the Costanzi, and one of *Lucia*, in which I also showed uncommon artistic ability. Poor Maestro Persichini had died a little before my debut, and thus could not verify with his own ears the ridiculous opinion he had of my voice. All the newspapers unanimously predicted a great career for me. Naturally, I spread the news of my success to all those who had been interested in me or had cooperated with me in some way.

When my engagement ended in Rome I was contracted to sing at the Arena Alfieri di Livorno (Leghorn) in *Trovatore* and *Lucia*. The impresario of this theater was named Alfredo Bini,[72] owner of two butcher shops, and it was said that he was very rich and loved to organize short operatic seasons as a hobby, for his own pleasure. The fee we agreed upon was 10 lire per day. I rented a furnished room in the Piazza Grande from a lady named Orsola, who, on account of her extreme skinniness, was nicknamed Torsola (cabbage stalk). My success in Livorno was such that when I stepped out of the house I was gawked at like some great personage. Profiting by my success, I told the impresario that I was not able to live as I should on 10 lire per day, so he generously offered me *caffellatte* in the morning and steak for my midday meal.

At the first performance a very distinguished-looking gentleman came into my dressing room, introducing himself as "Cesarino Gaetani, one of your colleagues, and an ardent admirer of your voice. I'd like very much to speak with you. Arrange an appointment, if you would be so kind, because I would like to present you to my Livornese friends, who would very much like to know you."

It was decided on the spot that on the next day he would call for me at my house, and we'd go to dine together at the Pancaldi.[73]

It was a brilliant July day. While waiting before a table set for the party of friends he had invited, we began to talk of art and the theater. Gaetani was great company. He cut quite a figure—classic Greek features with abundant chestnut hair; he was one of the most robust men of Livorno, a true athlete, and known as such by everyone. He was rich and married to a woman known for her grace and kindness. He was a mixture of Don Giovanni, poet, singer *manqué* and bohemian. His passion for opera was extreme—almost fanaticism. But Nature had been unkind to him in endowing him with a wretched baritone voice. Even so, he had spent a small fortune on singing lessons and flaunted a luxurious theatrical wardrobe. He had sung with mediocre success in *Ruy Blas* and *Carmen*. He was angry at his fellow citizens, accusing them of ignorance, yet his passion for opera survived his disillusionment. We saw each other often and became good friends. An enthusiast of Carducci and Pascoli, at times he declaimed their poetry beautifully—I mean, with impassioned simplicity.

He was popular in Livorno. Everyone hailed him with pleasure. Wherever he went women vied with expressions of love for him. So as not to glory too much in his powers of seduction he would often clutch at me and say: "Dear Titta, to make them all happy you'd have to be a man of steel. I have one now who doesn't want to surrender, but it's a question of time and I'll have her in my clutches." In speaking he scanned the syllables and appeared to be reciting. Sometimes cursing me in the Tuscan manner he would exclaim, "If I had your voice I would shake the whole world!"

"Not for long, dear Cesarino," I responded, wanting to call him dear bird of prey, "because with all the women you have in your hands, or better, in your clutches, there would be very little of your voice left for the public."

We had lively discussions on my interpretive conceptions of various personages and situations. I listened with great interest, and now and then I followed his advice when it appeared sound. Seeing me so young and inexperienced, he often said "I'm afraid you will end up doing just as many of your colleagues—Barbieri, Benedetti, Cioni, Casini and Gasperini. All beautiful voices, but not true artists, and therefore never reaching higher than halfway to the top."[74] Then, increasing the dose, probably venting his irritation with his fellow citizens, he added, "You too will never be a great artist."

To this ill omen I replied that the greatest living actor, Tommaso Salvini, no less, was a Pisan. Then Gaetani, to make me angry, insisted that Salvini was not a Pisan.[75]

Poor Cesarino! What an end was in store for him. I met him many years later in Moscow, where he was with a small touring company. He was after a young artist of the company with whom he was violently in love. I was singing the *Demon* of Rubinstein at the Imperial Opera. I had just finished encoring the aria (in Russian), creating delirium, when I saw him appear. I thought I was dreaming when I saw him. We embraced with great feeling. He had aged and had white hair and rheumy eyes. He had enthusiastic words for me, praising the position I had won for myself in the leading theaters of the world, and before leaving (the company was departing for Kharkov the next morning) he told me, "Please forget the evaluation I made of you in Livorno at the beginning of your career because you are now, in spite of my prognostication, a great artist." He embraced me, then added, "This is probably the last time we will see each other. You will surely read in some Italian newspaper that Cesarino Gaetani of Livorno has blown his brains out. Goodbye now, dear Titta, and pursue your glorious career, because you deserve it."

Sometime later I learned that he had finished much as he predicted he would.[76]

But back to Livorno: in the two months of my engagement there I became popular. The impresario had introduced me to various music-loving merchants in the food-purveying line who demonstrated their appreciation daily by sending me hunks of Parmesan cheese, flasks of wine, fruits, one thing or another, vying with each other. As I was continually invited out I left all these gastronomical homages, including the noonday steak that was provided according to the terms of my contract, to my voracious landlady. At the end of the season "La Torsola" was unrecognizable. I would guess she had put on at least fourteen kilos. Take me at my word: if one looked at her from the collar down she looked more like a barrel than a woman.

My last opera in Livorno was *Rigoletto*, in which I obtained not only a vocal but, given my youth and inexperience, also an artistic success which was very, very important. Thus a lasting memory of me was left in this city.[77] And my fame was spreading. In August I was put under contract by the Politeama of Pisa,[78] where I made my debut in *Trovatore*, followed by *Lucia*, thus confirming and extending my versatility and musical reputation.[79] Many came from Livorno to Pisa to hear me again. Gaetani in particular almost never missed a performance, and we spent many happy hours together discussing art and theater on the quiet banks of the Arno, lit by the September sunsets.

I was living in the house of my Aunt Ines and Uncle Lelio,[80] also an ironworker and a worthy pupil of my father. Both were well enough acquainted with music and art in general. I stayed about a month in their modest home, surrounded by their affectionate solicitude. They were very proud of their nephew and did not hide the fact, especially when we went out together.

At the end of September I returned to Rome, where I spent several days at home with the family. Although my earnings had been very modest, I always had enough to send help to Mother, and Father seemed to resent my absence and my brother's. The strife between him and Mother was more and more intense until it became unbearable; the discord was too painful. To justify his long absences from home, Father cited his abandonment by his two sons. And mother had to put up with the bitterness of such a life. I tried to cheer her up, assuring her that my love, like my help, would never lessen.

CHAPTER 10

In Calabria and Sicily with Cavallaro

THE MOST IMPORTANT STEP at the beginning of my career was the period I spent touring with the Cavallaro Company. In the year I was with them I was able to extend my repertory in the theaters of southern Italy to about ten operas, which served, so to speak, to launch me—since I was now quite at home and expert on the boards and knew my roles to perfection—toward the most important theaters of the musical world.

The tour opened at Catanzaro. The Teatro Comunale there was quite large,[81] and many artists of great renown had appeared there. The first person I met in the city was an old family friend I had known in my father's shop: the son of Alessandro Bencini, a noted public works contractor. The son, Angiolino, though called by the diminutive of his name, was truly a Hercules. He was thirty years old and with the Rossellini firm[82] was constructing a stretch of railway tunnel. Angiolino was loyal, generous, intelligent, as charming as could be. His social and financial position in the city was prominent, and in the Calabrian world, to use an expression in vogue today, he was "on the ground floor." Having read my name on the company roster he hurried to the theater to find me and during my stay was of great moral support to me. Without delay he took me everywhere to introduce me to politicians and the well-known people of the place, the friends at his club, the technicians working in his vast enterprise, etc., thus creating a warm aura of favor for me.

My first appearance was in *La forza del destino*. My Leonora was Ester Adaberto[83]—a splendid voice, beautiful, tall, with an abundance of black hair, surrounded by many admirers. Alvaro was sung with authoritative artistry by the Spanish tenor, Izquierdo[84]—the one who had got me the audition with Cavallaro, and who helped me to get my contract. We became good friends and sought each other's company all season long.

Cavallaro was very busy getting the company ready for its debut. Present at all the rehearsals, watching every detail, one could say he was really the stage director. He attached great importance to my personal success, as he had spoken (perhaps too much) in high terms of my voice to the subscribers, and also because I was the youngest artist on his roster.

My debut was a grand success for me and all the others; congratulations were unanimous among the regulars of the Communale, which Cavallaro received with great joy and pride. At the end of the opera he burst into my dressing room and clapped me on the back, saying in Sicilian, "Well, we showed them! Don Peppino is never wrong!" Even the prompter, an elderly Sicilian and an old trouper, came in and said, "Are you happy? A great success, my boy!"

If I was happy is needless to say. My voice had been appreciated by all without distinction of rank or station in life, especially at the end of the opera, where they wanted me for a solo bow. Bencini, who was there with his family, was radiant with joy and invited me to dinner the next day. I felt as if protected. The local press gave their seal of approval, with particular praise to Cavallaro, who had succeeded in gathering a company of such excellence, among whom my name was mentioned as an exceptional talent destined for a most brilliant career.

Without making himself conspicuous Cavallaro was watching my every move. He became, along with Bencini, a sort of behind-the-scenes patron saint. Every evening before the opera began he would come into my dressing room to offer his good wishes. Then he was always in the orchestra, sometimes seated and sometimes among those standing. When applause broke forth, he would look all around him, smiling and jubilant, making grand gestures of approval with his hands and head, as if the applause were for him. Then looking up to me on the stage he would make two or three flourishes of his right hand, as if describing a circle over his head, and with enough voice for everyone to hear, he would exclaim, "*Minchia*, what a phenomenon." That for him was the highest praise. He often told me, "If you listen to Don Peppino you will become the present generation's greatest baritone."

Taking advantage of his enthusiasm, I told him of the generosity of my Livornese impresario, who in addition to my ten lire daily also gave me breakfast and a steak dinner.

He made no comment, but next morning at a rehearsal of *Bohème*, turned to me and said, "I thought over what you told me about your Livornese impresario, and did some mental arithmetic. I will equal his terms till the end of the season, and between the *caffellatte* and the steaks, I will have paid you an additional 700 lire in that time. Your subtle speculation, however, had me in doubt. Are you, by any chance, Jewish? Because such an idea as yours could not have originated in a Christian head!"

Nevertheless, after the rehearsal, he took me by the arm and escorted me to a cafe in front of the theater. He called the owner over (whom he had known for many years) and told him, "Every morning this young man will come here for coffee, buttered toast, and so on. At the end of the week the bill should be sent to me."

I broke in immediately to say that sometimes, instead of the morning meal, I would prefer a snack after the performance. Cavallaro burst out, "That's the limit! If you are not Jewish, on my honor, your ancestors were!" The proprietor of the cafe, seeing it was all a joke, started to laugh, and we all remained in agreement.

So every morning before going to rehearsal, at just before ten o'clock, I would stop at the cafe, and sometimes instead of two buttered rolls I would have three or four, asking to have them added to the bill along with the tip for the waiter. At the end of the week when Don Peppino came to pay the bill, he found it too high and demanded an explanation from the proprietor (who on his own account was not above adding an extra item or two).

Annoyed, Don Peppino sent for me to confront the proprietor. I had foreseen that there might be some irregularity in the roll accounting, so I pulled out the notebook where my expenses were entered. I showed him my daily expense account, observing that on only two mornings, to compensate for the small size of the rolls being offered, had I taken a few more.

Then the owner of the restaurant accused the waiter of irregularities. The waiter, in turn, got angry, since besides not receiving one *soldo* in tips, he was being accused of theft. Cavallaro then covered the proprietor with oaths, saying that he was more of a Jew than I. Then, turning to me, he said, "You louse! Haven't you got at least the 10 *centesimi* for the tip?"

I took delight in egging him on, as by now I knew his character very well, and answered that my Livorno impresario was much more human than he because he did not make me feel the weight of these expenses, nor did he repay my small excess with humiliation.

BOHÈME WAS PRODUCED NEXT, and it was a great success for the artists. We had to repeat the second act scene of Musetta's waltz, where my voice, in the phrase *Gioventù mia*[85] was so enormous and powerful that Cavallaro compared it to Niagara Falls, and his hyperbole became a proverb. It really seemed so in the finale of the opera, where it eclipsed the orchestra and all the other voices. Cavallaro attributed the reinforced power of my voice in the finale to his *caffellatte*.

At the end of the opera the audience went out repeating sotto voce or whistling the theme of *Gioventù mia*. Thus *Bohème* became the favorite work at Catanzaro, and had a magnificent success, materially as well—the theater was completely sold out every time. I was glad of this, because it (the role of Marcello) spared my voice the fatigues of my heavier parts.

After the two-month winter season in Calabria, we went to Sicily. The first city on the tour was Catania.[86] We crossed the straits of Messina, an enchanting day. I stayed on the deck of the train ferry through the voyage with my long mane of hair, alas, blowing in the wind, and sang in the open air to applause from the sailors. A gentleman from Messina offered me some well-aged wine from Siracusa and Cavallaro drank to my coming success in Catania, the most beautiful city, he said, in the world. It is hardly necessary to add that he was a native of that city.

By now I enjoyed his complete confidence in our dealings. I joked with him all the time and was not afraid to remind him that Rome came first, then Catania. He answered that in Rome the streets were black with priests and for that reason he would not exchange one corner of Catania for all of the Eternal City. He added that the greatest geniuses were born in Sicily, particularly "The Great Swan," Vicenzo Bellini, whose divine melodies inspired even Wagner, adding that if Bellini had not been born, Wagner would have remained unknown.

To every one of his statements I made an echo with a loud *bum*. "And who was the greatest Italian poet? Mario Rapisardi."[87] I reminded him that he had forgotten Carducci and Pascoli, to which he replied undaunted that in comparison to Rapisardi, these were two babes-in-arms. Then he said that the greatest statesmen were Sicilian, and cited Crispi. And that Sicilians were the greatest orators. He then called to mind the name of a great artist—greater, he said, than Tommaso Salvini—one who was working at this very moment in a puppet show for a modest Catanese theater, but whose name in the not too distant future would resound over the entire terraqueous orb: Giovanni Grasso. In short, we were at each other's throats the whole time. I had a world of fun and not only I.

When we arrived at Messina we went on immediately to Catania, and I found rooms near the Teatro Nazionale,[88] where the company was to appear. That evening at the Cafe Trinacria Cavallaro introduced me to some of his friends, among whom I particularly remember an agent and secretary of his, one Ettore Sciuto, and a journalist, short, dark and ugly, who looked like an Arab, all pockmarked with smallpox. Then a handsome young man came to shake hands—he was brown-haired, distinctive, elegantly dressed, with two light, curved moustaches.

"This young man," said Cavallaro, pointing at me, "is my baritone, Titta Ruffo. And this," he told me, pointing at the young man, "is one of the most respected judges of Catania's courts. He is also the greatest orator of Sicily, Gigi Macchi.[89] Days from now he is going to speak in the Bellini garden, and we will go together to hear him."

In greeting me Macchi promised to come to the rehearsal the next day, as he was eager to hear me. The echo of my success in Calabria had already reached Sicily.

Gigi Macchi soon became one of my inseparable pals. He was highly cultured, a wonderful speaker, and besides these exceptional qualities he possessed a beautiful tenor voice and refined musical tastes. He loved art and the theater with a great passion, and if he had been dedicated to singing he would have become, by his eloquence as well as his voice, a great artist. He introduced me to his friends. I recall the deputy Peppino de Felice, an energetic man, a bold swordsman, a brilliant journalist, and a witty orator and conversationalist.[90] I also met Giovanni Grasso and Angelo Musco, hardly known at the time in Sicily, who in a few years time would become the most popular dialect-speaking Italian actors.[91] Thus I developed a circle of beloved and elect acquaintances. Gigi Macchi, however, always remained the closest to my soul and my heart.

I debuted as Marcello in *Bohème* with great success. Then in succession I sang *Ballo in maschera*, *Ruy Blas*, *Gioconda*, and *Rigoletto*, in which my vocal gifts, always getting stronger and becoming more polished, showed to good advantage. I became the city's favorite.

Macchi was happy for me, and when his work gave him a

few hours of freedom, he spent them in my company. He was always, therefore, in my dressing room. We discussed how the characters in the various operas might be interpreted, just as I had with Gaetani in Livorno, and his remarks were so tactfully made that I was never abashed by the overwhelming superiority of his culture and experience. He gave me some very valuable advice during these sessions. I treasured them, as every evening they proved themselves by enriching my performances. He was an intimate friend of the noted baritone Delfino Menotti,[92] and was trying to inspire me with all the beautiful qualities of the great tradition which he had learned at first hand from the illustrious singers he had known and appreciated.

Interesting artistic discussions flared up between us, and I acknowledge with gratitude all that he did during the Catania season to enrich my mind and further my knowledge of history, literature and art. What a joy it was to have him illuminate and explain so many things about which I had been in ignorance, with his clear, vivid words!

Cavallaro took advantage of Macchi's influence on me to beg the latter to intercede on his behalf and get my consent to sing some extra performances—without pay, of course!—and I didn't object. As a result Don Peppino actually had me sing twelve consecutive performances with one-day intervals.[93] Macchi then asked Cavallaro not to involve him in contractual matters, and began to take my side. Cavallaro, to show his high esteem for me, and what he could accomplish to please me, asked me which opera I would like to add to my repertory. I cherished a number of new characters, and proposed the Valentin in *Faust*, for example.

"Fine," he responded simply, "next week we will mount *Faust*." And he kept his promise. Every wish of mine seemed a sacred duty to him now. Then Macchi and I began to analyze the magnificent role of Valentin, exploring its depths and unearthing the most subtle shades of meaning. This procedure for Valentin was no different than the one I employed now for all the roles I ventured to interpret.

One evening during a performance Sciuto came into my dressing room to tell me that a beautiful, much-courted young lady was in one of the stage boxes listening to me: it was Cavallaro's daughter. He then added that she never missed one of my performances, coming always with her mother and applauding me with obvious enthusiasm. At the moment I did not attach any importance to this information, but it remained in my mind.

I should explain that when Cavallaro intended to wring some concession from me, he went all-out in courtesy, no matter how trifling the matter. For example, during one of our usual gatherings at the Cafe Trinacria he offered me a *cassata alla Siciliana*, which he knew I just loved. [This is a rich cake, made of ricotta cheese, candied fruit and liqueur, enclosed in a mold of sponge-cake and chilled, then decorated with more candied fruit. *Tr.*]

At one point in the conversation he winked at Macchi and said to me, "You can do something nice for me, and to be honest, I think I have it coming."

Smelling a rat, I interrupted. "I understand! The cassata is turning to poison. I will have to sing another free performance, that's the *nice thing*."

All this passed between us to the merry laughter of the rest. As a matter of fact I had not quite finished the *cassata* when Don Peppino asked me to do another *Ballo in maschera* on the next evening.

This was starting to get serious. "This is too much! Very quietly you are starting to exploit me!"

He began curling his mustache between thumb and forefinger as was his custom when he wanted to convince someone, and said, "Don't talk nonsense! I have never exploited anyone. One day, for everything I have done for you, you should erect a monument to me. And you'll sing tomorrow, I'm sure of it. You don't have the gall to refuse Don Peppino, who loves you like a son!"

I turned facetious and blurted out a teasing remark which was to have painful consequences. "Good! I accept! But only on the condition that *you will give me your daughter in marriage!*"

I should *never* have said that. He jumped to his feet, eyes flashing. "Upon my honor, *bella madre*," he screamed, "before I would give my daughter to an artist, I would take her down to the beach at midnight and drown her!"

"You're trying to say," I replied, "that tomorrow night *you* will sing my role in *Ballo*."

From my tone he understood that I had meant what I said as a joke, and told me to stop talking nonsense. On my part I was conscious of having committed a gaffe, and sought to ease the situation by declaring that of course I was ready, as usual, to sing whatever he wanted. However, my thoughtless outburst had some complicated consequences. Upon returning home Cavallaro recounted the whole story to his wife, while the daughter, who happened to be in the next room, hearing them talk of theatrical matters, began to listen and heard my words repeated: "I will sing if you give me your daughter in marriage."

In the young girl's soul a hope was then born, or should I say an illusion, which soon became a great passion. However, all this was kept locked in her heart. She never told anyone about it, with the exception of a very close confidante, who told me much later what had occurred, and the consequences.

Some days later a woman came to me, saying she was the company's laundress; if I wanted to make use of her, she would make me good terms. I accepted and sent her my laundry. When she brought it back, washed and ironed, her bill was ridiculously small. I begged her to come back again, and thus she became my laundress until the company moved on to Siracusa.

I had been about a week in that city when to my surprise one morning, as I was showing up for rehearsal, I saw my laundress standing at the stage entrance. She hastened to explain that her husband had been dismissed by the sulphur company, and that in order to earn a living she had to follow the company to this place. I felt sorry for the poor woman and told her to come pick up my laundry as soon as possible. She did not have to asked twice, and pleased by my disposition to help her, timidly added that she was a very good cook, and that at very little expense to me she would prepare my meals at home.

By good luck the quarters I had rented had a good-sized kitchen furnished with all the necessary utensils, and the landlady was out all day at work and only returned when it was late. Therefore it didn't take a lot of nerve for me to ask as a favor the use of her kitchen, and she quickly conceded it. Thus, at one stroke, the laundress also became my cook.

Hardly a week had passed before I had in her the very incarnation of the accomplished domestic. For one lira, or even less, I had wonderful meals. She made a most delicious spaghetti à la Siciliana, with steamed eggplant, and she gave me meat once a day which I washed down with an excellent Sicilian wine, and topped off with a cup of coffee. She also kept my room in order, and took care of my linens and clothes. At the end of May the heat began to be felt and the flies became my chief torment, never giving me respite. And what did she do about it? The dear soul made a paper fan of colored vellum to chase the flies, and after eating my midday meal, when I took a nap as a rule, she took it upon herself, without the slightest prompting from me, to sit next to the bed and patiently fan me during my nap to keep the flies from bothering me. By now she was more than a faithful servant, she was a devoted slave.

One day I happened to notice that a photograph of myself as Marcello in *Bohème* had disappeared. I began to suspect her, but hesitated to accuse her, even bent over backwards to exclude her. Upon reflection, the house was unattended at times. Some fan could have slipped in and made off with it.

Another day, while I was lying awake with my eyes closed, she—believing me profoundly asleep—bent over me, and I no longer felt the breeze of the fan on my face, but her own light breath, and her hand grazed my face with a light caress.

I lay quiet, my eyes closed, thinking over this extraordinary occurrence. How should I behave now? How could I fake an awakening? After a few minutes I got up and decided to speak frankly. I asked her why she had caressed me, and reproved her. I must confess that as a servant the woman was most precious to me, but as for the rest... Well, she just wasn't my type. So it wasn't hard for me to make a moral issue of all this, but I did want to spare her any greater humiliation.

The poor thing, who had not really done anything wrong, began to cry, begging my pardon, and tried, after calming down a bit, to explain that she had yielded, in a moment of abandon, to an impulse almost of veneration. Because for a long time she had considered that the life I led—honest, modest, and full of sacrifice—had made me seem like a saint.

I admonished her as gracefully as I could and told her that I thought it would be prudent if henceforth we stopped depending on each other and went our separate ways. Then she revealed the mystery, speaking clearly and simply over her own displeasure. She said she'd been placed at my side by someone who was deeply in love with me and who was suffering by my absence. She said that she had been in continuous correspondence with this person, keeping her informed about my life, and depicting me as a saint, in fact, who had never had a woman around except the one who took care of him and served him like a faithful slave. She finally revealed the name of the person who had sent her on this assignment, and this was, as you may already suspect, Signorina Cavallaro.

I was upset at the moment to discover that for two months I had been harboring, right at my elbow, a detective who was spying on everything I said and did. But other considerations quickly calmed me. The mystery of the photograph was explained. She confessed that she'd taken it herself to send to the lady, who had been insistently demanding it. Furthermore, the mystery of how I could eat so well and be served so well for a few *soldi* per day was also cleared up.

Poor woman! She was the only one, probably, who never cheated me when it came to expenses. From that day forth my thrifty existence was finished. With what I'd saved thanks to the good woman I'd been able to send more help to my mother, and even a little to my soldier brother. Apart from that, when I was alone I felt a great emptiness around me, and I don't mind confessing that when I returned to the bare squalor of my room at night, tears came to my eyes. The poor woman had filled my life, without my being aware of it. While she had been with me I had become quite used to her, or to say it better, I'd grown to like her a lot.

A little later, when I returned to the company of my colleagues who had not seen me for a while either at lunch or dinner, they asked me with a certain irony, "And the laundress?" Without giving the true explanation, which none of them would have believed, I simply said that her husband had asked her to return to Catania.

The first time he saw me in Siracusa the secretary of the opera company, Sciuto, had asked, "Well, Titta, when's the engagement to be announced?" I told him, in substance, that he was stupid to make insinuations of this kind, and I wouldn't stand for any interference in my affairs, even as a joke. I told him I would never marry anyone as I had more important things to think about. Sciuto knew very well what I was talking about, just as I understood that his allusion to an engagement did not refer to the laundress.

I spent the rest of the time in Siracusa in the company of a noble figure of a man, the concertmaster of the orchestra, Saverio Russumanno, a hearty Calabrian. I'd formed a bond of cordial friendship with him since Catania. We had a great liking for each other, always hailing each other in public, but we couldn't know each other better because we only saw each other in the evening at the theater. Now that the laundress had gone I went to live in his building, in a room near his, and from that point we became the closest of friends. He was about 38 years of age then, and led an exemplary life of great simplicity, uninvolved in either close friendships or love affairs. He was something of a skeptic in regard to both, and a good bit of a philosopher. For the rest, he was well educated, correct in manners, and incapable of taking undue liberties or speaking vulgarly. He dressed beautifully and for that, too, I called him "the Calabrian aristocrat."

Many times I asked him why he never married and he answered that he did not trust any woman, and the very thought that he might be cuckolded at any moment discouraged him from matrimony.

When I tried to hit back at his misogynistic pessimism, tried to convince him that not all women were the same—many were good wives and exemplary mothers—he justified his opinion by stating frankly that all the women with whom he had been intimate in his long career as a violinist had been married.

We parted in Catania, good friends, but I never saw him again. I learned later, by accident, that he was a victim of the terrible Messina earthquake, leaving a widow and a son. Some years later in Buenos Aires a lady with a little boy in tow came to my dressing room after a performance and was introduced to me by one of the orchestra men.

"Please excuse my impudence, but I have been wanting to meet you for such a long time," she said, drawing from her bag numerous letters and photographs. "I am the widow of your good friend Saverio Russumanno, and this is his son." Then she added, "My husband spoke of you with so much admiration and affection that I keep these letters and photos as relics. I left Italy after his awful death, and carry them with me always."

The little boy was looking at me as if mesmerized. He looked so much like his father that as I looked into the child's eyes I saw the father himself, the beloved friend who had perished so tragically. Returning for many years to Buenos Aires I was able to follow the development of the little boy. Now he is a serious young man with an academic degree, and one would say straightaway, Saverio reborn. He lived close to his mother, who carried her husband's memory close to her heart and did not remarry.

Russumanno! If you could see her today, so devoted and loving many years after your death, I would not need my optimistic reasonings about marriage and love to change your marital attitude.

Returning to Catania, we were there again in the first days of August, when the heat was African. Macchi, who was waiting for me at the station, immediately cleared up the situation regarding the new management installed at the Politeama Pacini in competition with that of Cavallaro.

We left after two days for Acireale[94] to perform some operas. We opened with *Ballo in maschera*, and as usual had a great success. In this little town it was inescapable to run into the other artists and musicians of the company at every turn, and since outside the theater I enjoyed being alone, the second day I went for a long walk along the marina which stood at the bottom of a high cliff which drops from the town. There were many fishermen, divided in groups, barefoot and roasted by the sun, who were working on their nets. Some others were seated at a coarse table in a cave excavated in the rock, eating fried fish. I approached and asked them if they would sell me some. A very wrinkled old man who was speaking an incomprehensible Sicilian shouted to a woman: *"Gna Marì,* give a plate of fish to the gentleman." And Marì brought me a good portion, right from the frying pan. She gave me in addition a piece of their black bread, and I ate all of it with great appetite. Another old man poured me a goodsized glass of wine which I was no less eager to consume. When I went to pay the bill, they acted as if they were offended: I was in their house and they couldn't accept money from me. I thanked Gna Marì, who asked me to come again. Well aware of the rusticity of my surroundings I didn't hestitate to say to Marì that, if she didn't have any difficulty cooking something for me every day, I would—paying, of course—gladly dine every evening with them. Gna Marì scratched her gray head: "Young sir," she responded, "we folk aren't accustomed to this, but if it would please you, come at one every day and I will prepare you something."

I offered a lira for each meal, but Gna Marì replied that that was too much; she didn't wish to profit from me; sixty centesimi would be enough. In short, in a few days I had become a regular at the fishermen's grotto. When Don Peppino and Russumanno and the artists of the company asked me where I went to eat, I made a great show of being well-acquainted, and told them that I was always invited somewhere. "Or could it be the laundress followed you here?" one of them asked. The fishermen knew that I was a singer, and believed that I was with a variety show, nor had I bothered to set them straight.

At the last performance, however, I took a notion to invite them to the Teatro Comunale.[95] None of them had ever been to the opera. I asked Cavallaro for ten complimentary seats in the first row. Too many! He denied me them, but when I told him that I had intended the seats as a homage to one of the great families of Acireale, who might be useful to him in securing the theater next year, he decided to give them to me, adding as usual, "By God, you will be the ruin of me."

That evening in the theater when Don Peppino saw the front row seats occupied by Gna Marì, dressed for a feast, her face resembling a carnival mask, and her husband, Ciccione, with his Corsican beret, who was careful never to uncover his head, and the other married couples, one more comical than the next, who were nibbling their little seeds and almonds, with their smoke stinking up the place, or calmly chewing tobacco and energetically spitting on the floor—merciful heaven! Cavallaro hurled himself into my dressing room, screaming: "Where is the stinker?"

I received him with Olympian serenity. He let fly with a low insult. "Great son of a... But who did you bring into the theater? Who are these people? And you scrounged ten free tickets from me for one of the great old families of Acireale? Swindler! This is a scandal! We can't begin the show. They'll be laughing at us on all sides! They'll sink us!"

I calmly replied that this was the good family that boarded me, and that for ten lire per day I certainly couldn't have recourse to the British royal table.

Cavallaro left the room in a fury, threatening me. "On my honor, I'll make you pay for this. You've ruined the last performance of the season."

But best of all was what happened a few minutes afterward.

When I appeared onstage Gna Marì, who recognized me in spite of my costume and makeup, began to scream to the others: "Hey, Big Frank, Paul! He, the young sir! Holy Mother, how beautiful he is!"

At the end of the first aria she rose from the front row, and approaching the orchestra, which was still playing she began to scream like a madwoman. A group of students, after the famous aria "*Eri tu, che macchiavi quell'anima*" offered me flowers. I threw part of them to Gna Marì, who was jumping out of her skin. The whole audience applauded, and she, completely beside herself, bowed endlessly in gratitude. The evening performance, instead of an extraordinary disaster, scored a success, so much so that Cavallaro himself ended by laughing with the rest.

I never saw so much good humor, so much happiness, in the theater.

The newspaper of the place underlined the exceptional nature of the performance, "embellished," it was written, "by the original intervention" of the fisher-folk. The following day, before leaving, I went to say goodbye to Gna Marì, Ciccione and their son Paulillo and the rest of the group. They wanted to throw a feast for me, offering me a beautiful meal with a stew of dried codfish and old Siracusan wine, which they kept hidden in the cave for very special occasions. I brought a photograph of me in costume and left it with them as a keepsake with the dedication, "To my dear Gna Marì and Ciccione." The son Paulillo, who was already around sixteen years old, hastened to nail it to the entry door in my presence, saying that it would be sacred to them for the rest of their lives. I embraced Gna Marì and Ciccione. I said goodbye to the rest of the company and finally left the fishermen of Acireale amidst a thunder of happy cheers from all present. They wished me all the good in the world, and continued to wave goodbye until they were lost from sight.

Fifteen years later, in 1914, I was in New York, singing a concert at the Hippodrome with Luisa Tetrazzini.[96] The hall was packed, for the most part with Italians, more than 7,000 people, approximately. The impresario had been obliged to fill up the area near the stage with a goodsized crowd. At the end of the concert, right in the middle of this crowd, one flustered fellow got up and began signalling and trying to get closer to me, shouting, in English strongly accented with Sicilian, "Mister Ruffo, I am Paulillo, son of Gna Marì and Ciccione, the fisherman; do you remember?"

Truly, I didn't remember, nor did I recognize this strange individual on the spur of the moment, and told him I didn't know him. But Paulillo wasn't so easily put off. He followed me to the Knickerbocker Hotel, where I was staying, and made it into the lobby, trying to refresh my memory by evoking a thousand circumstances regarding our old acquaintance, not omitting mention, naturally, of my portrait, which he said still hung from a nail at the door, preserved like a relic. I asked about his parents. The mother, Gna Marì, was dead from tetanus, following an infection she contracted after being wounded by one of the needles used for mending nets. Ciccione, the father, went blind. Now and then even in this condition, said Paulillo, he dragged himself, feeling his way, to the entrance of the cave, to touch my effigy with his fingers as if it were a talisman. And having heard in the papers, when he had someone read them to him, stories about me as I traveled throughout the world, acclaimed by multitudes, received by princes and emperors, he claimed that this picture represented the honor of his humble home.

Paulillo's story, with the sad end of Gna Marì and the even sadder misfortune of poor Ciccione—I can't possibly say how moved I was. I invited him to drink a glass of champagne. Then I introduced him to Caruso[97] who had made plans to do something with Tetrazzini and me after the concert.

Paulillo was ecstatic to see himself in our midst, as if all at once he had been raised to heaven and stood among a chorus of angels. Very soon after I had left Acireale he had shipped out on a ship of the mercantile navy and disembarked at Boston. From there he went to New York where he started working in Brooklyn, in an Irish bakery. He had learned English, and when the owner died, he had married the daughter, becoming thereby the proprietor of the business. He let me know, not without a certain self-respect, that he was very happy with his business and had eighty thousand dollars in the bank. What tricks destiny can play! Who could ever have predicted that the son of a fisherman of Acireale would leave his native grotto for the great city of New York, wed an Irish girl, become Americanized, and in addition, wealthy?

So as not to interrupt my story, I will record here that five years later, that is to say, in 1919, when I had scarcely finished my military service, I was contracted for an engagement in Mexico. I embarked on the Italian steamer *Re Vittorio*, which was bringing back to America about two thousand American soldiers who had fought on our front lines. There were very few civilian passengers on board. After a few days a man introduced himself to me: a handsome fellow, dark, serious, unpretentious: he was Major d'Anna, a medical officer of the American army, born in New Orleans of Italian parents, who asked me very kindly to sing something. It would have been discourteous and unfriendly on my part to have refused. I replied that I had never sung on a steamship, but that I would do it this time with pleasure, in homage to the American flag, which had waved beside our own. On board a party was organized with games, boxing matches, and the like. On this occasion I climbed a rope ladder, the better to be seen and heard by all, and sang several different pieces, among which were the Oberdan anthem and the Marseillaise, which created a universal delirium.

Dr. d'Anna was very grateful to me to have procured so much joy for his brave combatants, and invited me forthwith to say a few words to them in Italian. Though I couldn't boast of my oratorical ability I acceded to his enthusiasm and said, more or less, the following:

American soldiers, I am proud to have sung for you. This was the only tribute I, a good Italian, might offer you who so generously came to the defense of our ancient fatherland, guided with that sentiment of liberty which is the symbol of your great starry republic. I too am returning to America, after having modestly done my duty in the little city of Terni, in the 33rd artillery regiment. So it is that I feel myself one with you, in a bond of solidarity. I don't love war. For four years a collective folly has devastated the world, and men of all social and intellectual classes (except for a few) have competed with each other to do their part in the defense of their countries. The most awful carnage has cast gloom over the battlefields, where thousands and thousands of men have sacrificed their lives, and thousands more have been maimed in their limbs or deprived of their eyes, and will carry accordingly the horrible signs of this frightful and sad conflagration. Let us look ahead to civilization and the happiness of peoples and individuals, let us hope that we are the last actors in this monstrous tragedy, which has contaminated the planet: that is, that a similar scourge will never be repeated in the centuries to come.

I had scarcely finished my impromptu speech when a roar of applause exploded from the mass of soldiers. And all of a sudden there was Paulillo, the son of Gna Marì, who had joined the American army himself to come and fight for our cause. Leaving the middle of the throng, moved, he came to me and embraced me.

"Mister Ruffo," he said, "destiny has reserved for me the joy of seeing you again here on the high seas, in the midst of this great celebration!" Here too was a good Sicilian, intact beneath his American varnish. "*Minchia!*" he went on, "how you sang, and how you spoke! Neptune," who knows where Paulillo learned that name, "should have catapulted from the bottom of the ocean to embrace you!"

So as not to lose the thread that leads to the good and brave Dr. d'Anna, I want to tell of another interesting episode. He left me in New York, promising me that, if I should ever happen to be in New Orleans, he would be proud to present me to his father and his numerous friends. A year later I happened to be singing a concert in New Orleans, sure enough.[98] And as promised, there was Dr. d'Anna, who had come right away to visit me. By chance the American and Italian authorities of the city were giving a banquet that very day in honor of the very same Dr. d'Anna; the banquet was being promoted by our consulate to celebrate the presentation of the title, "commendatore"; nomination had just arrived from Rome. Very graciously D'Anna invited me to the feast, and I was even seated just to his right, while his father sat to the left of him. This act of deference touched me quite a bit, all the more since, having arrived the night before, I hadn't figured among the invited guests, and some might have considered me an intruder.

At the end of the dinner the Italian consul found words to express great thanks and praise for the beneficent contribution D'Anna had made to the war effort as a man of science as well as a combatant. He closed by saying that he felt very proud to be able to pin on D'Anna's uniform as an officer of the American army the emblem of the high honor which his majesty, the King of Italy, was conferring upon him. At the end of this highly respectful discourse D'Anna rose from his seat, pale with emotion, and with a hand on his old father's shoulder for support, and with a strong and incisive but vibrant voice, responded: "I thank the Italian consul for the courteous words that he has addressed to me, and I pray that he will convey to the King of Italy my profound gratitude for the honor that has been given me. I have only done my duty, and I have to declare, in the presence of the noble company gathered here today, that whatever good I have been able to accomplish in my life, I owe to my old father, who came to America fifty years ago, began humbly enough by selling bananas, but with the assiduousness, the tenacity, the self-abnegation and the diligence of the Italian laborer, was able to attain his dream of seeing me go forward and perfect myself in my studies, until he saw me obtain my degree from Columbia University. To honor him, then, I would like all present to raise their glasses: in honor, I say, of the little banana seller who, asking nothing of anyone, in the silence of his unappreciated labor, knew how to make a man of me who might be good for something today. Naturalized American though I be, my veins will always run with the good blood of a Calabrian."

A round of applause crowned his, so to speak, humbly proud words. He embraced his father repeatedly. He was carried thence in perfect triumph to his automobile. That evening D'Anna attended my concert, along with his father and many of the invited guests. I have never forgotten this episode, and the words pronounced by D'Anna in praise of the indefatigable but fortunate laborer seated to his left remain chiseled in my innermost soul.

BUT LET US RETURN to my earlier memories, in Sicily.

One morning, after the return from Acireale, Cavallaro came to my house with music under his arm and a mysterious air, and asked me jokingly if I knew Latin. In short he informed me that he was preparing a great artistic and religious event, namely the performance, in the Benedictine church, of Perosi's oratorio, *The Resurrection of Lazarus*. The author himself would conduct.[99] Cavallaro had been charged with furnishing the elements of the company, comprising orchestra and chorus, and my contribution was to be nothing less than the part of Jesus.

With patience and fervor I set myself to study all the Latin I needed to know for the part. After many rehearsals together, the performance was announced with great publicity. To go before the public I needed a black tailcoat, but I had nothing of this kind. Don Peppino offered to take me to a fine tailor, and before long he had made me the costume I needed.

When I asked Don Peppino how much I was to be paid, he replied that I ought to be paying him. In fact, for the part of Jesus, Perosi had intended to engage the baritone Kaschmann,[100] who had performed it many times, and only when he, Cavallaro, reminded him that he had furnished the rest of the elements of the production, on provision that I be assigned the part of Jesus—only then had Perosi given up on having his favorite baritone. There was no longer any question of being paid for my singing. I contented myself with the new tailcoat and the new patent leather shoes.

The day of the great event thousands of priests and seminarians had gathered in Catania from all over Sicily. The immense Benedictine church contained ten thousand of them.[101] The performance was a grand success. My voice, very suitable for the part of Jesus, and the Latin diction, and above all the musical interpretation, were much admired by Perosi. I had been put, along with the soloists and artists of the chorus, on wooden risers, specially constructed in the middle of the church. Cavallaro and Macchi had two of the front-row seats. At every phrase of mine Don Peppino gestured after his fashion, making signs of approval. The voice, notably amplified by the acoustics of the church, flooded the space like a huge river. At the evocation, "*Lazare, veni foras,*" Cavallaro could no longer contain his enthusiasm, and screamed out loud enough to be heard by Perosi: "Holy Mother, but this isn't the voice of Jesus Christ, it's a demonic voice."

Hearing the blasphemy Perosi shot him a resentful glance.

At the end of the oratorio, as I was passing through the crowd, the seminarians were looking at me as if enchanted. With my little beard, the beginnings of a moustache and my mane of hair I must have really seemed an authentic version of the Nazarene, though a somewhat young one. Cavallaro, making room for me, brought great authority to bear as he faced up to all these clerics, imbued with mysticism, and exhorted them to take my hand. "Kiss the hand of your Master!" They were so carried away by the performance that they were continually taking my hand and carrying it to their lips. Like an automaton I let them do it to the point that in the end my hand was wet with the many kisses of these devouts. We were scarcely outside the church when Don Peppino exclaimed, "Do you see how far I have brought you? On my honor, you should raise a monument to me. Here, in Catania, you remain immortal in the hearts of all these priests and seminarians, as the greatest Jesus Christ in the world."

In Catania a lot of things had changed. The public, in view of the suffocating heat, deserted the Nazionale and preferred the Pacini, an open-air theater, and quite a vast one.[102] The ruthless competition of the new company against Cavallaro had begun to affect the company's future. The proceeds were beginning to go from bad to worse. We were persisting with

Ballo in maschera and *Bohème*, the public favorites. I was singing four and sometimes five shows a week, and ended feeling quite exhausted. The admonishments of Macchi never ceased: if I were to continue at this pace, my voice wouldn't last much longer. I knew it very well, but what was I to do? I was engaged for another two months; I would be able to rest afterward in Rome.

Then one morning, behold, five British torpedo boats lay at anchor in the port of Catania, and all at once the town was full of British sailors. Don Peppino, who never let the chance to make money escape, announced a final grand gala at popular prices in honor of the British squadron, with clamorous publicity where my name stood out in huge letters. Relying on my perpetual compliance Cavallaro had taken this initiative without ever once consulting me. The following morning the messenger came with the call for me to sing in an evening performance of *Ballo in maschera*. Aware of everything that was going on, and that, among other things, the theater was already sold out, I waited.

For my evening call I let myself be found in bed with a towel around my neck. With a hoarse voice I beseeched the messenger to inform Cavallaro that the performance would have to be changed or postponed because my voice, since I took a chill the evening before, had completely deserted me. Soon afterward Cavallaro and Sciuto were barging into my room with a doctor. I refused the doctor, who wanted to put a spoon in my mouth to look at my throat, and I spoke with less and less voice. Don Peppino, sitting next to the bed, was regarding me with consternation, saying it was the evil eye, and that if I couldn't sing, it would be the ruin of everyone.

I kept playing my part. No sooner had the secretary left to see about a possible change in the performance than Cavallaro, looking me over searchingly with his eyes, asked, "But do you truly believe you are unable to sing this evening? It seems impossible to me. No one will believe you are indisposed."

Sure that no one was listening I replied, with a tragic expression on my face, that I would be able to make an extra effort if he would give me a hundred lire over and above my contract.

Don Peppino was onto my game. He accused me of being a *faker*, a blackmailer; he protested that he didn't merit such treatment. For fear of being caught *in flagrante* I started losing my voice again, saying that by now he knew what he ought to do, or if not, he should change the show, and without any more boasting or affront!

At this point Sciuto came in and Cavallaro blabbed the truth to him: namely that I was in perfect form and was blackmailing him for a hundred lire. I denied it to Sciuto's face, my voice breaking, saying that the blackmail was something Cavallaro had dreamed up. Cavallaro whipped himself to a fury, snatched the towel from my neck, and went completely mad, calling me a "swindler," a "clown," and threatening that if I were not present at the theater at the agreed hour, it would finish badly between us. Left alone I finally got up, did a few *vocalises* and waited till it was time to eat.

On the evenings I sang *Ballo in maschera*, which required a certain time to complete the makeup, I usually headed to the theater towards seven o'clock. That evening, when he hadn't seen me at seven-thirty, Cavallaro rushed to my house, and told me rudely that if I didn't go to the theater at once he would have to replace me with another baritone. I told him simply that he would give me great pleasure by so doing. Then a quarrel erupted between us that was far from friendly. I accused him of taking advantage of my health and my ingenuousness, and swore that, if I were not paid the hundred lire, his theater had seen the last of me.

It was almost eight. The show began at nine. Convinced that I was firmly decided not to give in, he seated himself at my little table, drew forth a thick roll of five-lira notes, and began to count: "Five, swindler; ten, coward; fifteen, disgusting; twenty, faker; twenty-five, miserable; thirty, delinquent; thirty-five, clown; forty, ungrateful..." And so it went, synonym after synonym, until one hundred, changing his name for me with every five lire. At the end he said, as if repeating it to himself, and not in a joking tone: "Dante was right to call Pisa *vituperio delle genti* [the shame of mankind],[103] because only a Pisano is capable of committing such a base and shameful act." Getting up, he concluded, "It's all finished between us."

I had listened unperturbed to this litany of insults, and finally, before he left, I sang to him the phrase of *Ballo in maschera*: "*E finita, non siede che l'odio e la morte nel vedovo cor!*"

With this lyrical conclusion, in truth not a very opportune one, he fled in a fury and slammed the door so hard that a small picture of Jesus on the wall came off as if in fright. I heard him screaming in the distance: "He even has the nerve to clown, that Judas, *vituperio delle genti.*"

I was happy. Tomorrow I would send the hundred lire intact to my mother. And with this thought I ran to the theater to put on my makeup. When it struck nine I still wasn't ready, naturally. The hall was stuffed with people, and with a number of British sailors, nearly all of them half drunk, who were screaming and banging their hands on the benches of the loges, shouting for the show to begin.

The first act unfolded amidst great applause and the continued request of *bis*. When I reached the end of the famous aria, which I repeated every evening, and to which the public had become habituated, a hellish din broke out, and the sailors screaming for an encore sounded like damned souls: *bis, bissss, bisseeee*. I had already made plans not to give them an encore, and I didn't. Then pandemonium broke out in earnest. Whether in the orchestra or the loge seats the people began to pound their fists in the same tempo. Hundreds of feet became one foot, and they began to scream *bis* with one voice. It seemed like the end of the world. Inflexible, I stood firm in the middle of the set, not intending to give in to the public.

Then Cavallaro ran hastily up onto the stage and from behind the wings began to inveigh against me, repeating all the abusive language he had used before. While the public, ignoring everything that was transpiring upon the stage continued to protest ever more clamorously, I took up the sword which had been placed on the table and resumed my argument with Cavallaro, saying that I wasn't obliged to concede an encore because it hadn't been covered in the contract.

Don Peppino's eyes had been injected with blood. From an onstage box Gigi Macchi saw that things weren't going well, and he too advised me to give them the encore, since otherwise the show could not go forward. I persisted stubbornly in my refusal, and told Cavallaro that, if he wanted an encore, he ought to bring me another hundred lire on the spot. An unbelievably nasty row ensued. If Gigi Macchi hadn't been nearby to catch hold of Cavallaro, the latter would certainly have hurled himself upon me right there in front of the public, and a new sort of episode would have occurred in the history of the theater. We didn't say a word about the incident in the theater that night for quite some time. We both wanted the contract to expire so that we would never meet again.

His company went through some tough weeks. The final profit for the season which was drawing to a close was realized in this last gala during which I saw one hundred lire all together for the last time. The public poured into the Pacini Arena. Cavallaro had become indebted to everyone, including me. I said nothing about it and resigned myself to the inevitable. He organized some concerts also, but the public hissed two different soprani in *Gioconda*, and some of the players in the orchestra went over to the other side after Cavallaro was unable to pay them. His adversaries were tormenting him in any way possible to bring him down. He was ruined as an impresario. We didn't speak to one another any more, but in my heart I suffered for him, and with him, in spite of our last disagreement. All his artists went, a few at a time, to the other side, so that, after a few performances of *Bohème,* he was forced to stop operating.

I was left with little money in my pocket. He owed me a hundred and fifty lire but I didn't have the nerve to ask him for it. When we ran into each other at the Cafe Trinacria we were both sad. The dishonest maneuvers of his adversaries, which had succeeded in putting him in a position where he couldn't continue, had as its principle goal securing Titta Ruffo for themselves and presenting him to the public in two new operas. And lo and behold, here was Sciuto himself, Cavallaro's secretary, who had been loyally taking his orders from Cavallaro for the last nine months, having seen that there was little or nothing to be gained from a star that was about to stop shining, accepted without a scruple the assignment of coming to make me concrete proposals. To be precise, he was offering me a contract in which the company, in return for my engagement to perform for a month in *Carmen* and in *Pagliacci*, pledged to give me in compensation one thousand, five hundred lire.

I thought about this advantageous offer for some time. The idea of earning a sum like that in such a short time, which had required months and months of work with Cavallaro, and of being able at last to send my mother a thousand lire, attracted me very much, but the offer was highly repugnant to my conscience. Sciuto, seeing me hesitate, tried to convince me and persuade me: it would be stupidity, especially in my desperate condition, to ignore such a contract... I took more time to think about it... I told him I would give him my response in the morning.

That evening, meeting with Macchi, who was current about everything, I was asked if I would accept the offer from the Pacini arena, and my response was the same I had given Sciuto. Macchi didn't intend to influence me in any way. Meanwhile, he espoused the reasoning that was holding me back: that is, that I was already under contract to Cavallaro, who, if he hadn't been able to pay me, was prevented by *force majeure*. In the last analysis this man had punctually maintained his end of the bargain for the entire season, and it didn't seem just to me to abandon him before the agreed time. While talking to Macchi my conscience prevailed over material necessity. It seemed to me that to accept such an offer would be on my part an act of ingratitude toward Cavallaro, if not worse, and I decided then and there to refuse it. Macchi was very happy with me. At bottom he loved Don Peppino, and while fully admitting the way he had wronged me, still he recognized, quite apart from his pure self-interest, that he had wished the best for me, as if I were his son, and was now suffering sincerely to find himself in disagreement with me and above all not to have been able to pay me.

The next morning Sciuto came accompanied by a baritone from the other company, an ex-classmate from my days as Persichini's student, Amleto Pollastri.[104] Though pleased to see me again, he too had come to induce me to accept. Sciuto had also received instructions to increase the offer up to one thousand, eight hundred lire, but by now I had made up my mind, and I resolutely told them my decision: I wouldn't accept for any amount of money. They went away disillusioned. After this resolution I felt much better: better than ever when I learned that my friend Russumanno, with his wholesome and ethical character, had been tempted in his turn by the Pacini Arena and had turned them down flat.

Later I had occasion to meet Macchi again at the Cafe Trinacria. Don Peppino was also there. Macchi advised me to bring him up to date on my refusal, that I would surely give him enough pleasure to compensate him sufficiently for all the pain he had suffered at the close of the season. I approached him from behind.

"Don Peppino," I exclaimed, "it's time for us to talk, to throw off our masks and read each other honestly."

I extended my hand asking him to forget the last incident, and I reassured him of my constant fidelity, telling him of the flattering offer made me by the Pacini Arena, and telling him how proud I was of having refused it, because, in sum, no other impresario in Catania had the right to sign me, except him, Don Peppino Cavallaro. He shook my hand then with strength, and made me sit down next to him. Then with a voice suffocated by despair he said, "My dear Titta, your words are opening my heart. What you want to do for me is most generous, above all because I still owe you some money, but it isn't possible for me to permit you to refuse a sum so important. I know you haven't got much in your pocket."

"Don Peppino," I replied, "don't make jokes. When I've finished the little that remains for me to do, with my *caffellatte* and my usual two buttered rolls, I'll be able to push ahead, and in so doing we'll manage."

Cavallaro's face lit up more than I can say. He seemed to have just received a sort of life-giving injection. Macchi was no less exultant and he assured me that, if I had gone over to the enemy camp, Don Peppino would have taken ill, since he knew by means of Sciuto, who was playing two parts in the comedy, that the Pacini Arena, in spite of the crowds, had found themselves always in debt because of the enormous expenses to attract them, and that they had offered me that large sum with the hope of raising their prices, speculating on my popularity.

Reunited now with the same spirit as in the beginning, we studied together what might be done to salvage the salvageable. We concluded that I would get a contract with some theater, if only to be able to leave Catania and to refresh my financial resources, which had just about dried up. The grateful Cavallaro swore that he had never doubted my nobility of soul, and that my action had been worthy of my voice. Therefore he headed for the telegraph office with Macchi and me, where he wrote the following dispatch:

> Teatro Municipale Salerno. Knowing of your brilliant new season, I propose Titta Ruffo, baritone of my company, the most beautiful voice in the world. Able to sing *Rigoletto*, *Faust*, *Bohème*, operas you have scheduled. Respond to Cavallaro Catania.

He showed me the telegram, adding, "This is nothing. Tomorrow I will write to all the theatrical agents of Milan, and the one thousand, eight hundred lire which you have generously refused for the good of your impresario, will be repaid to you in no time, I swear it to you on my mother's soul."

Poor Don Peppino! He was in severe anguish; I was told that to save himself he had even pawned his wife's jewels. Very well, but when we went to the port together that night to have supper he was beaming. Then we went to the Pacini Arena all together, where, when we were seen entering, they looked at us with wide eyes, knowing that for two months or so Cavallaro and I hadn't been speaking. Cavallaro chose the seats, and when the impresario offered him some complimentary seats, he scornfully refused, saying, "Thank you, but I don't need your generosity."

We put ourselves in the first row. After a bit the whole theater knew that we were there. A lot of artists who had been part of Cavallaro's company and had deserted him were ill at ease. They were performing *Carmen*. The performance was mediocre. Cavallaro was gloating. He pointed out every jarring note or inaccuracy in a loud voice. "It's an indecency," he screamed. "People who instead of pretending to be impresarios should be polishing shoes or selling peanuts."

The many people who knew him were laughing at his criticisms and were hailing him with friendly gestures. In the second act some of the audience in the gallery began to shout, "Titta Ruffo! We want Titta Ruffo!" The voices and applause grew louder and louder until they had become a veritable ovation, so that I had to stand to show my gratitude.

"This is going to ruin them," Cavallaro was continuing to murmur under his breath, "because the people of this city, and I know them well, will desert a theater fast when there's no idol on the stage. I can't wait to receive the telegram from Salerno. Even if they put you under contract for half what these mafiosi and thugs were offering you, we will have won the day, you with an action worthy of you and I with the knowledge that I haven't damaged you too much..."

I disclosed to him an idea of mine: namely that, if no contract with Salerno was concluded, we could organize a big farewell concert in our theater, and I would be content with a very minimal portion of the take. He received my idea with enthusiasm, but nothing further materialized.

While leaving the theater after the show, turning to the group of impresarios standing by the door, he said with a sarcastic air: "*Arrivederci*," and then indicating me, "The big fish hasn't been taken in. He's too heavy for your nets, which were woven by too many treacherous threads. That kind of thread is so fragile, it breaks so easily..." Then taking my arm we slowly took our leave.

Don Peppino accompanied me to his house and didn't want me to leave him. There was sadness and penury at his place. His daughter had been ill for some time. He loved her tenderly and suffered a lot from it. In broaching this subject, because it seemed I might have been somewhat responsible, I limited myself to advising him to consult some good doctor.

"*Titticieddu mio*, what do you want with doctors in some cases? This daughter of mine must be in love. That's my diagnosis."

The following morning, there was Cavallaro at my house with the telegram from Salerno. They were offering me six hundred lire for one month. With his agreement I decided to accept and responded that I would be in Salerno on Saturday evening. As we left the telegraph office, we met Giovanni Grasso who had learned that I would be leaving Catania the next Friday (it was Tuesday) and wished to invite us together with Gigi Macchi to spend an evening with him. He arranged an evening in my honor on Thursday at his puppet theater and we agreed that afterwards we would go to eat at the restaurant in the port.

On Thursday Macchi and Cavallaro came to get me and we went to the performance. On the door of the little theater was a banner with these words printed upon it: "This evening's performance in honor of the great baritone, Titta Ruffo. The story of Rinaldo and Ferraù will be interpreted through his miraculous puppets by Giovanni Grasso in a one-man show."[105]

Naturally we sat in the first row. The theater was crammed for the most part with children and young people, dirty, noisy and impatient, screaming their demands that the show begin at once. This was the first time that I had ever attended a performance of this kind. I didn't know the story of Rinaldo and Ferraù, and for all that Macchi did to enlighten me, I understood little of it and remember less, distracted and deafened by the infernal racket of these children who were never silent or still. I do remember among other things that at a certain point two splendid puppets, two warriors, with helmet and armor, and with their Durlindant swords [a type used by the paladins - *Tr.*] in their fists, went at each other ferociously, with Ferraù getting the worst of it. Grasso, in his first exchange between the two warriors, first had Rinaldo say in a white voice, "Tell me Ferraù, speak, reveal your secret: where is your Achilles heel?" And Ferraù, in a big, loud voice that resounded in the little theater responded: "Wicked Rinaldo, I don't fear you. My Achilles heel is a place you won't be able to hit..."

The epic contest was over, and the curtain was lowered in the midst of the screams and wild applause of all those fanatics, who had divided themselves in two parts, those for Ferraù and those for Rinaldo. Grasso, his head thrust out of the red tent that concealed him, uniting the five fingers of his hand which were still controlling the strings and bringing them back against his lips as if to blow me a kiss, exclaimed at the top of his voice, "Goodbye, *beddazzu*,[106] my brother, may God bless you and conserve your golden voice..." To see me respected and singled out in this way by Grasso, this bunch of brats began to look at me as a rare beast, and, I don't know how, the word got around that I was also a puppeteer. I was tremendously entertained, and Grasso was as happy as could be. We brought the evening to an end down at the port.

We were forcing ourselves to be happy that evening, but a rather sad image was very near the whole time: the little cargo steamer that would take me to Naples tomorrow, then on to Salerno. Cavallaro grew melancholy at the sight of it.

"Life is such a cruel joke," he said all at once. "Man would be better off with a stone instead of a heart. When I think that tomorrow evening that steamer will have taken you far away, and that you will never come back here again, and that distracted by your future triumphs, you might not remember anything more of us—when I think of it, on my honor, I can let myself weep."

Grasso on the other hand amused himself by giving me advice about my voice, advice of a physiological nature above all. Then all of a sudden he thrust his fingers into his hair.

"My brother, please don't forget, stay away from *affairs*. That was the ruin of Ciccio Cardi. He fell in love with a woman and left his B-flat inside her. Renunciation of women is the whole secret for a singer."

Gigi Macchi took to singing *"Cielo e mar"* from *Gioconda* under his breath, his favorite aria. Don Peppino was looking off into space, immersed in his sad thoughts. And I felt that I was leaving something of myself with these people, and would carry with me so many vivid memories from this long period of work and togetherness. A profound melancholy flooded my spirit.

They accompanied me to my house. A messenger from the steamship company came to inform me that the departure had been put off by a few hours, since some oxen to be taken on board had yet to arrive from Siracusa.

Friday morning, at Macchi's invitation, Cavallaro, Grasso and myself got together to dine in a trattoria on via Etnea, and spent the whole day together.

Toward sunset—the steamer was leaving at seven o'clock— I went home to collect my things, including in my suitcase the sad array of a struggling artist's costumes, with Valentin's sword tied transversely across. Accompanied by my friends I headed for the port.

When the captain gave the handful of passengers their orders to come aboard, Cavallaro brought a colored handkerchief out of his breast pocket and dried the tears from his eyes, then gave me the handkerchief, assuring me that the tears were sincere. The good man didn't want to leave me. How many feelings were at war within me! I remember that he told me, while we were with the others, "I don't have the heart to go back home, with that daughter of mine as sick as she is..."

Dear Macchi also had brotherly words of affection for me. He exhorted me to keep studying, since I had the future in my hands. Grasso, when the steamship was already a small distance off, with a thunderous voice, called to me: *"Titticieddu,* please don't forget what I told you! Remember! Stay away from females!"

Those were the last words I heard leaving Sicily. My friends remained on the beach looking fixedly at the steamship as long as they could still see it. I saw their outlines growing ever smaller until they faded into the last reflections of evening.

Thirteen years later, while waiting at the station in Pisa for a train to take me to Genoa, I noticed a group of strange people near the baggage truck. They were seated on old suitcases, or on sacks of cloth. All of them were half-asleep. I was struck particularly by a man who was very extravagantly dressed, smoking half a cigar, next to the wall. On his head was a cap of ordinary leather, and he was wearing a short, chestnut-colored jacket and bell-bottomed pants with a red sash that resembled somewhat the one worn by Alfio in *Cavalleria rusticana*. The man was none other than Giovanni Grasso, the old puppeteer, that I had left thirteen years before in the port of Catania, who later became a great actor in Sicilian dialect. Those gathered around him were the artists of his company: Angelo Musco, Spadaro, Majorana, la Aguglia...[107]

At a certain point Grasso began to stare fixedly at me, and I at him. We didn't recognize each other right away. He began to make nervous gestures, now pressing his hat down over his forehead, now over his ear. Then he threw his cigar on the ground and asked one of the ticket-collectors if I were the singer Titta Ruffo. When the latter said yes—he knew me well, as it happened—Grasso threw himself upon me, howling with his huge wolf's voice, "Little Titta, Little Titta, my brother!" He grabbed hold of me with one hand on my collar at the nape of my neck and an elbow on my shoulder, in such a way that I couldn't get away, and stormed me with kisses. Then he began to caress my face with his robust, lean hands—caressed me, I say, but I would do better to say bruised me, contused me—recalling Catania in excited language. His sash had already come undone and my hat had fallen off. Someone watching this scene from a distance might have thought it was a scuffle. Some of the actors had approached in curiosity, asking who I might be.

Then Grasso flung his hat down and seized Angelo Musco.

"My good friend," he screamed, "don't you remember him? The kid who sang *Ballo in maschera* in Catania, fifteen years ago, with Don Peppino Cavallaro? Titta Ruffo, then, the greatest baritone in the world, known by everyone..."

Musco, who was remembering nothing at all at the moment, with a comical gesture of his head, replied: "I never heard the name."

Grasso, infuriated, pasted him with a strong backhand slap, and reinforced it by calling him the worst names he could think of. "Ignoramus, dim-wit, you don't remember him?"

Then he went to Spadaro, and he too gave a negative response. "I'm sorry, comrade, but I don't know him."

And he earned himself a loud slap as well, though he was stooped with age.

In short, none of his actors knew me, including la Aguglia and il Majorana. Then one of the secondary actors came forward, saying that he recognized me from having heard me sing the *Resurrezione di Lazzaro* in the Benedictine church in Catania. To this summons Musco jumped up. "Ah, yes, I remember! Perfectly. You were wearing a little Nazarene beard and had long hair. Sure, he's the greatest Jesus Christ in the world."

Grasso was happy that someone had finally recognized me. When my train arrived I embraced Grasso and shook hands with his actors. Musco, mortified, asked me to forgive him for not recognizing me right away, and raising a hand to his face, told me: "Now I'll certainly never forget you again, not after that blow Grasso gave me, heavy as it was."

CHAPTER 11

From Catania to Salerno

To pick up the thread of my narrative: the crossing from Catania to Naples gave me my first experience with that terrible horror—seasickness. As we left the port of Catania in a lovely sunset I looked forward to a repetition of the delightful crossing of the Strait of Messina that I had so enjoyed a few months before, when the sea appeared to be an expanse of oil. But it wasn't that way this time! The little freighter had hardly left shore for two hours when a strong wind came up and the waves swelled enormously. The cargo of dry coal which was on deck in the open air was knocked about by the squalling winds and embroiled in them so that the entire vessel was full of coal dust. It penetrated the cabins, the berths, one's eyes and ears and every pore of the skin. In short, with no escape, we were reduced to looking like chimneysweeps or worse.

The twelve oxen on board had been fastened by hawsers to the bow of the little vessel for fear they would be washed overboard, and the poor beasts bellowed all night. Their laments seemed human, as though they were directed at those who had taken them away from their beautiful Siracusan fields and peaceful stalls. In the hellish darkness where I was during the cataclysm the groans of the beasts were no less distressing than those of the wind and the huge, surging waves. Naturally

I wasn't able to shut my eyes. It made me brutishly stupid, and even I, in the toils of such malign forces, was reduced to moaning somewhat less noisily, but in much the same manner as the unfortunate beasts.

When I saw Naples in the distance the next morning, at dawn, I felt myself returning to life, and near the port the storm was succeeded by a dead calm. The sun began very slowly to illumine these enchanted isles, emerging through a light mist over the entire Isle of Capri, with its famous rainbow of colors: green, blue and violet.

My first thought on setting foot on shore, with my suitcases and Valentin's sword and my face all black with soot, was to go to a barbershop near the docks and rid myself of all the gross dirt which had stuck to me all over during the crossing. I don't know which was blacker, the soot or my mood.

When the barber greeted my entrance with gales of derisive laughter of course I felt like responding with my fists. I was about to address him as he deserved, or better, to get the relief I deserved, when I saw myself in the mirror and calmed down right away. A more ridiculous, more grotesque man would be hard to imagine. I was blacker than one of the little moors who danced before Amneris in Verdi's *Aida*. The cautious but rather sarcastic barber wanted to know in advance how much I intended to give him for my cleanup, and blackmailing me, wanted to bargain over the price in advance. He was asking absolutely no less than three lire. I could only bow my head. Could I permit myself to be followed by the sneering laughter of all Naples? And it was into Naples that I was obliged to make my way.

When I had returned to my normal condition I felt as if I had been delivered from an incubus, and began to sing a Neapolitan song called *Malavita*. The barber, who was rinsing his basin, which by this time looked like a cesspool, had chopped off my hair in a fury; but hearing me sing appeased him, as if by an enchantment. However, although my song had increased my market value, he asked another lire of me since I had requested an extra towel to make myself presentable.

From there I headed to the station to take the train for

Salerno. No sooner had I reached my destination, and left my suitcase in the baggage room, than I ran to the Teatro Municipale in search of the impresario. He wasn't there. Then I was approached by three individuals—three young men from twenty to thirty years old, who were very, I would almost say excessively, ceremonious, dressed with an ostentation of arguable elegance—who asked me if I were the new baritone who had just arrived from Catania. When my response was affirmative they advised me and convinced me to go to the hotel facing the theater, along the sea. They accompanied me there themselves, recommending me to the owner. And one of them would have gone to the station to reclaim my suitcase if the owner of the hotel hadn't said that he had his own personnel for that. Joining me a little while later in my room the hotelkeeper himself told me not to have too much to do with these men, who were nothing but three hoodlums well known to the police for their affiliation with the *camorra* of Naples and Salerno, but in the same breath he told me not to make enemies of them now because they were part of the *claque* at the theater, and had boasted that two years before, at his debut, out of reprisal and wickedness, they had hissed at no less a performer than Caruso.

This fact impressed me quite a bit, without on the other hand unduly upsetting me. Certainly I listened to the advice of the hotelkeeper, but I boldly succeeded in deceiving them throughout the season. I led them to believe, feigning collusion, that before becoming a singer I had for some time been affiliated with the underworld of Livorno. This joke may have caused me more damage than good, and exposed me to troubles and risks that were anything but amusing. After my debut, in fact, they never left me. I had them always under foot, and I came to hate them, longing for the moment when I would leave the city. At all my performances a veritable revolution took place. They all got together, there must have been fifty of them, between the loges and the ground floor. They were coming and going in my dressing room as if they owned the place. They raised an infernal din, convinced in their minds that they were doing their best to honor one of their company and help him rise, though still young, to renown. They all celebrated, too, feeling that at bottom they were partly responsible for my success. I unburdened myself to the owner of the hotel, who, always kind and obliging, sought to protect me in clandestine ways. He feared them, knowing them capable of anything. At the last performance of the season, which was *Rigoletto*, every last one of them was in the theater, dressed to celebrate.

When the performance and the season were over, they had arranged a banquet in my honor in a low tavern by the sea, rather far from the center of town, where they would be met by their women, almost all of whom were of easy virtue. The police had already been apprised of this reunion. The hotelkeeper saved me from some real trouble. He got me a ticket for the first train to leave town. With an intelligent stratagem three policemen assured my three indivisible friends that I had already left for the tavern with another of them, and furthermore that they saw me leave minutes before the three of them arrived. Then the police helped me to flee through a back door.[108] I confess that I had wanted to be an invisible presence at their banquet in the tavern by the sea, together with their women—especially for the toasts which were sure to have been drunk, rising from the table to honor their old comrade in arms, risen so young to the light of stardom!

CHAPTER 12

To Genoa and Ferrara

AFTER SALERNO I RETURNED to Milan, and from there left many times to sing for brief periods in various Italian theaters: at the Brunetti of Bologna,[109] at the Garibaldi of Padua, the Regio of Parma, the Tosi Borghi of Ferrara,[110] and the Carlo Felice of Genoa. In the last I received a considerable fee—nine hundred lire for about two months. I had signed with the agent Zoppolato.[111] I had no success whatsoever in wringing from him the round figure of one thousand lire. I debuted with *Traviata* and followed it with a *Rigoletto*. Zoppolato recommended me to a good Genoan pension which was frequented by artists, and himself averted the proprietor so that he came to fetch me from the station.

Before going with him, however, I had the shrewdness to ask the price of his pension. He replied that he had made me especially favorable rates, compared to the others, contenting himself with only fifteen lire per day. I immediately put my suitcases down. How could I permit myself such luxury with the miserable contract I had? He stood there amazed. In Genoa I would not be able to live for less, not even in the most humble pension. When, to persuade him, I showed him the contract, he asked me how I succeeded in making both ends meet. I told him about my life a few months before among the fishermen of Acireale. He was offended by the comparison between

Acireale and Genoa. I assured him that I would succeed in finding some tavern down by the port where I could eat a good *minestra* for a few lire, and excellent fish. He waved goodbye, disappointed. When he was but a short distance away he stopped and retraced his steps. He asked me what I would have wished to spend, precisely, to live the next two months in Genoa.

I had already made my calculations. I responded that, to get to the end of the season without asking anything of anyone, the most that I would be able to spend was ten lire per day. The good Genoan, perhaps out of a sense of pity, decided to welcome me to his pension for only ten lire, adding that his wife had already prepared the room and had set a place for me at table. He begged me not to tell anyone about the favor he was doing me. I passed the season in attractive enough surroundings and, a strange thing, was treated better than the other pensioners who paid more than I did.

I debuted at the Carlo Felice in *Traviata* with artists who had already achieved celebrity. The house was full. The protagonist was Angelica Pandolfini, an exceptional temperament and a classy artist, especially great in the death scene.[112] Alfredo was the tenor, Elvino Ventura, who had made a hit at that time in the *Iris* of Mascagni.[113] My success in *Traviata* proved me worthy of my illustrious colleagues. I was often required to repeat the famous romanza "*Di Provenza il mare, il suol*" amidst a delirium of applause. This success convinced the administration to put on *Rigoletto* and entrust the part of the protagonist to me. This renewed, if it didn't actually increase, my success, winning for me a preeminent position among young baritones.

From the first performances in Genoa I became acquainted with Pier Giulio Breschi,[114] who was then the editor of *Century XIX*, who had for me and for my interpretations words that were quite flattering. He continued to write good things about me after the *Rigoletto*, predicting a great career. We became friends. I met him many years later in Rome where he was director of the *Messagero*. Our relationship was reinforced. In him my family had the most attentive and affectionate guest.

At the end of March, 1900, I went back to Milan.

My limited earnings hadn't permitted me to accumulate any but the smallest savings. I had in my billfold the last one hundred lire I had earned, and that constituted my entire fortune. In Milan I was overjoyed to embrace my brother again, who had completed his military service. He stayed with me for two days, then he continued on to Rome. I accompanied him to the station and divided with him the little money that I had.

The following day I was passing through the well-known Galleria in the expectation of a contract. I was approached by one of the many messengers, so abundant then, who asked me if I was free to sing *Ernani* at the Teatro Tosi Borghi in Ferrara. The night before the entire company had been hissed in that opera house, and the directors were looking for new elements to replace those who had brought disgrace. I accepted immediately and the Zappert agency drew up my contract, wherein it was stipulated that I was engaged for six performances for a fee of six hundred lire,[115] and that upon my arrival there I should have to receive an advance of one hundred and fifty lire.

I was happy, as if I had just signed a most important contract. The Ferrari tailor shop had made me a fine overcoat for the mid-season, to be paid off in monthly installments. I went to claim it and informed the tailor of the contract I had just signed, assuring him that upon my return I would pay off the entire bill. The tailor saw no problem, and even let me have the overcoat without asking for the first payment. I left the tailor's shop exultant, with the new overcoat of pea-green English cloth on my back.

On the morrow I left for Ferrara, not in fourth class, you can be sure, for the simple reason that the Italian railways didn't have it then any more than they do now. I took off my overcoat, folded it with great care and placed it near my suitcase. It represented the most precious object in my wardrobe. But for all that...

But for all that, due to a wretched case of amnesia, I left it on the train. I had scarcely left the station when I became aware of it, and I went back the way I had come, but the train had already left. I rushed with tears in my eyes to the stationmaster, imploring him to have it looked for, my new overcoat, the only one I had. The stationmaster did all he could, but the overcoat wasn't found. I interpreted the loss as a bad omen; I headed to the theater with ugly presentiments in my heart. And my heart wasn't playing tricks on me. At the door to the theater I met the conductor of the orchestra with despair on his face.[116] He asked if I was Titta Ruffo. We shook hands and he led me outside. I learned from him that the impresario had taken flight, leaving the company high and dry.[117] He now found himself completely destitute, with no idea how to get back to Milan. At this news I felt the blood leave my veins.

In addition, as if this weren't enough, rain began to pour from the skies and we had to take refuge in a little cafe. We were asked, naturally, what we would like to have, and were obligated to order two cups of *caffellatte*. I only had ten lire left in my pocket. Now, while with tears in my throat I was telling the maestro of my own misadventures, two distinguished and charming young men whom we had heard at a nearby table came forward and introduced themselves. These were the Magnaghi brothers of Ferrara. In a well-mannered way they showed their distress over what had happened in their city, and invited us to dinner at their home.

It seemed to me indiscreet to accept, but the conductor, a man of a certain age who knew how to get on in the world, encouraged me like the good Neapolitan that he was. I conquered my reluctance and we both followed the two young men, who took us to their house and presented us to their father and their entire family, and offered us a succulent dinner, washed down with a wine that would have brought the dead to life.

After dinner they bid us enter a music room where there was a grand piano. The maestro, who had not had the chance to hear me in a theater, asked me to sing some excerpts from *Ernani*. The Magnaghi family, lovers of song and theater, insisted as well. At heart I had no other wish than to reciprocate their courtesy in some way. At the end of the recitative of the third act, one of the brothers opened the window which gave onto the street. After the romanza *"Ah de' verd'anni miei"* and the aria "*O sommo Carlo*"[118] an immense crowd was applauding frantically. Then I sang the romance of Rotoli, "*La mia bandiera,*"[119] amidst a roar of acclamations. The senior Magnaghi and the conductor, after hearing my sample presentation, started chatting amongst themselves in private, and in short, that was how the company, with its artists and extras, was reorganized,[120] so that before two days had passed my debut was announced under the new impresario, Magnaghi.

Then on the morning of the performance I saw my name on posters with the following advertisement: "This evening *Ernani*: the part of Carlo V will be interpreted by the celebrated baritone Titta Ruffo, direct from his triumph at the Carlo Felice of Genoa." This type of publicity really made me furious. I ran to the Magnaghis and asked them to destroy all the posters. I insisted that I was only a young artist undergoing his first trials, however fortunate they might be; I didn't intend to exploit the good faith of the public; I absolutely could not sing under the appellation "celebrated." The publisher of the Ferrara newspaper, who was present at the discussion, also advised the Magnaghis to postpone the show till the following day; in the meantime he would explain why to the public, which would have a certain value, putting me in the best light where public opinion was concerned. And so it was done.

The next day a magnificent article appeared in the paper exalting my good sense and my artistic conscience. My popularity soared. I was very nervous when I went to my dressing room. The theater was packed. By good fortune the success was greater than all of our expectations. In the end Magnaghi offered me an evening in my honor, where he presented me with a laurel crown. In addition he gave me a thousand lire and a new overcoat, so that I left Ferrara without any of the bitter tears over the coat I had lost when I arrived. Through his generous gesture he had saved the company from ruin and at the same time he had earned for himself, with eight performances, twelve thousand lire. On the way back to Milan I thought I was Julius Caesar. And my first concern was, of course, to pay Ferrari the tailor for the pea-green overcoat, lost by misfortune on a train.

CHAPTER 13

From Genoa to Santiago

GOOD OLD MENNINI, my restaurant host in Milan, the friend of artists, was delighted with the initial stages of my career. One evening he introduced me to a theatrical agent named August Conti. He would have been about 55 years old, and was small in stature, thick-set, with little hair on his head. He was a Florentine and spoke an exaggerated Tuscan. However, on the whole my impression of him was quite favorable. Barba introduced us by saying, "This is just the man for you," and he invited me to audition for him. Conti offered me a five-year contract, with an obligation to pay him five percent of all the contracts he obtained for me. I accepted without having to think twice about it.

The following day I was in the Galleria relaxing. The weather was splendid; Milan was festive. Lots of artists, agents, messengers, conductors were seated at the Biffi restaurant. I was there watching Puccini go by with Tito Ricordi and Leoncavallo with his turned-up moustaches[121] when all of a sudden there was Barba to tell me that Conti was looking for me because an impresario wanted to sign me up for Chile. We went together to track them down.

Conti made the introduction to this Latin American impresario, whom everyone called, behind his back, Don Juan, and so shall I. Indeed, the fellow was a fine gentleman,[122] who could boast of having brought Adelina Patti to America for the first time,[123] signing her for 30,000 lire per performance, while at the time the contract was being drawn up he hadn't a penny in his pocket: this should be enough to give an idea of the intelligence and craftiness of this man.

He looked me over from head to foot and asked me why I wore my hair long. I answered, somewhat taken aback by such an indiscreet question, that I wore it thus out of artistic and economic necessity. Since I was often required to sing as Marcello in *Bohème*, it served to spare me the expense of a wig, which, with what they paid me, was nothing to be cheerful about, but that with my first important contract my hair would go the way of Samson's. He invited me to be heard in an audition at La Scala, saying that, if he was pleased with me, he would sign me for Chile.

I went to the audition. I sang the recitative and aria from the second act of *Trovatore*, followed by the aria from *Ballo in maschera*. Don Juan, seeing that the reports he had of me were more than truthful, led me together with Conti to a little room in the Hotel Rebecchino.[124] He asked me if I would like to leave for America two days later, and inquired as to my monthly fee.

This was a solemn moment for me. I objected to the time of departure because I wanted to go to Rome first to see my mother. He told me that that would be impossible, since the company had to embark at Le Havre three days hence. I would therefore have barely enough time to get everything ready for the operas I was to sing. I had no choice in the matter. As for my pay, I asked three thousand lire per month. Don Juan looked at Conti with an enigmatic expression, and observed that that was a bit too much. We finally settled on 2,700 with the last fortnight in advance. Thus I signed my first important contract.

That same evening Don Juan and Conti took me to a supplier of theatrical furnishings. We selected a number of different costumes and accessories: breastplates, helmets, swords, boots, belts, ornaments, shoes of all kinds necessary for *Aida*, *L'africaine*, and *Otello*, and we filled a large trunk with them, which was then closed and shipped to Paris together with the rest of the company's equipment. To pay for all the things, they handed me a promissory note to sign for 3,500 lire which would fall due upon my return from America. I didn't want to sign it but Conti told me that the value of what I was buying was double what I was paying for it, and that it was a big advantage to have found so much that was just right for me—and, what was more important, these were things that would be of use to me throughout my career. I gave in. Reluctantly—this was the first and the last promissory note I ever signed.

We left with the understanding that the next day I would show up at the station a half-hour in advance of our express train's departure for Paris. Then, alone with Conti, I signed a contract he had ready, authorizing his representation, without so much as reading the stipulations.

From there, we quickly returned to Barba's for dinner. The dear old lady told me: "My dear Sciur Titta, with this contract your career is now assured. You'll see, they will call you to La Scala afterward. They're already speaking about you as an extraordinary artist..."

As I waited anxiously to depart I occupied myself in preparations; wrote to Mother; I bought various personal effects; I said goodbye to the Casinis, who were also very happy with the turn of events. When they learned the amount of my pay Casini assured me that, had I asked five thousand lire, they would have found the money and paid it to me. In fact, Don Juan had signed Delfino Menotti—who, along with Cotogni, Maurel and Kaschmann, was one of the most famous baritones of the epoch[125]—at nine thousand, the most ever given to a great baritone at that time; but at the last moment he had taken ill. In any case Casini, who, himself, aspired to go to Chile, told me that the contract represented, just as it was, a big step up for me. The next morning, not before stopping to say goodbye to Mennini, I left for the station, this time by coach. Don Juan was already there with the company: orchestra musicians, corps de ballet, soloists and chorus members. There were a hundred and sixty people in all.

In the middle of this hubbub, amidst baggage of every sort,

while everyone was anxiously trying to find the most comfortable place to sit, I felt lost. But I revived quickly enough. Among all these more or less agitated forms I spotted a fine gentleman who was carefully shaved, a type more Russian than Italian, who was called Paolo Wulmann.[126] He was the first bass of the company and was going to a lot of trouble to place the artists, each in his compartment. Don Juan presented me to him, and urged him to take care of me, and to see that I traveled in his first-class car.

WULMANN SHOWED ME every possible courtesy, though he regarded me as a youngster. While accompanying me to my berth, he spoke to me as if he might have to be my tutor during the entire voyage. When I arrived, the porter, who had been carrying my luggage back and forth from one car to another, exclaimed, "My God! Finally! What you got in there, lead? Damn!"

I gave him a tip because, truly, the bags were heavy—there was even an iron in one of them.

By the time we departed I was more dead than alive. With such a hurried departure, everyday matters had to be concluded as quickly as possible: writing or saying goodbye to this person or that, running here and there to get things done, all this had worn me out. I fell asleep for a few hours. Wulmann, who was seated close to me, woke me up to tell me, "Baritone, it's time we go eat." I had no appetite. I stayed behind.

Left alone in my compartment I began to count the money that was left me. Between my immediate expenses and the money I had sent home, and telegrams to my father exhorting him to be patient and convincing him that my career was seriously taking off, and so on, the sum, which had seemed enormous to me, was reduced to a very small nest egg. After dinner the compartment filled up with people I hadn't had the opportunity to observe before, since I had been half asleep. Wulmann hastened to introduce me. We exchanged a few words, and then I fell back asleep, and slept until nearly four in the morning.

It was already the middle of June and suffocatingly hot. At daybreak I began to walk the length of the aisles; I felt alone, downhearted and numb for having slept the whole night in an uncomfortable position with Wulmann close by, who had been snoring like a motor. As daylight gradually flooded the car, I began to ask myself if it had been worth the trouble to have changed directions and set off to fight who knows what battles, among people I didn't know, who didn't know me, far from my family, where I couldn't even embrace my poor mother. A tremendous dismay came over me. I wanted to unburden myself to someone. The splendor of the sun, which was burning its way across the beautiful French countryside, instead of giving me courage, overflowed the vessel of my soul, and I felt the tears hot down my cheeks.

Near Paris we continued on for Le Havre. Our steamship, a modest British vessel called the *Lorellana*, was already at anchor, ready to leave the following morning. I lodged in a little hotel near the port, where a dirty little room fell to my lot that gave off a stink of bestial humanity, and some French sailors were staying in the room next to mine. They came in late, half-drunk and their revelry didn't stop till dawn. Some sang themselves to sleep with the Marseillaise. I need not add that I went the entire night without sleeping. And that morning, too, when the sun came up, some tears slid down my cheeks.

On board at last I saw Wulmann busily taking the company's belongings on board. I was shown to a cabin for four people—namely Wulmann and me, the baritone, Cerratelli, a Florentine,[127] and the fourth, a Southerner, the assistant conductor, I believe, whose name has completely passed from memory. When the company had settled in and been assigned their places in the dining room, they proceeded to the regular ceremony of introductions. Of the sizable company, I was the youngest. For the first time, then, I met a brown-haired woman of fascinating beauty who had, I learned, sung two years before at La Scala in Milan, creating great enthusiasm. She would have, as I will shortly relate, an extraordinary influence on my life as a man and on my mettle as an artist.[128] I will speak more of her in due course. Now I shall return to Don Juan.

Don Juan was taking along a singular young woman. Singular in her name, as well, for she was called, or wanted to be called, Ireos Myrtea.[129] She was very slender, had sea-blue eyes, a tempting little mouth, very fine golden-blonde hair, and was always wrapped, perhaps in keeping with her name, in iridescent veils. Taken altogether she appeared ephemeral. She had been personally engaged by Don Juan and occupied a cabin which communicated with his.

Don Juan, profiting from his position as a great impresario, took some beautiful young creature to America with him every year, always a different one. He was then about sixty, but he had kept himself well. Still a handsome man he was tall, strong, with a fresh complexion, and two long sideburns always carefully sculpted by his razor. His behavior was distinguished. He treated his Myrtea with an almost servile gallantry. Always, but especially when he was gazing at Myrtea, he physically resembled one of the fauns of Rubens or the tritons of Arnold Böcklin.[130] He succeeded in charming everyone and never lost his temper. For him everything that happened in life was a joke. He had already made a hundred crossings, always leading the life of a *gran signore*, even though he hadn't much money. He was a valiant trencherman, and on his long voyages he always kept himself well supplied with tinned meats in oil, truffles, caviar, special wines and sweets, and almost every other gourmet item apt to satisfy all the gastronomic caprices of his *odalisque*. In sum he was what's called an epicurean of the first order, refined, sensual, intelligent, diplomatic, and endowed with a most brilliant and charming wit.

I had the privilege of being assigned to his table, where at every meal Myrtea was regaled with caviar on toast, tins of tuna, candied fruits and fine liquors. We passed the first days in perfect harmony. Through Myrtea's courteous intercessions I was also able to taste some dainty morsels, or a little glass of something, and if I refused to accept her largesse—and I refused regularly—then Myrtea, in a voice that seemed to have descended from heaven or gushed forth from her iridescent veils, pronouncing her *e* very closed would say: "Help yourself, please; we have so much more."

I thanked her obsequiously, and didn't know how to conduct myself. But I felt myself always more ill at ease because, with the strain of all the compliments our whole table had adopted an affected manner, all smiling somewhat, if not actually pronouncing their words the way she did. I longed for dinner to be over so that I could resume my normal behavior, and when I was finally able to leave the dining room, I heaved a great sigh of relief.

Sleeping four to a cabin was for me, throughout the voyage, an indescribable hardship. Wulmann snored with such vehemence that prior to sleeping I had to stuff my ears with cotton. Besides I had the misfortune to have to sleep above the assistant maestro already mentioned, who stank so badly that sometimes, especially below the equator, he turned my stomach. By good fortune I had a little window next to my bed, and when the sea permitted it I could thrust my head outside, and purify my lungs with the ocean breezes.

There was a bath next to our cabin. One day I ordered one. When the steward came to tell me that my bath was ready, the substitute conductor, annoyed because I had to put a foot on his berth when I was descending from my own, asked me where I was going, and finding out, rubbing the sleep from his eyes, exclaimed "What stupidity!"

At my second bath he roused himself again to say, "Jesus! Another bath! You're going to ruin your health; you're crazy..."

Furious to have to submit to the stench of this man, completely beside myself, I replied "I'm not crazy, but you are smelly!" ["Io non son *pazzo*, ma tu sei *puzzo!*"]

He was profoundly offended, and when I told him that, out of respect for us at least, he ought to take a bath himself, he replied that he was clean by nature, and that only those who were dirty by nature had to take baths. So it was that in the forty-day voyage from Le Havre to Valparaiso he didn't wash himself once.

One day the sea was very agitated. I walked back and forth on the bridge with an upset stomach. A lot of passengers had retired to their cabins. At the end of the bridge a seventeen-year-old girl named Lisetta, from the corps de ballet, was feeling very sick. I went up to her to help her empty her stomach. I put her head outside the parapet, pressed my palm against her forehead. Pale, cold, she appeared about to faint, and I saw to it an orange and some sugar were brought to her, and when she had some relief I lifted her onto a bench. She was grateful that I had helped her in the extremity of her sickness; she addressed affectionate words to me and laid her head in the crook of my shoulder, saying, "Excuse me for permitting myself this liberty, but I simply can't—"

There was nothing I could do but remain in this position until she should recover a little. In that moment Don Juan came by with Myrtea, and the latter, seeing me in this position, shot me a look as if she wanted to strike me with lightning. I accompanied the poor girl to her cabin, and since I too suffered from seasickness, was soon imitating her. However, I decided not to go to my cabin, thinking of my companions, and above all of the one who didn't wash himself because he was "clean by nature."

At the mere idea of that stench I felt as if all the waves of the ocean were mixing together in my stomach, and I preferred to remain on the bridge in a deck-chair. I didn't even have the strength to get up to eliminate by mouth the bitter bile which almost always precedes vomiting.[131] What I suffered at that point was unspeakable. I finally began to scream like a man in agony. I swore that I would never again commit the blunder of accepting a contract for an overseas engagement. I cursed Christopher Columbus and his lugubrious discovery. I remained nailed to my chair, for how many hours I don't know. Who can preserve notions of time in such a state? When it seemed to me that the pitching and rolling was a bit attenuated, I got up to walk a little, hanging on desperately to everything in order not to fall, and saw with joy that my friend, the assistant conductor, the man who was clean by nature and fragrant by education, had just sat down not far from me. He was in such a state, my God—he appeared to have come down with cholera. Traversing the corridors I could only hear cries, laments, sobs and death-rattles. From the half-closed cabins such violent sounds of retching erupted from time to time that

I don't know how, from one moment to another, intestines with their sad contents intact didn't burst forth.[132] The stenches were so raw and sour that they would take the breath out of a giant like Goliath.

Well, in spite of the anguishing irritation of my stomach and nerves I had the strength to reach my cabin where, would you believe it?, Wulmann was snoring in the middle of this apocalypse with his usual obstreperous calm, as if we were navigating in perfectly calm seas. I am not going to say I envied him. I undressed in haste, plugged my ears with the customary cotton and tried to get to sleep. Alas, my mind was vacillating between the need to sleep and the desire to die! Oh, why hadn't the Inquisitors contrived a machine to inflict the most terrible of all tortures, seasickness? Perhaps none of them had ever suffered it. Or perhaps one of them had thought of it but the mechanics of the time were not sufficiently advanced to produce it. After two days Neptune decided to placate the waves, and thus very slowly all the passengers emerged from their cabins, pale and half-dead. Myrtea, leaning on Don Juan's arm like the Santa Teresa of Bernini, was decidedly spectral. He, on the other hand, was in fine fettle. After so many voyages he had become inured to the ocean's caprices. Particularly prostrate was the little ballerina I had helped two days before.

At the dinner hour nearly all of them returned to the table. This time, however, even though Don Juan and Myrtea served themselves the usual delicacies, they did not invite me to participate. She didn't address so much as a look to me. I pretended not to be aware of the change. She was evidently offended, but I did not succeed in discovering why. He, going along with the attitude of his companion, showed himself no less haughty. The other diners noted the behavior, so, finding myself more ill at ease than ever at this table, I decided to change after two days. The abandonment of my assigned seat worsened my relationship with Don Juan, who asked me why I had done it. I responded harshly that I found no pleasure in being in heaven to spite the saints. I should have said to spite the *saint,* but he understood the allusion all the same and I thanked him with all the same courtesy with which he had honored me.

We had already been at sea eighteen days. Lisetta, the young ballerina that I had aided in that terrible predicament came to me often. Some evenings at sunset I found her near me, and she often spoke to me, competing with me in her admiration of the vastness of the sea and the supreme spectacle of the sun setting. And I, slowly, so as not to seem like a bear, and all the more because she was very sweet, showed myself to be always more affable. We got along well together, like two good children, and we were, I believe, the youngest of all the passengers. We conversed at length about all sorts of innocent things. The familiarity began to be noticed by Don Juan, and especially by his company, creating a pretext for vulgar and malign assertions, whose principal origin was without doubt the tongue of Myrtea.

One morning Don Juan, wondering if this familiarity could hurt me, and hurt him as well, called me into his library and made me a sharp reproof. I should think about my responsibility, which implied his as well. Acting thoughtlessly I would compromise us both. Meanwhile he prohibited me from talking to Lisetta; and, if I should not obey him, he would have me put off the ship in Rio de Janeiro. The threat was grave, however unjust its imposition. But Don Juan was far from realizing with whom he was dealing.

I replied that I was much amazed that he had permitted himself to meddle in my intimate affairs, and that it meant nothing to me to be put ashore in Rio; moreover, it would have pleased me since I had the artistic means to earn my living wherever I might go; and that as far as he was concerned I had no other obligation than to acquit myself as an artist when we arrived in Santiago; and that I had no intention of depriving myself of the innocent company of Lisetta along the way. Then I left him in the lurch, quite irritated.

On the bridge I met Lisetta, whose eyes were red. The ballet mistress, to whom her well-being had been entrusted by her mother back in Milan, had forbidden her to speak to me. My fury rose to the heights. I persuaded her that, on the contrary, she shouldn't let herself be influenced by anyone; that we had done absolutely nothing wrong; and that we were free to act as we pleased; whereupon I took her under the arm and we promenaded together here and there along the bridge for around an hour.

The next day the following notice was put up in the salon by the stage director: *Tomorrow at ten-thirty rehearsal of* L'africaine *with all the artists.* I immediately set about running over some *vocalises.* I was most anxious about what had happened and it was important to me that tomorrow the company should hear my voice at its best. This was necessary above all in front of Don Juan, whom I had shown I was a man and not some spiritless boy. When it was time for the rehearsal I sang the principal music of Nelusko, my part, at full voice. My voice gushed power in its entire range. All who heard me were profoundly impressed, even Myrtea, who, near-wife of Don Juan, acted like the director of the company.

Among the ones who heard me then, the one whose praise I coveted the most was the "brown-haired woman" who had sung in Milan two years previously, bewitching the public with her beauty and her art. This woman, who will be called Benedetta from now on in my narrative, had roused in me the most ardent attraction, joined with a higher, almost sacred, reverence. This complex feeling, which sustained me right from the beginning, I jealously guarded within me as if it were a secret that I feared to reveal—let it be said: even to myself. I saw her as so superior to me, so far and lofty that the hope of winning her heart, or at least her attention, seemed to me a ridiculous fantasy. I was twenty-three years old, she was thirty-three. Everyone was courting her, flattering her. She sat to the right of the commander at table and he, too, and this says it all, was paying court to her, although, being an Englishman, he did so most discreetly. Then Wulmann, who liked to play at being a gallant and irresistible ladykiller, was madly in love with her, and was paying court to her almost to the point of being insolent and offensive. I remember his saying occasionally in our cabin, "I'll have her yet! When we're in Chile, things will be different. Here on board everyone's always around and

I can't be alone with her for a minute..." His common boasting sent the blood to my head and it was hard to resist the temptation to show him my contempt.

At the end of the rehearsal—the idea of singing full voice had proved most felicitous—I found that I had gone way up in the estimation of all my colleagues. Even Benedetta came to shake my hand, congratulating me. I responded: "Thank you, signora, your praise is very precious to me." Although I pronounced these words with a special accent that should have conveyed how I felt inside, she didn't give, or didn't appear to give, any importance to them.

Wulmann with his usual protective air was telling me, "When we're in Santiago, I will introduce you to my journalist friends, and I will think of everything. Relax; I'll see that you have a big success."

Even the tenor Castellano[133] recognized something extraordinary in my voice. While admiring the diamond on his finger, he told me, with a certain protective air, half-joking, half-serious, "You will have the honor to sing with Edoardo Castellano."

The tenor Izquierdo, who was truly a great Vasco di Gama, told me in his turn: "You will hear my *Africana*. It's a pity we couldn't sing it with Cavallaro in Sicily. The last time I sang it in Spain I had to encore *O Paradiso*."

Such, or very like these, were the discourses and manners which occupied us on board the *Lorellana*. Let's forget them...

After the first few days of the voyage the first antipathies began: the first disagreements, words of gossip and betrayals. Insinuations, slanders and criticisms rained down—about behavior, conversations, the way one walked and dressed. Imagine what existence on board must have become after forty days of such a voyage. There were outcomes of all kinds; it would take an entire book to tell it all. As for me and Lisetta, notwithstanding my bold reaction against Don Juan, I decided, compelled by the appearance of wrongdoing, that for her peace and mine it would be best if I stopped talking to her. We limited ourselves to a salutation with a simple wave of the hand. Surely it was Myrtea, with her wicked tongue, who had created such a situation; accordingly, my silent dislike of her grew daily.

One day after our meal—we were below the equator and the heat was suffocating—I found myself face to face with her, enveloped in one of her lightest veils, as she crossed the corridor to go to her cabin. She looked at me like an exasperated cat. Fixing her with my eyes I addressed these two words to her: "Viper! Witch!"

I should never have done it! She was overcome and fainted, falling full-length onto the floor. I distanced myself, going quickly on deck. She was carried bodily into her cabin.

Don Juan, furious, was looking for me everywhere. There followed an angry dispute between us. I contrived to convince him that, while I was rehearsing the part of Marcello in *Bohème*, she had had the misfortune to pass right in front of me at the very moment I addressed those two words to Musetta, in the third act. Don Juan prevailed upon me to go to signorina Myrtea, explain the misunderstanding to her, and ask her pardon. This was truly the only thing left for me to do to avoid unmasking my lie.

To bring Myrtea to herself had required the vinegar of the Seven Thieves.[134] I found her in a state somewhere between agony and ecstasy. Upon hearing my explanation she began to cry, and between her tears she told me that during the first days of the voyage I had been kind to her, but that when that ugly slut had crossed our path, my friendly manner had altered. I restrained myself, so as not to aggravate the situation, but I can't say how badly I wanted to make her eat her words, specifically the word "slut" for a young girl so innocent and pure, an especially insolent accusation inasmuch as it was coming from the lips of someone like her. I didn't refrain from telling her, however, that Lisetta was someone quite different than what she had judged her to be, and that in any case I hadn't spoken to her for many days. To calm her I dried her eyes with her handkerchief. Then looking fixedly into my eyes she whispered, "It's a shame our trip has been embittered in this way," and desolate she leaned her head on my shoulder.

We were thus almost embracing when Don Juan, seeing

the ceremony unnecessarily prolonged, had approached on tip-toe, and suddenly appeared before us. I wished the earth could have opened under my feet. He closed the door and watched us with his eyes as big as a faun's, then he screamed at me: "This is the limit! Get out of here this instant!"

I reassured him: nothing bad had happened. Taken unawares by another fainting fit, I'd been obliged to help her up in this fashion, and that was all there was to it. Myrtea, to extricate herself from this embarrassment...fainted again. Humiliated, I left the cabin, and until we reached Santiago I didn't once open my mouth either to Don Juan or Myrtea.

Life on board continued to unfold from one bit of viciousness to the next with the most boring monotony. We no longer knew how to kill time. I resorted to passing long hours on the bridge near the English officers' cabin. Ignorant of their language I had to be satisfied with observing the helmsman, the compass, the ocean charts. Then one day I noticed, near the captain's quarters, that the only luxury cabin was occupied by two newlyweds on their honeymoon. No one had ever seen them. They had been living apart and eating in their cabin. They were two very handsome young people, tall and distinguished. He was fair-skinned, brown-haired, with big eyes; she was a Swedish blonde with regular features, a little cold, but attractive. They passed long hours looking at the sea, sitting side by side, hand in hand, and sometimes caressing each other with such tenderness that they appeared to be in perfect physical and moral harmony. I watched them as if I were looking at a beautiful painting, and the painting seemed made for its stupendous frame, the sea and sky, and they for it. Watching them admiringly I felt less isolated.

Often when I was near them, without being seen, I formed an image in my mind of the ideal companion, in harmony with my nature—and Benedetta fired my imagination. I dreamed of her, she, too, next to me, and compared the two couples: the blonde and the brunette. If the young British gentleman was superior to me—and without doubt he was, and not only in elegance—his blonde companion, on the other hand, when compared to my ideal companion, was totally eclipsed by her. Benedetta may have been less tall, but the nobility of her face and the perfection of her figure had no equal in the world. Her mysterious voice was enchantingly suave. Her head was splendid, with a spacious brow framed by seven exquisite points formed by her hairline, the most pronounced in the middle, and the other three on each side, forming a slight descending curve to her ear. A glimpse of her ear revealed it to be small and perfect under the thick undulations of her black hair. Her eyes were black, large, luminous, even more beautiful for a light shadow around them and her long, thick lashes. Her hands were small and well-modeled. She dressed with elegant simplicity and did not wear jewels. I talked with her in spirit for long hours every day. Above all it pleased me to look lovingly at her in profile from a hidden vantage. In profile she had the grace of an antique cameo, and in certain moments, when she looked down, it seemed she might have been sleeping.

I will recount the following anecdote to give an idea of the power that this woman had acquired over me. One morning I was playing quoits on the bridge with two other passengers, and it became a game to decide who could throw the farthest: there was practically no one around. The *signora bruna* was sitting apart with a friend. Unfortunately a quoit thrown by me struck her friend's foot and gave her quite a bit of pain. I hastened to make my apologies, but the signora, feeling for her friend, said, "This isn't the place for games like this!" and went on, "What sort of fellow are you? What are you going to do with that beautiful voice? When we arrive, you'll understand the responsibility awaiting you, and with this long hair and that eternal flowing tie, what a sight you'll be!"

I dropped the quoit and, humiliated, I started to think over the deserved observations she had made on my account, and although they hadn't been the most appropriate, I went to my cabin and looked at myself in the mirror. I didn't see myself with the same eyes as before. I found myself ridiculous, with my exaggerated mane of hair, and that tie of mine, and without wasting any time I ran to the barber and had him cut my hair like any other fellow's, and replaced the bow tie with a long tie purchased in Milan.

Afterwards I returned to the bridge—the two women were where I had left them—and addressed myself to Benedetta. "Look," I asked, "does this please you?"

She, without realizing the importance I had given to our conversation, seemed surprised by my rapid metamorphosis, and was pleased to exclaim, "Now, yes, you're quite a gentleman, and when they see you they will have quite a different opinion."

The other artists too all thought I looked better. Don Juan, even though I wasn't speaking to him any more, perhaps attributing the change in me to the suggestion he made during our encounter in Milan, improved his attitude toward me. From that day forward I was no longer capable of playing around or joking. A new personality was emerging in me.

The most tedious and tiresome part of my first, long Atlantic crossing was that between Montevideo and Valparaiso. In the Strait of Magellan a violent storm came upon us, and we passed some very unhappy days. Better not to speak of them. When we reached Valparaiso all the passengers disembarked amidst the confusion of visiting customs officers, journalists and photographers. Along with the stupor that overtakes one after setting foot on terra firma after such a long and arduous voyage, I was invaded by a deep sadness. It seemed to me a folly to have come so far, to this ugly country, into this brutal climate, humid and oppressive, which was affecting my head and making me sick.

As I watched my big chest being unloaded, the one containing all my theatrical goods, my eyes casually fixed on the strange figure of a man all in rags, with a beard growing out almost entirely white, with the expression of someone about to die, who by means of a wooden bar across his shoulders was carrying two baskets full of lemons. He put the two baskets down and accosted me with two large lemons in his hand, asking me if I wanted them, and offering them to me for a few *soldi*. What an incredible surprise it was to find that... But here, before proceeding further, I must beg the reader to take more than a step backward with me.

At twelve years of age I was an ironworker in my father's shop in Rome, as has emerged from the preceding narration. Among the workers who had left their mark in my heart—I recall all their names, though forty-seven years have passed— were Vittorio Cataldi, Pietro Cardolini, Tarabo the stammerer, Mastro Righetto, Fabrizio, Pizzini, De Pretis, Spadari and Pietraccio.

The last-named was the oldest of them all. He had a mild and generous character, and was particularly attached to me, the youngest of them all. He called me *Ruffetto*. Some Saturdays after my father had finished paying them, he used to take me with some of the others to an old tavern on via Merulana called the *Bocconottaro*, where, besides an excellent wine *de li Castelli*, one could eat sweets called *bocconotti*, whence the name of the establishment. I was most content to find myself in that Roman environment, frequented by the ordinary working class. I used to return home slightly tipsy—in truth, one glass was enough to do the trick—and I recounted excitedly to Mother everything I had heard and seen at that place. But she didn't show herself to be the least enthusiastic. She considered that habit harmful to my health and my developing character. Finally she had Pietraccio informed that he was not to take me any more. And Pietraccio had so much respect for my mother that she didn't have to tell him again.

One evening, to my surprise, Pietraccio announced to us his imminent departure for America, saying that he was going aboard at Naples a few days hence and sailing from there to Chile. My father and many of the workers advised him against taking such a trip blindly and without any concrete means of support so far away, leaving the certain for the uncertain. He didn't pay attention to any of them, firmly persuaded that before a few years were out he would be returning to Italy without ever needing to work again.

Prior to his departure he wanted to buy my father and the other workers a drink at the *Bocconottaro*, and wanted me to come along in spite of my mother's prohibition. Accompanied by my father, I accepted with pleasure. Among the many toasts bidding him goodbye and wishing him well, Pietraccio raised his glass, saying, "I embrace Ruffetto for everyone, because, without meaning to offend anyone, my greatest sadness in leaving Rome is for him."

Everyone applauded him. He kissed me then, visibly moved, and not because of the wine! In the years that followed no one ever learned what became of him.

And here was that wretched man, carrying two baskets of lemons on his back suspended from a wooden bar, and putting the baskets down, offering me two big ones for a few coins—the very same Pietraccio. "Pietraccio!" I shouted.

When he heard his name he paled and asked me who I might be and how I happened to know him. I invited him to look me over carefully and see if he didn't recognize in me a person very dear to him. Shaking his head he replied that he had never seen me before. Then I recalled to him his little friend Ruffetto, his workmate at Oreste's shop, his companion at table in the *Bocconottaro*... I hadn't finished evoking these memories when he let the lemons fall from his hand and we threw our arms about each other, both of us moved to tears.

I had three hours before our departure for Santiago. I passed them with him. He told me his whole unlucky story. Luck had been against him from the time he left us.

Embarking at Naples on his sailing ship, he had been at sea for three months, stopping in all the smallest ports of the Mediterranean. When he finally reached Santos in Brazil he wanted to disembark because he could no longer stand the wretched life on board. But some old sea wolves, taking advantage of his meek and good character, obliging him to perform the most humiliating services, did not permit him to land. Thus he had been forced to continue his voyage to Rio de Janeiro, Montevideo, Buenos Aires, until, crossing the Strait of Magellan, after many hardships, exhausted for lack of nutrition, he arrived at the port of Valparaiso. He lived those years in the most abject misery. Incapable of reacting against his cruel fate he was living for some time like a poor stray dog. In his desolation the only comfort he received came from a small Japanese dock worker, who helped him with his lemon business, and had contrived for him to sleep clandestinely in one of the port's big warehouses, between bales of cotton and sacks of coffee.

His sad story made me so despondent that I intended to save him any way I could. At the moment of my departure I wasn't able, owing to my scant means, to leave him as much as I would have liked, but I recommended him to the secretary of the Milan Hotel in Santiago, a gentleman who had already come to meet us in Valparaiso, a likable Piedmontese who had settled in Chile many years ago and who was now to lodge the best part of our company in his hotel. Very generously the good Piedmontese promised me that he would occupy himself with my friend as soon as he arrived in Santiago. And in fact... But it is now time to pick up the thread of my interrupted narrative.

After a three-hour respite, then, the heavy boredom of which was alleviated somewhat by Pietraccio's story, although it was a lot sadder than entertaining, we left for Santiago and finally arrived there late in the evening. A small crowd was awaiting us at the station: journalists, photographers, the personnel of the Italian consulate. Also present was the owner of the Hotel Milan. He asked for me right away. He had heard good things about me from the artists of the last season. He covered me with compliments and invited me to come directly to his hotel, where he had prepared a beautiful room with bath for me, set apart from the others and very quiet. We left together in the same coach.

As soon as I arrived at the hotel the first thing I asked was if the lady who interested me so much had also arranged to stay there. I was given the list of client's names, and read there with joy that of Benedetta.

The following day the first rehearsal in the theater was held. Since the theatrical commission was there to hear us, everyone was singing full voice. I just marked my part from beginning to end, which did not make a good impression. The president of the commission came to order me to sing out also. I refused, adding that, because of the terrible voyage, very tiring to someone like me, new to the sea, my voice wasn't in perfect condition.

At the second rehearsal—I don't know what got into me—it was the same thing. At the third, the general rehearsal with orchestra, quarrels broke out between Don Juan and the commission because I insisted on singing *piano*. The commission accused the impresario of having brought over an artist with no voice and no sense of responsibility. So Don Juan was forced to break the ice with me, and mounting the stage along with the president of the commission, who wore a long, black beard, he solemnly told me, *if I didn't sing the entire part in full voice, he would have to summon another baritone from Italy.*

I wasn't terribly upset by this for two reasons. In the first place, I was very secure in my part—I had shut myself up in a remote room of the hotel every day, where the owner had put an old piano at my disposal, and I had carefully gone over the score, and sung the most difficult parts full voice; in the second place, it would be a bit difficult to bring another baritone from Italy to take my place. Taking advantage of my young age—I looked even younger than I was—I managed, as they say, to pretend ignorance so as not to pay the penalty. My strange behavior led the subscribers to distrust me. Don Juan, to unburden himself of all responsibility, was finally reduced to imploring me to sing just one phrase. I replied that I was sorry not to be able to accommodate him, but I had to keep all my vocal resources in reserve for my debut. Only the public was in my heart, I was highly unconcerned about the theatrical commission. At the general rehearsal the theater was packed as if it were a performance. Maestro Padovani,[135] responsible for the outcome in front of the onlookers, came to implore me, for the love of God, to sing the opera in full voice. In substance I responded as I had to Don Juan.

The rehearsal was a disaster for me. Everyone sang *forte*. The soprano, Mazzi, in the role of Selika, continued, as usual, to sing full voice, and the tenor, Izquierdo no less than she. His aria "*O Paradiso*" excited a delirious enthusiasm. The bass Wulmann, who was playing Don Pedro, gathered abundant laurels with his robust voice and gigantic physique, well-suited to the character. I was the kill-joy of the evening. The president complained to Don Juan, "What a shame that this stupid and irresponsible boy had to ruin a splendid performance." Don Juan alternated between fury and humiliation. The subscribers went to congratulate all the artists in their dressing rooms, and since they were obliged to pass in front of mine as well, expressions such as the following came to my ear, and not seldom: "Tomorrow that boy is going to have a bad time of it, the poor fellow!"

I cannot conceal the fact that these words made a certain impression. I feared that I was playing a bad joke. As soon as I was in the hotel I shut myself in my room; I opened the chest with all the necessary accoutrements from the theatrical supplier in Milan; I brought forth my make-up materials, the wig, the undergarments, the sandals, and though it was already very late, I transformed myself completely into Nelusko, putting on even the sweater with the padding over my chest. Finally I placed upon my head the diadem of the Indian's feathers, and stood a long time in front of the mirror to study the effect. I would have given two years of my life to go right then to the theater and discredit the story that I had no voice.

I took off my makeup, took off my costume and put everything back in order, then I slipped into bed. I passed the night in a very agitated state and didn't get off to sleep until dawn. In compensation I slept late. Scarcely had I got out of bed, it was around one o'clock, when I did my usual *vocalises*. That day my voice gushed forth limpid, powerful and secure, as was my will to triumph.

I went down to eat and the owner of the hotel, who had been present at the general rehearsal, found me a special meal and exhorted me—in truth, even he was very nervous—to be strong.

When I was in the theater, made up and dressed, the stage director came to beg me to be ready.

"Yes, by God, most ready!" I responded with the obdurate scowl of an Indian. "I can't wait to get this load off my shoulders."

I entered the set descending some stairs at a bound with the agility of a man of the forest, as the part required. At the first notes that I had to sing, two *"No"*s on a B-flat and a D-natural, I filled the hall with powerful vibrations. I felt my voice was free and easy, and only awaited my will to unlock itself and burst out in its full force. From the first phrases, *"Oh, non parlar! Regina"* and *"Se andate per comprar un bue da lavorar"*—above all at the end of the last, where I cleanly emitted a sustained G-natural resolving in a middle C, the public burst out as one in formidable applause. I remained immobile in the middle of the set without acknowledging the ovation so as not to destroy the illusion that I lived as my character and his spirit was real to me. On leaving the stage I noted that an animated dispute had broken out in the stage box of the commission, of which I understood I was the subject. The man with the black beard was repeating over and over, "This man has been pulling everyone's leg!" [*"Este hombre nos ha tomado todos por el pelo—"*]

In the second act, after the prayer (*"O Brahma, O Dio possente"*), the public broke out in great applause, but the height of my success was defined by the phrase *"All'erta marinar,"* and after the famous ballad *Adamastor*, which I had to encore. By this time I had conquered my public. The last wheel of the cart had become the first. But the image isn't appropriate. I must say that I had become the *idol of the crowd.*

Don Juan was beaming. He ran to embrace me, declaring that I had won a great battle. Everyone came to congratulate me. The president with the big black beard, which stood out even more against his white shirtfront, thinking that he was doing me a great honor, came with Don Juan to salute me, announcing himself, naturally, by knocking on my dressing room door and stating his name and his title.

Fortified by my success and mindful of all the unfavorable or even offensive evaluations that had been made of me, I responded by saying that I did not want to be disturbed by anyone. He insisted, and thinking I hadn't understood, repeated that he was *Don Pedro de Vargas, the President of the Commission.* Don Juan hastened to beg me to open, but I replied, in a loud and clear voice: "Impossible!" Nor did I keep from adding that the visit of signor *Pedro de Vargas* was not welcome and I did not intend to receive him. Big-beard went away protesting and claiming that he would have full satisfaction from me and from Don Juan for the insult I had brought upon his person.

Then Don Juan brought all his diplomacy to bear, and he was very capable in that respect. He issued a profusion of apologies, saying that artists were abnormal beings and generally not responsible for their actions. When I was ready for the fourth act I went to the artists' hall and there met Don Juan, who told me that I'd gone too far with the president, and after the performance, I should go and offer him my apologies.

At that moment I saw big-beard with Myrtea on his arm standing not so far away from us that he wouldn't be able to hear my voice well. Therefore I responded to Don Juan in a loud voice that it was ridiculous to beg the pardon of a man who had, the very first evening, offended me in public, called me irresponsible and stupid, and so on. From the expression on big-beard's face I understood that he had already forgotten everything, enraptured as he was by Myrtea and her veils, as she smiled artfully with her affected, debauched little mouth.

At the end of the performance when, free at last of the fervent homage of the thousand admirers I had never seen before and tired of shaking hands, I was about to leave my dressing room, I was surprised by a visit from Lisetta, my companion of the crossing—my companion in misfortune. She arrived all dressed up and made up like a cheap little princess, loaded with diamonds on her ears and at her wrists, with a large white fox fur around her neck, her face rouged and her lips a fiery red like Myrtea's. I already knew that she had left the ballet and had come under the protection of some bigshot. I received her very coldly. She made me a thousand compliments in her Milanese dialect.

"How you sang! What a beautiful voice you have! The public was delirious!"

Seeing her so young and already fallen so low, I felt so sorry for her that I couldn't refrain from speaking harshly to her. I told her that I preferred her in her simple little dress on board the ship, without rouge, without lipstick, and that, dressed as she was, she was parading the price she'd paid for her honor. Then I brought her mother into it, asking her what her mother would think of her if she could see her reduced to this condition, incapable as I was then of thinking that her mother herself had perhaps pushed her into it, letting her go alone to such a faraway place, in such dangerous society as that of the theater.

I returned to the hotel a little sad because I had not seen the *signora bruna* at the show, and I asked the hotelkeeper about her. Thus I learned, with the most vivid displeasure, that she had remained the entire evening at the hotel because she had undergone minor surgery on her larynx. Strongly affected, I confided to him then the constant fascination which had bound me to her from the first day I saw her, and I begged him therefore to go to her in person the next morning to get news of her.

The news that she was ill kept me awake nearly the entire night. I had wanted to be close to her, to share my success with her, to comfort her. Having received the morning newspapers in my room with the review of the performance, which was full of praise for my voice and for my interpretation of Nelusko, I would have wanted to go to read it all to her myself, because fundamentally I had sung with all my soul...to show her that I wasn't as much of a child as she had judged me on board.

In the meantime I was invited to one of the first rehearsals of *Ballo in maschera*. Before going, knowing that she should have been present but would be unable to make it, I decided to write her a letter. In it I said:

Gentle lady, it will surprise you to receive this from me, but I learned of your indisposition by chance, and am very saddened by it. I had wanted you to be present at my success. I nurture a feeling of profound gratitude for you—for the kind and earnest advice you gave me on board our ship. Your words had the power to change my personality. Now I feel that I am more serious, more of a man, and I would like to express in spoken words what I feel inside, but I wouldn't have the courage. Forgive me. Get well quickly, I beg you, because your being brings light and the joy of living. With all my devotion: Titta Ruffo

I accompanied this somewhat puerile letter with a bunch of roses. I learned later that my homage had found her heart most receptive, all the more since it had reached her in a moment of depression. In fact the directors of the theater had informed her that, because she had exceeded the six days provided in the contract without joining the rehearsals of *Ballo in maschera*, her contract had been annulled, and thus she would have to leave, or according to the self-interested advice of Don Juan, accept the protection of the president of the commission. She gave them a flat refusal. The beauty of her spirit was no less exalted than the beauty of her body. I would have done anything in the world to help her.

I went down to the salon where, among others, I met the tenor Castellano. After complimenting me on my performance, he repeated, somewhat sarcastically, "Soon you will also have the honor of singing with Castellano."

This time I didn't let him finish the phrase before replying dryly, "And you will have the honor of singing with Titta Ruffo."

Like a good Southerner he never lacked for a rejoinder, and told me that I had a long way to go before I would be able to concede that honor.

"Certainly," I replied, "but when you've come to the end of your career, I'll still have, if God wills it, a lot more years left to continue with mine."

Our unchivalrous verbal duel was interrupted by the arrival of Benedetta. She had finally returned, and with a sad and disheartened expression. She scarcely greeted those present with a nod of her head and was off to see the conductor, the only one among them all who might be concerned about her painful situation.

I was able, thanks to the kindness of the latter, to find myself face to face with her; she, too, wished to speak to me. She thanked me for my letter, which had surprised her, as had the beautiful flowers, and she congratulated me for my success. She promised me that, prior to leaving, she would do everything possible to come hear me in the theater. She foretold a great future for me. I seized the opportunity to open my heart to better advantage. I told her that I had sung *for her*, in order to be considered a man *by her*, and that I felt myself capable of helping her without the slightest ulterior motive, but only out of gratitude for the impression she had roused in me ever since our first encounter. She had understood; and by helping me to clear my overheated young mind of dreams and illusions, she had caused me to reflect seriously on the reality of things.

The following evening the second performance of *L'africaine* was on the program. However, since one of the artists was sick, Maestro Padovani thoughtfully came to advise me that if the indisposition of the artist was prolonged, we would have to change the performance. He asked if, in that case, I felt myself sufficiently in form to go on and do *Rigoletto* without a rehearsal. I didn't try to hide the fact that in my opinion it would be hazardous, but I had brought the score with me. We went to the piano and *sotto voce* I marked all the important music of the opera. He was quite happy when he left me, asking me to keep myself ready just in case. I brought to his attention the fact that I had the right to a rehearsal with piano and one with orchestra, and that I would therefore be due extra-contractual compensation. Without giving importance to my words he went his way saying that it was the same thing whether I sang *L'africaine* or *Rigoletto*. Later Don Juan came and announced that we needed to change the show, and that the only opera that would content the subscribers was *Rigoletto*, where I would succeed in winning a new success.

Beautiful words, I replied, but to venture such a program I

would require an additional one thousand, five hundred lire, to be paid to me prior to going to the theater. Upon hearing my request Don Juan had turned to stone. He looked like Don Bartolo of *Barbiere*. I repeated, stressing each syllable, *mille-cinquecento lire*.

"But you're raving mad!"

"Quite otherwise! I am a man of wisdom to be kept free and unconstrained and you'll see it from the facts. If I am going to sing *Rigoletto* tonight, that means you will have brought me fifteen hundred lire, and not a soldo less. After all, it doesn't cost you anything. Didn't you dock the sick lady fifteen hundred lire? Then you will give me fifteen hundred. It's the law of compensation."

"But what do you know," he went on, "of things concerning the administration?"

I told him that, faced with the case of the sick lady, and the possibility, already described to me by Maestro Padovani, of changing the opera, I immediately read my contract. I knew very well that Article 7 gave the artists the right, for every opera, to one piano rehearsal and one with the orchestra, not only that—on the day of performance the artist was not obligated to rehearse. Therefore he should make up his mind since, if I hadn't received the requested sum by four o'clock, I was leaving the hotel and would be returning in my own good time. Don Juan left me flat without adding a syllable.

At exactly four o'clock, however, who should come but the administrator of the company to hand me the equivalent of fifteen hundred lire in Chilean pesos, and not a *soldo* less. I saved the money in my traveling kit and at six o'clock was in the theater getting ready. I sent for the barber to adjust my wig, and slowly, with great calm, I began to vocalize on the stage, while watching the stagehands who were striking the *Africaine* set and replacing it with the one for *Rigoletto*. Toward seven the other artists arrived. Castellano, who ought to have been debuting with *Manon*, was against his will constrained to make his first appearance in *Rigoletto*. He wasn't nearly as arrogant as he had been the day before. Not having sung this Verdi opera for a long time he felt himself unprepared, and he was unable to conceal his anxiety. I, on the other hand, had sung it not very long ago—the last time at the Carlo Felice in Genoa, to be exact—and had kept the entire part perfectly clear in my mind. If not, how could I have taken on such a responsibility so readily?

After the third act of my second role here my complete success had been confirmed and consecrated, placing me definitively in the first rank of the company's artists. When I returned to the hotel, the manager seemed to have gone out of his mind. He was jumping up and down in the salon, exclaiming in his energetic Piedmontese: "*Dio faust*, what fanaticism!"

I longed to tell Benedetta of my new triumph and to vindicate her. I ran to my room, took the fifteen hundred lire in pesos from my traveling case, and entered the salon, which was crowded with artists and hotel guests. I called the proprietor and asked him to please summon the signora, if she was still awake, since I had the most urgent need to speak to her. Don Juan entered quite haughtily at that moment with his Myrtea. Then just a little later, Benedetta arrived. A lot of artists were present and all of them, openly or otherwise, were accusing me of extortion. I pulled out my pesos then, saying to Don Juan that I had intended to convey this sum to the signora, and that therefore I had never wanted to extort money from the management. Rather I had carried out a just and comradely act. The signora didn't want to accept the money. She felt that what I had done, however innocently generous, might have been given a malign interpretation. I then consigned the money to the manager of the hotel, begging him to take charge of it, for it belonged to the signora. The censure of the other artists changed into admiration. Embarrassed, Don Juan withdrew with his Myrtea. Still the signora persisted firmly in her refusal. In front of everyone, without reticence, I repeated that what I had done was only inspired by a deep sense of solidarity and deference, and I couldn't have acted differently, because the act had made me a bigger person.

My life in Santiago unfolded as it had elsewhere; it was monotonous, between my room at the hotel and my dressing room at the theater, between rehearsals and studies and exercises, always more or less to earn the favor of my public. Sometimes I sought relief from my tiresome work with a restorative walk, and to familiarize myself with my surroundings and with works of art if there were any. Sometimes my companion in such walks was none other than—you can't imagine!—Pietraccio.

The good Piedmontese, secretary of the Hotel Milan, where I resided, faithful to the promise he had made me while we were still in the port of Valparaiso, had remembered my friend, and a week after our meeting there, he was at his service. I bought him a suit and made him shave his beard and moustaches; I made him like new. On evenings when there was a performance, with the agreement of the proprietor, he carried my case and remained with me at the theater. He was amazed to hear the performances. As he expressed it, to find his little Ruffetto after so many years transformed into an artist, acclaimed by the crowd, exalted by all the Chilean newspapers—he said it seemed to him that he was part of a beautiful, continuous dream.

One Sunday I took him with me to visit the zoo. Near the lions' section, in an iron cage, there were, as I remember it, two bears. The old one was bald and broken down, the other was little more than a cub, lively and playful, an excellent acrobat, and the visitors clapped their hands. Pietraccio enjoyed himself very much, and found a similarity between the two bears and the two of us. It's not necessary to say who met the conditions of the first term of the comparison, and who the second.

On holidays, too, he was always bustling through some corridor or room of the hotel; I would look for him so that we could chat together somewhere, and we would recall days gone by, days of sadness, of comfort, of learning, remembering our friends at the shop, the vicissitudes of fortune from that time on, sometimes tragic, sometimes ridiculous, which prepare men in silence for their destiny.

In these three months Pietraccio, in his new situation, had been able, with his salary and the liberal tips he received, to save a little money. Leaving there I would have wanted him to go back to Italy with me, but he wouldn't hear of it. It might have been the old illusion, now come back to life in him, that he would return to his country with a certain fortune, if not the fantastic one he had envisioned prior to his expatriation, or it might have been the new affection he had discovered for a certain waitress by the name of Mercedes who also cared for him and habitually called him *"my angel."* I left him, persuaded that I would be returning next year to the Chilean capital. I didn't return for twenty-eight years, that is, until 1928. Pietraccio had been put to rest already quite some time ago in the cemetery of Santiago. I wanted to render him a last honor by placing on his grave a marble stone with the inscription: *Al caro Pietraccio il suo Ruffetto.*

CHAPTER 14

A New Tour in Italy

WHEN I HAD COMPLETED my engagements in Chile, alternating performances between Valparaiso and Santiago, always with great success, assisted by my perfect health and my vehement passion to climb ever higher, I embarked with the entire company for Europe. We traversed the Strait of Magellan with the sea as stormy as usual, amid great suffering. Prior to arrival in Buenos Aires the sea calmed. I immediately went looking for Benedetta. I passed the time in her company with the greatest joy. She welcomed my feelings of devotion with great goodness and sweetness. I was happy to have won the esteem of someone who had been the ideal companion of my dreams only a few months ago. She was the angel right behind me during the most difficult years of my career, and with a sure hand she guided each step toward my goal.

In Montevideo an impresario came on board who offered me a chance to sing in Buenos Aires in a second-class theater. Perhaps my inexperience pushed me to accept, but she, for many reasons, advised against it, since in Argentina it was the official opera theater[137] in which, one day, I would hope to be engaged.

The voyage continued with the calmest of seas and we arrived in Genoa at the end of October. The money which I had earned during my American season was just sufficient for my subsistence, for paying the debts I had contracted before leaving, and for helping my family. Once in Milan, after having traveled over a great part of the world, I felt a deep sadness. I recommenced daily visits back and forth to the Galleria in search of a good contract. I thought I was worthy of one. My personality had been much transformed—for the better, I feel. Other than the head of hair which was no longer *à la bohème* and the tie which was no longer flowing, I had assumed a more serious aspect, more intense, as one who had begun to perceive how difficult the path of art could be, and how facile the illusion of sudden riches. After a number of days of going back and forth I was signed to sing the part of Iago in *Otello* at the Teatro Verdi of Pisa: a part which I had studied and adapted magnificently to my voice and to my temperament.[138]

Some doubted that I would know how to succeed, young as I was, in such an arduous role; but, after the first performance, even the most severe critics recognized in me, not only a singer privileged by Nature to have a voice, but also an artist who had intelligently combined acquired gifts with his innate talent. In fact, prior to presenting myself to the public, for about a month I did nothing but study *Otello*. I had procured the translation in verse of Giulio Carcano[139] and there I was every day with the Shakespearean tragedy in my hands. And inasmuch as the creation of such a profound character required much more, I believe, than one month to be penetrated and understood completely, in just a month I found it possible to assimilate it well enough. Certainly the success was great both in the theatrical world and in the press.[140] From then on I never stopped studying the great English dramatist. He was the high point of my creative evolution. After the performance in Pisa of *Otello*, I went to Siena to the Teatro dei Rinnovati, where I interpreted Carlo V in the *Ernani* of Verdi,[141] and from there I went to Palermo.

I was called there to substitute for two great baritones at the Teatro Massimo who had to leave for Buenos Aires, Mario Sammarco and Eugenio Giraldoni;[142] for one in the part of Rigoletto, for the other in the part of Scarpia. Both Sammarco and Giraldoni proved to be very kind to me: they were true gentlemen in art and life.

I ought to have opened with the *Rigoletto*, but that was impossible because of *force majeure*, therefore I had to debut in the part of Scarpia, a part that was more difficult and risky, as well as, most important of all, new for me. In the second place, it had already been performed by the singer whom the composer himself had selected for the part. In the third place, it was my lot to have to go on stage without an orchestra rehearsal, with nothing more than a simple piano run-through. The day following my arrival was to be the last performance of the aforesaid opera.

Thus I had the time and means to know Giraldoni more closely. I asked to be introduced to him and he received me with the utmost cordiality. I asked him to forgive me for disturbing him, but I believed it was too audacious of me to go before the public in the Teatro Massimo right after him, the first and best interpreter of the character, without the aid of his expert advice. I was permitting myself to inconvenience him to gain some insight from him, particularly into certain particulars in the second act. He received my plea with great generosity of soul, and although that same evening he had, as I have indicated, his last performance, he went with me to the theater, called one of the assistant maestri, had a piano brought onto the stage, and for around an hour wore himself out being a stage director, illuminating the whole second act for me down to the smallest particulars with a tenderness worthy of the highest aesthetic conscience, which was innate in him. Thus the secure grounding I needed to confront the judgment of the Palermo public was given to me. This behavior of Giraldoni's was deeply etched in my heart, and many years later, at the Teatro Colón in Buenos Aires, I was happy that a propitious occasion presented itself to demonstrate my gratitude to him, not in words, but in deeds.

Palermo signified an important step up in my career.[143] At the time the impresario and patron of the Teatro Massimo, their Maecenas, was the renowned Ignazio Florio.[144] He had invited me there with a flattering telegram, and when I arrived, as was the custom, wanted to know what fee I might be asking. I responded that, except for the expenses of travel and hotel, I would consider myself more than sufficiently compensated by the pleasure and the glory of singing in his theater and knowing the best-loved and most honored man of Sicily. I took part in six performances and after each one had the pleasant surprise of receiving from the Florio administration an envelope with a thousand lire in it.

Nor was that all. Prior to leaving Palermo, the Casa Florio threw a big party, where the entire aristocracy of Palermo took part, and I was invited too on this occasion and asked to sing a few arias. When the brief concert was over the secretary again gave me the usual envelope with a thousand lire in it. I refused, saying that I had been amply paid by the honor of being able to participate in such a gathering. Yet at the moment I was taking my leave I had another surprise, and one more pleasant than ever. Florio was wearing a gray, tailcoat and a cravat, in which was stuck a tie pin with a splendid pearl of obvious value. He came up to me accompanied by his beautiful wife, Donna Franca, to thank me for the pleasure of having me sing in his house. She added her thanks to those of her husband and, I believe she was already aware of my refusal of the thousand lire, she removed the splendid pearl from her husband's tie and stuck it into mine, with the wish that I would accept it as a remembrance of my success in Palermo. This was the way guests were treated in the *Casa Florio!*

After Palermo I went back to the Fenice of Venice, where I appeared in *Trovatore* and scored a resounding success.[145] I was then entrusted the part of Lucifer in the opera *Il santo* by the Venetian master Francesco Ghin, one of the strongest of musicians, a pupil of Smareglia. The author of the libretto was Count Sugana.[146] As for the musical performance, I studied the part with Ghin and he was enthusiastic about it. He even declared that no other artist would have been able to give the role a better interpretation. As for the dramatic performance, Sugana found me too young to play Lucifer, too slender and too immature from the standpoint of experience.

Likewise he doubted that I was sufficiently knowledgeable

about mythology, and was quite frank in telling me so. I protested that I didn't understand a great deal about mythology in general, but for all that, as regarded Lucifer I was sufficiently informed, and I urged him to trust me completely.

I was required to go on in the first act in the costume of a Roman gladiator, carried on a large shield on the arms of four centurions, and to start singing a Bacchic song to great melodious and dramatic effect. At the rehearsal Sugana certainly realized that my voice was what he had longed for to express diabolical power, but in spite of Ghin's enthusiasm he continued to maintain that my slender form was still inadequate. The count had a point, but he didn't know that I had had an undershirt constructed in Milan which gave my chest and my entire body the powerful lines of a gladiator of old, an authentic king of the abyss.

At the general rehearsal everyone was dressed and made up. I waited impatiently for the four centurions so I could climb onto the shield when lo and behold a very nervous Count Sugana appeared before me, accompanied by Maestro Ghin. I found myself face to face with him.

He was so myopic that he didn't recognize me, and indicating me to Maestro Ghin, he shouted "This is the way Titta Ruffo should be!"

But Ghin had recognized me. "Oh, can't you see?" he interrupted, exultant. "That's exactly who it is, in person?"

Sugana was stunned. It seemed impossible to him that my boyish figure had been transformed all at once into the body of an athlete, even a Titan. Squeezing my artificial muscles he exclaimed, "It's a miracle!"

My success was immense, especially in the monologue, which was the most important piece of music in the opera. It was delivered at the finale to the Sphinx of Egypt—in the background of the magnificent set the pyramids could be seen in the distance—and I crowned it with one of my best baritone notes. The public exploded as one person into a loud ovation. The authors of the melodrama said that the performance was in every way everything they had dreamed.

CHAPTER 15

To London and My First Vacation at Home

MY ARTISTIC PATH took me ahead without interruption. Some weeks later I was appearing at Covent Garden in London in the *Barbiere di Siviglia*. My colleagues were Maria Barrientos, Alessandro Bonci and Antonio Pini-Corsi, and the conductor was Luigi Mancinelli. This was the first time I had sung the part of Figaro. Pini-Corsi was a great help to me, he knew all the traditions. For my second opera I sang *Lucia di Lammermoor* with the same artists.[147] One day management asked me to assume the part of Rigoletto, which ought to have been taken by Antonio Scotti,[148] but he had fallen ill. The part was proposed to me even though it wasn't in my contract. I accepted right away, happy with the offer, which gave me the opportunity make myself appreciated in London also in a role of the first rank, and one already perfectly familiar to me.

This Verdi opera was being performed in honor of *Madame* Melba, the artist most favored by the British public at that time.[149] I was presented to her, but at the orchestra rehearsal I was obliged to sing the duets alone because, although she had come to the theater, she didn't want to take the trouble to mount the stage, and remained hidden in a stage box with the conductor. After I had sung my monologue, Maestro

Mancinelli, quite annoyed, asked that *Madame* Melba join in, but she absolutely didn't want to leave her box. Thus I began to rehearse the third act, which I sang almost entirely in full voice. After the aria, "*Miei signori*" I was applauded by the entire orchestra. At the finale the entire chorus joined the orchestra, ringing out a true and justified ovation. Some of the old choristers of Covent Garden swore to me that they had not heard the part of Rigoletto sung with so much ease and joyful expansion of voice and feeling in many years. Returning home I was happy to be able to sing the role I preferred over all others in my repertoire in the great English theater. My name had already appeared in the papers and been advertised on the streets. I passed the night too agitated to sleep.

Yet on the morrow an ugly surprise was waiting for me. When I showed up at the theater I saw that my name had been removed from the program, and that Scotti's had been put back in my place. Acutely resentful of the unjustified affront I hastened to see management. I was received by Maestro Messager[150] who, after my energetic remonstrances, maintained that he was ignorant of the reason for the change, but believed that it had come about because Melba wished it, along with the director of the theater.

I became furious. The half hour or so, or a little more, that I had to wait for his arrival seemed like a century to me. Then finally I was able to unleash all my indignation. What they had done to me was neither thoughtful nor generous nor legal, since I had given management a helping hand so as not to interrupt the flow of the week's performances.

To this the director, who was an Englishman,[151] replied with the customary British phlegm that *Madame* Melba did not intend to sing with me because I was still too young to carry a part like that, and she had consequently begged Scotti to make an effort to sing the best he was able, and Scotti, with great sacrifice, to do her the favor, had acquiesced.

I was so beside myself that I did not refrain, even though I was in the man's office, from excoriating the director with some choice language. Since he didn't understand Italian he had these words translated and they sounded so offensive that he decided to have recourse against me in English law.

I had been back at my pension for a few minutes when I was joined by my good colleague Pini-Corsi, and he exhorted me to leave London as fast as possible if I didn't want to meet with serious difficulty because of the director, who had been insulted in his own office.

I left in the afternoon. Pini-Corsi, accompanying me to the station, gave me to understand that the reason for the stink had been my decision to sing in full voice at the rehearsal. The ovation of the orchestra and the chorus had been paid for with the suppression of my name from the program and the advertising. My bitterness was very great at the time. My destiny, which had always been good to me, not too far in the future gave me the means for revenge. So as not to interrupt the thread of the narration, I will relate it now without delay.

Some years later,[152] when I had already acquired stature in the world of art, I was put under contract by De Sanna for the Teatro San Carlo of Naples. I sang there for a number of seasons in important operas. A Neapolitan morning newspaper announced the visit of the celebrated artist, Nellie Melba, just back from visits to Amalfi, Sorrento and Capri, who was then about to embark on a voyage back to her native Australia. So it was that one evening in which *L'africaine* was being performed, the diva turned up at the San Carlo, invited by De Sanna to share his box (De Sanna was then directing the fall season at Covent Garden)[153] and she showed unlimited enthusiasm for my interpretation of Nelusko. The diva returned there a second time, when I was singing in *Hamlet*, always invited by De Sanna. After the third act De Sanna came to my dressing room to greet me and tell me that Melba was applauding frenetically in her box, and she had asked him to arrange a performance with me where she would be Ophelia. Naturally De Sanna was enthusiastic about the idea.

I then replied, assuming the same coldness of the Anglo-Saxon in his London office: "Tell Melba that she is too old to sing with me."

Melba, with a little mental exertion, remembered well the time when she didn't deign to sing with me in *Rigoletto* because I was too young.[154] In truth I didn't like the reprisal or the retaliation. But it does appear to me that the blow given in London by Nellie Melba was answered well by the response given in Naples by Titta Ruffo. Even De Sanna, who at first was amazed by my rudeness, thought that I had a point and, when I asked him to deliver my words exactly as I had spoken them, was faithful to my wishes.

From London, after a brief stop in Milan and some days with my family in Rome—I had such a desire to hug my mother and show her how much money I'd saved for her—I went back to Milan and from there I went to Brunate[155] to give myself up to pleasant solitude and reinvigorate my powers, to study new operas and equip myself with a little general culture, the lack of which goaded me ever more sharply. Prior to leaving Milan I acquired a quantity of literary and historical books which were, in my two-month parenthesis of leisure, the bread and butter of my spirit. At Brunate I stayed in a quiet pension, a sort of Swiss dairy farm. I occupied a room under the roof from where I was able to see a large part of the lake and enjoy the enchantment of dawns and sunsets. I got up early in the morning, and took long walks, carrying with me my books, in which I remained immersed with infinite pleasure for hours and hours on the grass of the fields, under the serene sky, ecstatic with the beauty of this pastoral life.

At the end of my reading my mind had opened to wider horizons. I reviewed the tragedies of Shakespeare and all of the characters created by his immense genius. I was struck above all by Romeo and Juliet, by Hamlet and Ophelia. I could say that the pale Danish prince became my constant companion and I was already dreaming of being able to portray him someday on the stage.[156] I resolved to learn by memory his salient traits and had some discreet success in doing so.

I read all the plays of Victor Hugo, and reread *Les Misérables*. Nor did I omit from my reading the less august authors whether they were modern or not. I quickly devoured *La Nouvelle Héloïse* of Rousseau and much of Guy de Maupassant and Alfred de Musset. Of the modern authors I was most enraptured by the sentimental and philosophical elo-

quence of Michelet, which so resembled our own Giuseppe
Mazzini, the thinker and political agitator. From Russian literature I learned to admire Leo Tolstoy. Dostoevski with his
Crime and Punishment pleased me more, carried me away
outright, if not artistically speaking. As for the Italian authors,
the reader shouldn't think that I would neglect them out of
respect for foreign literature, as some readers were in the habit
of doing out of a stupid snobbery. I learned by heart as much
as I could of the poetry of Carducci, Pascoli and D'Annunzio.[157]
I preferred the first and the second to the last. Even less then,
as everyone understands, did I omit the cultivation of my voice.
Profiting from the hours when the pensioners went for a walk
I would go to a little music room where there was an old yellowed piano, where I vocalized and sang countless pieces of
Rossini and Mozart to refine my technique and my art.

In the entire period of my working vacation I lived isolated from everyone, but not from the *signora bruna*. Her presence—not actual, but ideal, of course—never abandoned me.
Often she helped me with her letters. She had only one purpose: to shape me or reshape me according to her ideal; to
create in me, or perfect, the man and the artist.

Man has two stars that follow him on his path through
life. Apart from the one at birth, the superstitious one, there is
the woman who is indicated by destiny, who can make of him
a beast or an angel, raise him to heaven or consign him to the
abyss. In my life I had the rare privilege of finding in this woman
the luminous star, so that with her constant devotion, and the
finesse of her tact, and above all with her spirit of sacrifice—
in fact, during the most difficult years of my life she lived always in the shadows, uniquely aware of the high mission that
she had undertaken—she knew how to make of me, really
almost from nothing, a man and an artist, if not of the type
that left nothing to be desired, at least one not far off. With
my reading and her sacred presence and her letters full of comfort, advice and warning, and upon occasion, reproof, I must
have spent hours in a dream, in heaven, during that period in
Brunate. But it was soon time to rouse myself, to return to
daily work and life's usual battles.

CHAPTER 16

In Egypt

A WEEK AFTER RETURNING to Milan I signed a contract with the impresario Luigi Gianoli for the winter season of 1901-02 in the theaters of Cairo and Alexandria in Egypt.[158] I embarked at Brindisi for Alexandria. The voyage was sad for me. Only in the thought of Benedetta could I find the strength to persevere on my hard path. I often went over my happy months at Brunate, remembering her advice to study, to read, to persist in cultivating my mind with all that could enrich it with beauty and goodness. And thus I succeeded at least in part in making my burden lighter.

The voyage was terrible. We were tormented more or less continually by storms and afflicted by horrible sufferings. I arrived at Alexandria exhausted. But I prodded myself suddenly as soon as I saw, seated on one of the wharves of the port, my dear friend whom I'd left many years before in Calabria: Angiolino Bencini. While the steamer drew nearer I saw that he was hailing me joyfully. It sufficed to hear myself called by name in that thunderous voice, and to see his open smile, to rouse me from the prostration brought on by the voyage.

It seemed that my family was welcoming me. Bencini, one of the most loyal and generous men that I had ever known in the world, had also won great popularity for himself in Egypt, where for many years he had been engaged in work for the port of Alexandria, and enjoyed a splendid position. He lived with his family in a beautiful mansion, where I was a guest many times prior to leaving Alexandria for Cairo, for dinner, supper, conversation, for my studies, and I would gladly be staying there still.

This city made a surprising impression. I seemed to have been removed to an entirely new world. The sight of those white robes, those red turbans, that heavy, sweet perfume which emanated from the Orientals, excited my imagination. Immediately I wished that I were dressed as they so that I might be assimilated and adapt myself to this strange new ambience. The Arab mentality had remained immutable for centuries; there was something at the very heart of this land which had remained unchanged since the time of the pharaohs. The Roman conquest, the Napoleonic dominion, the Anglo-Saxon colonization might be said to have passed like a cloud that, according to the proverb, leaves things unchanged.

In Cairo I put up at a French pension in front of the Teatro Khediviale,[159] owned by a very distinguished elderly woman. Though I was warned not to go out in the evening, that it was very dangerous for those who weren't used to the dampness at night, curiosity prevailed over prudence. I wouldn't listen to anyone's advice, and wanted to go visit the Arab quarter with my friends. It was about nine o'clock. I had on a light overcoat, and the humidity was ever more dense and oppressive. At the entrance to the Arab quarter a phantasmagorical spectacle of light and music opened in front of me. I proceeded into a labyrinth of narrow streets, crowded with people of all races, who were expressing themselves in the most unexpected and incomprehensible languages. The air was more pregnant than ever with strong, cheap perfume, and among these odors the smell of the Negroes was particularly strong. Many, right on the ground, with crossed legs, were working by the light of acetylene torches, making curious objects of copper that they ornamented in the arabic style. Behind mysterious shop entrances young men were playing continually, uninterruptedly, upon flutes and bagpipes and cymbals, emitting strident or deep, hollow sounds, amidst the voices of a thousand merchants shouting from the doors of their shops to attract the foreigners, and producing a din so deafening and unnerving that I longed to escape from that horrible confusion.

I asked the friend who was acting as interpreter to let us visit the most important or characteristic sights, and he accompanied us to a place below street level where women, more or less nude, with turgid breasts and bare stomach were dancing lasciviously, undulating from head to toe so that they appeared to be human serpents. This wasn't a house, but a pocket of hell. Vendors were offering us little bottles of scent, and the contents were so strong that, having sprinkled a few drops on my clothes, the effluvium stubbornly remained there for many weeks.

Afterwards we traversed other little streets that were even narrower. Old men with a somnolent air about them were sitting on carpets, smoking enormous pipes with long rubber tubes and humming monotonous songs through their closed mouths. It was a mournful spectacle. The idea came to me that these mummies might at any moment surround us and drag us down into some subterranean labyrinth. When this strange fear came over me I no longer restrained myself from begging my companions to take me home.

I returned home stunned, weakened, exhausted. And the morning after I awoke with a powerful headache. The Arabic domestic, who could express himself a little in all languages, lifted the mosquito net and looked me in the face when he brought me my breakfast and said immediately, "The signor is sick." He ran to get the thermometer from my hostess. In fact, I had a fever of 39 degrees centigrade (102 degrees Fahrenheit). Small black macules had sprung up on my hands, on my arm and on my face. I was profoundly disturbed, as if some negro from the Arab quarter had cast some sort of evil spell upon me.

The lady who owned the pension, who had taken me much to heart, assured me that the illness wasn't grave. I had dengue fever[160] and, if I followed the right remedy, I could be cured of it in a week.

I had to debut in *Aida* and go to the rehearsal which customarily preceded every performance. Therefore I found myself having to inform the theater management that I was unable to attend because I was in bed with dengue fever. Management was obliged to change the schedule of performances and to replace me with another singer. This turn of events was so injurious and made me suffer so much that, finding myself alone every evening in my room, in a foreign country, where I knew no one except for the old lady at the pension and her Arabic domestic, I confess that I wept. On the third day of my fever the doctor administered a medicine as bitter as poison, guaranteeing that, with a spoonful three times a day, I would be free of my dengue at the end of the week. Notwithstanding my intolerance of this vile medicine, at the thought of being quickly cured, I stoically gulped it down three times a day.

Indeed, after a week the fever went away and with it all the black spots. Naturally I informed the management of my cure, saying that I was ready to debut. What a bitter surprise it was then, when I went to the theater, to see that no one bothered about me. The colleague who had substituted for me in *Aida* was refusing to yield the part of Amonasro to me, and management didn't know how to resolve the issue. I addressed myself to my colleague, a singer of world renown, but whose voice was used up by then.[161] I entreated him to consider that I had been ill with dengue. But he responded with an indecent phrase that rhymed with *denga*. This baseness of spirit and language amazed me, humiliated me and irritated me enormously. It seemed impossible to me that such a great artist could be capable of such vileness. I didn't fail to respond in kind, but I was very sad when I returned home, and I scarcely slept at all that night. My nerves were so shaky that I could only predict ruin for myself.

I went back to the theater the next day and spoke with the conductor of the orchestra, Alessandro Pomé,[162] and asked him with the utmost courtesy when he intended for me to debut and with which opera. He also received me with little respect, and responded evasively that the only opera possible for me would be *Sansone e Dalila*. Although I rather disliked having to debut in the part of the priest which would fall to my lot, I already knew the opera a little and still had five days to show up at the rehearsal, so I accepted on the spot. It was urgent for me to gain ground any way I could. Woe to the poor artist, especially at the start of his career, who has the bad luck to become ill! It's all over for him. Everyone feels sorry for him, and everyone competes to send him to the bottom. Rarely will someone be found who tries to give him a hand and save him from disaster. If he is gifted with a magnificent voice, they will find that he is not hardy, and it even happens that some chari-table colleague will spread the word that he has tuberculosis, or that he has ruined his voice because of some other more mysterious malady. In sum, pray, O artists! Pray that you will always be in good health; otherwise you will pay dearly.

After a week of pain and doubt I finally succeeded in de-buting in *Sansone e Dalila* in the part of the priest. My col-leagues were the tenor Carlo Barrera and the already famous Virginia Guerrini, a stupendous Dalila.[163] Though the part con-fided to me wasn't, as I have said, completely to my satisfac-tion, I produced something quite other than a mediocre effect since the role was most suited to my voice, and in succeeding performances I even began to be fond of it.

Following this debut both management and Maestro Pomé changed their attitude toward me. For the second performance I had to content myself with a return to Marcello in *Bohème*,[164] but I also obtained great satisfaction from it, above all in the *concertato* in the second act and in the duet of the fourth, where I had the leisure to demonstrate all the beautiful quali-ties of my voice, and in a few evenings the picturesque charac-ter of Marcello had won me the same popularity I had acquired the first time out in the theaters of Calabria and Sicily with Cavallaro's company.

I no longer had occasion to encounter the ungenerous col-league who had vulgarly rhymed my being sick with dengue. He continued to sing my part in *Aida*. Then I was unexpect-edly informed by management that I should get ready to sing the opera that very evening because my illustrious colleague had taken ill, and, by strange coincidence, it was the same sickness that had overcome me when I first arrived in Cairo; that is, dengue, which raged over all of Egypt that year. This news gave me great pleasure, not for the man's sickness, however much he may have deserved to have Destiny chastise him in this way, but because it gave me the opportunity to take back the part of Amonasro, the renunciation of which had caused me so much suffering, since I had studied it with such passion, and it belonged to me by right.

After a few days the first general rehearsal of *Otello* was announced, in which my colleague ought to have taken the role of Iago. But my colleague wasn't well yet. Management was then unable to change the performance and requested me to substitute for my friend in that part. I came to the general rehearsal with my voice at its most effective. My position in the Gianoli company thus became increasingly solid and eminent. In the end they even came to offer me the magnificent part of Telramund in *Lohengrin*, which I performed with a new consciousness, as I did likewise in the part of Kurwenal in *Tristano e Isotta*, whose protagonist was the great and celebrated Borgatti.[165]

After my unfortunate illness I led an exemplary life. I was animated, or should I say driven, ever more powerfully by ambition, meaning a desire to achieve celebrity one day. I used my hours of repose to write to my mother and to Benedetta. To Benedetta I wrote of everything that was happening to me, be it for good or ill. I sent her reviews of my work that had appeared in the papers. At the time she was at the Teatro Regio di Torino for the winter season.[166] She wrote me frequently, urging me never to abandon the "religion of art." Her letters were a beneficial dew for my spirit. She also sent me some beautiful books, among which I remember one that was most dear, *I grandi iniziati* by Edouard Schuré, a work which seemed marvelous to me. The ardent and brilliant evocations of the mystical writer exalted me indescribably, above all those of Pythagoras, Moses and Christ. I went to read this book on the banks of the Nile; passed the Ghisira bridge; continued on toward the pyramids. This was my favorite walk. In the magnificent sunsets on the sacred river, in my silent contemplations, so many phantoms stirred softly in my soul, and severe reflections occupied my mind. Mother often appeared to me, aged, sad, always waiting to hear or read something good of me, and, with her, the *signora bruna*, united always in my feelings as authors and inspiration of the maxims which governed my artistic and moral life.

Much of my heart and all of my being suffered and consumed itself when I looked too deeply into human motives and passions. But how was the artist, or the man as man, to repudiate or avoid sadness, if this is the supreme source, if not the unique source, of his greatness?

With this emotion my mind returns to the time of my youth and my career. It seems impossible that thirty-three years have passed! When I look at myself in the mirror, at my head, which is about to be covered by frost, and compare my appearance now with what it was then—slender, pale, with a mass of wavy black hair and the light down of two small moustaches—even though I don't feel old at all, I am taken unawares by a good dose of melancholy. Already by then my face had begun to show the characteristic traces of the theatrical mask.

My season in Egypt ended a complete success and, before leaving, I had the pleasure to sign a contract for the following year for the figure of 6,000 lire per month, which was quite a lot for the time—and double the sum I had received the first time. With great courtliness Constantino Sinadino cooperated in my reconfirmation. He was a great enthusiast of Italian opera, patron of the Teatro Khediviale, and he never missed one of my performances. It was he who had incited Gianoli to concede me whatever I asked for the next season. During my Egyptian sojourn, besides my acquaintance with the great Sinadino, who was loved and esteemed by all, I met some other important people, among them the pasha Shery, the bey Shery and the pasha Tito, by whom I was often invited on diverting day trips or hunting parties. With them I visited the pyramids, the tombs of the pharaohs, the museum.

Among my colleagues I most dearly remember Giovanni Paroli of Brescia.[167] He was then in his fifties. A handsome and attractive man: openhearted, frank, loyal. He had lived a lot, maybe too much. But, at least his having lived too much in his younger years had helped him find the balance which sustained him and the manner which distinguished him now. An artist of value, he had known in his brilliant career the greatest personalities and kept vivid memories and portraits of them. He loved to recall the first performances of *Otello* and *Falstaff* at La Scala of Milan, where, in *Otello*, he was chosen by Verdi himself to take the part of Cassio. He had great faith in my career, and often gave me wise advice: which I wisely never failed to follow. At the general rehearsal of *Otello*, in which I was playing Iago, he described for me in the greatest detail the first *mise-en-scène* of Verdi and Boito with Tamagno, Maurel, Pantaleoni and Navarrini,[168] that is to say, with all the first interpreters of that opera, himself included. In those two Egyptian seasons, in sum, his company was of great comfort to me and very helpful. We loved and cared for each other reciprocally like two brothers.

CHAPTER 17

Again in South America

IN APRIL OF 1902 I embarked for America, directly for Buenos Aires, this time. I found myself on board with a pleiad of artists with great reputations. The impresario of the big company, which I knew only by reputation, was Bonetti, the concessionaire of the Teatro de la Opera.[169] The conductor of the orchestra was Leopoldo Mugnone.[170] I don't need to say what a Neapolitan type he was, how energetic, exuberant, extravagant. I was introduced by Bonetti before anyone else. He barely shook my hand; he looked me up and down as if he were sorry for me. He considered me too young and immature to be singing in such a theater.

Then I was introduced to the major artists of the company. I met the *primo baritono* Mario Ancona. He was at the apogee of his career, a veteran of the Metropolitan Opera of New York and the Covent Garden of London. He was very elegant: he wore a beard in the Edward VII manner, and boasted that the prince was a friend of his, and he had a tie pin which he said was a gift to him from the Queen of England.[171] Then I met Ericlea Darclée, the Rumanian artist, an elegant and beautiful woman with a splendid dramatic soprano voice;[172] the celebrated tenor Edoardo Garbin and his wife, the diva Adelina Stehle, two artists of the first rank, admired by the majority of operagoers the world over for their interpretations of *Bohème*,

Manon, *Fedora*, and the modern operas in general which had won them their reputation for the romantic repertory;[173] then the tenor Borgatti, already known to me, the great interpreter of Wagner, charming and original; the celebrated contralto Alice Cucini,[174] a fascinating Dalila; the bass Remo Ercolani,[175] a Roman artist whose talent was much appreciated in Italy and South America as well, and others whose names I no longer remember.

The voyage was tiresome enough. In the midst of all those *divinities* I felt like a fish out of water. I was worried to note that my personality did not come across as attractive to Maestro Mugnone. During the voyage he had cordial and happy conversations with Ancona, going to and fro together on the bridge, arm in arm like two old friends. From the beginning I greeted them by first taking off my cap in the most deferential way, but when I saw that they responded with an ever so slight inclination of the head, as if they were giving me alms, I stopped greeting them altogether.

Alas, I saw that I was going to be swimming against the current, and would have gladly gone back. The season of the Teatro de Buenos Aires began badly enough for me. A few days after my arrival I was called for a rehearsal of *Aida*. I came there punctually expecting to find the whole company in the hall. Instead there was no one. I remained there for about a half hour, waiting in a place that was ugly and sad, a low-ceilinged room where the stench of tobacco turned my stomach. Finally the Maestro entered with half a cigar in his mouth, smoking like a Turk.

He was very nervous. I said good day to him and he responded with something incomprehensible muttered with his cigar clenched between his teeth. After a long silence he came out with the question, "What's your name?"

I felt offended. He still didn't know my name, as if I were a simple chorister? Suppressing my resentment I replied very dryly, "Titta Ruffo."

He, in his pure Neapolitan accent, commented, "A silly name," and continued to ask me questions as if I were a conscript in front of a general. "What part of Italy are you from?"

I knew that his wife was also a native of Pisa[176] and, thinking I could gain his sympathy thus, replied: "I am from Pisa, the same as your wife."

At my response he opened wide his two terrible eyes and he exclaimed with contempt, "Great town!"

My response had been an error. I didn't know how to contain myself. I felt that some hostility toward him was ripening in my soul, and that the rehearsal would finish very badly. However, I restrained myself. My apparent calm disquieted him and encouraged him at the same time to continue with his sarcastic tone. Finished with his *toscano* he tossed the stub into a corner of the room, and finally seating himself at the piano, asked me if I had ever sung *Aida*. When I said yes, "Well, then," he warned me, "remember that in this opera you are not a Pisan but the King of Ethiopia."

My state of mind as we began the rehearsal can well be imagined. And not only in the first rehearsal, but all during the early part of the season I had to remain on the alert to avoid letting myself commit ill-advised acts that would make my position worse than it already was. Evidently Mugnone nourished a profound antipathy for me; but in time he began to change, and by the end of the season we had become the best of friends. I have already noted—and who would deny it?—that he was a very eccentric type.

There were in him two quite different personalities. The artist was impulsive, intolerant, caustic, villainous, but free of any wicked feeling whatsoever, to whom it seemed natural to let loose anything that came to mind, and he was therefore offensive, humiliating, insulting—sometimes in front of the orchestra—without a single scruple or sign of self-restraint. And right beside the artist was the man, who loved to make a game of life, who told jokes, who laughed immoderately, who wanted to be addressed with the familiar *tu*, who lavished his friendship upon you with both hands full, who became a veritable child, a street urchin, a rascal.

After the first part of the season he wanted to rehearse with me, playing the piano part himself, the part of Cascart in

Zazà of Leoncavallo, which he was premiering in Buenos Aires. I must say that he put all his interest, all his artist's soul, all his maestro's science and insight into helping me penetrate to the comicality and sensibility of the character. After having sung in *Aida*, in *Trovatore*, in *Africaine* I appeared in this opera together with Ericlea Darclée and Edoardo Garbin. The opera was a huge success. I was by then secure in the affections of Mugnone and my voice profited from my serenity of spirit. From the first performance, after having been admired in every aspect of the role, I was obliged to repeat the aria of the fourth act, "*Zazà, piccola zingara*" three times. Even Mugnone prompted me from his director's stool, with signs of his head, his eyes, his beard and everything else about himself, to comply with the public's repeated requests. Certainly *Zazà* availed me of my grandest triumph in the Argentinean capital in that, after six years of absence spent in Russia, I was invited to inaugurate the most important theater of the republic, the Colón.[177]

Upon returning to Italy, after two months in residence at Milan to study *Proserpina* and *Fedora*, I sailed again in the direction of Egypt for the winter season 1902-1903.[178] Thus I spent another winter in a delicious climate. I found my good old friends there, and lived in generally friendly and benevolent surroundings. I was able to save a middling sum that season which permitted me to furnish a small apartment in Milan, and to spend the summer in repose, dedicating myself to the study of new roles.

Returning this time I found mother very ill. Her only joy was to know that her son was advancing ever further along his lucky, though risky path. After fifteen days of great pain and worry I had to leave her. I urged her to have patience, as I was planning to buy her a little house on the outskirts of Rome, since it was her supreme desire to have one, with a small garden and a chicken coop. I embraced her with this promise, and with this promise I left with uplifted spirit. How strange is destiny! If Mother, who dreamed of having a modest little house with a kitchen garden and a chicken coop, had been able to imagine the luxurious dwelling where I imagined my-self welcoming her in her old age, it would have seemed more a folly to her than a dream. I lived in that dwelling with regret always in my heart.

CHAPTER 18

Milan at Last

ONE DAY IN MILAN I was sitting at the Cafe Biffi when a badly dressed man came up to me, someone I knew by sight, an old messenger, and he asked me if would consider auditioning for Maestro Toscanini.[179] I wanted to know the reason the reknowned maestro might want to hear me. He explained that he had heard a conversation between him and Tito Ricordi about a possible performance of *Rigoletto* at La Scala, and Toscanini himself, who was looking for a young, intelligent baritone, had said my name. How could I refuse? The messenger went immediately to the maestro to report my acceptance.

The audition was fixed for four o'clock on the same day.[180] I returned home agitated by thoughts of the scrupulous examination that was awaiting me. And I was no less agitated when at three o'clock I left for the theater with my music under my arm, looking for a maestro to accompany me. I found Lorenzo Molajoli[181] and asked him the favor. At precisely four o'clock I was there in front of Maestro Toscanini and the engineer Gatti-Casazza, who was then the artistic director of La Scala.[182] They went to sit in the orchestra in the middle of the hall, I mounted the stage. I began the audition with the aria from *Ballo in maschera*. The voice was in top form. Having understood by the end of that piece that I had produced a favorable impression, I asked if they would like to hear me in the aria from *Dinorah* of Meyerbeer.[183] When I'd finished with the second piece the maestro asked me to sing Rigoletto's monologue and the aria of the third act, "*Miei signori, perdono, pietade!*" and I put all my power and feeling into it. I produced a great effect. Toscanini and Gatti-Casazza complemented me with very flattering words.

They recognized that my voice was perfectly suited to sing *Rigoletto* in their theater, and they offered me a contract for the 1903-1904 season, engaging me for about six months for ten thousand lire to sing that opera, the *Germania* of Maestro Franchetti,[184] and the *Griselda* of Massenet.[185] I accepted, moved, and without discussion; a half-hour later the stipulations of the contract had already been made and the contract signed. I left after I thanked Toscanini and Gatti-Casazza, and assured them that I would do my best to be worthy of a contract that brought me so much honor.

I left La Scala drunk with joy. I was only twenty-five years old. My most cherished dream was at last rapidly, more rapidly than I could have wished, become a reality. I crossed the Galleria, going over my first arrival in Milan and the long odyssey that preceded my first debut. I telegraphed the great news to Mother, then ran home to expatiate upon all my jubilation about the great event in a letter to Benedetta. The following day my contract was common knowledge in the theatrical world, provoking the most diverse comments, of course, according to the admiration or emulation or envy that it dictated. During the waiting period I went to spend two months of rest in the Ledro valley.[186]

My continual success was rousing in me an ever stronger will and aspiration for something more than vocal preeminence pure and simple. A beautiful voice is certainly indispensable to the singer, but prior to his complete musical development the artist must analyze, elaborate and assimilate the characters he will take on stage, to be able to rouse a more vivid emotion. When he has achieved entire mastery of vocal technique in the studio he should forget singing and develop the interpreter in himself, the actor. In this regard I prefer an intelligent actor with a mediocre voice to a perfect singer without the spark of intelligence. My secret ambition was to incarnate new characters on stage. The artist needs to renew himself continually, to deepen the characterizations he has already created in performance, to approach ever closer to perfection, even if it is not within man's ability to attain it. Thus, in my month of rest, I recommenced studying the complex character of Rigoletto.

I got a hold of a translation of Victor Hugo's tragedy, *Le Roi s'Amuse*, for Rigoletto is none other than Triboulet. Reading the original text, which places the tragedy in the court of François I of France, I understood how all or nearly all singers had made a serious mistake by not taking this circumstance into account. I have never seen a single tenor of my generation, for example, capable of bringing the historical type of the French monarch to life on stage, or even coming close to it. It is true that in Verdi's opera he has been replaced by the Duke of Mantua, but this is no reason for the actor to transform his character and physiognomy. I ascertained a need for reinforcement of certain recitatives in the second and fourth act monologues, since in the original drama the hunchback soars to more striking heights of tragedy. Thus I sought to accustom myself to a more personal style of declamation, without distorting the Verdian melody, prolonging some pause, when I found it justified, and letting the word of the thinker take precedence, to imprint on the listener the virtue or soul of the actor more than the virtuosity of the singer. In saying this I am not trying to assert that my *creation* of Rigoletto—dare I style it thus?—should be exempt from criticism for having reached perfection, but certainly the figure I created acquired more intensity and humanity and dignity.

In the same way I acquired *Le Barbier de Séville* of Beaumarchais while I was in Milan, and came to know all the characters through their literary sources. I had already sung the Rossini opera at Covent Garden in London, but without the slightest historical or analytic preparation, relying solely on the intuition and versatility I had by nature. With this guide I now rehearsed the score of the opera, and was with full consciousness able to modify some recitatives where Rossini's melodrama seemed too conventional, and the musical comicality, with which the Swan of Pesaro's entire opera pulses and flashes, wasn't lost, but rather gained extraordinarily.

During my sojourn in the Val di Ledro, other than all the theatrical works of Beaumarchais, I read or reread the best part of Victor Hugo's. I also rededicated myself with growing passion to Shakespeare, always seeking to better penetrate the soul of Otello and Hamlet and King Lear and Macbeth. As I had at Brunate I continued my deep study of the personality of Hamlet, which was most harmonious with my temperament and my soul, and mysteries were revealed to me which I strove to interpret and render fully in the performances which would follow.

My life was spent in an active and contemplative serenity, always helped by the comfort of Benedetta's letters, which were often enthusiastic. Every day, as I had in Brunate and in Egypt, I took long walks. In the beautiful evening sunsets I sat at the lakeshore reading or meditating upon the characters that I would create before the public.

Nor did I neglect to study human nature directly. One evening at a crossroads I met a man who had come down from the mountain, dragging a bundle of wood behind him by means of a rope wound around him under the armpits. He was a very strange man: of medium height, with eyes inflamed by conjunctivitis, a nervous tic affecting his right shoulder, a mouth with boils on the lower lip and missing some front teeth, reddish hair, a low forehead—all the attributes and behavior of a mental defective. His jacket was in tatters and he wasn't wearing a shirt; his hairy chest was covered, though marginally, by the shreds of an old undershirt. He breathed like an asthmatic and had the rattle in his chest of someone with chronic bronchitis. He came near me to rest, and I addressed a word to him, but his only response was to look at me with a half-witted smile on his face, revealing his toothless gums.

Returning home I wasn't able to shake the image of this poor devil. The following evening I returned to the same crossroads in the hope of meeting him again, and in fact, after a time, there he was coming down off the mountain with his usual wood trailing after him. And he stopped to smile at me with his usual weakminded smile. A few minutes later a peasant girl, about twenty years old, happened along, herself carrying on her head a bundle of wood. He stared at her with an expression that was between anguish and desire, and when he was near her, he addressed incomprehensible words to her—on top of everything else, he stuttered. He made to touch the girl but she avoided him with repugnance. The unhappy one remained thoughtful, following her with his eyes full of sadness until she had disappeared in the evening shadows.

I asked him why he was pursuing the peasant girl. How to describe the expression which came over his grotesque mask? I asked him if he loved her. At this he began to tremble, and came up with a prolonged monosyllable that wanted to be a *sì*, but was neither a *sì* or a *tì*.

The innkeeper told me who he was. He was the son of no one, a poor bastard, who lived in a thatched hut belonging to shepherds who further humbled him with the way they made use of him, giving him in return mere crusts of bread.

I waited again in the same place at the usual time to talk to him, if that was the right word, and to know what he wanted in regard to the young peasant girl. In this last encounter I advised him in a friendly way to leave the girl alone, not failing to mention, though I did so in the most charitable way I could, that in his condition he couldn't aspire to have his love reciprocated.

What a revelation! The halfwit's eyes instantly filled with tears, so desolate and despairing that one less sensitive than I could have been moved to pity. I put a hand on his shoulder and stroked him consolingly, and I gave him some money. He looked at me with an air of stupefied recognition, as if this were the first time in his life that a human being had deigned to come near him and console him for the misery of his lot.

I wanted to describe minutely the episode involving this luckless person because later he served me marvelously well in portraying, on stages all over the world, one of my best-received and most admirable creations—Tonio, the halfwit in

Leoncavallo's *Pagliacci*. I faithfully reproduced that very same face, that very same behavior, and in the love duet with Nedda when Tonio says, *"So ben che difforme, contorto son io; che desto soltanto lo scherno e l'orror,"* a shudder traverses my being, bringing a profound agony, recalling to mind the very desperate tears I had seen engorge the eyes of that poor bastard in the Val di Ledro.

I left the Val di Ledro very reluctantly, engaged in Venice by the Teatro Rossini for six performances of *Nabucco*. The relaxation I had obtained during these two months had been very useful to my voice. It gave me the ease to put myself before the public in my best form, at my most efficient, and this was a public which was conserving a vivid record of the Lucifer I had given six months before, and was now impatiently awaiting me as the protagonist in Verdi's melodrama. I sang with all the fervor that was in me, lavishing the exhausting part of the biblical king with all the vigor of my voice and my soul. The enthusiasm of the Venetian public was such that I was obliged to sing some performances in addition to those fixed by the contract.

When the hour of my debut in *Rigoletto* at La Scala di Milano had finally come, I went to the first rehearsals and was informed that Maestro Toscanini would not be able to conduct my performances. I was deeply saddened because I very much wanted, as it's easy to understand, to sing the opera under his magical baton. I was presented to the Maestro Cleofonte Campanini,[187] who would substitute for him.

Called to the rehearsal hall I saw, seated in the stalls, (besides Maestro Campanini) Maestro Franchetti, the Viscount of Modrone,[188] Tito Ricordi, and the engineer Gatti-Casazza. And I was the only other person in the hall. I understood immediately that what was at stake here was not a simple rehearsal but a dangerous examination. Ricordi and Campanini asked me to sing the entire part in full voice. I began to sing the first recitative sotto voce. Tito Ricordi then jumped out of the stall and in an imperative tone told me, "My boy, don't play around. It's necessary to hear you because it seems to me that Rigoletto is a part quite beyond your capabilities."[189]

In truth I didn't know how to make out why, in the time since I had been chosen by Toscanini for the part, Ricordi—and others, evidently—had considered me too immature for the role. What happened was, as I came to know afterward, two very famous artists were hostile to me and were plotting behind the scenes, hoping to replace me and to be able to obstruct my career, which had been proceeding for six years at top speed.

I quickly intuited their plan, however, and foresaw just what a great danger I was running. Without letting Ricordi's imposition intimidate me, I replied calmly that I was ready to submit to scrutiny by the patrons of La Scala, but not to that of Maestro Franchetti, who filled me with awe—and for the rest I hadn't imagined when I had signed the contract that I would have to pass such an arduous test.

Franchetti thought my remonstrance just, got up and invited the Visconti di Modrone to leave with him, beseeching Ricordi and Campanini to let me audition in calm. When I was alone I began to sing my part with less agitation, and when necessary, I put out my full voice. It had to be thus to hit back at the hidden forces working against me.

When I had finished the rehearsal of the third act, Campanini was convinced that Toscanini's judgment of my voice had been exact and dropped any remaining hostility he may have felt on my account. Franchetti, who with the Viscount di Modrone had been present at the rehearsal all the same, listening from the wings, gave his approval, and I thus definitively gained his approval too to sing his *Germania*.

Several days later we began rehearsals together. Tito Ricordi always took part whether it be in a piano rehearsal or during the staging. We sometimes spent the entire day on one act. Then we began the stage rehearsals, and then the insistence of Ricordi became obsessive. He demanded that everything always be sung full voice, as if the human throat were a barrel-organ. Discussions were breaking out which hindered the tranquil and serene unfolding of the necessary preparations. To give an idea of the working conditions I had to endure before my debut, it suffices to say that, after having rehearsed for fourteen consecutive days, morning and evening—yes, I'm saying morning and evening, fourteen days—I was constrained to sing three orchestra rehearsals, including the general rehearsal, the entire opera at full voice, made up and dressed, while to face the La Scala audience one piano rehearsal and one orchestra rehearsal would have been more than enough. At the first performance I felt exhausted and couldn't display all the energy required for a debut of such importance. To save myself and follow through on my work I availed myself of all my shrewd experience and my perfect knowledge of the entire opera, not just the character assigned to me.

Critical opinion wasn't always kind to me. But in the course of the season—I sang, with *Germania* and *Griselda*, twenty-seven performances altogether, with sixteen of *Rigoletto* among them—I succeeded in establishing myself fully. Several tenors and sopranos were replaced but no one substituted for me as Rigoletto.[190] At the end of the season I was invited to take over the part of Valentin in *Faust*, but I didn't feel I was ready for the part and turned it down decisively.

In one of the last performances of *Rigoletto* the impresaria and director of the Teatro Municipale of Odessa came to hear me at La Scala, Signora Lubkoska, with the intention of signing me for the next winter season there. She offered me a very favorable contract for appearances in the Verdi repertory, in the *Demon*[191] of Rubinstein and Leoncavallo's *Zazà*.

In between times, that is, while waiting for the Russian season to begin, I went from Milan to Florence, having been signed by the Teatro della Pergola, where I performed *Rigoletto* four times. The Florentines lavished me with unforgettable welcomes. Then I returned to Milan where I concentrated my energies on studying Rubinstein's *Demon* in depth, and the music of the maestro in general. I fell boundlessly in love with it. I started by singing mournful passages which put my soul in a sad state and repeated them, looking for sounds that were in harmony with the meaning or, better, with the feeling of each word. The Demon is one of the most complex figures of the Russian repertory.

One night while I was deep in this study I was awakened by a ghastly nightmare. At that moment I had sensed my mother expiring in my arms.[192] I was unable to get back to sleep. I left the same morning for Rome. I ran to my house. Nella came and opened the door to me. She was pale and troubled. She embraced me crying. I hurried to Mother's room. I found her seated on the bed, breathing painfully, with a hand on her heart. There was nothing left of her but a shadow. I took her in my arms and urged her to be calm. I told her that I had come to take her away with me. She smiled bitterly at my words, a pitiful lie. Her condition was obviously grave. There was no point in trying to deceive ourselves. Nor did the doctor pretend that her end would be delayed. He assured us that she had only survived till now because of her great strength of soul, which was much greater than all the resources of science, or through her desire—more a superhuman will than a true human desire—to see me once more before leaving us forever. I scolded my family bitterly for having hid the reality from me. If Mama hadn't appeared to me in a dream, I would have been deprived of the satisfaction of embracing her again while she was still alive. I looked around me. The house was squalid, bare, lacking everything. The resources of the family, which came only from me since my father had been gone for a year, had not been enough to provide all the necessities of life.

The following day Mother's spirits had rallied somewhat. She was stretched out on a chaise longue. I walked around the room trying to cheer her up with the story of my successes, shortening the recounting of anecdotes and jokes, smiling, hiding all the anguish of my heart from her. She was ecstatic as she looked at me, and asked me so many things; finally, with a barely audible thread of voice she asked if I had been able to save any money. Her greatest cross was that I was carrying the entire family on my shoulders. I told her another lie. I came very close to her as if I were revealing a secret and told her that I had fifty thousand lire on deposit with the Banca Commerciale di Milano. Her face shone and she said with a great sigh, "Now I die happy."

With inexpressible force I tried to restrain my tortured feelings. I'd brought sufficient personal effects with me, hoping to stay close to her for a time. She wanted to see all my clothes and wanted me to put them on one after the other for her. How could I refuse? Poor Mother! With each change she said, "How well you look. How handsome you are!" She saw me with the eyes of a mother. At one point, overcome with joy, she put out her emaciated arm, pulled me to her and dissolved in tears. In her son she saw that her old dream had been attained. She advised me not to touch my savings for any reason, because we were always in the hands of God at least a little, and when the day came that my voice failed me, my daily bread would be secure.

The next day at four in the afternoon she wanted to get up from her settee, acknowledging a great weariness and need of rest. When she was on her feet she begged me to let her walk unaided into her room. So as not to contradict her I only accompanied her with my eyes. But she had hardly crossed the threshold when she bent over, and she would have fallen if I hadn't reached her in time to hold her up. I lifted her in my arms and stretched her out on the bed. She was looking at me fixedly, looking intensely into my eyes as if she wanted to leave hers in mine. Her last words were, "I entrust my children to you." A short time later she passed away.

This grave loss obliged me to move the family from Rome to Pisa. These were days of infinite sadness and desolation. After having spent a month in our new residence I went to Recoaro[193] so that my sadness would find a refuge near Benedetta. With her great soul she knew how to find words of consolation and encouragement necessary for me to resume my studies with energy. I established myself in a pension, as usual isolated from the town, requiring me to bring a piano from Vicenza. After several days I was joined by Maestro Viscardo Ucelli, a great pianist and very knowledgeable about operatic music. For ten years Ucelli had been the accompanist of Angelo Masini, the great Roman tenor. I had with me the score of *Demon* and of *Hamlet*.

I spent three months at Recoaro tirelessly applying myself through painful, rigorous exercises to the refinement of my voice and the expression of my soul. I had found certain small defects in my voice, for the most part in the low register— such as the emission of sounds that were too closed or guttural, for example. I nearly always rose at dawn, took a brief walk, kept company by the memory of my mother; afterwards, back at the house, I sat at the piano and vocalized patiently, seeking to track down the natural virtues of my voice which had been compromised when I was led astray by the advice of too many voice teachers. I started to vocalize like a student again, beginning with the light sounds, taking the voice as far as the intonations of tenor character. The maestro came every morning at ten and stayed about two hours. Every day we rehearsed the important parts of *Barbiere* and of *Don Giovanni*, operas that lent themselves very well to modulating, rounding and coloring the baritone voice, with great technical and artistic benefit. Then we began to rehearse *Hamlet*, and since that time I began to sense the effects that I would be able to obtain with my voice in this melodrama.

After three months of study I was able to easily accomplish agile and wonderful modulations in my *pianissimo* and my *fortissimo* notes. With my special technical means it was my ambition to create a veritable palette of colors. With clearly defined variations I was creating a white voice, then a dark, more intense sound that I called blue; enlarging the same sound and rounding it I sought the red; then the black, too, the tone with maximum darkness. To obtain this iridescent palette I formed sounds which I called *suoni di bocca* (mouth sounds) which is to say *verbal* and not *vocal* sounds.[194] In this regard I am able, after my rich experience, to state with authority that a singer who wants to make a long career without forcing his larynx and respiratory apparatus, ought to adopt more verbal sounds than vocal sounds, even if he has at his disposal an extraordinary vocal endowment.

Given my technique I was able to continue, for a period of twenty uninterrupted years, to sing in all seasons and all cli-

mates, in Russia at thirty degrees below zero and in the hot-
test weather of Egypt and Havana. Wherever I went my voice
was always ready and dependable.[195] In the most active period
of my career I passed eighteen consecutive winters without
ever knowing a summer.[196] Indeed, I went to South America
where I found winter, returned to Europe where it was still
winter. I don't believe that any other artist of my generation
was so gifted with the same efficiency for thirty years, crossing from one corner of the world to the other and performing
a repertory of such imposing size and responsibility. Except
for Japan and Australia I am able to boast of having sung in
all the principal theaters of the world.

CHAPTER 19

In Russia

I N THE AUTUMN OF 1904 I returned to Milan to sing a completely modern repertory in the Teatro Lirico. I obtained one of the biggest successes of my career there in the part of Cascart in Leoncavallo's *Zazà*.[197] From the first performance, after having been applauded enthusiastically in the course of the whole opera for my comic interpretation of the character, I was constrained to repeat as many as three times the famous aria of the fourth act, "*Zazà, piccola zingara,*" where my voice stood out in special accents and a wealth of indescribable vibrations. I was on the alert to leave for Russia at any moment where I had been engaged with a regular contract. Meanwhile many Italian impresarios were disposed to pay a fine just to make me stay with the Italian theaters. I didn't allow myself to be convinced. It would have been improper, if not downright dishonest behavior, toward impresaria Lubkoska, who had reassured me already and reassured me now that she would do the impossible to present me in her theater with the highest honors. So I left for Odessa in the middle of November.

I encountered a terrible cold. The city covered with snow made a desolate impression: squalid, silent, sepulchral. Along the long streets every sort of sleigh was sliding, drawn by magnificent smoking horses and driven by men all bundled up in furs and blankets. The unexpected tinkling of bells attached to the harnesses roused a momentary sense of joy as they accentuated the contrast with the infinite silence. I felt as if I had left the world as I had known it and was lost on some distant planet.

I found lodging in a pension near the theater, with the Svetlov family, composed of the mother, two daughters and a son. The son was a handsome young man, more than six feet tall, a real giant, who possessed a colossal baritone voice and had already sung in different theaters of little Russia, but he was not given consideration by the State Theater because of his Jewish extraction.

Later I went to the theater. Signora Lubkoska, who was there, welcomed me very nicely and immediately introduced me to her husband, proprietor and director of a great Odessa newspaper, and to her son, also a very handsome young man who possessed a delicious tenor voice. Then she saw that I was wearing a simple overcoat, though a heavy one, and she asked me if I was provided with a fur, since, without one in this climate, which was not only extremely cold but also damp or humid, I would be running the risk of becoming ill. I replied that I would think about such a luxury after my first appearances, and she understood and politely had her son accompany me to a large furrier's establishment. A beautiful fur was wrapped around me, which gave me a feeling of suffocation, it was so thick and heavy. And when I asked the price of it the young Lubkoski told me not to worry about it, that everything would be arranged later. Feeling myself so effectively protected I also found myself in better spirits to acquit myself of my artistic duty.

I debuted in *Rigoletto*. I was a resounding success and the critics were very kind. I am not going to say if and how much Signora Lubkoska might have been pleased. I sang without interruption, sometimes as many as four performances a week, alternating *Rigoletto*, *Barbiere*, *Ballo in maschera*, *Trovatore*, *Zazà*, and the *Demon* of Rubinstein.[198]

In this last I faced my public for the first time. Maestro Kharchov was a great help, a noted musician and pianist. He also wanted to teach me—supported by my fervor, with his kindness and patience he succeeded—the big aria of the third act in the Russian language so that later I would be able to sing it in public with the correct pronunciation.

At the third performance, which was *Rigoletto*, after the third act, I had the good fortune of meeting Delfino Menotti, one of the most celebrated baritones of past generations. I was introduced in my dressing room by Signora Lubkoska. Menotti was, besides being beautiful in his person, tall and slender—and the gray in his hair and moustaches took nothing away—besides being truly fashionable, of an uncommon culture and versatility, uniting in himself the virtues of a valiant singer, painter, lecturer and most eloquent orator. After retiring from the stage he had settled in Odessa where he directed his own school of singing, loved and respected by all. After that day I went to visit him. He had the most kind words for me and entertained me for a long time; we became the best of friends. When his duties permitted we passed hours together discussing the art of singing, and the most significant figures in the theater, and such topics. I keep the very dearest remembrance of him.

Returning to the *Demon* of Rubinstein, I understood what a responsibility this opera was, but I had already studied it in Italy and gone over it again now thoroughly, so that I could perform it in such a way that it would crown all the popularity that I had earned at Odessa in the preceding performances. The echo of this great success extended well beyond the circles of this city. Even the newspapers in St. Petersburg were writing enthusiastically about my interpretation.

At one of the last performances Maestro Cavallini was present, an Italian, invited expressly by the directors of the Conservatory Theater of St. Petersburg to hear me, and possibly to sign me for the forthcoming Lenten season. I didn't displease him, evidently, since after the third act he came to my dressing room accompanied by the Signora Lubkoska, and offered me a contract for ten performances at his theater, with compensation of six hundred rubles for each one. I accepted right away, all the more because I was eager to know St. Petersburg, and to make myself known to the public in that capital.

I also debuted there in *Rigoletto*. Afterwards I sang *Pagliacci, Trovatore, Otello, Barbiere,* and *Demon*.[199] As the Demon I acquired such mastery that I ended by being able to perform it without the slightest hint of exertion, easily, naturally, as if I were the Demon himself, in person. In this same season, as with every year, the big Italian company was active in St. Petersburg, and on the stage of that theater[200] the most famous singers in the world came through: Angelo Masini, Enrico Caruso, la Boronat, Battistini, Marconi, Navarrini, Anselmi[201] and so on. My success at the Conservatorio aroused a vivid interest among the artists in the Italian company, and many controversies and discussions among the *divinities* of the capital. And every new interpretation of mine roused them all over again.

The last opera I sang before leaving St. Petersburg was *Linda di Chamounix*.[202] That evening the same opera was given concurrently at the Italian theater with Mattia Battistini, who had long since been one of the most-discussed idols there. The following day a critic from one of the biggest papers, with little regard for my colleague in art, wrote that since the epoch of Antonio Cotogni there had never been heard a baritone voice as beautiful as mine, the only one worthy of comparison to him. He was saying that in *Linda* he had met the great singer again in me. The appreciation of the famous critic, disagreeable as it may have been because of the comparison with Battistini, gave me perhaps the most satisfaction of my career, because Antonio Cotogni had been, at the time of golden voices, one of our miracles, the only one who could compete with Adelina Patti and Angelo Masini. The satisfaction was all the greater inasmuch as it was a question of two singers of the same voice type.

I met Antonio Cotogni about a year later in Rome. He occupied the post of *maestro di canto* at the Conservatory of Santa Cecilia. I was singing *Hamlet* at the Teatro Costanzi, and after the third act he did the honor of seeing me in my dressing room accompanied by his pupils.[203] He embraced me, congratulating me for my voice and for my "deserved success." He told his students to take me for an example, and then he came very close to me, with the most delicate tact, and told me sotto voce, so that the students might not hear, that he had to give me a word of advice. And he reproved me, as a father might do with his son, because in the *concertato*, during the reprise of the drinking song, I had emitted a high B-flat that hadn't been indicated in the score. And he urged me to avoid this note, not only because it was foreign to the baritone register, but because nature had granted me a voice so beautiful and rich that I had no need to borrow effects elsewhere.

I thanked the great maestro for his valuable advice, and in the innumerable succeeding performances of *Hamlet*, I guarded against further emission of this extreme note. Sometimes, returning to Rome from my long peregrinations he was very kind to me, and as a rule I didn't fail to visit him in his house in via del Bufalo. Nor, may I be pardoned for saying so, did he receive me with less pleasure.

CHAPTER 20

In Paris

I LEFT ST. PETERSBURG with a real feeling of nostalgia, and swore that I would return. Meanwhile I had been put under contract in Paris by the Teatro Sarah Bernhardt for the season of Italian opera sponsored by the Publisher Sonzogno.[204] This season remained memorable in the annals of this illustrious theater. Competing in solemn appearances were all of the great celebrities of the epoch.[205] To give an idea of the importance of the event it suffices to cite the principal names. Mascagni, Giordano, Leoncavallo, la Pacini, Masini, Caruso, De Lucia, Garbin, Bassi, Kaschmann, Sammarco, Baldelli.[206] I was signed directly by Sonzogno to sing the part of Gléby in the *Siberia* of Giordano, a part that I'd already performed with success the year before at the Lirico of Milan. So I went to Paris.

The impression that I had seeing the great French metropolis for the first time is difficult to describe. I installed myself at the Hôtel Palais and from the window of my room, which gave on the Seine, I descried many bridges and enjoyed a magnificent view. But the immense city also inspired a sense of fear. Would I not then be lost in it? I had several days to wait before the debut. I profited from them by visiting the Louvre, the Luxembourg Palace and Gardens, Fontainebleau, Versailles, the Palais des Arts and private museums. I spent my day in a fever of discovery of all the most interesting things that Paris had to offer. I returned to the hotel at dusk dead tired and at the same time drunk with enthusiasm. But a week before the debut I reentered my methodical life of a singer. I got up early, did my physical and vocal exercises, took my usual walk.

I usually walked along the rue de Rivoli, l'avenue des Champs-Elysées, as far as the Arc de Triomphe. Sometimes I proceeded as far as the Bois-de-Boulogne. Paris was at the height of spring. The soft riding grounds were overrun with horsemen and lady riders. Rich horse-drawn carriages attended by servants were trotting along tree-lined avenues. It was a festival of richness, elegance, luxury, joy of which I had never seen the equal. I don't know whether to say I was more ecstatic or intimidated by the spectacle.

The coming debut preoccupied me greatly. Notwithstanding the valid proof given in all the great cities of the world it seemed to me that Paris should be the most decisive step, and for that the riskiest of my career. I sustained myself with the firm will to triumph. This powerful energy came to me from the equilibrium of my intimate life, and from the religiosity, I say, with which I professed my art.

The character of Gléby had entered into my veins by now, since my portrayal of him at the Lirico di Milano. In the serenade of the first act and in the subsequent scene I reaped a flattering success, but I reached the culminating point in the third act in the narrative, *"La conobbi quand'era fanciulla."* The narrative ends in a cadence that goes from F-sharp to a sustained G-natural. At this point the public broke out in noisy applause, and asked for an encore with such persistence that I was obliged to repeat the whole passage from the top. I was truly against encores, above all when it came to breaking the thread of a dramatic development which ought to palpitate beyond self-gratification and musical acrobatics. But the applause was so intense, the request so persistent that, urged by the conductor of the orchestra, Cleofonte Campanini himself, I reprised the narrative without delay, because otherwise the performance would have suffered an even more injurious interruption than that of an encore.

Siberia, as performed by the Italian opera in Paris, represented the greatest success of the season. At the end of the
performance I had the honor of receiving Victorien Sardou[207]
in my dressing room, accompanied by Umberto Giordano. Enthusiastic, they embraced me, both of them. Sardou kissed me
on the forehead and addressed the following words to
Giordano: "*Voilà un artiste qui fera beaucoup parler de lui
dans le monde entier.*" ("Now there's an artist who will have
the whole world talking about him.") And Giordano recognized that my personal success contributed immensely to that
of his opera.

Now I don't remember at which performance of this work,
toward the end, the Countess Château came into my dressing
room accompanied by the famous musical agent Astruc,[208] and
asked if I were disposed to sing in her concert at the Bois-de-
Boulogne. Other illustrious artists would participate in the festival, among whom, for example, was the celebrated violinist
Kubelik,[209] who had all Paris saying his name. I had a happy
inspiration; addressing myself directly to the countess I declared that to be presented by her to Parisian society was for
me an honor to equal, even to surpass, any compensation
whatsoever. The countess looked at me in surprise and responded, "That's very kind on your part, Monsieur Titta Ruffo.
You will be well received in my house, but I do not wish to
profit from your most agreeable kindness." And she left, adding, "All my congratulations for your immense success in Paris
as a singer and an actor."

The concert to which I had been invited fell on a Saturday
evening. At nine on the dot I found myself in a palatial drawing-room, waiting for the concert to begin, talking to Kubelik.
This was the first time I had participated in a private concert,
and I didn't know the customs. It was very disillusioning for
me. It fell to me to wait an hour. That evening the Châteaus
were putting on a diplomatic dinner, where the Parisian *haut
monde* were present; it didn't end until around ten-thirty.

Kubelik was announced first on the program. He entered
and extracted from his violin the prodigies that were known

to all the world by this time. He returned to the drawing-room after a real ovation, received an envelope from the major domo, politely said goodbye to me and left.

When it was my turn the major domo invited me to enter the salon and proceed with my part. I refused, wanting first to speak to the countess. The major domo, surprised, immediately averted her and after a few minutes, while I was intent on admiring some beautiful paintings by Boucher,[210] she came, visibly upset. With great calm and coldness I showed my resentment for having been made to wait almost two hours, like a domestic servant, and declared that I did not intend to undergo the humiliation of seeing myself given an envelope for my singing and being excused without the slightest consideration of me as a person. I reminded the countess that I had accepted her invitation refusing material compensation in the conviction that, since she deigned to come personally into my dressing room, she might treat me with the regard due an artist, and might present me in her house as a guest. Nothing remained for the Countess Château but to offer me her arm, and with her habitual refinement, to escort me to the piano— and, when the program was finished, to introduce me to her guests.

Instead of the three arias on the program I was obliged to double the number in the midst of unanimous enthusiasm. On this occasion I met, among the most conspicuous bright lights of the world of Arts and Letters: Rostand, Maeterlinck, Saint-Saëns, Massenet, Richepin, the sculptor Troubetzkoi and others I don't remember.[211] As for the political world, I was introduced to all the ambassadors present, and, most notably, to Tommaso Tittoni[212] and his amiable wife, Donna Bice, who were full of affection for me.

I must make special note of the meeting I had then with the Baroness Ernesta Stern,[213] who, in her magnificent house on Faubourg St. Honoré, often gave receptions, along with unforgettable musical performances, in the presence of the most elite cosmopolitan society. This lady was most friendly to me. In the years in which I sang at the Casino of Monte Carlo she often invited me to her castle in Cap Martin, and as a much more significant proof of the affection she had for me, when my daughter Velia was born she expressed the desire to be her godmother. In a bittersweet intermission—very bitter at the beginning but sweeter than sweet at the end—the concert at the Château Palace propelled me into many of the grandest Parisian salons, where I acquired fame and prestige.

Returning to my performances, after *Siberia* and *Fedora* I had the good fortune to sing at the Sarah Bernhardt theater in *Il barbiere di Siviglia* beside Angelo Masini, the greatest tenor of the past generation, and Regina Pacini, who was worthy of comparison to Adelina Patti. The famous comic bass Baldelli was the Don Bartolo and Don Basilio was the bass Oreste Luppi,[214] well-known for his beautiful voice. Masini gave me learned advice during the rehearsals of *Barbiere*. With great tact he invited me, during our scenes together, to harmonize my voice with the pianissimos, and with the perfect modulations which were made possible by his agility. I was glad to be on the same stage with him. He was a man of few words, Masini. A misanthrope, he was on friendly terms with no one. I met him often during my walks along the Seine, with his soft felt cap *alla Romagnola*, and his indispensable cigar in his mouth. Sometimes I would want to tag along and keep him company, but I never had the nerve—such was the fear and respect that he inspired in me.

From Paris I went to Pisa where, as I indicated previously, I had transferred the family after the death of my mother. I lived in an apartment in Palazzo Agostini,[215] one of the old Pisan houses from the seventeenth century which had a marvelous view. Indeed, from there it took in the panorama from along the Arno up to the medieval fortress near the *Porta a mare*, and in certain luminous sunsets I could make out the battlements of the tower which projected fantastically from the depths of the horizon: a magical scene. The enchantment of this vista brought back so many memories of early childhood, and in particular the theft of the cherries and all the blows my mother gave me, the little Gemmina, the distant companion of my childhood games in via Carraia, and similar images and episodes of my childhood. I remained a while with my sisters, then departed for Milan, where I had to sing the season at the Lirico.

I rented an apartment on via Sant'Antonio and began to study *Le jongleur de Nôtre-Dame*, the opera of Massenet, which was to bring me back before the judgment of the Milanese public.[216] I had to interpret the characteristic part of Fra Bonifazio, the convent cook. I studied it deeply. In the mystical aria *"Fioriva una rosa sul margin della riva,"* I believed it best, after much contemplation, to look for tenor-like modulations with a lightly reinforced tone, and I found them, without sacrificing the baritone color of my voice. I sang this melody five or six times a day, and mastered it perfectly. What a joy it was when I could verify my success in fully dominating my voice, and in perfecting the most difficult colors, blending the white and the blue with the red and the black in a harmonious mixture.

Some readers will find it strange that I once again speak of the colors of the voice, but for me it's the most natural thing. Without wanting to fall into aestheticism, I regret not being able to give a persuasive demonstration. But for my part I believe that a student of singing, after having the fundamentals firmly implanted in his voice—namely, sounds that from the lowest notes to the highest are composed, free, supported, united above the palate, without muscular contractions, sustained only by natural respiration—I believe, I say, that every student of singing, if he be endowed with feeling and imagination, and finally, with talent, would be able with practice to form all the colors of a palette of sounds, and thus express every one of the emotions of the soul in all their tints and shadows. Surely it is not easy to do or quickly done. To perfect the human voice, as one of the most original and gifted artists, Antonio Cotogni, once justly remarked, would require two lives: one to study, the other to sing.

CHAPTER 21

From St. Petersburg to Lisbon by Way of Monte Carlo

ONE AFTERNOON, WAITING at home for Maestro Gaetano Coronaro, who was coming personally to rehearse me for the part of *Enoch Arden*,[217] I had the surprise to see him arrive in the company of Victor Maurel, the great French baritone. He had met him at the Duomo, having arrived just then from Paris. They hadn't seen each other in many years and had been evoking the past as they walked together as far as via S. Antonio. Maurel, after learning that Coronaro was going to rehearse his opera with a young baritone, and being given my name, expressed a desire to know me personally, and so they came together to my house.

That day I was wearing an old work jacket and was without a collar. The presence of Maurel–a most distinguished man between sixty and sixty-five years of age with an expressive mask to be found on no other performing artist—made me nervous and I asked him, embarrassed, buttoning my jacket hastily, the reason he was paying me the honor of a visit.

He had heard me in Milan and Paris in *Siberia*, in *Barbiere*, in *Rigoletto* and in *Zazà*, and he wanted to know me out of a keen interest in my voice and the artistic way I used it. The conversation suddenly became packed with meaning, full of warmth and interest. To hear him speak, my mind filled with new ideas and images, one more elevated than the next. Friend of Boito[218] and the preferred artist of Verdi[219] during the period of the maximum evolution of his genius, he called to mind the figures of a time during which *Otello* and *Falstaff* were first performed: memorable evenings in which Maurel had shown himself to be the worthiest interpreter. At a certain point, leaning on the piano, accompanied by Coronaro, he began to mark a few pieces of these two operas and of *Simon Boccanegra*. Although he didn't raise his voice, I immediately noted the grandeur of his genius and of his art.

He asked insistently that I let him hear my voice again. Although nervous, whether because he had surprised me so badly dressed, or because of the awe he inspired, I agreed and sang the aria from the *Demon* of Rubinstein which lent itself to demonstrating the whole range of my vocal colors. At the end he embraced me with enthusiasm and swore to Coronaro that he had never heard a human throat as prodigious as mine. I confided to him my future artistic aspirations, and especially my ambition to go onstage with the *Hamlet* of Thomas and *Falstaff*. He proposed that I leave the theater temporarily and follow him to Paris, where he would teach me himself with all his enthusiasm this opera and others, such as *Simon Boccanegra* and *Otello*, be they in Italian or in French, assuring me that at the end of a year under his discipline I would have the whole world at my feet.

I listened to the flattering offer a bit dreamily, and looked at Coronaro, without knowing how to respond.

Coronaro exclaimed: "As you see, dear Ruffo, I brought you luck."

After having seriously reflected, I told Maurel what I thought. In substance it was this: "To accept your generous offer I would commit a grave error. Given, for one thing, my outstanding gift for imitation and assimilation, and for the other, the powerful influence which emanates from your temperament and your talent, in the end I would have done nothing more than bring into the world a copy of Victor Maurel. And then, would that be possible? Because," I added, "there is only one Maurel, and his memory need not be profaned by counterfeits, even if they are not at all unfaithful, and might be brilliant. I prefer, then, to remain with my personality, no matter how defective."

Psychologically, as I think about it now, I find no fault with my response, but logically I do, since I failed to reconcile my admiration for Maurel with my awareness of my own worth. Perhaps I succeeded in disguising, between the folds of formality, a certain resentment I may have felt that Maurel wanted, at heart, to remand me to school, no matter how great it might be for being his, while I no longer aspired to be a scholar, even if I was not yet a maestro, as he was.

Perhaps Maurel saw nothing of this in my words—or perhaps he was only giving the appearance, in his finesse, of not perceiving anything in them, because having listened attentively, he addressed Coronaro and limited himself to saying, "Perhaps he's right; each of us ought to keep his personality and follow the nature of his temperament."

He took his leave embracing me with affection, and predicting for me all the good fortune that my voice and my sincerity merited.

I looked at the clock. Our conversation had lasted seven hours, from three in the afternoon till ten at night. I have to regret having no more to report of it than some little excerpt.

The season at the Lirico, unfortunately, did not have a happy end. The impresario Ludovico Heller had mounted too many operas and brought in too many foreign artists who didn't interest the public. I was contracted for few performances. After *Le jongleur de Nôtre-Dame*, where I obtained a considerable success, I ought to have created the *Enoch Arden* of Coronaro, but, to my intense displeasure and that of the author, since management didn't have the money to pay a large number of artists who brought in nothing, the season had to close. Now my agent, Conti, wanted to sign me up in Italy for successive seasons of carnival and Lent, and had initiated deals with the San Carlo of Naples, who offered me, for a half-year of performances, twelve thousand lire.

But I, with the *idée fixe* of returning to St. Petersburg, did not want to make up my mind to accept, and was always waiting for the arrival from Russia of Prince Cereteli, the impresario.[220] After some weeks of hesitation my agent became very uneasy, saying that I ought to consider myself lucky to be able to sing in such a theater for such a fee. Always counting on my return to Russia I replied that I wasn't hasty to sign contracts for Italian theaters, when he, I mean Conti, gave me a Milanese newspaper, where printed on the first page in large letters was "REVOLUTION IN RUSSIA—State of Siege in St. Petersburg and Moscow."[221]

The news made me lose all hope of seeing realized my dream of going to Moscow and yet I was still reluctant to be bound by other contracts. My hesitation was exasperating to Conti. To him, my indecision was madness. But madness it was not. No more than two days later, finally, I received from St. Petersburg a telegram from Prince Cereteli which offered me six performances at the Teatro Conservatorio at fifteen hundred lire for each. Considering that I would have had to sacrifice six months to earn twelve thousand lire at the San Carlo, while I could pocket nearly the same amount in two weeks at the most, I responded immediately to Cereteli that, as soon as I received an advance of three thousand lire, I would accept right away.

A week later I left for St. Petersburg. After two days and a half I reached the Russian frontier. The stationmaster absolutely did not want to let me proceed further, affirming that no one was traveling because of the state of siege. The only departing train was commandeered by the police.

I felt lost, but I insisted, and after stating my name, showing the contract and the amount received in advance, he decided to let me leave on the train. However he declined, as they say, all responsibility for what might happen to me. I am not going to hide the fact that the stationmaster's words made me very uneasy. But I summoned my courage and entrusted myself to Destiny, if it is not better to say that I defied it.

The train began to move. It made me desolate to see the immense car empty. At every station I saw pitiful scenes. The trip was interminable. The Russian capital was in a full state of siege, exactly as the Milanese journal had reported. At the station no one was available to help me unload my baggage, and there was not one sleigh to take me to the opera house. The great city, covered with snow, twenty-eight degrees centigrade below zero, made a fearful impression. For an instant, or perhaps for more than one, I was discouraged. But my nature prevailed. I armed myself with holy patience; I took my two heavy suitcases, and sank my feet in the snow, which penetrated my galoshes, and arrived panting at the Teatro Conservatorio.

At the sight of me the doorman was shocked, and asked me by what means I had arrived. He directed me to the stage. The stage was deserted, the curtain was down; only a white cat crossed the stage. But from the orchestra I heard some feeble sounds of stringed instruments leak out. There were a few instrumentalists who were rehearsing the *Demon* by the faint light of their music stands. This wasn't a musical rehearsal, it could sooner have been a funeral ceremony, a burial.

I asked for Prince Cereteli, Maestro Cavallini. No one had anything to tell me. When the orchestra learned that Titta Ruffo was in the theater, behind the curtain, they didn't want to believe it. They all began to play.

I asked one of the technicians to raise the curtain. No sooner had the instrumentalists seen me than they leapt up from their benches, put down their instruments, and after the invitation of Maestro Kharchov, began to clap their hands.

I returned to my old pension, and two hours later was joined there by Cereteli. He was amazed. How had I arrived safe and sound? He confessed that he had sent the advance with the idea of mortgaging my future, but was sure that I wouldn't be there until the general strike was over. I also had a visit from Maestro Cavallini who, to my doubts on the possibility of putting on the performances, told me that the newspapers were *au courant* about my arrival, and assured me that for my six performances the theater would be sold out.

My debut in the *Demon*, that came about five days later, was announced with articles, where much was made of my courage for coming, in such dangerous circumstances, to sing in their country, and recalling to mind my numerous performances of the year before. The theater was mobbed when I sang. It seemed impossible that with a revolution in full swing the public might forget the danger and come pouring out to be at every one of my performances, which were attended as in normal times. When my six performances were over—they were *Demon, Rigoletto, Trovatore, Pagliacci, Barbiere* and *Otello*—Cereteli offered me a contract for another ten. I accepted with great delight.

In my first month in residence at St. Petersburg I sang in fourteen performances, leading the life of a prisoner engaged in the most intense and serious work. House to theater, theater to house, that was my only diversion. The other theaters were closed. No other Italian artist had the courage, that year, to come to Russia.[222]

When my performances in St. Petersburg were at an end I went on a tour—always under the auspices of Cereteli, who was earning a lot of money and had all the regard for me one could imagine—with a company composed exclusively of Russian artists. I was at Kharkov, Kiev, Moscow, and so many other secondary cities of the Ukraine which I do not recall.[223] We returned finally to St. Petersburg in the dead of winter, with a cold which sometimes descended to thirty-three degrees centigrade below zero. Nevertheless I never suffered the least touch of illness or other seasonal inconvenience.

One morning Cereteli came to propose that I sing, the following Sunday, a morning performance of *Rigoletto* at the Teatro Conservatorio, and one in the evening of the *Demon* at the Teatro Imperiale, promising me a thousand rubles for each of them. I hesitated a little because this was a question of enormous strength, perhaps more than I had. But I had faith in my youthful energy, and delighted by the possibility of earning almost five thousand lire in one day, I decided to say yes.

The following Sunday evening, however, at the end of the two performances, I began to count my earnings, which had been paid in ten-ruble gold pieces, it seemed to me that I could never aspire to a greater sum. But I was exhausted. I went to bed more dead than alive. The huge effort obliged me to keep to my bed for three days. No matter how much money I was offered in the future I would never attempt such a feat of strength a second time. But it was true: after only five months' residence in Russia, and after sixty-six performances, I had accumulated a hundred thousand lire: the first hundred thousand. But I was no longer sure of my strength. I was no longer able to resist this climate which was so heavy, dismal and sad. I had become neurasthenic, and told Prince Cereteli that I needed a change of scenery, and rest. Finding my desire just he announced my last performance right away. Aided by various ladies he prepared an extraordinary surprise for my farewell performance.

After the third act of *Rigoletto*, behold the stage inundated with flowers and thirty-six stage-servants, among whom a number of impassioned singing students had mingled, each carrying a rich cushion upon which was a small box containing a gift. From the first moment—I knew other artists that had that weakness—I had believed this was some staging for the sake of publicity. But I saw now that it was quite different. I went out to thank the enthusiastic public, and since Cereteli was the organizer of this magnificent festival of art, I invited him to present himself to the public with me. Since he had a timid character, he was hesitant. I dragged him forcibly to the middle of the stage, and the enthusiasm of the crowd grew to demonstrate their gratitude to him for having contracted me for their theater and to have given diversion to their spirit at such an anguished moment in their national life.

I had lived in these long months with all the comforts that the hard life of someone in my position was permitted. Every month I had sent my family the money they needed. Between times I had moved them to Milan to be closer when I returned to Italy. And I had about two thousand rubles in cash and had deposited one hundred thousand lire in a bank. In the midst of all this grace of God, only one desire was strongly stimulated in me: to see the sun again, the sun of my land. There weren't riches enough in the world, nor glory, to compensate me for its absence.

Before leaving St. Petersburg I received a telegram from Pacini,[224] director and impresario of the Teatro San Carlo of Lisbon, who asked me to sing four performances of *Hamlet* there—and one from D'Ormeville, the dean of theatrical agents, who was proposing some performances for me at the Casino of Monte Carlo.[225] These interesting offers reached me in a moment in which I had a great need of a little rest, but the thought that, after so many years of study, I would finally be able to realize my dream of creating Hamlet on the stage, and the idea of enjoying a gentle climate in the process, after months of ice and dimness and almost perpetual night, induced me to accept both engagements.

Opportunity passes only once in life, one needs to profit by it and continue on the path without resting on one's laurels. *Ogni cosa lasciata è persa.* ["Every opportunity left behind is lost."] After three days I left St. Petersburg directly for Monte Carlo.[226] By order of I don't know who, the train had put at my disposition a first-class compartment that I found all decorated with flowers. An admiring crowd was at the station to see me off: men, women, subscribers, students, friends, enthusiasts. When the train began to move I felt a huge emotion leave my heart.

In the six months that I remained in Russia I had lived the rigorous life of an ascetic because of my dedication to art, a total dedication at the cost of any sacrifice. Arriving in Monte Carlo I had regained my health and strength and was ready to face another battle, sure of victory. I sang a few performances in the magnificent Casino. I was first heard in *Ballo in maschera*; I followed that with *Don Pasquale*; I took my leave with *Barbiere di Siviglia*. Before I left the country, Raoul Gunsbourg,[227] the artistic director of the Casino, offered me a contract for ten performances the following year.

I then left directly for Lisbon. There Benedetta joined me, giving in to my insistent demands. I was just about to put myself forward in *Hamlet*. Thanks to the comfort of her spirit and the help of her advice, this character creation had deepened over the years. In this solemn hour of supreme challenge

I wanted the woman of my dreams, the wise and faithful inspiration of my career to be present. Her coming gave me a
great spiritual energy. There isn't a man in the world who can
make something beautiful and big without the spiritual torch
of true love. It was she, and I can never repeat it enough, who
comforted me constantly throughout my evolution, and who
supported me and when necessary corrected me in order to
transform the boy she met by chance on a little British boat
into an artist and a man, in the deepest sense.

In the repetitious and tiresome rehearsals of the opera I
had frequent discussions with the conductor of the orchestra,
Luigi Mancinelli. He did not approve of certain details of my
interpretation, nor of certain pauses, and still less of certain
additions that I was making, above all in the third act. At the
first general rehearsal—that evening he was quite nervous,
perhaps for reasons that had nothing to do with the performance—he demanded that I sing the opera full voice. I didn't
find it necessary and refused, so that we came to words that
were rather violent.

At the first part of the monologue where I changed some
words he interrupted the rehearsal, noting that the words
weren't in the libretto, and screamed at the prompter to prompt
me well. But I had told the prompter, instead, to keep quiet
the whole time, as I had no need of him, and it bothered me to
hear his voice. The maestro erupted in all his fury at this point
and screamed that this was ridiculous, that he had conducted
Hamlet with the greatest interpreters: Maurel, Kaschmann,
Pandolfini[228] and Menotti, and he was not going to permit,
especially from me, who had performed less than they, any
innovations. I should therefore perform the tempi as he was
taking them, according to the contents of the libretto, not according to my free will. There was a great silence.

I went close to the footlights and told him that, for a man
of his artistic eminence, it was not generous to humiliate me in
front of the orchestra, and that by so doing he himself was
putting me in an inferior position. As for his famous artists, I
made him note that they were, alas, dead, at least artistically,[229]
and that he should have to content himself, therefore, with

what the present generation had to offer. On the other hand, my interpretation was the fruit of long years of hard and conscientious study, nor was I so stupid as to face public opinion in a theater with such glorious traditions without having complete certitude of a happy result.

At the end of my tirade Mancinelli exclaimed, in an unexpectedly soft Roman accent: "Know what I've got to say to you, my son? Do as you please. You'll answer to your public. I wash my hands of it."

Calming myself a little I replied, smiling, that with that phrase he had showed himself to be a worthy descendant of Pilate. At this retort, generalized laughter burst forth from the orchestra, and the rehearsal continued with everyone in better spirits.

At the first performance of *Hamlet* the theater vibrated with electricity. When the stage director came to ask if I was ready, I could no longer feel the blood in my veins. I seemed no longer to have a body, and my voice had vanished. I took Mother's portrait and kissed it, invoking her spirit to give the necessary force to triumph in this terrible battle. Benedetta, who had never stopped praying for me, kissed my forehead, and making the sign of the cross with her own hands, gently pushed me out of the dressing room. Some of the artists, while offering their routine good wishes—*in bocca al lupo*—cautioned me that the Lisbon public was very cold, and for that I shouldn't be alarmed if I didn't hear applause.

Hamlet's entrance in Thomas's opera is preceded by an *adagio* in the cello part. When I was in the middle of the stage there was a glacial silence. This public was seeing me for the first time; I certainly wasn't expecting to be welcomed by applause. Still, it was always alarming, seeing yourself before a new public which has the air, not of having come to proclaim a triumph, but to judge you severely, and is only waiting for the chance to show you their hostility, maybe even by hissing. It is then that the crowd seems to you like a *ferocious beast with a thousand heads*, which some novelist described in famous pages.

I attacked my recitative, almost *parlando*: "*O vano duol!*

fuggevole affetto!" The color of my voice was white, sick, monotonous, which always appeared the most well-adapted to express the unhappy state of the hero's soul. The first melodies started to unwind, and in the duet with Ophelia I displayed my voice in all its vigor. This availed me a loud burst of applause which sufficed, so to speak, to normalize the circulation of my blood and to fill my Benedetta with joy, who had been looking on with anxious expectation.

In all the scenes that followed, my success intensified more and more until it was time for the drinking song. This affords a cadenza of such vivacity that to sustain it (naturally, after indefatigable study and exercise) in one breath, with unbelievable acrobatics, one goes, I dare say, almost into the realm of the supernatural. And the enthusiasm became delirious then. Even before the end of the aria the public interrupted me and buried me with applause. Asked to encore it, out of respect for the authority of Mancinelli I didn't dare, without a sign of encouragement, but he himself, in the depths of his artist's soul, was enjoying my success and urged me with an energetic gesture to sing it again. I must confess sincerely that in my heart, and according to my taste, this bacchic song is really not so pleasing to me aesthetically, but in the minds of the majority of the public my Hamlet was linked unfailingly to this aria.

This demonstrated that what counts most for the crowd, in an artist of the opera stage, is always vocal power and vibration. I have known some singers of my generation to give interpretations of high mastery, of an exquisite originality, but the public, while admiring intelligence, remains unsatisfied and exclaims, more or less, "What a shame he didn't have more voice."

For my personal taste, then, the most powerful passages in *Hamlet* are in the third act when all my sensibility has the means to extend itself completely, that is to say precisely, in the monologue, and in the scene with Ophelia, and in the dramatic duet with the mother. I was obliged, out of hatred for convention and love of naturalness, to introduce some modifications. I do not claim that my interpretation of Hamlet should be immune from censure, but I can in good conscience affirm that it legitimately belongs to me alone. I stole nothing from the artists of my time; I am referring to that which my long study and great love of art, together with the fervent words and insights of Benedetta, inspired me and obliged me, I would almost say imposed upon me.

When I had fulfilled the terms of my contract at Lisbon, Pacini, cheered by my continual triumphs, offered me the chance to sing five more performances of *Hamlet*. I accepted the invitation, in part because I wanted to make myself wholly the master of the role, which was my favorite. For the ninth performance the theater had already been sold out a week in advance. When it came time to leave Lisbon, where I had created the character that I love more than any other in my vast repertoire, it would take another pen than mine to describe my emotion.

CHAPTER 22

Milanese Parenthesis

UPON MY RETURN TO MILAN[230] I found my sisters and my brother had already moved from Pisa. I am not saying they were happy to see me again. We were stirred by so many events and memories that were recalled to mind, above all that of our dear mother. I informed them that two cases ought to have reached them from St. Petersburg containing all the gifts I had received from that place upon my departure. The following day I went to the bank to cash my Russian check for one hundred thousand lire. The director of the bank wanted to know me personally, and advised me to transform this sum into securities that would yield a modest income. For the moment I wanted to have the entire sum in banknotes, and so the cashier issued me one hundred thousand-lire banknotes, not without warning me that it was dangerous to carry such a large sum on my person. As a precaution I placed the large packet against my chest, under my shirt.

After I left the bank I stopped a taxi and indicated with an excited voice the direction of my house, and reaching my front door, so as not to lose time, I gave the driver ten lire, instead of the four I owed him, telling him to keep the rest to drink a glass to my health. The taxi driver, who had the nose of a heavy drinker, in the fashion of Ferravilla's Tecoppa,[231] raised his hat to me and exclaimed, "By God, if everyone was like you, there would be less misery in the world!"

We lived on the top floor and there was no elevator. At the top, winded, I stopped for a while on the landing to catch my breath. Taking from my breast the precious packet, I placed it in my pocket and rang the bell. In the house there was a big hubbub because, just as I had advised, the two boxes of gifts from St. Petersburg had arrived and had already been opened. In the parlor, on the furniture, on the piano, on the chairs, on the floor, everywhere, it was a full-scale invasion of small boxes. The most splendid of all the objects was the silver crown with leaves of laurel which was meant to symbolize my glory.[232] My brother and sisters were dazzled. No sooner had I entered than they attached themselves to my collar, kissing me without stopping, without a word. The most sensitive, Nella, was openly crying. To complete the scene of family joy was the illusion that the spirit of our mother, hovering over her children, was able to see everything. I had the windows of the drawing room closed. I took the packet from my pocket and hurled it into the air. The bills fell back, scattering themselves here and there among all the beautiful objects, and were strewn all over the floor, of course. The scene was so strange that it didn't seem real; rather a dream from the *Thousand and One Nights*. I don't have to say that this manna from heaven, this fruit of my hard but victorious labors, did not long remain there on the floor, or still less that this constituted one of the most moving episodes of my life. True, in my career I would come to earn sums greater by far, but none ever procured me a more intense satisfaction than this.

I continued to embellish my new abode with *objets d'art*, some canvas of a certain value, some little bronze. I began to love painting. I visited the Galleria di Brera, rich with so many beauties. I didn't neglect the Exposition of modern art, however I sensed in myself a more lively attraction to that of antiquity, and above all, to Renaissance art, and in particular that of Florence. I was delighted besides by the old churches of Milan. I returned many times to the Duomo, remembering the dark days of my apprenticeship. Now I had come to observe everything in a different spirit. I found a great harmony of line in this immense forest of stone: not so much on the outside where all the spires appeared too bunched together, but inside.

Again I gave myself to reading. At that time I had in my hands the biography of Leonardo da Vinci. I wanted to see, naturally, the famous *Last Supper* and, oh, how ill it made me to see such a great masterpiece almost destroyed by Time! Sometimes I paused a little to observe, more attentively than I had ever done before, the monument of this genius in the Piazza della Scala, which, with his copious undulating beard and long hair à la Nazarene, gave the impression of being a divinity. But the life I led in my new residence didn't please me in the end. Benedetta's health was deteriorating, and I was profoundly preoccupied by it.

I hastened to join her then and took her to Venice, where we remained for several days. She had been born right there in Venice, though she had left it after infancy. Her father, constrained to flee for political reasons had carried her and her mother with him. They boarded a sailing ship and took refuge in Andalusia, and lived there for a number of years. In reality her face seemed to marry the qualities of Venetian beauty with the mysterious enchantment of the women from that region. During our brief sojourn on the lagoons we visited together the ducal palace and the principal beauties of the city.

She wanted to see her parents again. I waited for her in the Piazza San Marco at the Caffè Florian. She returned after about two hours, pale and weakened as I had never seen her. It was then and only then that, feeling almost near death, she confessed to me how for some time she had been harboring an incurable illness. She asked me to take her back home.

The last rays of the sun were shining on the golden dome of San Marco. She looked at it fixedly, the poor, dear one, as if lost, and exclaimed in an anguished voice: "What a shame that I have to leave life so young!"

She was just thirty-nine years old. When she spoke these words I felt as if I were dying too. I made myself strong; I sought to comfort her; I implored her not to be disheartened, not to see things more tragically than they were. Looking at me with extreme sadness in her eyes she made me understand that by now there remained very little time to live, and that this would be the last time that she would see the sky of her beloved Venice.

I had to be strong; I had to find a reason.

I took her to Milan where she submitted to a medical evaluation and here I learned the whole horrible truth. A surgical intervention was necessary. But for the moment she didn't have the strength to expose herself to such a danger, and wanted to postpone the matter till later.

At the beginning of autumn I resumed my activities for the maestro Walter Mocchi at the Lirico di Milano, performing in the *Zazà* of Leoncavallo, that had roused so much enthusiasm two years before. Again I had as my colleague Emma Carelli, the greatest Zazà of her time, and the tenor Piero Schiavazzi.[233] We sang a good eight performances with the theater always packed.

One evening, who should come to my dressing room but the *Intendant* of the Teatro Imperiale of Vienna, accompanied by Mocchi, who proposed a singing engagement in Vienna opposite Enrico Caruso, and asked my impresario to grant me freedom for four days. Mocchi consented. All Vienna was anxious for rehearsals to begin so that they could hear the two Italian artists together in the Verdi opera. The honor to sing beside my great colleague, with whom I had shared the success of *Fedora* in Paris, filled me with the most fervent enthusiasm.

This Viennese performance turned out to be a veritable feast of art, and a grandiose one. The show was crowned with an immense ovation.[234]

The show had scarcely closed when I had to leave, the same night, for Milan, where I was awaited for other performances of *Zazà*. Carlo d'Ormeville was pressing me to sign a contract for the opera of Buenos Aires, against compensation of seven thousand lire per month. Though at that time the sum might seem more than modest, and even baritones of great renown were not paid more then, the offer seemed unacceptable to me. I countered to D'Ormeville that I had opened a path for myself in Russia by this time which yielded much more, and for that, and for the conditions, they might as well forget my name in the theaters of South America. So in the winter of 1906-1907 I returned to Russia and sang at the Aquarium Theater of St. Petersburg.

I returned to Milan in Spring, and spent many weeks amidst great anxiety. Benedetta was deteriorating more with each passing day. Surgical intervention had become urgent. I took her to the clinic with sad foreboding. Indeed after five days the sacred star of my life was spent.[235]

I went through months of an anguish that has no name. I had sunk into a state which resembled madness. In that inexpressible calamity my faith in her was no help... I found neither refuge nor remedy. I had been very nearly an abstainer, if not from alcohol in general, at least from absinthe; now I continued to poison myself with this malefic drink, which reduced me to stupor and an artificial oblivion. I lingered for entire hours beside her grave, and thus, between sadness and vice, I was destroying myself more and more.

In this terrible predicament the face of an old friend from my youth reappeared to comfort me on my path: Amleto Pollastri. From then on he followed me for many years all over the world like a faithful dog. He had been one of the baritone students of Persichini, during the brief period that I had frequented the Conservatorio di Santa Cecilia. Nature had endowed him with a beautiful voice, but incapable of making the sacrifices that the career of a singer required, after a few years he had fallen behind in his course, and ruined himself as an artist. Then I took him for my secretary.

In the years he stayed with me I gave him all my trust without limit; I treated him like a brother; he sat at my table like a member of the family; he lived the same life I did. He was my factotum: secretary, cook and, to save time, also my accompanist. He looked after my voice as though it were his. In sum he reciprocated the love I had for him. In the hard battles in Spain and Buenos Aires where there existed organized *claques* who wanted to blackmail me with the threat of disturbing the performance, he confronted the leaders at opportune moments. Endowed with Herculean strength, he scared them in his turn with threats of exemplary punishment. He even climbed to the gallery with a less-than-reassuring scowl on his face to intimidate them. "Anyone who goes after Titta Ruffo better beware," he would repeat as he went. "Unless they want something to remember me by."

In these years of intense activity I confided important sums of money to him. He collected money from management on my account and deposited it at the bank. Some envious, malign persons who wanted to occupy his post insinuated that he speculated on the stock market with my money. I listened to no one, and must say that Amleto Pollastri dedicated his work and his affection to me without reserve or ulterior motive. He was a perfect gentleman. We left each other, we divided up, it's true; but why? One day he fell in love with a beautiful Roman girl who was also an artist,[236] and became her husband and secretary: that's why. Destiny was all that separated us.

Returning to my personal calamity, this caused me to abandon the theater for some months. I wandered here and there at random throughout Italy—without purpose or comfort. My health got progressively worse, and all that had formed my life's dream heretofore became completely strange to me. Where was the ardor I had once felt for art? By this time all the fires in me were out. I went to Milan of course, but did not want to live with my sisters so as not to inflict my sadness upon them, and limited myself to visiting them every so often.

I often went to a bar near the hotel where I had taken lodgings, and sat in a corner. I ordered liquors, five or six at a time, and absinthe by preference. The waiter who served me knew me very well, having applauded me at La Scala and at the Lirico. He regarded me with a sense of pity, and moved by pity, certainly, he forced himself finally to advise me not to abuse the drink I've named, which was noxious to the health and ruinous to the voice. Some of the regulars at the bar, who were in the know about my situation, accosted me and with the gentlest words urged me to leave off poisoning myself that way. I replied that it was the only medicine that was worth anything to lift my spirits and make me forget.

There were days when I drank as many as ten glasses of absinthe. Then I felt a light sweat flood over me and the most pleasant possible coolness traverse my entire body, providing an extreme sensual pleasure. I went back to my room; threw myself on the bed fully clothed; went to sleep weeping over the image of the dear one I had lost.

One night when I did not succeed in getting to sleep I stood behind the window of my room, which gave on the Corso. It was late. I began to observe the rare passersby, and the strangest images began to take fire in my cloudy imagination. My gaze followed these few nocturnal walkers from the great tumult of Milanese life. They seemed dead to me. In the hallucination I undressed them, and besides taking off their clothes, I removed their covering of flesh, so that I was seeing real skeletons pass by, and I could even hear the quiet grating of their bones. When the macabre vision had come to an end, or rather when my brain's morbid vertigo had—it's hardly necessary to add that all this was caused by the poison that I'd ingested over the months of perpetual intoxication—I left my hotel and set off for the Piazza del Duomo.

In the Galleria a group of artists, the ones who lived their lives at night, upon seeing me called out in a high voice, and perhaps expressly so I would hear, in their high voices took compassion upon my misery and my declining health, nor did they refrain from passing judgment to the effect that I was by now a ruined artist and that I owed my ascendant career entirely to the undue influence and help of the *signora bruna*. I retraced my steps and stopped before the group of mediocre singers, and with arch coldness hit back at their malice and their foolishness. I protested that I wasn't a ruined artist, but simply one that had been immensely saddened, and that my future wasn't closed. They were embarrassed.

Meanwhile a healthy reaction had shaken my spirit. The reality of life began to waken me. I reflected that all of us are born to die after a brief appearance in the world, that life was a battle, that before dying each one of us needed to fight with strength and courage, without letting ourselves be vilely brought down by the blows of Fate.

Returning home I called to mind all that had poured out of me to the crowds, and that the crowds had received from me with so much enthusiasm; and the siren of art reappeared flattering and propitiatory on my path, the harbinger of new victories. I determined from that moment to abandon the abuse of alcohol. I reentered my room and put out the lights; I got down on my knees in an attitude of prayer, and invoked her spirit with mine, praying that she might appear in whatever form, might advise me, might pardon me, if I had drifted so far away from her sage precepts, and promising her to again follow the path that she had so luminously shown me. It was difficult to break with my longstanding habit all at once, but by gradually diminishing the dose I finally succeeded in doing without the deadly substance.

One day I received a personal letter from Edoardo Sonzogno calling me urgently to his office. I didn't hesitate. He received me coldly, which was his habit; he shook my hand and invited me to sit down. He reproved me severely for allowing myself to drift away from the theater, and above all to be given to drinking. He urged me gently then to return to my path, whether from respect for the art which I served, or from a sacred duty of gratitude toward the woman who had helped me so much to travel that path gloriously thus far.

I expressed my gratitude to Sonzogno for his affectionate interest, and gave him my word that I would return to the straight and narrow. In addition I asked him, since the *signora bruna* was the great source of my interpretation, to help—and he could do it—to have *Hamlet* staged for the Teatro Lirico. Sonzogno, the generous soul, got up and shook my hand, and, although he had little confidence in the success of *Hamlet*, promised to satisfy me. In seeing me off these were his last words: "I am doing it for her, for your good, and for the good of our lyric theater."

From that day not one drop more of absinthe, or of any similar liquor, entered my stomach.

My will, unexpectedly reborn and vibrating in my spirit, to take up the path of art again and go back to face the crowd after so many months of morbid deviation, gave my life a new direction. I sensed the paramount need for a point of support to anchor my fluctuating life, and the necessity of a moral purpose to continue along the retaken path to higher good, and the urgency, finally, of having my own family. And I took a wife.[237]

The chosen woman had all the virtue and talent necessary to accompany me and help me efficiently in the future stages of my laborious march. The profane public does not know how many harsh renunciations and generous sacrifices, how many secret heroisms are interwoven into the existence of someone who is the companion of a man totally dedicated to art. This woman fulfilled both my needs and my dreams. Of our marriage two children were born, Velia and Ruffo, who were and are the source of all my truest joy and all my highest inspiration; both of them, together with her, of course, their adorable and adoring mother. My career after this step, and thanks to it, was more and more triumphant, and for all that I wished it, it was impossible for me to escape from the light of clamorous publicity that is wont to surround an artist's life when he is called great by the world. But, although following me closely in the theaters, in the salons, at the parties and the worldly receptions, she continued to remain, as a rule, in the shadows. There wasn't the slightest ambition or vanity in her.

Even her name pleased me. She was called Lea. Even if she had not had the gift of beauty, though in truth she wasn't deprived of it, she was and is someone with such a penetrating, blue-eyed gaze, and such nobility of countenance, urbanity of style, softness of voice, agility of mind, mildness of character, that she could, nevertheless, when necessary, compensate, if not surpass, that gift. And she learned how to transmit her rare spiritual quality to her children, who in the moment of their moral development thrived under her guidance. The arduous though sublime mission of motherhood can be fulfilled, even surpassed, with abnegation and tenderness alone; the intelligence that she has brought to the task has won for all of us the prize of a happy existence. I—together with my children, who are the light and the life of our house—never cease blessing the destiny which has given us the privilege of a companion so elevated from the ranks of ordinary women.

CHAPTER 23

From Milan to Monte Carlo by Way of Madrid and Other Theaters

WE NOW COME TO *HAMLET* which Sonzogno upon my request had agreed to produce at the Lirico of Milan. The last interpreter of this opera had been Victor Maurel,[238] who had been much admired and applauded many years before by the Milanese public at the Dal Verme theater. However, despite the outstanding skills of the French baritone, the opera had not aroused much interest. Milan was now awaiting my performance with intense curiosity.

With fraternal enthusiasm I had been helped with the staging from the first rehearsals by Ruggero Leoncavallo. I had begged Edoardo Sonzogno to find me an attractive singer for the part of Ophelia. And sure enough, at the first rehearsal with piano, he presented to me a marvelously pretty creature, Liliana Grenville.[239] Shakespeare could not have wished a more poetic woman to embody Ophelia. She was American-born and had studied in Paris. She had a lovely soprano voice, slightly lacking on certain high notes, but, having studied her part with diligence and love and aided by the effect of her physical charms and her musical talents, was able to gain the admiration of Milan. There were many blocking rehearsals, and Leoncavallo was always with me. It was he who studied the distribution of the crowds in the coronation scene as well as in the scene of the comedians and of the madness of Hamlet.

Sonzogno wanted to invite the entire press to the dress rehearsal. I advised him against it, thinking it unwise to have critics witness the inevitable mistakes and weaknesses which are almost always part of dress rehearsals. Only one critic was allowed in the theater: Romeo Carugati of the newspaper *Lombardia*. Although we were tied by a deep friendship dating back many years, our friendship did not prevent him from judging me with severity when he deemed it necessary. As I found out from my secretary, he feared that, as before with Ricordi and Campanini in *Rigoletto*, I was too inexperienced to perform such an arduous role in Milan; and, if some errors were evident in my interpretation, he intended to cite them.

Well, when the rehearsal was over he came to my dressing room with my secretary and, clearly moved, said to me: "Bravo, Titta Ruffo. You may face the audience with confidence, because your interpretation of *Hamlet* will be a triumph, I am sure of it. I did not believe that you would have known how to take on this character so completely when he was the stumbling block not only of the greatest baritones but also of the most famous actors in the world."

All the artists who were in Milan at the time came to the theater for my performance, among them many baritones: Renaud, Sammarco, Giraldoni, Amato,[240] and more than a few other renowned ones. This success marked an artistic peak for me. The next day, on the stock exchange of lyric theater and singers of the F clef, my shares were the highest. They had gone up from one hundred to one thousand, and the largest companies in the world wanted to purchase them.

After the show I was visited in my dressing room by many distinguished celebrities. Edoardo Sonzogno wanted to greet me before anyone else and expressed his utmost satisfaction, and I thanked him, moved by all that he had done for me. After him came Leoncavallo with Colautti,[241] Mascagni, Giordano, and other figures of the theater world. My agent Conti then came to announce that the managers of the new Teatro Colón in Buenos Aires were waiting outside for the end of the customary ceremonial visits so that they could come in and discuss business matters. The managers were Cesare Ciacchi, Luis Ducci, and two Argentine gentlemen who later managed the Colón in association with Walter Mocchi and Faustino de Rosa.[242] Conti told me to hold firm on a high price and not to accept contracts for less than twenty thousand lira a month.

Although I was aware of the importance that that great theater could have for my career, I thought it preferable not to show excessive enthusiasm and responded that I intended to secure and consolidate my position in Russian theaters; however if they would reciprocate with an offer of fifty thousand lira a month, I would accept a two-month contract. The managers of the Colón looked at Conti as if to ask for an explanation of my exorbitant terms. Then they left me sitting there without even discussing the matter. Conti was quite annoyed and told me the success of *Hamlet* had surely gone to my head, and I did not see him again for several weeks. At that point all hope of resuming negotiations with the Colón seemed lost.

Meanwhile, at the end of October 1907, recruited by impresario Jean Feder, I began a season at the National Theater of Bucharest. He was an intelligent man and was able to present me to the audience in an aura of great prestige. I received very festive welcomings in that capital. I sang many operas from the Verdi repertoire. My success reached exceptional heights, and Feder made a lot of money with me. At the closing performance, in order to express his admiration for and gratefulness to me, taking advantage of the enthusiasm—or should I say fanaticism—of the university students who crowded the theater each night, he arranged for them to carry me in triumph to my hotel after the show. So, when I had just exited through the stage door, I was surprised to see an unusually large crowd awaiting me. I felt myself being lifted up in the air by strong arms, as if I were a small toy—and I was not a small toy—and a thousand people began to cry out like madmen: "Hurray! Hurray! Long live Titta Ruffo!"—I was carried by that crowd which overflowed with youth and enthusiasm in a phantasmagoric torch-lit procession, and the sight instilled joy as well as fear in me.

Another pleasant memory of my stay in the Rumanian capital was my personal acquaintance with Ermete Zacconi, who with his incomparable creations was enjoying the endless admiration of the playhouse audiences of the time.[243] In order to celebrate the comtemporaneous success of Italian lyrical and dramatic art, an official banquet with two hundred guests was offered in our honor. That was an unforgettable evening. I was proud to hear my name exalted along with that of the great actor for whom I had always harbored the deepest admiration. Both of us were staying in the same hotel and spoke together often. I eagerly cultivated his friendship.

From Bucharest I went to Warsaw with a repertoire of *Hamlet* and several Italian operas. I bid my goodbyes to the Polish audience with the *Barbiere di Siviglia*. My interpretation of this comic figure, so distant and different from my other roles of a more tragic nature, happily secured my reputation as an actor and singer. From Warsaw I went to Lisbon, to the same São Carlo theater where I had left behind so many wonderful memories. I sang in a ten-performance series. I spent one month in the capital of Portugal, joyfully captured and enraptured by my art. From Lisbon I went to Madrid. It was the first time that I was heard in that city and in the famous Teatro Real where the most renowned artists in the world had succeeded each other, and where the memory of Patti, Masini, Gayarre,[244] Marconi, Maurel, Cotogni, Pandolfini, Menotti and other such champions of the era of *bel canto* was still alive.

The public's curiosity was tremendous in anticipation of my entrance on the stage upon which the feet of so many immortals had tread. My series lasted one month, and I had to sing in ten performances, as before in Lisbon. Ten days had gone by since my arrival and the management had not yet made up its mind to announce my debut. So I decided to let it be known that I would not be able to, nor would I want to, sing in all ten contracted performances with only twenty days remaining, and that I intended to be paid for all ten performances even if they did not all take place for lack of time.

At the time the impresario of the Teatro Real was a retired colonel who in my opinion had neither the intelligence nor the ability to successfully fulfill his duty. He attempted to justify the delay with the following reason: that Mattia Battistini, considered then the king of baritones, had just finished a series of performances there, naturally achieving great success, and that to avoid damaging comparisons it would be prudent to wait some time before presenting a new colleague of the same register, especially one awaited with such curiosity. Thanking him sarcastically for his sense of diplomacy, I made him aware that I was a simple artist at the beginning of my career and that I had no intention whatsoever of competing with anyone. As for his pretense of keeping me ten days beyond the end of the contract, I informed him that I had already consulted a lawyer, and that for that reason delaying my first appearance could prove very costly to him. Seeing my firm intention of having the terms of my contract rigorously respected, the manager changed his mood and his tactics.

Indeed the following day I was asked to attend rehearsal, and there I read on the program announcements at the entrance of the theater: "*Coming soon:* Rigoletto *with the famous tenor Giuseppe Anselmi.*" Giuseppe Anselmi was one of the darlings of the Madrid audience, and his name was written in bold capitals, while that of the other artists, including mine, was in small type. Evidently, even though I was to play the protagonist in the Verdi opera, the main attraction of the performance was Anselmi. This impropriety towards me greatly offended me, but I did not show any resentment.

I entered the rehearsal hall with my usual serenity. The great singer Anselmi barely greeted me with a slight movement of his hand, as is done with someone considered inferior. I sang my part in a lowered voice; the impresario made frequent signals to Anselmi which expressed a lack of confidence. When the rehearsal was over, Anselmi bid goodbye to the others with the same air of foolish haughtiness, and when the impresario asked him thoughtfully at what time the next day he wanted the rehearsal with orchestra, he replied in a light falsetto: "At eleven." His desire was made into law.

Although I had been well-acquainted for some time with the petty schemes of the theater world, my serenity had given way to disgust. However, confident in my mature discipline and in the abundance of resources granted me by nature and reinforced by my studies, I waited patiently for the opportunity to defend myself appropriately and finally to have myself respected.

The next day at exactly eleven o'clock I was on the stage of the Teatro Real, an anxious and largely ignored unknown. Anselmi arrived late only to be flooded with everyone's reverences as if he were some kind of god.[245] The following day the opera was performed, and only someone present at my debut could describe the significance of the success which I achieved. If I were to convey it myself, malicious people would call me conceited, or, as is said in theater jargon, a self-promoter. I am not a self-promoter, but if, as a result of a gift from nature and not of will, I was able, with the privilege of an exceptional voice, to make something of myself in this world, why hide it? Why should I not have availed myself of this gift using all my energy and shown my worth? I would have been ignorant with regards to the generosity of Mother Nature and foolish with regards to human maliciousness.

I can affirm that I have received the greatest display of enthusiasm of my career from the audience in Madrid. Even King Alfonso XIII and Queen Vittoria Eugenia[246] were present at the opening. They stood up at the end of the third act, applauding loudly. When I was alone in my dressing room, about to remove my hump, the impresario came, moved, to embrace me. He reproached himself with not having presented me to the audience two weeks before and for having been advised badly; and he happily informed me that the next performances were sold out.

I was hired by the Real for many of the following years[247] and I appeared in fifteen operas there. I sang—and I quote them in order to give a clear notion of the range of my artistic activity: *Trovatore, Linda di Chamounix, Don Carlo, Africaine, Tristan und Isolde, Barbiere di Siviglia, Falstaff, Bohème, Gioconda, Tosca, Andrea Chénier, Pagliacci, Hamlet* and *Rigoletto.* With every year my name gained greater prestige and popularity. Several times I was honored with an invitation to the royal court where I received magnificent gifts from the very beautiful Queen Vittoria Eugenia and the Queen Mother, Maria Cristina.[248]

On one occasion there was a small celebration which only the members of the august family attended, and I was invited as well. After a brief conversation, the *infanta* Isabella[249] sweetly asked me to imitate, as I had done before in her home, some actors of the Italian theater. I agreed to the request and, improvising some scenes, recited the same lines in the manner of Novelli,[250] Zacconi, and finally Angelo Musco, to the great pleasure of my listeners.[251]

Another time King Alfonso became interested in finding out what my pastimes and activities were outside of theater. At that time I was putting together a stamp collection and already had many of great value. So I told him about my philatelic passion; and, a bit indiscreetly, knowing that he happened to have one of the most important collections of the time, I expressed my desire to be given a stamp as a souvenir and as a symbol of all the honors bestowed upon me during his reign. The sovereign kindly granted my request. And after a few days, minister Romanones delivered to me, by order of the king, an envelope containing the first four stamps of Spain.

I often moved from Madrid for performances in Valencia, the luminous Mediterranean city. There I met one of the greatest contemporary painters: Sorolla.[252] I visited his studio and admired his canvases which were more intense with sun and light than I have ever found in another painter. I appeared during several seasons in the Liceo theater of Barcelona as well, always accompanied by fortune and glory, singing in many performances of *Rigoletto, Hamlet, Barbiere,* and *Pagliacci.*

The land of song, dance, and *toreros* became almost a second homeland to me: the more I was loved and celebrated there, the more that country pleased me. The artistic satisfaction which I enjoyed there was infinite. The funny events and adventures that I experienced were countless. It would take too much time to tell even the most significant ones.

During a *corrida* in Barcelona, the famous toreador Gallito wanted to kill the animal in my honor. The custom, though somewhat barbaric, is the most meaningful expression of affection and admiration anyone in this Spanish environment can offer. Gallito, before bestowing the fatal blow upon the bull, came towards my seat: he threw to me as a gift a very beautiful cloak embroidered in gold, pronouncing these words, naturally in his native tongue: "My friend, my brother, for you, for your father, for your mother, for your wife, for your children, for all of those who love you as I love you, for your wondrous art, I dedicate the bull in homage to your glory." At the end a crowd of fifteen thousand people came to its feet with formidable applause, crying out my name. Afterwards I was taken to my hotel by several toreadors in a convertible car and spent a joyful evening in the midst of those expansive and exuberant fellows. Later that night they took me to one of their taverns where they danced their traditional dances and where I felt a little like a toreador myself.

Another time, during one of the evenings in my honor at the Real of Madrid, the great toreador Mazzantini offered me his most lavish costume, which he had worn in his last *corrida*. That night the honor was bestowed upon me, I do not know how or where it was earned, of receiving the High Military Order of Spain, equal to the rank of honorary colonel in the army, from the Duke of Tovar by order of King Alfonso XIII.

From Spain I went to Monte Carlo. I stayed in that heavenly nook of the Côte d'Azur for about one month. I sang in *Linda di Chamounix, Cristoforo Colombo, Otello, Gioconda,* and *Barbiere di Siviglia,* and my artistic aspirations were fully satisfied.[253] I lived in a little white villa which basked in the sun, with all comforts. Despite this, during my walks when I watched that cosmopolitan world enjoying a worry-free existence, I felt envious. I couldn't—I'm afraid—do otherwise. When an artist becomes aware of his responsibilities—and he should beware if he neglects them!—he becomes a slave to the audience. He is an unhappy man: he can no longer enjoy anything with total abandon. Sometimes this provokes a certain reaction in him: he would like to break the chain that binds him to the unmovable Sphinx of Art in order to savor the joys of life and his natural rights. He cannot. It seemed to me in those moments that I was making a useless sacrifice and that I was repudiating or desecrating that which existence holds as most beautiful. I was destroying the best years of my youth, and for what reason? For the desire for glory, a glory of the most ephemeral kind: that of a singer. A serious error which one realizes only when the invaluable treasure of youth is spent. Only one who lives intimately with an artist can understand the existence he is forced to lead, how much will power and how much self-control are needed to move through a long career, to maintain one's place in the world: and the more an artist possesses certain rare faculties, the more this discipline is required—for the audience then expects a new miracle from him each night.

At my second performance of *Cristoforo Colombo* I had the surprise of seeing in a row of seats all the managers of the Teatro Colón of Buenos Aires[254] whom I had not seen again since their visit after my first performance of *Hamlet* at the Lirico of Milan when my request for 50,000 lire per month caused them to rush off as though escaping from a madman. But after the second act, there they were in my dressing room congratulating me for my success and inviting me for a glass of champagne at the end of the show. It was not my custom to go to night-clubs after a performance. Instead I usually returned home and took my usual precautions: drank *caffelatte* then went immediately to bed in order to be ready with a light stomach for the following day's work. So I apologized, thanking them, for not being able to accept their invitation. Instead I invited them over for tea the next day. They came and lingered until after sunset, nor did they want to leave before having persuaded me to sign a contract for the opening of the Teatro Colón. At eight o'clock in the evening the contract was all drawn up and signed. I was engaged with this contract for thirty performances in three months in South America, with a remuneration offered by them—would you believe it?—greater than that which I had requested that first time after *Hamlet* in Milan and which had made them flee horror-struck.

Thus at the end of April 1908 I boarded ship in Genoa with a great Italian company composed of the most renowned artists that lyric theater had at its disposal at the time. The sea was calm all the way, and I spent those eighteen days of crossing enjoying the rest with a certain abandon. How many images, how many dreams on that boat in the middle of the ocean, in those enchanting moonlit nights below the equator! They were not always happy images or rosy dreams. Sometimes I would spend long hours on the prow, alone, going over my past, thinking of loved ones who had passed away, and I would think to myself with tears in my heart: "Why do you cry when you should be completely happy? Be grateful to Providence who continues to protect you with Her blessed hand and always leads you to greater heights; who brings you to this Argentine city to inaugurate one of the greatest theaters in the world. What more do you want to satisfy your ambition? Besides wealth, fame is with you, and will follow you for many years." My reflections were correct, but what can a man do if he has been made in such a way by his forefathers that sometimes he cries without wanting to, and asks the reason why? The soul of an artist is incessantly surrounded by so many ghosts, by something that comes from afar, or rather from the inside, from deep inside, and this something from which the most beautiful flower of beauty springs forth—perhaps I am repeating myself—is called pain. Man carries with him, until the end of his journey, the heavy burden of memories. In order that he be able to enjoy a certain happiness, he would have to find, instead of the elixir for a long life or an eternal life, a way to forget the past; to begin again at each stage in his life. But unfortunately life begins from the day one is born and each stage is linked to the other by unrelenting memory. All our actions form a chain which does not break.

We finally arrived in Buenos Aires. I had a presentiment that the greatest fortune would smile on me in that country. I immediately went to the Teatro Colón, curious to see the new building. I found myself standing before a huge structure which rose up next to a large square and towered over all the other buildings like a giant. I entered the theater. The stage alone was so wide that it was almost frightening.[255] Many stage-hands were already busy putting up the sets in the midst of a deafening noise. At a certain point all the lights of the hall were turned on. There appeared a crown of stars, a kind of celestial vault over and around us, with all of its suns flaming.

After a few days I made my appearance in that great theater with *Hamlet*. The staging of the French opera stirred up some controversy. There were some critics who judged that *Hamlet* was not the most suitable opera with which to highlight my voice. In the same period an old theater was also operating where an opera company in competition with the Colón was seeking by any means possible to disparage and to defeat the new theater.[256] The rivalry provoked unbelievably deceitful plots, and the target they most wanted to hit and knock down was Titta Ruffo.

Since the hall's opening performance of *Aida* had not had great success,[257] the future of the new theater depended on my debut and my debut was anticipated for that reason. Everyone can imagine in what state of trepidation and anxiety— despite all comforts and even, I should say, the confidence that came from my past success—I lived through those days as I pondered the vital task that weighed on my shoulders. Repeatedly at the rehearsals I saved my strength as best I could in order to approach the battlefield fresh and ready.

The success of *Hamlet* was decisive. My voice, in full power, spread through the immense hall, dominating with great facility. My interpretation of the difficult character was admired and exalted. And the theater was always sold-out for the following performances. The scalpers made a fortune. Instead of the thirty contracted shows I sang forty-four during that season. I received the greatest applause in *Hamlet*, *Rigoletto*, and *Barbiere*. As I had sensed, that season marked the beginning of great success and endless popularity for me. In the following five years, from 1908 to 1913, I sang in nearly forty performances each season and eighteen benefit concerts. Nor did

I rest on my laurels. Rather I came out every year with some good interpretations, even if from a previously-sung repertoire. Besides the operas mentioned I sang in *Otello, Pagliacci, Paolo e Francesca, Gioconda, Africaine, Aida, Don Giovanni, Don Carlo, Falstaff, Boris Godunov, Thaïs, Demon, Andrea Chénier, Cristoforo Colombo, Tristan und Isolde, Tosca,* and *Bohème*: a good twenty-one operas[258] in which I released my most ardent enthusiasm for art.

After a year of rest—I had fought victoriously but certainly not without great fatigue—I returned to Buenos Aires in 1915 when Italy was already fighting in the great war. Enrico Caruso was also contracted at that time, since he had made up his mind to leave his North American admirers for a few months. We sang *Pagliacci* together, first at the Teatro Colón and then at the Teatro Solis of Montevideo.[259] Those evenings were, as is said in theater jargon—but how can one say it differently?—sensational, unforgettable. The prices of seats rose to unbelievable heights. The theater was always booked days in advance. There was always a contest between Caruso and me for who would sing the best, but also who was the most nervous since we both understood the serious responsibility incumbent upon us. The two principal parts of the opera, the *Prologo* which I sang and the *arioso* "*Ridi, pagliaccio*" which Caruso sang had been recorded and were therefore extremely well-known. People came to the theater to hear again the same vocal effects that they already knew from the record, and one had to be careful—given the price they had paid—very careful to give one hundred percent to that crowd hungry for musical emotions! One bad note would have been enough to get devoured! The Latin audience jeers without mercy, and the very same fanaticism which has raised an artist to the altar a few days before, a few days later knocks him into the dust.

I returned to the Teatro Colón in 1926, 1928, and 1931; then, for reasons not dependent on me but on the effects of all sorts of schemes plotted by malicious people, I was no longer able to get a contract with that temple of art where I had battled so valiantly during the best years of my young adulthood. The last time that I went to sing at the Colón was solely for the satisfaction of showing my latest artistic experiment there as well, *Edipo re* by Leoncavallo, which had already provided me with so much success in Chicago and New York.[260] It proved completely impossible to stage due to the deplorable negligence of the artistic management, and I had to content myself with repeating the operas from my old repertoire. On May twenty-fifth, the Argentine national holiday and the most solemn evening of the season, I was implored in the name of everyone from the president of the Republic to the last subscriber to sing *Hamlet*. Considering this character was my favorite, the request seemed a dream come true; and naturally I stirred up the same enthusiasm that I had in the first performance twenty-three years earlier, an enthusiasm that was highlighted in the national press.

Only one reporter, a fellow countryman and vile hack writer whose name I shall not mention in order avoid soiling the honest pages of this book, had the impudence to send to his newspaper—and the paper published the false information—the news that on May twenty-fifth the performance of *Hamlet* had been replaced.[261]

In the first five years performing at the Colón, at the end of every season, before going back to Italy, I also gave performances and concerts in the major theaters of South America. I sang in Uruguay, in Montevideo—and in Brazil in Rio de Janeiro, Santos, and São Paolo. In this last city I received the honor of inaugurating the marvelous Municipal theater, and I chose for that my most beloved Danish prince.

In the year of that inauguration, I was at the head of a lyric company composed of artists of high regard: among them Maria Barrientos and the great tenor Alessandro Bonci. I had created a partnership with the concessionaires of the Teatro Colón, Cesare Ciacchi, Giuseppe Paradossi and Vittorio Consigli, and we organized a long tour under my name. I went to Tucamán, Cordova, Rosario di Santa Fe, Montevideo, Rio de Janeiro and São Paolo. I sang in nineteen performances in thirty-four days: a grueling effort to make after the work at the Colón. That year was the most depressing of my career.[262] I bring attention to the fact that, upon my return to Europe, I still sang in many performances in Italy, Spain, Portugal, and elsewhere, and always in the most demanding operas of my now famous repertoire. No surprise. I had a cast-iron constitution, a voice of unalterable timbre which was effortlessly pliable, rich in all nuances, with a sure pitch, and infallible; a gift of nature, certainly—and I thank Providence for it—but also the product of my constant dedication and of that strict self-discipline which was regarded as exemplary in the lyrical milieu. And if I enjoy holding this up to the light repeatedly, it is not simply to boast.

I had wanted, following the order of events, to push ahead this narration of my South American activities to 1931, going seven years past the boundary which I had set for myself. However, now I must, as has been necessary for me to do on other occasions, go back several years, because I interrupted my activities in the American hemisphere several times to go back to ours not only to rest but also to sing either in concerts or operas. One of the first ones I like to remember, in particular because of a strange thing that happened to me, is the performance at the castle of Racconigi;[263] of the others, two of my interpretations of *Hamlet* which I consider the most important for me—important for reasons which, as the reader will see, are not wholly pertinent, although not wholly irrelevant, to art.

In 1909 I lived in Rome in Pietro Mascagni's villa. One day my distinguished host telephoned, telling me that he had been charged by Queen Elena with organizing a concert at Racconigi castle in honor of the Czar of Russia, Nicholas II, who was in Italy for an official visit,[264] and asked if I would be willing to participate. Naturally I accepted and we agreed to meet in Turin. A few days before the concert both of us were there, guests at the Europa Hotel.[265] I was in a room close to that of the maestro. He had had a piano brought to his room in order to practice with all the artists—Maria Farneti, Parsi-Pettinella and Grassi the tenor[266]—the music of the program he had put together. Thus I had the opportunity to acquaint myself with him a little more closely. I had heard talk of his eccentric personality and I was proud, as well as curious, to share a little of his life. Every morning, with his kind consent, I went to his room and enjoyed the use of his piano for my vocal exercises. We were almost always together for lunch and dinner. I took the liberty of asking him questions of an artistic and musical nature, and he shed light on everything with an easy eloquence and broad culture. It was a delight to hear him speak in his Tuscan language which not even the noted linguist Petrocchi[267] would have wished to be more pure or more vivid. There was not a time, when I went to the piano for my *vocalises,* that I found him in a black or gray mood. He was always cheerful, always witty. The day before the concert we again went over the program. The last ensemble number was the quartet of *Rigoletto*, which we had to practice several times. When the time had come, we left on a special train for Racconigi: a train full of ministers, generals, statesmen and court dignitaries.

At the entrance of the magnificent royal castle we climbed a splendid stairway of very low steps. At the end of every other step stood liveried servants with white wigs and even whiter gloves, stiff as pokers, looking like statues. And right there, in that monumental double row, I recognized to my great surprise an old friend from the orphanage of Rome by the name of Pizzini. He was naturally stock-still like all the rest. When I reached him, I stopped and, calling him by name, held out my hand and asked him how he was. He did not know what to do, but his excitement was stronger than all the ceremonial duties, and, quickly deciding, he reached his hand out to me as well, shook it effusively and told me in Roman dialect: "It feels like I'm dreaming, seeing you after all this time."

Mascagni, who was behind me, shot out like lightning upon seeing this private interaction: "Titta, what are you doing, for Heaven's sake! Are you going mad? Are these things proper at court?" His words were also heard by Giolitti,[268] who was climbing the stairway near Mascagni. I answered calmly to the maestro that I was not committing any crime, that that servant was a childhood friend of mine, and that, seeing him after so many years, I could not act any differently. Pizzini's companions, who had observed the exchange, asked him who

I was in a hushed voice: "He's a friend of mine," answered the good Pizzini.

When I was on stage, which had been transformed into a great hall for the occasion, I saw on both sides two servants in the same statue-like pose, one of whom was Pizzini himself. At the end of each piece, when I was being applauded, he stole meaningful glances in my direction equal to loud applause. At the end of the concert, our sovereigns, the Czar of Russia, the Duke of Aosta, Princess Letizia, the Count of Turin and finally all the members of the court came to congratulate and shake hands with all the artists.[269]

My friend Pizzini was beside himself with joy at seeing me celebrated by such majesties and highnesses; and, as soon as he got the chance, he moved near me and said: "Who would have known, when you were in the workshop, that one day you would be shaking hands with kings and emperors. Dear Ruffo, as soon as you saw me and shook my hand like when we were in the workshop, you gave me great joy, and you did something that brings you more honor than your glory as an artist."[270]

In 1911, on the occasion of the Great Exposition, thirteen years after my first debut with *Lohengrin* as the Herald, I returned, presented to the Roman audience in the midst of much clamor, in order to embody once again on the stage of the Costanzi the most complex of my theatrical figures: that is, Hamlet. There were several performances.[271]

At one of these I found out from an old friend that my father, having come expressly from Carrara where he had moved his business, was seated in the orchestra and was the object of much curiosity on the part of many spectators and several journalists. We had not seen each other for many years and had stopped all correspondence. The death of my mother seven years before and so many other painful episodes suddenly came to mind. I continued the performance, quite troubled by these memories. But the thought of my father prevailed over other thoughts. I saw him everywhere, I saw his look fixed upon me, I would have liked to interrupt the show to embrace him once again. This unusual state, far from diminishing them, magnified all my expressions, and, in the most dramatic moments, with the apparition of the ghost, and in the scene of feigned madness and in the scene with Hamlet's mother, my interpretation became more evocative than in the previous evenings: nor did this escape the notice of the audience, which lavished me with enthusiastic ovations.

At the end of the performance my father came to my dressing room with his friends, who congratulated him. I cannot convey how full of emotion our embrace was. Both of us remained still for several moments without uttering a sound. Even those present, aware of our relationship, were clearly moved. His demeanor however betrayed a deep exhaustion. I had him sit in a chair. His hair was already almost completely white, his wide forehead already grooved with deep wrinkles, his eyes full of unspeakable sadness. He had changed so much from the man I knew before! But in his spiritual expression he appeared quite a bit for the better. It seemed to me that suffering had refined his soul. "Dear father," I said, stroking his forehead, "you cannot fathom how happy I am to see you again after so many adventures and so many struggles. The thought of you has followed me during these long years around the world, always; and sometimes, when I would come out for the applause of the crowds, I would imagine you there, sharing in my success. Tonight my dream has come true."

My father broke the silence by telling me that it seemed impossible to him that I had imbued Hamlet with such tragic strength and reached the heights I had that night, and he asked who had taught me all this, who my teachers had been. I answered that all the beautiful and the good that I had accomplished in my life and in art I owed mostly to him, and that he alone had been my truest teacher. He looked at me as if caught in a dream; and having turned to his friends, confessed that, instead of supporting my career, he had always thwarted it, and, convinced that I would never succeed as a singer, he had never wanted to spend even one cent toward my musical education.

I answered him that, leaving aside the many privileged physical and spiritual qualities that I had inherited from him, his very contrariness and opposition forcing me to wander the world to earn my bread on my own at fourteen years of age had ended up being an invaluable gift, since I was able, through this process, to become a sure expert and master of life and of art.

He declared at that point that he was still under the influence of the last scene of the third act between Hamlet and his mother. "He must have had to study intensely," he exclaimed to his friends, "in order to express the pain with that inflection and that demeanor, as if he were really feeling it." The expression of my character and my gestures and inflections, I replied, could be attributed less to any lengthy study, as he thought, than to a life endured in early youth, recent painful experiences and precocious responsibilities.

And I recalled some of our family episodes when, in order to express feelings of anger, of pain, of rebellion, and similar emotions, I, impulsive as I was at the time, would pound my fist on the table, would interrupt him with bold words which were inexcusable, even if from the mouth of a child: now I asked him a thousand times for forgiveness. In the scene with Hamlet and his mother, where my father had felt such emotion, I was doing nothing other than reproducing the feelings of my childhood; except that now, I did not rudely pound my fists on the table, nor did I disrespectfully raise my voice. I was no longer the uneducated boy of before, but the pensive prince of Denmark, for whom every attitude and nuance must be nobly pliable, always marked with dignity and majesty, even in anger; but the emotions of all human beings are essentially the same.

The following day we were seated at a rustic table under an arbor at the *Osteria Scarpone* at San Pietro in Montorio. It was one of those luminous days whose equal can only be found in Rome. Midday was sounding and the numerous tolling bells of the Eternal City were reawakening in my heart a sweet nostalgia for faraway times. The image of my mother reappeared in my mind, while my father watched the Rome of his youth with an expression more sad than happy, absorbed in his thoughts by perhaps the very same vision. I tried to keep him in good humor. We ate with good appetite and drank abundantly: especially he, stirred up more than ever by the novelty of finding himself alone with me. Often I would rest my hand on his so he could feel my tenderness towards him. I told him many things about my life and my vertiginous ascent to fame. He listened, sighing deeply as if all this unexpected good pained his heart.

But perhaps other reflections made him grieve. "When one's blood no longer runs boiling through one's veins," he said in reply to one of my more implied than expressed questions, "man becomes aware of his errors, but it is too late. The destiny which he builds for himself with his own hands inevitably drags him through a whirlpool from which he cannot escape, if one can say escape, other than through death. My dear son, I am just sixty-two years old, and I confess to you that for some time already I have been going to sleep many nights wishing and hoping never to wake up again."

We lingered under the arbor of the old *osteria* until almost sunset. Then we walked towards the top of the Gianicolo and stopped on the large terrace that dominates almost the entire City. A mysterious dusk was spreading the last gleams of light through the immense city; here and there sounded the last tolls of the Ave Maria. We hastened back.

The following day we were together at my house. My children, Velia and Ruffo, were playing on the grass. Instinctively he moved towards little Ruffo, picked him up off the ground, squeezed him in his arms, rested his brow against the little curly-haired head and kissed it several times while repeating: "He is so beautiful!" The child looked up at him with some curiosity and smiling, stroked his face with his little hand. Velia on the other hand was now somewhat reserved with him. In the evening I accompanied him back to the train station. He was going back to Carrara where, as I have noted, he now had his business and lived, well-liked and respected by all.

About two years after that episode I was at Montecatini in the La Pace Hotel. My father joined me there. His face was emaciated and his voice almost a whisper. He said that, feeling himself close to death, he had had a great desire to see me again. I urged him to remove that ugly notion from his mind and that I would have him examined by Doctor Grocco who was nearby.[272] In the meantime I accompanied him to his usual hotel. We stayed together the whole day and recalled many things of the past. He confessed openly to me that he had asked Destiny several times to allow him to pass away near me. He was in fact extremely depressed. He wanted to introduce me to the owner of his hotel: "This is my great son, the pride of my life." In the evening that man brought us a special Chianti wine reserved for solemn occasions. I begged my father not to drink any, saying that in his condition it could be harmful to him. But he begged me in turn to let him drink freely, that his health had been ruined for a while now. Those were perhaps his last glasses of wine, and he was happy to savor them in my company.

We left each other with the promise that we would see each other the following day to consult a doctor. I had just reached my hotel when I was compelled to rush back to his hotel, having been informed that he had suddenly taken ill. I found him lying on his bed. Doctor Grocco, who had been already notified of the emergency, told me he had had a stroke: the cerebral hemorrhage had already done its damage and there was no longer any hope in saving him.

His agony lasted three days. In my distress I was unable to shed a tear. It seemed that my heart had turned to stone. I did all that was necessary in the matter. Closed up alone in his room, I stroked his forehead and hands several times. I accompanied him to his final resting place.[273] Upon my return, while going through his personal belongings, I found tucked in the pendant of his watch chain a small portrait, on the back of which was written in his hand: "My little Ruffo."

IN 1912 I WAS IN RIO de Janeiro in a Swiss hotel along the bay: a peaceful place surrounded by very high age-old palms, a true corner of paradise. I was to sing the last two performances of a long tour of South American theaters; a tour which had included a good forty-five performances,[274] and from there I would a few days later set sail for Italy, where I had plans to enjoy a month of rest—I had, I believe, earned the right to it—when I received a telegram from my impresario and director of the Imperial Theater in Warsaw, Mr. Raychmann, passionately urging me to accept an engagement for two performances of *Hamlet* at the Paris Opéra, it also being his personal ambition that the audience of the French capital should have the opportunity to applaud me in my best role.

Despite my aforementioned plan and my extreme need and desire to follow it, my ambition to establish myself on the stage of the greatest French theater, while interpreting my favorite role as well, compelled me to accept. And after a brief escape to Rome, I went to Paris and stayed at the Grand Hôtel, waiting with enthusiasm and apprehension for rehearsals to begin. I had as fellow performers for Thomas's opera Yvonne Gall[275] and Marcel Journet, two artists of widespread fame; this stimulated my sense of pride even more strongly. My reputation in Paris had already been secure for several years, but the success of *Hamlet*—the *pièce de résistance* of the greatest French baritones—not only confirmed it, but heightened it to such a point that, after the two contracted performances I was invited, or rather insistently begged, by the management to sing others as well. Although I was reluctant, feeling over-exerted, I accepted, but at the third performance I arrived at the theater in a feverish state.

I received a visit from Jean de Reszke, the famous tenor in whose house I was often welcomed with affectionate sympathy,[276] and I confided in him my preoccupation with this state of nervous exhaustion. I shouldn't worry, he said upon leaving, because by now I had completely conquered the public and that I could have allowed myself anything that I wished with impunity. And in fact, even during the third performance my faculties responded perfectly to the demands of the audience and to those of the art, to the particular satisfaction of Raychmann who was always nearby, proud of my success since he was the show's promoter.

Having reached the third act, my weakness was so acute that it made me seriously fear that I would not get through to the end of my part. Just after preparing myself and putting on my makeup, I went, as I usually did, onstage to verify personally that everything was in the place that I had indicated. I lay down on the crude bed near the table where the scene with the recitative and the following famous monologue "To be or not to be" begins. The stage director asked me if it was time to signal to the orchestra to be ready; I asked him to wait.

I tried to shake off my exhaustion with a little coffee, and then I lay down again. My straying gaze focused on the decorations of the large theater's interior acoustical arch. Suddenly I beheld a strange vision. I was no longer on stage, but at the other end of the theater, and, observing the gloomy scene onstage, I saw myself lying asleep in the feeble light of the oil lamp, with the white skull placed on the heap of books and the portraits of two kings, my father and his brother, usurper of the throne. I was no longer an actor but a spectator and almost a critic of myself. Why—I asked myself—continue along the same wearisome path only to continue playing the same roles? A work of art expresses itself in a single and unique act, and reproducing it so many times inevitably makes it a convention, intolerable to the imagination of a true artist.

And thus the desire, I would almost say the sensual attraction, of death came into my heart. A few more times, while I was immersed in these thoughts and feelings, the stage manager came to ask me if I could begin; and a few more times I pleaded, for the sake of my exhaustion, that he wait a little; and I invoked all the forces that watch over us and over human affairs to bring an end to my life at that very moment, conceding to me the ultimate joy of death at the apex of my career, before the curtain was raised. In the intensity of the fever that consumed me I felt the orchestra begin its assault, I saw the curtain go up, and, at the moment in which the actor must go on with the performance, I saw everything stop; the orchestra stop playing; a great panic invade the stage; the stage director come out pale and agitated to the audience to announce my unexpected death, the large crowd at its feet discussing the fatal event amidst consternation and lament. This strange vision persisted until the stage director came to tell me that the third act was about to begin. I did not respond. The orchestra hinted at its first harmonies, the curtain opened. Relentlessly I once again had to take up the usual drama of theater.

Having determined that in my conception of Hamlet, in order to distance myself from affectation, the first recitative go on while I am sleeping, the first words: "*Potea svenar quell'assassino, e risparmiato l'ho! Perché mai tardo ancora...? Punir lo deggio omai!*" were pronounced in my sleep as if I were tormented by a horrible nightmare. At that point Hamlet wakes up, and, with the vision of his father still before him, moving his gaze around in the empty space as if to search him out, adds: "*E tu! sparito sei, tu padre mio?*" Then I began the monologue "To be or not to be."

Never as during that evening, in which I struggled in distress between life and death, never, I repeat, did I render with such truth and power the sublime monologue which has wrapped itself around and moved the human spirit through the ages. I split myself completely in two. I undoubtedly was Hamlet: the Hamlet whom Thomas's talent put to music in his melodrama, whom the genius of Shakespeare created in his immortal tragedy. But, to speak my mind truthfully, this Hamlet was also something more. He was also me. I, with my past experience, with my present anguish, with, in short, my solid personality intact. And, it seems to me, with something better: something which I cannot analyze clearly, but which I feel clearly, and which, although it left my limited and ephemeral being unchanged, freed it from all limits of space and time: it carried me into the infinite.

CHAPTER 24

In North and South America

I WANTED, DRAWING FROM a free association of ideas, to push the parabola ahead across South America to the very end, again surpassing by several years the limits which I imposed on myself in this book. It is now fitting, as is usually said in fairy tales, to take a step back, or rather more than a step back; that is to move back to when I began my performances in North America. I went there for the first time in 1912, accompanied by my old friend Carlo Younger[277] and contracted by the impresario Andreas Dippel,[278] general manager of the Chicago Opera Company at the time. After long and tiresome negotiations, I had signed a contract with him in Monte Carlo for fifteen performances. Dippel was accompanied by the influential banker Stotesbury[279] of Philadelphia, who became guarantor of the contract. My terms were much higher than the usual remunerations given my colleagues who were already established in North American theaters. In order to justify this enormous and unusual agreement Dippel, with the financial help of Stotesbury, released an astounding advertisement two months before my arrival.

In it he claimed to have contracted the greatest baritone in the world. The details of my contract and the exaggeration in the advertisement stirred up widespread and lively polemics in the American theatrical milieu. Dippel provoked many bitter reactions on the part of other artists for having allowed a baritone to receive a salary that was throwing their theatrical and financial policies into disarray. Especially resentful was the Metropolitan of New York, where the only artist remunerated with extraordinary sums was Enrico Caruso, who had been the darling of the audience for years already; who, however, had had to undergo a long trial period before reaching that level of pay.

Given the American-style advertising campaign that Dippel had organized and that had flooded all the newspapers there with my name, upon my arrival in New York there was a throng of photographers and reporters awaiting me. Moreover, Dippel immediately organized a banquet in my honor, with a press conference. Having finally succeeded in freeing myself from that yoke, I went to stroll on Broadway, where I saw my name announced in the program at the Metropolitan. The distribution of my fifteen performances was left to Dippel's discretion in the contract, and he therefore was under no obligation to inform me in advance. Still I was left unpleasantly surprised when I saw my name announced at a theater of another company. Dippel explained to me that the Chicago Opera had an agreement with the Metropolitan through which it would give a performance with its own artists in that theater every Tuesday. So at the first available opportunity Stotesbury had included my name at the Metropolitan.

Thus the next morning I thought it my duty to visit the general manager of that theater, Giulio Gatti-Casazza, with whom I had not had the opportunity to meet since my performances at La Scala in 1904. He received me in his office rudely, even hostilely. Twisting his gray beard he began to speak disparagingly of Dippel. He warned me that the impresario had played a dirty trick on me by including my name on the program at the Metropolitan since I was clearly unwanted at his theater, nor did he feel inclined to put up with me because of the salary I had been allowed, which was undermining his policies and finances. He swore that I would only sing there one evening, and he promised that it would not do me any harm, but neither would it do me any good. I was left, if there is a need explain it, quite mortified at being so poorly welcomed, and I understood immediately and perfectly the fight that awaited me in that star-spangled country. While exiting Gatti-Casazza's office I ran into maestro Giorgio Polacco, the conductor of the Metropolitan orchestra at the time, and he greeted me coldly as well—perhaps he still bore a grudge for a personal matter which I had long since forgotten.[280]

These were my first interactions at the Metropolitan. I armed myself with patience and courage. I was accustomed to doing battle with loyalty, in the light of day, without having recourse to the petty schemes and tricks characteristic of the world of theater, and, indeed, the world at large. Calmness of mind had become second nature to me, and I always tried to rise above the maliciousness and misery with which life so frequently trips us up. Younger was a great help and comfort to me. He followed me everywhere in the United States. I did not have the advantage of speaking English, and Younger, besides being a friend, also served as an interpreter. With his aristocratic figure, his friendly personality, and the authority of a true gentleman, Younger knew how to create an atmosphere of great prestige around me before managers and directors in all the theaters where I appeared.

The Chicago Opera Company had already inaugurated the season several weeks before at the Metropolitan of Philadelphia. Maestro Cleofonte Campanini, who was then the artistic director, awaited my arrival there and had already had my appearance in *Rigoletto* announced. For that occasion no less than a new train service, a special train from New York, was added. The entire music world and all the members of the Metropolitan management of that city, headed by promoter Otto Kahn,[281] were present at the performance. I spent several days in a state of extreme uneasiness. It was entirely too evident to me that, if I produced negative results, I would have no other choice than to take the first departing steamboat and leave the United States forever. Instead, luckily, I was able to win my battle clamorously, and this served not only to justify the sensation Dippel had created with his advertisements, but also to give me the satisfaction of my first important contract with the Victor Talking Machine Company of New York to produce the records that have made me so popular in the world.

And now there was the occasion of my *Hamlet* at the Metropolitan of New York. Opposed by all the conflicting factions, my entry here was not welcomed by anyone. No one was supposed to approach me. It was said that it would be my first and last performance there. In order to intimidate me, on the eve of the performance, there appeared before me—obviously sent there—two ugly-looking types, dressed like gentlemen, who warned me not to appear to the audience because they would surely boo me. Almost all the artists of the Metropolitan attended the performance, but no one dared to come greet me. Only Geraldine Farrar,[282] almost in secret, came kindly to wish me great success: in secret because I was almost under surveillance.

I leave to the imagination in what conditions my nerves were when the time came, when I had to confront the famed thousand-headed monster—the audience. Even Younger, with all his Anglo-Saxon calm, was extremely nervous and could not conceal it. When I went onstage I could not feel the blood in my veins. I did not have the strength to emit a sound, but fortunately I was able to regain my stamina thanks to the thunderous applause that greeted my first appearance and which in truth I was not expecting. All the Italians who were in the theater, and there were many, had wanted to show me their affection thus. My success was, without exaggerating, tremendous and so much more amazing considering the thousands of difficulties and all sorts of opposition to its attainment.

At the end of the show I had the flattering surprise of seeing in my dressing room the great Victor Maurel, whom I had not seen since our first meeting in Milan. We recalled, moved, that unforgettable day when we began to share a perfect spiritual and artistic rapport. At that time I had been nurturing—and I had disclosed it to him—an ambition to take *Hamlet* to the stage, and here was my ambition now, crowned with the most splendid success. Maurel told me that he had followed my progress since that day, and that now he was happy to be able to congratulate me for such a victory.

The next day the New York press gave conflicting reviews of my interpretation. Many critics, loyal servants to special interests, endeavored with unsubtle arguments to belittle my art and my incontestable success. There was one person, however, Henderson, as famous as he was honest, who wrote these words: "After having heard the new artist Titta Ruffo in his performances of *Rigoletto, Ballo in maschera* and *Barbiere* in Philadelphia, I was waiting, before speaking of him, for his performance in *Hamlet* at the Metropolitan, a performance which marks a memorable evening in his career. Titta Ruffo unites in his voice the beauty of Caruso, the classicism of Jean de Reszke, and the power of Tamagno."[283] Before leaving New York, I signed a contract with Dippel for the following year for fifty performances and concerts with the Chicago Opera Company. I therefore returned to Philadelphia with Charles Younger, both of us overjoyed at having won the greatest battle in the United States, and we drank several glasses of whiskey to celebrate the triumph. I continued my performances, free now of even the smallest worry, because, having carried off the victory, a new field of action was opening up before me, devoid of any obstruction, completely open to future progress.

The following year, 1913, I also brought my brother to the United States, who with his merit and intelligence was able to found an important voice studio under my name.[284] I remained in North America until 1915, singing a grueling repertoire without a pause and organizing another two tours of operas and concerts, one of those concerts together with Luisa Tetrazzini, the famous emulator of Adelina Patti. I traveled for these tours to Pennsylvania, Texas, California, Washington, Oregon, Colorado, Missouri, Mississippi and to New Jersey where I closed.

During the North American season something odd happened to me, one of the strangest things in my life. I was singing in *Cristoforo Colombo* by Franchetti in the midst of the greatest enthusiasm. The character of the Ligurian hero adapted itself perfectly to me both physically and vocally. Now Dippel, for publicity reasons, had had my portrait, in full costume, published in all the newspapers with the caption: "Titta Ruffo,

God of Voice." This photograph, making its way around the United States, was most striking—and I will explain the reason shortly—to the American Indians of Colorado.

During one performance of *Cristoforo Colombo*, there in fact arrived about fifteen Indians accompanied by their prince (chief) expressly to hear the greatly extolled God of Voice. The Indians of America, now that their forefathers have been decimated by the "pale faces," enjoy a very great respect today. They were received in the theater by the opera patron, McCormick,[285] who had two boxes put at their disposal. Dressed in their magnificent costumes, they stirred up great curiosity in the hall.

After the performance, which they watched without batting an eye, they were led to my dressing room and wanted to shake my hand to congratulate me for my success. The chief expressed his wish that I receive him the next day at the Congress Hotel, where I was staying. I willingly granted his request. My friend Charles Younger served as an interpreter, and the next day, in the main room of my suite I received the chief of the Indians with many honors. The reason—he told me—they had come to Chicago was solely because they had read the epithet "God of Voice" in the newspapers. And this is why:

A few years earlier—the prince said—an odd thing had happened to him. The weather was very bad, and blustering winds raged across their land, damaging it. During the storm a huge black bird had crashed down near their encampment, and a young boy, having managed to capture it, blinded it with a red-hot iron. This cruel act provoked indignation, or rather horror—an almost mystical horror—in the whole tribe. The young boy, perhaps to amend his own fault, asserted that the bird had been shooting horrible lightning bolts from its eyes, enough to make one think it was an evil spirit. The bird seemed crazy with pain. The chief of the tribe ordered it to be freed. It had barely been let loose when it quickly took flight up to the sky and disappeared. Its cries however could still be heard after it was out of sight. The young boy received the punishment of *contrapasso*, as Dante would say, or the law of retribution as we would say, and suffered the same torture that he had inflicted upon the animal. But the howls of the blinded bird often echoed atrociously near the village. Were they perhaps the work of spirits? Or was the mysterious bird, trapped in its own darkness, actually flying nearby? Those howls struck a superstitious terror in all. They predicted that a bad omen would fall sooner or later upon their harvest, on their fruit, and they lived long months with the nightmare of the threat of divine punishment.

But, much to the contrary, the harvest that year was very abundant, and this, according to them, was due to the just punishment given to the inhuman torturer. After that, when someone claimed to have heard the mysterious lament of the bird, people began to say, "He is the God of Voice." That is why, when the epithet appeared in the newspaper under the expressive image of Titta Ruffo Colombo, it had impressed them and prompted them to attend the show of the man described as the God of Voice.

A large banquet was offered for them at the Congress Hotel and was surprisingly interesting. The prince—I was seated to his right—gave a speech at the end. The words that he and others of his tribe pronounced, animated by a vivid sense of humanity and morality, deeply moved the listeners.

The next day I was brought by Dippel to a grand exhibition. There was a vast wooden oval construction with bleachers. And in the middle, for the occasion, was a platform. There upon it the Indians were performing their traditional dances. I also was tattooed, or more accurately, marked on the face as they were, with a tattoo that seemed natural and was purely symbolic. They invited me to climb onto the platform, where in the midst of howls and uproar, using sharp knives, they began making strange and dangerous movements around me. It was the ceremony, a very long one, of my election as honorary chief of their tribe. This done, they embraced me and called me their brother.

Upon bidding them goodbye I promised that I would go visit them in their mountains. And I would have kept my promise if the outbreak of war in Europe had not prevented me from it. They wrote me that they had prepared a very beautiful white horse for me, lavishly harnessed. They sent me two little Indian suits for my children. After having spoken with the prince I can confirm without fear of exaggeration that the most civilized men that I have ever met in the world are the Indians of Colorado. This happened in 1914.

After four years of tireless work I was invited in the Spring of 1915 to inaugurate the new Teatro Nacionál in Havana,[286] and afterward I returned to New York to depart for Argentina, where I was contracted by the Walter Mocchi and Faustino de Rosa management. The steamship on which I was supposed to leave had broken down, running aground on who knows what Northern coast. The boat company deceived me for ten days, constantly reassuring me that I would be able to leave on the same boat. Walter Mocchi meanwhile, seeing the growing delay, ordered me by telegraph from Buenos Aires to leave with the first steamer, and that otherwise he would sue me for damages.

In order to avoid this danger, I boarded, together with my wife, the first steamer departing for South America: a Brazilian boat weighing roughly four thousand tons, the *Minas Gerais*. The crew was Black. The passengers were very few.

After a few days we were caught in a terrible storm in the middle of the Gulf of Mexico which kept us between life and death for twelve days. When the surges took on alarming dimensions, more alarming than I have ever seen in my many sea voyages, they confined us to our cabin. My wife was tied to the bunk with straps. I protested and did not allow myself to be tied. After having run the risk many times of being swept away by the billows, I reached the captain on deck. I had dragged myself to him in order to find out exactly what kind of danger we were in. He flew into a rage upon seeing me because they had not prevented me from leaving the cabin; and, in order that I not risk going back there, he had me tied to the pilot bridge with a thick rope, next to him.

We barely made it. We remained there for about seven hours, almost continuously engulfed by gigantic waves. I wore, tightly tied around my neck, a small purse holding thirty thousand dollars in bills that I had not been able to deposit in New York before boarding. It was purely by chance that the precious savings did not get thrown to the fish in that storm. Time and time again, in the frequent submersions, I felt the strap that held the little sack around my neck slip up around my head up to my forehead. Whipped by the wind's freezing gusts and by the assault of the surges, my body had become livid. The constant image of my wife locked up in the cabin and tied up alone, faint with fear, was driving me mad.

At one point I could not stand it any longer. Exhaustion defeated me, and I gave up with a convulsive cry. The sprays of water slashed my face like points of steel and were blended with my desperate tears. They were more desperate than ever and burned even more each time that the image of my two little children, far away and alone, came to my mind alongside the image of my wife. Finally—finally!—the gale began to abate. The captain gave orders to let me loose. One sailor rubbed me with alcohol, since I was more dead than alive. Then the hatches were opened. I rushed to my wife. We held each other and remained still and silent, crying from emotion as if we had both been brought back from death.

We arrived in Buenos Aires several days late. I could have easily, during those long hours, those endless hours that I spent completely soaked and exposed to the blustering winds of the storm, have caught pneumonia or another similar ailment. A miracle! For none of that happened, and, although it may be hard to believe, it is a fact that my voice did not show the slightest change. I immediately went to the theater, where I told the story of the unhappy odyssey which had resulted in part from the order to leave with the first steamer out of New York.

The following day an artist came to see me who had traveled on the same steamship with a manager of the Colón, and he informed me that the manager had declared in conversation that my delay would be reported as a breach of contract, and that the management had decided to sue me for a very large amount of money as soon as I had performed.

Grateful to the actor for his well-intentioned warning, I immediately ran for protection. I hired a renowned attorney, letting him in on how much was being plotted behind my back. The lawyer immediately solicited a statement from the management which would concede that the delay was due to an act of nature; and he justified his request citing my wish to settle things contractually before my debut.

The management bluntly refused. It was clear that my good artist friend had said nothing but the precise truth. I was to appear in *Africaine* in the role of Nelusko. I thought it wise at that point to personally warn the management that, until they had released the statement requested by my attorney, I would present myself to the audience not in the costume of Nelusko in which I was supposed to appear, but in civilian clothes, and that I would speak to the spectators from the stage, unmasking the management's schemes.

That group, having taken full advantage of my name and that of Caruso, had succeeded in making colossal season-ticket sales. The wait was very intense. A huge scandal might have followed. The attorneys on both sides clashed violently until eight o'clock in the evening. My defender was unshakable.

He was thus able to wrench the document from them, and so I appeared before the audience of the Colón not as Titta Ruffo, but as Nelusko. The immense crowd literally filled up the theater, unaware naturally of how irritated I was after the nuisance of the legal storm and the horrors of that ocean. So much strength and courage are needed to maintain one's name at the height to which fame has raised it! A pretentious word, a tremendous weight is fame, so serious, so burdensome on the shoulders of him the world has chosen to bear it. Often the true artist would prefer to remove it. And woe to him if, when he is no longer able to carry it, he does not unload himself of it in time and retreat back into the shadows. He inevitably will end up crushed by it.

CHAPTER 25

Military Intermission

THE WAR IN EUROPE had broken out and was a raging fire.[287] Arriving at the critical moment when Germany was seriously threatening to prevail, Italy as well threw herself into the conflagration. I was thirty-nine years old in 1916 and had finished the usual lyric season at the Teatro Colón in Buenos Aires, when there one morning I read in the newspaper *La Patria degli Italiani* the news that all those members in the third section of my conscription unit were being drafted.

I was supposed to embark a few days later for the United States, where I had been engaged with the Chicago Opera Company for a concert series and other important contracts, and I had already reserved a cabin on a Dutch steamer. But I preferred to go pay my respects to Ambassador Cobianchi, with whom I had a very good rapport, and although he, aware of my engagements in North America, courteously assured me that I could settle my military situation without giving up those contracts, I decided on the course that would take me back to Italy.

Although I actually was not particularly keen on military fanaticism, I did not heed his words, feeling that if I did any differently, I would be failing to fulfill a sacred duty and would be betraying all the men in my unit who were less privileged than I. Though the ship navigated under the constant threat of

German submarines, I arrived in Barcelona after a beautiful crossing, interrupted only by a stop of a day or two in Rio de Janeiro. Since I had about one month of time to present myself to the recruiting office in Rome, I continued by train to Nice with the intention of spending that month on the Côte d'Azur.

It was there, while strolling one day on the Promenade des Anglais, I met a dear acquaintance of mine, *Mademoiselle* Carmen Tiranty, to whom I had been presented in Paris by Baroness Stern. Besides being a superb musician and singer, Tiranty was one of the brightest and most cultured women of French society, and rich and generous as well. She had a magnificent villa near Nice, Villa Schifanoia, and had turned it into a military hospital during the war. In the beautiful halls of her home many wounded were sheltered, and she was the most beloved benefactor and nurse. She asked me therefore to bring some relief to her wounded with my voice, singing something for them.

It goes without saying that I accepted with all my heart. After a short time I was at Villa Schifanoia where, accompanied on piano by Tiranty herself, I sang several arias amidst the enthusiasm of all those suffering souls. When I was taking leave, she expressed much gratitude and I promised that I would always be at her disposal for similar events. It was thus that she, along with General Lama, head of the French Red Cross, organized a benefit concert using my name at the Eldorado theater which raised a considerable amount of funds.

Later she asked me to sing in the villa of noble King Alberto of Belgium[288] which had also been changed into a hospital and where five hundred of his troops, injured by poison gases, were being tended to. A grisly spectacle: young men ruined forever— some poisoned, some wounded, some blinded or with other injuries. I had not conceived that war could cause, besides death, such agony, such horrors. I spent my month of waiting singing in almost all the military hospitals, and I witnessed events so painful that they would be enough to open the hardest and most invulnerable heart to compassion.

When the time came to fulfill my duty, I left for Rome and

presented myself at the recruiting office. From there I was sent to barracks in Prati where I underwent the medical examination. And *voilà*, the much-applauded singer changed into an anonymous soldier in a rough gray-green uniform, with two sturdy boots of hard leather on his feet, and on his head a large, long-visored cap that came down to his ears. When I was in full uniform, I looked like a raw recruit straight out of Cuttica's comedy skits.[289]

Placed in a row along with hundreds of other soldiers with a rucksack on my back and other equipment of new conscripts, they made us cross Rome and we were housed in the Ferdinando di Savoia barracks next to San Lorenzo. I remained in the two-hundred seventh battalion M.T. for some time. We would wander around the large courtyard of the barracks for hours and hours, waiting for mess and the evening outing. I would then run home to embrace my family; my children, seeing their father in such awkward attire, looked at me as if caught in a daydream. I lingered there during all my free time; I would then return to the barracks, always hoping to reach a better destination some day or another, that is, a less monotonous one.

The military exercises began. We would march for great lengths of time up and down the courtyard under the command of a sergeant major who shouted with a thundering voice and the authority of Napoleon. When things were limited to "Platoon forward, march" things went smoothly enough, but "About face" produced such a bustle that it became impossible to make any sense of the situation: some turned to their left, others to their right, some stayed back to tie the straps that had become undone, others ended up rolling around on the ground: all were men from older units, most of them already so overweight and weak that they seemed fifty years old.

The day came when the 207th Battalion received the order to depart immediately—I barely had the time to give a last embrace to my dear ones—for Umbria. We traveled—as, unfortunately, is often done in these cases—in cattle cars. At the Termini station, from whence we departed, wives and numerous children ran to see off those departing, and created unbe-

lievable chaos, crying as if Umbria were Pasubio or Carso.[290]
After three hours we reached Terni. They had us get off and
march for several kilometers. We were headed for Cesi,[291] a
small mountain village where, as soon as we arrived, we were
divided into groups and sheltered, for better or for worse, everywhere: some in the peasants' homes, some in the stables,
others in cellars. Some even in...church. Precisely where I, along
with another fifty soldiers, found myself. The church was naturally completely empty. The only sacred emblem left there was,
up high in the choir, a large cross of rough wood. We made
ourselves comfortable on abundant but humid straw in rows
along the two sides of the church.

I lay down exhausted on my bedding. I found myself between two men who were very different from me in their character, state of mind, and education, and when speaking with
them I experienced a strange sense of dissatisfaction. I was
convinced or, rather, reconvinced that until man has reached a
certain level of intellectual and moral equality, brotherhood
and happiness will remain a utopian ideal, and will perhaps
remain a utopian ideal forever.

To my right slept Count Boni of Siena, a refined reveller
who, after pursuing a very excessive and wasteful lifestyle,
had found his balance in a happy marriage. He did not possess the powers of adaptation to tolerate the discomforts of
military life. He had, as he said with tears in his eyes, too
much of an aristocratic nature to be able to live in the midst of
this human stench; and, with a voice full of lament, he exclaimed: "*Appena vidi il sol, che ne fui privo!*" ("The moment
I saw the sun, I was deprived of it!")[292]

I found out then that he had married a beautiful and
wealthy American a few months earlier and had had to leave
her right in the middle of their honeymoon. He confessed to
me that after having known so many women in his illustrious
life, he had fallen deeply in love with her and truly missed her.
This confiding bothered my neighbor on the left who, unable
to fall asleep, snored as loudly and as often as he could in
retaliation, in the manner of the *trombetta di Barbariccia*.[293]
Then, in a mocking voice, he said in his Roman dialect: "Sir

Count, if only you could sleep, dogs be damned!" I had my neighbor note that his obnoxious music was more bothersome than the other's conversation. And he too told me his story.

His name was Remo Prosdocimi. He was a carter and lived in Trastevere. He had left his fiancée pregnant without having been able to marry her, and he feared that her father, who had a violent character, might kill her if he discovered his daughter's dishonor.

The third of our group was a fanatical admirer of Gabriele d'Annunzio who, in the middle of the night, by what strange exaltation I do not know, perhaps to rout the extreme cold in the church, began to recite one of his poems loudly. At that point a rebellion broke out against that possessed man who was preventing everyone from sleeping. They hurled several insults at him and his forebears, such as "your forefathers be damned!" Boots flew by; and, if one of them had hit its target, it would undoubtedly have cut off the lyrics in his mouth, if not the lyricism in his heart. He soon became silent again, and then Boni told me in a low voice: "How repulsive vulgarity is! Here we are right in the middle of it. I prefer madmen and delinquents."

I urged him to adapt to this new life. I encouraged him, making him understand that, although I had not been born an aristocrat as he had, I nonetheless had become accustomed in my art to living in the guise of a prince, king, emperor, or also of a poor man, and that I had left a life of comfort, lodged in the best hotels with every luxury and refined consideration. I explained to him that I had come back to Italy to fulfill my duty although I could have remained in America if I had wished. But, despite living in this den among those people, mostly commoners, I felt perfectly calm; I even felt a sort of delight. I had agreed to come and be a soldier and live among men who were not yet or at least not completely refined by art or tainted by artifice and also to experience what I had not been able to experience at twenty years of age. All that I saw and observed almost rejuvenated me and provided me the opportunity to know my fellow man more closely and to enrich my spirit, analyzing what good and bad, what beauty and ugliness existed in them. Boni readied himself for sleep with these words: "Dear Titta, I do not share your philosophy..."

After the first night I changed quarters, moving from the church to a modest peasant home. A friend of mine whom I had not seen for many years came to live there with me: Adolfo Pineschi, an agreeable fellow. Agreeable to a fault, actually, but also intelligent, kind, and honest. Count Boni accompanied me to the same house, and two contributors to the *Giornale d'Italia* joined us as well: Bazzani and Sgabelloni, distinguished and friendly men.

One morning we were visited by several officers of the thirty-third artillery regiment of Terni. They arrived in the village on horseback to conduct an inspection, and the whole regiment was assembled. Suddenly my name was called by one of them. Nearing them I recognized my superior as Vincenzo Tanlongo. A man of swift intelligence, of exemplary compassion and generosity, whom I had met—mountains are stationary, but men keep wandering—before the war, in Boston, where he had started his singing career with a very beautiful tenor voice.[294] He was now carrying out his duties as adjutant, loved and esteemed by all from the colonel to the soldier of most modest means.

A FEW DAYS LATER he had me transferred to his regiment,[295] keeping me under his direct protection. Many of my fellow soldiers were sent to dig trenches in the Edolo mountains.[296] I was assigned to anti-aircraft defense in Terni's aviation field, as a so-called machine-gunner of the Queen. My friendship with Tanlongo brought me some privileges, such as that of sleeping outside the barracks. He would hasten to assure me that he was not, in so doing, breaching military regulations. These favors, according to him, were well-deserved. He had recently married and would sometimes invite me to his home where we played music, nostalgically recalling theater life. Also participating in our dinners and accompanying us on piano was Angelo Caccialupi, a Roman who had also been given the rank of corporal major in the same regiment. Caccialupi and I became inseparable companions during those long winter months spent in Terni. A talented musician and pianist, a cultured man with a farcical spirit, he would with his pleasantries and witticisms instill in the group that kind of good humor that cheers up and distracts even those most reluctant to be happy.

But do not think that my military life did not consist of anything military other than its name. There was never a lack either around me or within me of the opportunity or the will or the impulse to *do*: in the most energetic sense of the word. Although I was thought to be part of an older unit, that period took me back to when I was twenty years old. Full of, if not spilling over with, strength and courage and daring; no task seemed unworthy to me and no risk frightened me. There were days when, sent on this or that mission, I would go through the mountains on horseback with an endurance and courage that I believe was a little greater than that when, in my rehearsals as a singer, I worked to master the difficulties of a particular musical score. I became a good driver, and I remember having delivered large trucks full of military equipment from Terni to Foligno several times, having ridden on motorcycle with the adjutant for inspections, having repeatedly flown over the aviation field with Debolini, the Tuscan lieutenant, a distinguished veteran and, in spite of his name (*debole* meaning weak), an excellent aviator, having accompanied the famous ace Salomone[297] up in the sky, who amused himself by performing—and thus having me perform—acrobatics that were, as I saw, slightly more arduous and audacious than those notes with which I had amazed the audience from the stages of the world in *Barbiere* and *Hamlet*. The circumstances of war disbanded the group. I do not clearly remember the destination of the others; not even of dear Caccialupi. Vincenzo Tanlongo was sent to the front where he heroically fulfilled his duties until the end of the war.

With him gone, I lost all my privileges, and I was immediately put, with the rank of corporal, in command of a anti-aircraft machine-gunner unit which protected the blast furnaces, where the material necessary for the defense of the country was feverishly being smelted. With machine-guns pointed at the sky, I was always on the alert for enemy planes, wishing for the opportunity to perform some act of valor, or at least be useful, but while I remained in command, no enemy plane neared the furnaces. I slept along with six men in an old *malga* hut on the mountain of Campomicciolo. I was rarely given leave to go into town.

Others in my place as an unavoidably inactive machinegun sentry would have gotten sick with boredom, or perhaps turned into uncivilized brutes. Not I. In the midst of the gunners I too felt like a boy, all the more from my contact with those—and there were a few—who were about twenty years younger than I. I avoided the stuffed-shirt distancing sulk of one who fears losing, otherwise, his authority; rather, I preferred to be with my men as much as possible and to live the same life. We would get up at dawn and put the machine-guns in order; and then away we went to wash our naked torsos as I had done before in Velletri with my boiler-room companion Pilade Bellatalla, in the nearby creek, no matter the season. Sometimes—and not too seldom—I felt the impulse to sing and my voice of bronze passed over the mountains, and roosters from all parts of green Umbria responded as if with an echo: *chicchirichiii.*

During the day, though I was not unaware of the enormous tragedy that was throwing Italy and the world into disarray, or rather because of that, I would try to raise my spirits and those of my soldiers by reading good books or telling jokes, so that the time for mess would arrive almost unexpectedly. Some evenings I would go with a few of them to a farmhouse not too far off where those good peasants would be waiting for us and would play my records on a gramophone. Entertaining us was a celebration for them. On Sundays and other holidays, those dear girls, on their way back from church, would come to our hut with wildflowers and would offer them to us with the courtesy of true ladies.

How I miss those distant days of Campomicciolo! And you young friends Manzotti and Scarsellini, Prosciutto from Naples, Perego from Milan, Fanfulla from Piedmont, and Paoli from Cagliari! A strange, absurd irony to have to realize that one of the few relatively happy times of my life was spent during the most tragic years in modern history.

I would be lying, however, if I said that, despite the joyful contrast of my life in Terni, a violent longing for the theater did not take hold of me at times.

And suddenly it was my good fortune to be officially requested by the management of the Opéra of Paris, through the Minister of War, to sing in a benefit performance for the French Red Cross. I thus found myself transformed for a few hours from machine-gunner to the Prince of Denmark. After the show, I put on my dress uniform, on which for the occasion I thought it appropriate to pin my medals. I went back onstage to sing several patriotic anthems in French and Italian. The theater was packed. A mighty applause broke out: *Vive la France! Vive l'Italie!* I was elated, I felt truly proud, despite not having performed any act of valor, of being Italian and of taking my personal contribution abroad.

When the enthusiasm for the anthems had abated, I was invited to sing a few songs. I had a piano brought onstage, and I intoned two arias by Mario Costa.[298] The brilliant author of *Histoire de Pierrot* was in the theater. I had noticed him in a front-row seat. He was not expecting such a surprise. When I finished singing his melodies in the midst of general acclamation, I pointed him out to the audience with these words: "Ladies and gentlemen of the audience, this applause does not belong to me, but to Mario Costa, who created the beautiful melodies you have just applauded." The audience paid tribute to him with such an ovation that it visibly moved the dear maestro's sensitive soul. When he came to my dressing room to thank me for the happiness I had given him, he said he had cried with joy at seeing his name united with mine in celebration of Franco-Italian art.

Two days later I appeared at the Opéra Comique in a benefit and sang in Leoncavallo's *Pagliacci*. The two evenings raised a total of two hundred seventy thousand lire. The following day I left for Campomicciolo, where the six gunners were awaiting me with the deepest longing.

I stayed in Campomicciolo for some time, then I fell ill and spent one week in the military hospital. The doctors prescribed a change of climate. I was transferred to the command post of the Florentine anti-aircraft defense. My departure from Campomicciolo left—why hide it?—a deep void among my comrades-at-arms. In those long months I had accustomed them to a lifestyle that was much different from a military one. Every fortnight I had delivered to our *malga* cases of Neopolitan pasta, good wine from Grottaferrata, and parmesan cheese from Rome. Their daily ration included a generous bowl of spaghetti and a glass of undiluted wine. And before leaving them to go sing in France, I arranged that during my absence they would be able to enjoy the rations to which I had accustomed them. The gratitude of those six men was such that upon my departure they cried as if they were losing a beloved brother. In this manner I would try, and also in more efficient ways, especially financially, no matter where I was, whether at the Ferdinando di Savoia barracks in Rome, the 207th Battalion in Cesi, or the 33rd Artillery Depot in Terni, I would try, as I said, to lift up the spirits of the many family men who were my contemporaries and fellow soldiers, as well as the spirits of loved ones left behind, for the most part without any resources.

In so doing it seemed to me that to a certain extent I was paying back my debt to nature and fortune, which, compared to those men, had bestowed so many gifts and so many favors on me. But I must say that, however much I gave, I got back ten times as much in gratefulness and love from my so simple and coarse yet kind comrades-in-arms whose burden during those times I had the fortune of lightening. This left me with the satisfaction of a clear conscience, which never lets one down and means more than any reward. In Florence... But I am unable to leave behind my memories of Terni without relating three more episodes—and I think it is worth it—each one more singular than the other.

I have mentioned the comic characters of Cuttica to give an idea of the grotesque spectacle produced by those few drafted men from my unit and category. One day I actually did, or rather attempted to, imitate one of those characters and I was, as you will hear, quite successful. I preface this by saying that, since the Minister of War had authorized simple soldiers to wear non-military medals on their uniforms, I enjoyed decorating myself and I adorned my breast with a quantity of ribbons of all colors; among them stood out the ribbon of the High Military Order of Spain, equal to the rank of colonel, with which the Duke of Tovar, as the reader will remember, had decorated me on behalf of King Alfonso.

Now one morning, when I was strolling in the barracks courtyard, an inspection unit of superior officials appeared in order to recruit artillery batteries to send to the front. The person who struck me the most out of those characters was the figure of a lieutenant general with a large curly moustache that reminded me of Umberto. Among the numerous decorations that he wore on his breast was the very same High Military Order of Spain which I had been given. As I passed him I naturally gave him a very respectful salute. He rested his gaze on my breast with a certain amazement, mostly because of the ribbon that stood out among the others in competition with his. He called me back. I, having pulled my cap down to my ears to change my physiognomy, had instantly taken on the appearance of an idiot, not unlike the characters brought to the stage by the previously mentioned Cuttica. I planted myself in front of him, loudly tapping my right heel against the left one just as required by strict disciplinary rule, and, having raised my right hand to my visor, remained stock-still at attention, or, in the jargon which all journalists like to use today, stiff as a corpse, looking like a man of clay.

The general, frowning, asked me: "What is your name?" Inverting my battle name and switching my first and last names in order better to conceal my identity, I answered: "Ruffo Cafiero Titta." He then asked me why I had been decorated with so many honors. Fixing my gaze upwards over his head, I replied simply: "*Mah...*" In response to that monosyllable and that attitude, the general, suspecting that he was dealing with a madman or a half-wit, asked me what feat I had accomplished in Spain to deserve the same honor as he. Keeping the same pose but moving my gaze from the sky to the ground, down on my boots, I told him that once, when I was invited over for tea at the royal palace of Spain, I had played the guitar, and as a reward...

He did not let me finish. Completely convinced that he was dealing with an idiot, he called the adjutant major and asked him in an agitated voice: "But why is that corporal wearing such a quantity of honors for which he cannot offer any plausible justification?" The adjutant major, who had recognized me even in that disguise, quickly responded: "General, he is the famous artist Titta Ruffo." The general repeated: "Titta Ruffo? Impossible!" And turning to me: "Are you really the famous singer Titta Ruffo?" "Yes, sir," I replied. "I am truly disappointed," added the general. "There must be some kind of mistake."

At that I immediately abandoned my Cuttica-like role and, having taken off my cap, I smiled, showing my true self. The good general understood that I had wanted to play a trick, and, shaking my hand, exclaimed: "Ah, these artists can act their parts so well in comedy and can transform themselves so adeptly... Didn't I take him for an idiot?" We then launched into a friendly conversation in which I specified when and how I came to be decorated with the High Military Order of Spain and he told me that he had admired and applauded me many times in *Barbiere di Siviglia*, in *Zazà*, and in *Hamlet*, and that he was happy to have made my personal acquaintance. In this theatrical manner I more or less facetiously managed to console myself for not being able to wear military decorations on my breast which were more suitable for a soldier.

While I still was part of the 33rd Artillery Regiment of the anti-aircraft defense of the blast furnaces, I was called one morning to the adjutant Vincenzo Tanlongo, who asked me if I would accept an assignment to take a deserter, a certain Pasquale de Carolis, who was in the military prison of Terni, to Bologna. He informed me that if I accepted I would be taking on a large responsibility as we were dealing with a very dangerous man whom it would therefore be prudent to handcuff. I accepted the assignment, convinced that with good manners I would be able to tame him and bring him to his destination without having to handcuff him.

When I had received the travel documents—third class naturally—I went to meet and inform this man. Having entered the prison I called out in a loud voice: "Pasquale de Carolis." Instead of answering immediately (as he was supposed to) with "Present!" he let a few seconds pass, and then said with much coolness and nonchalance in Neapolitan dialect: "That's me." He was a young man about twenty-five years old, of average build, with a shadow of a beard and thick black hair which was all tousled. His eyes were pitch-black, his pupils quite dilated, which accentuated the whites of his eyes and gave him the look of someone hallucinating. But his shabby and dirty clothes, along with that disheveled hair, made me think more of an outlaw.

I informed him that I was to take him to Bologna to his regiment's prison and that we would leave within the hour. He looked at me at length from head to toe, insolently, resting his gaze on my simple rank of corporal, and then exclaimed arrogantly, "Mr. Corporal! Be a good boy and take me to Bologna." I did not allow myself to be intimidated either by that attitude or by that tone, and I answered simply: "We'll see about that!" And I left to prepare for the trip.

One hour later I was at the prison gate in complete regulation battle gear, that is with my saber on my left side, a large loaded pistol on my belt, a green-gray winter coat which came down to below the knee, and the strap of my cap tucked under my chin. A pair of handcuffs from the prison headquarters was given to me. Instead of putting them on De Carolis—the thought of doing so repulsed me—I threw them in my pocket. I do not hide the fact that the damned soul instilled a certain anxiety in me. But I tried to conceal it, and, having taken him by the arm, we headed towards the station. On the way I reprimanded him, not harshly but seriously, for his lack of respect at our first encounter and I warned him that, if he ever got the urge to escape, I would have six ways—and I showed him the six-shooter on my belt—of ridding him of that urge, and if he was well-behaved, I would treat him like a brother, not like a prisoner. And, in order to prove my words I said,

"See," taking out the handcuffs, "I could have put these on you, but instead I spared you them."

He listened to this speech with his head low and, at the end, with the same insolent and sarcastic tone as before, replied: "Hey, Corporal! How good you speak! You remind me of a lawyer."

Meanwhile we had reached the train station. We boarded the train from Ancona. We had to get off at Falconara and wait there three hours until the troop-train came to take us to Bologna. During the trip from Terni to Falconara I was unable to get a word out of De Carolis. He seemed like a deaf-mute. Perhaps he was planning some kind of trick. At one point, near the station, he asked me for permission to go to the lavatory. Despite his reassurance that it would not be necessary, I made it my duty to be present while he tended to his business, which, among other things, threatened to last forever. I asked him to cut it short and get moving.

When we reached Falconara late that evening, we entered the station restaurant. I promised a large tip to the cook if he would prepare a good dinner for two. My companion—I explained in a hushed voice—was a deserter who might be sentenced to death by firing squad, and I wanted to treat him in the best possible way. After about an hour, dinner was ready. The first course that was placed in front of us was a large dish of lasagna with tomato sauce and abundant parmesan; it was absolutely exquisite. I wanted to serve the prisoner myself. He tore into his food like a starved wolf and was not satisfied with just one bowlful. The second course which came to the table was roast chicken with potatoes and white Romaine lettuce. Then followed cheese and fruit, and, as a finishing touch to the meal, coffee with Tre Stelle brand cognac. A Lucullan dinner which—is it necessary I point it out?—was washed down with a flask of lively Chianti which I poured with my own hands as often as I could into the wretch's glass.

By now the mood and face of my deaf-mute were changed as if from day to night. But he still remained, if not deaf, mute. I asked him if he was content, if he had enjoyed his meal. He was silent at the more general question; he was silent at the specific question. Only when I asked him if he wanted a smoke did he smile, barely, with the look of someone who wants to accept, and answer with a subdued "yes." I purchased cigars and gave them to him, and after smoking half of one, he fell asleep with his elbows on the table.

There were still two hours before our departure. I had him laid out on a couch in the waiting room, and sat down next to him. I woke him when the next train came. He got up with a start and seemed a different man. He thanked me for dinner, saying that he had never eaten so well in his entire life and that these had been the most peaceful and happy hours he had spent since he had been in the army. He did not feel capable of doing me harm or of saying anything offensive, and he would go with me docilely, wishing the trip would never end.

I then began to speak good-naturedly to him. I made him understand that this duty of taking him to prison was not a pleasant one for me. I considered him a man of flesh and blood like me, and his status as a deserter made me more sorrowful than scornful. When I paid the check, the cook offered us a pleasant punch with a generous shot of rum. That was the *coup de grâce*. Totally dazed, the poor man would not stop thanking me for my generosity.

I left him alone for a few minutes in order to check on our train. The station was almost dark. The few electric bulbs were tinted blue to escape detection by enemy planes. The prisoner, seeing that I had not come back—although I never stopped keeping an eye on him—came out from under the shelter in search of me, crying "Hey, Corporal, I'm here, don't run away, don't leave me." He was the one who was looking for me, as if I were the prisoner! I returned to him and helped him—he was stumbling, half drunk—board the train. Despite the bitter cold, he fell back to sleep immediately, and I spent the night, almost until dawn, with his head on my shoulder. Finally he awakened and exclaimed: "I have always wanted to end my life with a happy memory, especially after going through two years of horrible suffering in the trenches." We traveled the entire day and in the various stations and stops I did not miss the opportunity to offer him a good breakfast and a good lunch.

By the time we arrived in Bologna, to make a long story short, De Carolis had already told me his whole life story and without hesitation bared his whole soul to me. After he had spent about two years in the trenches, his mother fell ill and he requested and was granted permission to go back and see her in Pompeii, his native town. The poor woman died two days later, leaving to her only son, Pasquale, her small property: a little house with a small garden and four pigs already fattened and ready for slaughter, a total value of about ten thousand lire. In order to protect his modest fortune from the greed of his relatives, he stayed on leave for several days beyond the allowed time and thus became a deserter. Those same relatives, with the intention of claiming the pigs, which were perhaps the most valuable portion of the inheritance, accused him and reported him to the *carabinieri*. He was then arrested and taken to jail in Perugia. During the trip he fled, not to avoid his duty as a soldier but to avenge the inhuman and unjust act perpetrated against him by his relatives, which he considered a desecration of his mother's memory. After being recaptured and brought back to prison, he again managed to escape.

He wandered for several days with the intention of avoiding police surveillance and reaching Pompeii, but he fell into the hands of the *carabinieri* in the Umbrian mountains and was given over to the 33rd depot in Terni. This was the first time since he had been declared a deserter, he confessed, that he had been treated with a little kindness; he began to cry. As the story unfolded I saw emerge from beneath the insolent mask of the deserter the honest face of a Southern peasant who was perhaps volcanically impulsive, but a good man after all, exasperated by the adversity of fortune and poisoned by human maliciousness and indifference.

I tried to calm him and help him forget the bad treatment he had received from his relatives who—he should be sure of it—would be punished, if not under the law, which results from man's imperfect judgment, then under God's infallible will. I advised him that, as soon as we arrived in Bologna, he should send to the military command a letter, which I would compose for him, faithfully telling his story and the true motive of his desertion and asking to be sent back to the front for his own honor as a soldier, since he did not feel in his conscience that he deserved such an infamous label. He took my advice and sent the letter, excited though still resigned.

We arrived in Bologna at four o'clock in the morning. I handed him over, according to orders, to the prison of the 35th Artillery. I did not have the heart to leave him looking shabbily. Since it was almost Christmas, I left him my holiday bonus so that he could drink a glass of wine to our health but not spend the rest except in case of dire need. I promised him finally that I would write him and that I would keep myself informed of his case from afar. I do not remember ever in my life having encountered a more sensitive and grateful soul than Pasquale de Carolis. By now he would have thrown himself into fire for me. When we said goodbye he threw his arms around me, crying like a child, leaving me with these last tearful words: "Corporal, my brother, may God bless you for what you've done for me and forgive me if I offended you when we met!"

The reader can well imagine what range of emotions afflicted my soul as I made my way back to the station. It was intensely cold and a thin layer of snow covered the city. Sadness overcame me. But, when I reached the station and was walking under the shelter waiting for the train, I had a surprise which managed to lift my spirits. I made out, standing in front of the restaurant, an artillery captain whose face looked familiar. I finally recognized him as Ignazio Florio, the distinguished Sicilian gentleman whom the whole world knows for his fame and, having seen him, no one has forgotten. I approached him with my hand raised in a military salute. He recognized me immediately, remembered those wonderful days in Palermo and, without any sort of formal ceremony, Captain Florio embraced Corporal Titta Ruffo like an old friend.

If Pasquale de Carolis would have willingly thrown himself into fire out of love of me, there was one man, a Sicilian, a certain Nicosia da Randazzo, who was planning, instead, to kill me with the same motivation. I told the strange story to a friend years ago; Virgilio Brocchi[299] heard it from my friend and published it in his book, *Gioia di raccontare*. Given that the famous novelist added little more than the ornament of his style, all I have to do is reproduce his narration, except for some small modifications—a narration which adeptly frames the episode in the setting of my Umbrian life as a draftee which I sketched out a few pages back.

Hindrance is not the right word; neither is nuisance. But that brown-haired soldier, burnt like lava, instilled in me a disturbing curiosity that was closer to uneasiness than to diffidence. Although we were safe, or mostly safe, none of us had any reason to be especially happy: we were all men forty years old or almost, and each of us had a family at home which we were unsure we would see again. Yes, we were safe for now, or so it seemed: on guard in an anti-aircraft battery without yet having had the occasion to fire a single round.

Still, in that idleness it became even easier to get stuck in the contemplation of one's own troubles. I was no less than a corporal, and for that reason it was my duty to keep my six men happy, and, with the help of guitar-playing, jokes, *tagliatelle*, flasks of wine, and excellent advice, assisted by a bank check or two to be sent home to the family, I often succeeded. This duty was costing me an arm and a leg and I had to write home for money so often that my wife became convinced that I was spending all those thousands of lire gambling. None of my men even suspected that I was anything more or different than Corporal Titta: a good-humored comrade whom everyone addressed with the informal *tu* when the sergeant was not there, and around whom the most exuberant ones now and then put their arm to slowly direct him toward the *osteria*.

But that other man, the Sicilian soldier from Randazzo, stood apart from the rest, silent, frowning, harboring who knows what kind of ill will, and I was unable to soothe him or make him smile or even make him cry by speaking to him of his family. He watched me with a dark look much like the one I have sometimes seen Giovanni Grasso give his beloved onstage, as if he were about to plunge a knife into her chest. I confess that at certain times it made me shudder and ask myself if I had not unknowingly committed one of those offenses that a Sicilian will not forgive for all eternity.

One day, precisely in order to get out of this situation, I cheerfully went up to him and took him by the arm, saying, "Come on, Nicosia, let's go lighten our hearts with a glass of wine. We'll drink to your children's health." I have never seen a smile break out so rapidly to transfigure a face, and immediately disappear as if that dark and rigid face had turned to lava. He followed me but kept his distance, as if he were scared or repulsed by the idea of touching me. "Nicosia," I said, upset, "you know me well!" "Yes, General." "General?" "Your excellency, yes! These idiots don't know a thing, and should be pitied. But I, I...Corporal, you? For who has the right to be a general if not you, your excellency? My heart aches with sadness, your excellency. I've heard you sing *Cristoforo Colombo* and *Boris* in Buenos Aires, and one time I walked from Randazzo to Palermo to hear you sing *Rigoletto*. Those are your roles: king or admiral or at least a general. Corporal!" he huffed with a disgusted expression of protest. "And tomorrow, if they send us to the trenches, the Germans will shoot at your excellency, just as they will shoot at me. Oh no!" he snarled threateningly, "I would kill you, your excellency, before letting the Germans shoot you!" I tried to laugh, but I was aghast; I asked: "But what have I done to offend you? Why would you wish to kill me?" He answered me, transfigured: "For love, your excellency!"

COMING FINALLY TO FLORENCE, which marked the last stage of my military life, I was put to work, after being assigned to the protection of the David in Piazzale Michelangelo for two months, at a desk job in one of the headquarters offices in via Lamarmora under the supervision of Major Marquis d'Adda. I remained there until the end of the war and was treated by him with utmost courtesy. I have kept a very fond memory of that time.

But the two weeks that I stood guard over the David remains etched in my mind like the memory of some supernatural dream. On those evenings with beautiful sunsets, from that height where one dominates the City of Flowers, I would lean on the parapet of the vast terrace surrounded by all kinds of figures of artists, martyrs, heroes, poets, merchants crowded around me, figures She created and donated for the joy, the glory, and the imagination of the world. When night began to fall, little by little the city would light up, and the reflection of the lights would come up to the top of those superb monuments and Giotto's belltower, Brunelleschi's dome, the tower of Palazzo Vecchio would rise up then in their most spellbinding beauty. If one adds to this enchantment the last tolls of the bells, one does not have to be a pilgrim on either land or sea to feel oneself touched by love and moved to tears. Divine Florence! In front of such majesty and such enchantment, on that deserted *piazzale*, at that place and in that hour, I too shed tears and I confess it without shame.

1

2

3

1. *(previous page)* Titta Ruffo
at age 12, when he worked in
his father's shop.

2. Amabile Sequenza,
Ruffo's mother.

3. Oreste Titta, Ruffo's father.

4. Father Oreste at work in
his shop.

5

6

5. The house in Pisa (via Volturno 31) where Titta Ruffo was born on June 9, 1877. A commemorative plaque was affixed to the façade in 1954.

Works in wrought iron produced in Titta Ruffo's shop:

6. Wreath offered by the Italian government to the French Republic in honor of President Sadi Carnot; placed on his tomb in the Pantheon (Paris).

7. Barred gate of the Caetani Palace in Rome.

7

8. Ruffo at age 16 with his brother (on the right).

9. Ettore, Ruffo's brother.

10. With his sister Velia.

8

9

10

11

12

13

14

11. Brother-in-law Giacomo Matteotti (1912).

12. Sister Velia at the time of her engagement to Matteotti (1913).

13. Titta Ruffo's wife, Lea Fontana.

14. Giacomo Matteotti between Lea *(r.)* and Velia *(l.)*, Ruffo's wife and sister (Abetone, 1912).

15

15, 16. Adelina Fanton
(Benedetta).

16

17

17. Young Titta Ruffo trying out various expressions
for the camera, *before* his stage career.

18

19

18. At 21.

19. The 22-year-old Titta
Ruffo in *La Risurrezione di
Lazzaro*, by Perosi, in Catania.
This is Ruffo's first known
photograph as a professional
singer.

20. At 26.

21. *(opposite)* Titta Ruffo as
Cascart in Leoncavallo's *Zazà*.
Milan, 1904.

20

21

22

22. In Rubinstein's *Demon*.

23, 24, 25. Three fairly early
publicity photos.

23

24

25

26

26. In the title role of Franchetti's
Cristoforo Colombo in Buenos Aires
[1909?].

27. As Jack Rance in *La fanciulla del
West*. Paris, 1911.

27

28

28. Titta Ruffo as Figaro and Dimitri
Smirnov as Count Almaviva in *Il barbiere di
Siviglia*, Paris, 1912.

29. Titta Ruffo and Antonina Nezhdanova
in *Rigoletto*. Paris, 1912.

30. As Figaro in *Il barbiere di Siviglia*, Paris,
1912.

29

30

31

31, 33. Titta Ruffo as Rigoletto.
Chicago, 1912.

32. As Rodrigo in *Don Carlo*,
1912.

32

33

34

34. As Escamillo in
Carmen.

35. Escamillo in
Carmen (1915).

35

36

36. As Mephisto in Gounod's *Faust*. Budapest, 1913.

37. As Barnaba in *La Gioconda*. Havana, 1915.

37

38

38. In the title role of Hamlet.

39. Titta Ruffo as *Boris Godunov*.
Buenos Aires, 1916.

40. As Hamlet in 1916.

39

40

41

41. Hipólito Lazaro, Enrico Caruso and Titta
Ruffo after a performance of *Cavalleria Rusticana*
and *Pagliacci* in Montevideo on August 16, 1915.
Lazaro sang Turiddu in *Cavalleria*.

42. Titta Ruffo, soldier. World War I, 1916.

42

43

43, 44. As Tonio in *Pagliacci*.
Chicago, 1919.

45. In the title role of Leoncavallo's
Edipo Re. Chicago, 1920.

44

45

46

46. Titta Ruffo as Iago in
Otello. The photograph is
inscribed to the soprano
Rosetta Pampanini.

47. As Neri Chiaramantesi in
Giordano's *Cena delle Beffe*.

47

48

48. In Chicago, 1919.

49. In 1921.

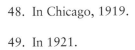

49

50. Titta Ruffo and Mattia Battistini.

51. Titta Ruffo (third from right) in the
company of baritone Carlo Galeffi (third
from left) and tenor Galliano Masini
(second from right).

52. Titta Ruffo portrait, Caracas.

51

52

53

54

53, 54. Ruffo mugging for
the camera.

55. At the beach. (Rimini?)

55

56

56. Participating in NBC's opening four-hour radio program of stars of opera, stage and concert hall, broadcast from the Waldorf-Astoria in New York.

57

57. Titta Ruffo and Fedor Chaliapin strolling through the streets of Milan during the basso's guest appearance in *Boris Godunov* at La Scala (three performances) in February, 1931.

58. Ruffo photographed two weeks before he died.

59. Victor Maurel.

58

59

60

60. Francisco Vignas (Viñas),
Titta Ruffo's first great co-star and
one of his greatest admirers.

61. Enrico Caruso. Inscribed
"To dear Titta Ruffo as a souvenir
of the memorable evening of
Rigoletto in Vienna on 6/10/06."
[October 6, 1906]

62. Titta Ruffo and Enrico Caruso,
courtesy of the Metropolitan Opera
Association.

61

CARUSO AND RUFFO

63. Fedor Chaliapin in the title role of Boito's *Mefistofele*. Inscribed to Titta Ruffo in Monte Carlo on March 8, 1911.

64. Indian Chief Fred Big Top, admirer of Titta Ruffo, honoring him with an inscribed photo. Colorado, April 23, 1914.

65. A sample of Titta Ruffo's handwriting.

To My brother Titta Ruffo
Chief Fred Big Top
April 23
1914

64

Lea cara — sono giunto a Parigi in perfet-
ta salute, la vita senza di te è un po
tristo. Ti prego di mandarmi dei libri
coi avrò da passare il mio tempo in
cose utili.

Titta Ruffo

65

66

66. Program page from the Teatro Colón,
Buenos Aires. Thomas's *Hamlet* with Titta
Ruffo and Graziella Pareto. August 7, 1910.

TEATRO COLON Temporada Oficial de 1909

Adm. Sdad. Teatral Italo-Argentina —— Dirección: C. CIACCHI

GRAN COMPAÑIA —— LIRICA ITALIANA

Maestro Concertador y Director de Orquesta

Com. Luigi Mancinelli

Domingo 8 Agosto

61 Función de la temporada

23ª. DE ABONO DEL SEGUNDO TURNO

La ópera en cuatro actos del maestro G. VERDI

RIGOLETTO

REPARTO

Il Duca di Mantova...... A. BONCI.	Il Conte di Monterone.. A. VETTORI,
Rigoletto, *suo buffone di*	Marullo, *cavaliere*......... L. BALDASSARE
Corte..................... TITTA RUFFO.	Borsa, *cortigiana*........... G. BONFANTI
Gilda, *di lui figlia.* ...... G. PARETO.	Il Conte di Ceprano .... L. GASPERINI
Sparafucile, *bravo*........ G. MANSUETO.	La Contessa, *sua sposa*..., M. ALEMANNI.
Maddalena, *sua sorella*.... E. LUCCI.	Usciere di corte.......... N. N.
Giovanna, *custode di Gilda*. M. MANFREDI.	Paggio della Duchessa.. N. N.

Cavalieri, Dame, Pagge, Alabardieri

Compañía Nacional de Calefacción

TUCUMAN, 768.— BUENOS AIRES

instalación de calefacción y ventilación del Teatro COLON es hecha por esta Compañía

67

67. Program page from the Teatro Colón, Buenos Aires. *Rigoletto* with Titta Ruffo, Alessandro Bonci and Graziella Pareto. August 8, 1909.

68. *(next page)* Titta Ruffo in 1912.

68

CHAPTER 26

From Mexico to New York

WHEN THE WAR ENDED, favorably for us, I regained full freedom. Impresarios rushed to snatch me up again. I accepted an engagement in Mexico, a country which I passionately wanted to visit for its natural beauty and its age-old history. After a two-year interruption in my artistic career, I again took up my methodical and disciplined way of life. But it was quite difficult at first to reacquire all the qualities of my voice. There is trouble in store for a singer who lets his delicate instrument be forgotten for a long time! He risks not finding it again at all!

After a period of diligent vocal and musical exercise, I left once again for the battlefield. I boarded ship in Naples, bound for New York. When I arrived in New York I rested for a few days and then continued on, taking a good five days by train to arrive in Mexico City. It was a very beautiful city, situated roughly seven thousand, five hundred fifty-five feet above sea level. The altitude prevented me from breathing normally, and it was quite difficult for me to acclimate myself. Many artists with engagements in the city had had to give up their contracts for this reason. Nevertheless I sang a good twelve performances beginning with *Pagliacci*, with which I attained great success, and continuing with *Barbiere di Siviglia*. I was accustomed at that time to singing the *cavatina* while skipping about from one side of the stage to the other with spontaneous lightness, but up there, at that altitude, I could not sustain prolonged notes, nor could I repeat those movements. I had to make an extra effort to sing, especially *Barbiere*, and I had to deploy all my strength of will to bring my performances safely into port.

During my days off I would take long walks in the large park of Chapultepec, which had extremely long avenues lined with millenary trees.[300] I fancied pausing in the famous *Avenida de los poetas* with its double row of giant eucalyptus trees and similar tropical plants. There, in the midst of the singing of thousands of birds of every kind and color, I would wait for evening to come upon me. Of all the natural wonders that I had seen in the world the *Avenida de los poetas* was one of the ones which most intensely stimulated my imagination and remained most strongly imprinted in my memory. It was in that spellbinding place that I read the verses of Rubén Darío,[301] the great South American poet. I could not have found a more romantic place in which to fully savor their delicate and profound beauty.

After I left Mexico I spent a few days in New York, where I was engaged to appear in *Rigoletto, Otello, Pagliacci*, and *Tosca*[302] and to sing in Leoncavallo's new opera, *Edipo re*,[303] with a libretto by Giovacchino Forzano[304] based on the Sophoclean tragedy. He had composed his last opera expressly for me, and I had promised Signora Berta at the deathbed of her illustrious companion that I would take it to the stage at the first opportunity.[305] So I immediately informed Mrs. Leoncavallo that I was finally in a position to keep my promise, having had *Edipo re* included in the program of the Auditorium Theater in Chicago and the Manhattan Theater in New York.

Since my new contract did not begin until the following year, I returned to Rome in the meantime to rest more peacefully in the company of my family. Spending that time redecorating my home with tasteful artwork and thus making it even more beautiful served as a gratifying and refreshing distraction. That had been my one ambition since boyhood, when my father's picture gallery consisted only of a portrait of Garibaldi and an oleograph of *Il trovatore*. When the time had come for my engagement with Cleofonte Campanini, I embarked once again for New York. But no sooner had I arrived than I learned with deep regret that he had died. He had wanted to make the Chicago Opera a predominantly Italian institution and with his skills, not to mention his theatrical and orchestral expertise, had been able to overcome the negative influences and schemes favoring French and German theater.[306] The general management of the Chicago Opera had been entrusted to the young and already well-regarded conductor Gino Marinuzzi, but I feared that Marinuzzi's authority, as great as it might be, would not be sufficient to preserve the traditions established and maintained by Campanini through many battles.[307]

In Chicago I received a visit from the president of the Victor Company, who asked if he could produce more records with me. It was that year that I had the joy of recording the second act duet of *Otello* with Enrico Caruso—a duet which was sought throughout the world for several years and which continues to circulate around the globe.[308] That season was mostly spent staging *Edipo re*, and not without difficulty since Campanini had died before writing the stage directions. I thus addressed myself directly to McCormick, a patron of the Chicago Opera who had been very attached to the greatly missed maestro, and asked him to intervene personally with the management in order to expedite *Edipo re* and encourage rehearsals with the chorus, which played an important role in the opera.

This was not done in vain. *Edipo re* was finally performed with great success both in the Chicago theater and in the Manhattan in New York. The critics, extremely generous with regard to the production, were not as generous with the music, which they found in certain moments to be lacking in orchestration. But they conceded that the role of the protagonist created marvelous effects with its *cantabile* and spontaneous melodies. In my opinion the musical conception of the charac-

ter corresponds perfectly to the power of the Sophoclean tragedy, and this was the fundamental intent of the author, who
aimed at recreating Oedipus using the characteristics of my
personality and voice.

The Chicago Opera changed completely for reasons of
personality differences too delicate for me to repeat. As of
1919 the munificent patron McCormick had lost interest. After that the entire organization, created with such toil and
painstaking diligence by Campanini, dissolved. The general
management was entrusted to Mary Garden, and the position
of conductor was given over to Giorgio Polacco in replacing
Marinuzzi. With these two new managers the prevalence of
Italian artists, aside from some Semitic participation, ended.
Even I, on account of old personal grudges, was blackballed.[309]

I stayed on in New York for a few days, during which I
went to the Metropolitan, invited by the manager, Gatti-
Casazza, to his box to hear Caruso perform Eléazar in Halévy's
Juive. This was his last and greatest role, though to say great
is to say too little. He was tremendous that night. He knew
how to create a character full of suffering and worry; he conveyed the anguish in his soul with such a mysteriously sugges-
tive expression that many spectators cried, and I was among
them. I returned to the Chicago Opera in 1920 for a few performances and from there continued on to California for two
concerts. But before leaving New York I went to the Metropolitan to hear Caruso again in *Juive* because it had moved
me so much the year before. I noted regretfully that the great
artist's voice that night indicated that something was amiss.
There did not appear to be fatigue but rather physical suffering in his voice. He gave the impression that at any moment
he might stop singing and collapse onstage. I left the theater
dismayed.

After a few days I heard that Caruso had taken ill while
performing *Elisir d'amore* at the Brooklyn Theater.[347] His performances were cancelled. The doctors confirmed that he had
pleurisy and declared that they would have to operate. The
news elicited distress throughout the world and especially in
the United States, where he was absolutely idolized. Immedi-

ately after the operation I wrote him an affectionate letter rejoicing that he had been saved from danger and upon returning from my tour in California I went to visit him at the Vanderbilt Hotel.

I left the hotel quite struck by the state in which the operation had left him. He was exhausted. The once magnificent torso from which the magnificent notes of his golden voice emanated was no more than a skeleton. Returning to my hotel I recalled with sadness those glorious evenings in Paris, Vienna, Montevideo, and Buenos Aires during which I had shared with him those successes that had represented such triumphs for our art and our homeland. I had the presentiment that the king of singers, my very beloved friend, would not experience them again. He had come to his end; before long he would no longer be. Only a miracle could have given him back his precious vitality.

Two days before leaving, I received a visit from Gatti-Casazza. He came accompanied by my ex-secretary Pollastri and offered me a contract to sing in ten performances at the Metropolitan for the 1921-22 season, telling me that it was his intention and Caruso's wish to stage Verdi's *Otello*. I accepted, hoping finally to be able to sing the Verdi opera at the Metropolitan with my great and beloved colleague. In the meantime I sang in Europe that year at the Royal Opera of Budapest for the third time and at the Popular Opera, playing Mephisto in Gounod's *Faust*.[311] When my engagements in the Hungarian capital were over, I returned to Rome, from where I almost immediately went to rest in Fiuggi—I believe I deserved it.

I was there, at the Palazzo della Fonte, playing cards with some friends, when all of a sudden the hotel manager appeared and gave me the news, which he had read in a Neapolitan newspaper, that Caruso had died. The tragic news saddened everyone. The game was ended; I put the cards on the table, and went to close myself up in my room, where I collapsed on my bed, crying. My wife, also very upset, urged me to cheer up, especially since I too had not been feeling well the last few days. As much as I had sensed his imminent end when I visited him at the Vanderbilt Hotel, I could not comprehend how that man, still young—he was barely forty-eight years old—that artist who had gathered so many laurels, who had inspired such enthusiasm throughout the world, could be no more than a cold body, a memory. It seemed to me that his premature end was the prelude of mine as well and was hastening its arrival. I went to the window and looked out at the chain of mountains that surrounds the village. An infinite sadness engulfed me. That evening I did not go down to the dining room; I was incapable of touching food.

The hotel owner, *commendatore* Della Casa,[312] offered to take me to Naples the next day in his car—Caruso had come back to his native city to die—in order to pay our last respects to my artistic companion in person. Very grateful to Della Casa for his kind gesture, I naturally accepted. We arrived in Naples amidst suffocating heat. The body of my dear friend was laid out before the public in a hall at the Vesuvio Hotel which had been turned into a mortuary chapel for the occasion. All of Naples wanted to go before the coffin of her glorious son, of the street-urchin who had become the most popular singer on earth and who had, using his golden voice, illuminated the hearts of all people with the fire of his volcano, the splendor of his sky, and the iridescence of his sea. I entered the hotel; I gazed at his stiffened face. A sob stuck in my throat. I was unable to stay long. I placed a flower on his breast, and left. I was asked to sing at his funeral mass, but declined: I felt that emotions would have overwhelmed me.[313]

I returned to Fiuggi at midnight; I had a fever. The ride in a convertible car wearing a light suit had taken its toll. My wife, who was anxiously awaiting me, was very upset. The next morning my fever had gone up to thirty-nine degrees centigrade (104 degrees Fahrenheit). It was bronchitis. I stayed in bed for fifteen days. From my window I would observe the mountains; I would spend hours and hours lost in gloomy fantasies, although it was not always thus. At sunset sometimes, true to my recollections, my dead friend would reappear in my mind no longer dead but still alive—alive and triumphant. The glorious evenings in Vienna and Paris would come to mind, but those times seemed so far away! Toward evening, when the fever would increase considerably, I was overcome by a sense of resignation and a desire for death.

During that illness I became convinced that one can cause one's own death with willpower. It was enough to want to leave this world, and all medicines and scientific resources became useless. My thoughts on this subject corresponded to a similar one of Goethe's, who claimed that one dies when one wants to die, and not before. I spent a few more days in a state of extreme exhaustion. I could not and I did not want to eat; I often broke into tears. My wife would urge me, although suffering along with me, to be active again, to be myself again. She would sometimes try to determine if some other reason might not be keeping me in such a desolate state of exhaustion. She put my children's portraits on the bedside table and, touching me tenderly, would conjure up and depict for me the wonderful future full of the joy of grown children that still awaited us. She did not have to wait long for an energetic reaction. After three days of complete fasting, I asked for champagne, gulped down two glasses of it and fell soundly asleep. The next day I was already beginning my convalescence with the determination to get well and to live and take up my artistic activity again.

Having recovered somewhat from the bronchitis, I left for New York in the middle of November. It was bitterly cold there. The sudden change in temperature affected my voice and my lungs. The fire of the Fiuggi illness, not completely extinguished, was rekindled, and I was forced to delay the opening for the time being. Gatti-Casazza, having been informed of the delay, ran to my house and begged me to make an effort to make my debut, that otherwise it would bring about the ruin of the series and, above all, my name. Upon my refusal he declared that, rather than change operas, he would replace me with someone else. Distressed by this development, I reminded him of the misfortune of Caruso, who the year before had triumphed at the Metropolitan and who now lay in a cemetery in Naples, perhaps because he relied too heavily on his own resilience or had complied too closely with the management's demands. I concluded that, compared to these risks, all his administrative concerns and my replacement seemed insignificant to me: I valued my health and life above all else and it was not worth it to me to sacrifice them for anyone. Another artist took my place and fulfilled his duty like a good soldier and was crowned with glory. I postponed all my performances.

That season was not a brilliant one. In the years following, until 1929—I add this in order not to lose the thread of the discourse, which does go past the limit which I have imposed on myself—my name was included in the Metropolitan's program in very few performances. Because I wanted to play some of my favorite characters, I asked Gatti-Casazza to produce *Demon, Hamlet,* or Leoncavallo's *Edipo re,* but always without success. Gatti-Casazza, who was omnipotent at the Metropolitan at that time, had, to my misfortune, a personal dislike for Thomas's *Hamlet,* was unaware of *Demon*'s artistic importance, and was leery of reviving *Edipo re;* I thus had to abandon my ambition for the time being. In the last seasons I was given the role of Neri in Giordano's *Cena delle beffe,* based on Sem Benelli's play, and I was thus able to be appreciated in the role of a modern character of great consequence which was perfectly suited to my voice and temperament.[314]

But at this point, which does lie beyond my pre-established limit, I would regret it if I ended my recollection of my last North American season without mentioning an event that occurred during that time, that is in '23, and which struck me in the deepest recesses of my heart. I speak of the death of Victor Maurel.

In 1918, on my way to Mexico after a three-year absence, I stopped in New York and I had the chance to again embrace the great maestro who over time had become more than a dear friend—during the time of my engagement by the Metropolitan I had had the opportunity to speak with him quite often. His health was beginning to deteriorate, and, because of the intense cold of the winter season, he sometimes could not leave his home. One evening, together with our mutual friend Duval,[315] his student and a famous voice instructor,

Maurel attended one of my performances of *Ernani* at the Metropolitan. After that evening I did not see him again for about two weeks. Very worried about his prolonged absence, and wanting to know the reason for it, I went to his house on Seventieth Street. On the way I ran into J. Thorner, the famous voice instructor and intimate friend of the old baritone. When he learned that I was going to visit Maurel, he accompanied me so as to give his regards as well.

When we arrived at his home, we rang the bell several times without response. We then knocked on the neighbor's door to ask for information. An old woman came to the door. She had known Maurel since the time of his glorious evenings at the Metropolitan, and from her we learned that Maurel was ill; his wife had left early and had not yet returned, and it was certainly impossible for him to get out of bed. I left my calling card, bid goodbye to Thorner and returned to my hotel. That evening, around five o'clock, prompted by a morose presentiment, I went back to Maurel's house with the hope of finding his wife at home, but, to my surprise, no one answered this time either. I began to be seriously worried. I spoke for a second time with the old woman from before who, upon seeing me so upset, told me that, if I wished, I might be able to enter Maurel's home by climbing up the balcony. Using my wits and skill I went up over the balcony and reached the window of his room; the window was closed. I broke it and entered the home of my poor friend.

I found myself before a sad spectacle. He was lying in a small bed, in a cold and dark room, faint with weakness. He fixed his gaze on me as if he were hallucinating and broke into uncontrollable sobs. I went to him and lifted him up by the arms. After he had calmed down a bit, he asked me, stupefied, what I was doing in his home and how I had managed to get in. I found the light switch after groping the walls, and finally a lamp, a lone lightbulb in the middle of the room, lit up and allowed me to see the scene better. Struck by this strange state of deprivation, I gently reprimanded him for not having informed me of his condition, since human kindness does not consist only of words but also of actually helping others through life's critical moments. From that sad sight I understood why Maurel had preferred to see me at my house.

Victor Maurel, a great gentleman offstage, a prince onstage, had lost his entire fortune in a financial fiasco in Russia and now lived in that wretched room, forsaken and forgotten by all, not asking anything of anyone. Pained at having to uncover the truth of his situation, he exclaimed, "Now, my dear friend, you see the reality of my tragedy." His faithful companion, the adopted daughter of Victorien Sardou, had devoted herself to writing screenplays for the cinema in order to provide some help for the poor man who had been forgotten by others and was spending her days in related pursuits now in New York. She would leave the house early in the morning not to return until late in the evening, exhausted, because she too was far along in years. I sat down at Maurel's bedside. I did my best to comfort him. I was going to sing in a concert in Boston the following day; I would dedicate it to him. The next day at nine o'clock in the evening, the time of the concert, he should turn his thoughts to me and my spirit would be with his, like that of a son, united in the fervent wish for a rapid and complete recovery.

I went back to his home right after the concert. I found him in better spirits. His exhaustion had been more moral than physical. After one week I arranged for him to leave for the gentle climate of California where he would spend several carefree months. I tried to comfort him as often and as best as I could in my letters since I could not do so in person. His replies were so dense with concern and affection that I am unsure whether more of the man's sensitivity or the artist's greatness poured forth from those letters. When I left New York I pleaded with him to come to Rome and said that I would be happy to have him as a guest for several months. He could not—he wrote me—accept my generous invitation because he could not leave his old companion alone and because his advanced age prevented him from making such a long trip.

When I returned to New York in the fall, the very morning of my arrival, I received a telephone call from my friend Duval who told me that Maurel had passed away a few hours earlier.

I immediately went to his house. The great interpreter of Verdi's most brilliant creations was now on his deathbed with his arms crossed, still and silent. Despite my deep sorrow I was incapable of shedding a tear, just as at my father's death. For a long time I watched his waxen face, composed in its eternal sleep, and it seemed to me that I could see etched upon it the motto with which Iago concludes his famous credo and which Maurel had sung marvelously so many times.

His companion was the very picture of pain. When we went back into the mourning room she gave me two mementos that Maurel had left for me. They were the earrings which he had worn in his first opening in *Guarany* at La Scala di Milano,[316] and his tuxedo cuff links. She said to me: "This is all of value my poor Victor has left. Before his death he asked that I give it to you in remembrance of his devotion and profound admiration for his great, dear friend Ruffo."

I sang in Maurel's funeral mass accompanied by organ in a New York church. That day the sun lit up the city and the large gothic polychromatic stained-glass windows filtered its rays which then reflected on the catafalque set up in the center of the church. As I observed the mournful scene from above, I opened the coffin in my imagination and saw the old man's noble forehead illuminated as if by a halo. When the ceremony was over, I wished to be among the few who followed the convoy to his final resting ground. Before his dear mortal remains were closed up in the marble monument I was unable, as a friend and as an Italian, to keep from reminding those present that, with the death of Maurel, Art had lost one of its best champions. His name, however, would never be forgotten, linked as it was to the immortal glory of Giuseppe Verdi, as one of the artists most admired and loved by the sublime maestro.[317]

CHAPTER 27

Last Tour in Central America

IN 1924 THE IMPRESARIO and conductor Adolfo Bracale, who had entered into a deal with a Cuban financier by the name of Ortega, offered me a lucrative contract for a tour with *Hamlet* through the theaters of Central America.[318] I accepted with much delight, eager to visit that part of America where I had never traveled. And as soon as I had finished my engagements at the Metropolitan I left for Havana, where the company was being assembled and where the series was to begin. I was contracted to sing in forty performances, alternating between *Hamlet* and *Barbiere*, *Pagliacci*, *Andrea Chénier*, and *Tosca*.[319]

We made our debut at the National Theater with great artistic and, because it had been possible to sell seats for very high prices there, financial success. But in the minor theaters of the island the revenues were not sufficient to cover the company's expenses as well as the high salary I was owed, and so some discussions arose between the management and me. I accused them of having swindled me by offering a remuneration that they knew full well they would be unable to pay. They justified themselves by claiming that, in comparison to the rest of the company, my salary was too high. This put me in an awkward situation vis à vis my colleagues. And to make matters worse the revolution began and devastated the whole island of Cuba from one end to the other.[320]

When we arrived in Santiago, the situation was desperate. I did not want the company to be defrauded in the same way that I had been by the management, and to save everything I decided to concede to a considerable reduction in my contracted pay. This transaction allowed us to continue the tour with much prosperity. We went from the island of Cuba to that of Puerto Rico, and from there we set sail for Venezuela on a small steamer. It was a very delightful trip. A certain spirit of unity had already been created, and everyone contributed his good will and made every effort to preserve the company's balance and reputation.

We stopped in Caracas, the capital of Venezuela, for about forty days. I made my debut at the Teatro Municipal, a huge building, with my favorite opera, *Hamlet*, and I had extraordinary success, artistically speaking, and also good results financially. However, after the third or fourth performance a national economic crisis made it impossible to continue with the tour.

Things constantly became more complicated. So, in order to continue the tour without leaving so many people short of money, I took an audacious initiative. I assembled the company along with the chorus and orchestra and proposed that we form a cooperative, establishing a partnership with the impresarios who would not have the right to interfere alone in the administration, but everyone in the cooperative would have the right to audit the financial records. This act of justice and professional solidarity earned me increased affection and respect from the others; however, this did not please the management—especially Ortega who, as financier, wanted to get out of all financial responsibility. But in order to save everyone I stood firm and did not yield. I fought without respite with such vehemence and steadfastness that I forced the management to go along with us until the end of our tour.

But one morning on my way to rehearsal I received two telegrams from Rome that put me in a state of grave apprehension. One was from our family doctor informing me that it would be necessary for my wife to undergo a difficult surgical intervention within forty-eight hours and asking for my authorization. The other, from my children, was even more distressing. I went to the telegraph office with a heavy heart and sent my authorization. That night I was scheduled to perform in *Barbiere di Siviglia* in a theater which would be more crowded than usual because the President of the Republic, General Gomez,[321] was to attend. Naturally I informed the management that I absolutely could not sing that night. Who would give me the strength to take on the clownish guise of Figaro? But the management ordered me to sing at all costs and if I didn't, it would be the end of the tour.

My performance that night was not brilliant. How could that have been possible? Throughout, I kept seeing my beloved companion under the surgeon's instruments, risking death. When I returned to the hotel I was completely undone. I was unable to sleep all night. At dawn I went out and wandered around the silent city with a dismal presentiment in my heart. I would have liked to escape, flying across the many miles that separated me from Rome. I headed towards a high ground very close to Caracas and I ventured into a wood. The sun was coming up, and little by little the huge disk began sending out its glittering rays through the fretwork of branches.

I stopped in a clearing where the sun dazzled my eyes. Spontaneously, without knowing what I was doing, I threw myself down at the foot of a giant eucalyptus, took off my hat, closed my eyes, and, in an act of supplication, like an Oriental man, I invoked, crying, the Force which rules over the world, completely absorbed in the thought of my dear companion and of our children. I remained in that pose, pronouncing their names repeatedly, for I do not know how much time. The agonizing effort of that performance and that sleepless night had worn me out completely.

I returned to the hotel, barely able to stand upright. I thought I would go mad. I threw myself on my bed. I spent the whole day and the following day in a state of desperation, constantly flooding my family with telegrams which were more like letters. Finally I received one from my children and one from the doctor letting me know that the operation had been a success and that they would inform me every day of the state of her health.

Rather than calming me, these telegrams frightened me. I remembered that unfortunately, many years before, a person very dear to me had undergone the same operation; the operation had gone very well but five days later, she was no longer.[322] I telegraphed the doctor directly who, after several days, which seemed a year to me, reported that my wife was out of danger and was beginning her convalescence. Not too many days later I had the immense joy of receiving a telegram from the clinic, dictated by my wife herself, saying that my telegrams were the best medicine, that her quick convalescence was a result of them. She encouraged me to continue on with my work with a calm mind.

Before leaving the Venezuelan capital, I visited the house and the museum dedicated to the memory of the heroic figure, Simon Bolivar. General Gomez, president of the Republic, wanted to receive me in the government palace, and I was decorated by him with the Cruz del Libertador.

THE FIRST ITALIAN COMPANY organized as a cooperative was founded abroad by me with the help and collaboration of my colleagues and of the manager, all of whose names I recall here to honor them: tenor Angelo Pintucci, bass Vincenzo Bettoni[323] and Adolfo Bracale. The management worked with us to the end. I had bound them to my arrangement, just as they had bound me to theirs, in the presence of the company which, without this protective net, would have remained far from its homeland, and some without money, without the possibility of going back.

The company visited two cities, Barranquilla and Cartagena. I appeared before the audience in *Hamlet*. The theaters were already sold out two weeks before my arrival. Thomas's opera produced a great sensation everywhere. My interpretation was admired and considered exceptional. The intellectuals of the city, before my departure, wanted to honor me by having marble plaques put up in both theaters in memory of my success and my passage through those faraway countries.

We proceeded through Bogotá, where the company remained about twenty days and then disbanded. I appeared in eight appearances making my debut, as I have indicated, with *Hamlet* and finishing with *Rigoletto*, which was neither on the program nor in my contract, but which the season-ticket holders had requested from manager Bracale as a favor.

During this last stop, after I had sung in a good forty-two performances, more very serious news came from Rome,[324] on account of which I was unspeakably saddened and I lost the strength and the courage to finish the remaining performances—especially for *Rigoletto*, which came first—with the necessary enthusiasm. I therefore decided to cancel the performance. But the management had agreed to offer this non-subscription performance in lieu of the one scheduled and for a very high price; the receipts would have been enough to repatriate the whole company. Several scalpers had purchased a quantity of seats and resold them at exorbitant prices. The show's cancellation created an unsettling situation for everyone, and I became the scapegoat for the whole affair.

When the crowd that had been waiting anxiously for me in the theater got wind of the cancellation, pandemonium broke out. The popular contingent in the audience was roused into a frenzy for revolution and poured forth to the hotel where I was staying. Many even came armed with sticks and stones, as if I had committed some crime that warranted my lynching. The windows of my room, which looked out onto the street became the targets of more than just the eyes of the furious crowd. Traffic was forced to stop.

I was saved by a miracle. The hotel manager called the police and several squadrons of guards on horseback were sent immediately to break up the crowd which was shouting uncontrollably. The chief of police came up to my room to question me. I explained to him the reason that had compelled me to cancel the show, and he understood. But in the meantime the violent situation which had developed had to be remedied in some way. I was compelled to formally pledge to sing *Rigoletto* within two days.

On the agreed-upon evening I was onstage before a hostile and impatient audience. The slightest hesitation on my part would have been enough to set that herd of wild animals upon me in a frenzy. That would have been my demise. But...no hesitation. Unprecedented success. At the end the entire audience, as if driven by the wish to offer compensation for the injustice committed, seemed overcome by paroxysm. They did not want to leave the theater. I was forced to speak, and finally a normal psychological state was reestablished. After the sad misadventure in Bogotá I excluded *Rigoletto* from my repertoire forever, not so much because of the memory of the unjust actions of the management and the frenzied audience as because of the motives which prompted them.[325]

I have often heard psychologists and great experts of criticism discuss the nature of art and the need to present oneself to the audience with a serene state of mind in order to channel one's thoughts, to adequately express emotion and successfully play out one's interpretation. Now then, what soul could have been more distraught than mine in that last performance of *Rigoletto* in Bogotá? And yet, without fear of exaggeration, that night my voice was of matchless purity and strength, and my interpretation was so harmonious and profound that it allowed me to produce the most miraculous effects. My soul and that of the tragic jester were not two but one that night.

That night I made—I do not feel presumptuous in saying this—a true creation, and the entire press took notice. The incident in Bogotá prompted other reflections. Will men of future generations, especially those of inferior classes, ever—I ask myself thinking about it again—be able to attain a certain degree of civility? Will they ever rid themselves of the atavistic ferocity which broods in their hearts and which is so ready to explode wildly, especially in collective action? And going over history from the story of Cain to the present, as I would sometimes in those days, I felt that I had to respond in anything but an optimistic manner.

I am in better spirits today, as I try to fill the idleness of my days writing these memoirs—in somewhat better spirits, I say, having reached a more mature age and a more mature experience. I wonder, if the history of mankind up to now incurs more fear than hope, what space can the lengthy past occupy in relation to the indefinite future? But the world is still young. I would rather imagine, even if I am not entirely convinced of it, the path of humanity not like a parabola, as mine has been, which slowly subsides into the future, but rather like an ever-expanding and every-rising spiral.

The Incident in Bogotá
and Thereafter

RUFFO TITTA, JR.

A PART FROM A FEW REFERENCES relating to later events, my father wished to end his autobiographical narrative at June, 1924. There remained thirteen years until the publication of the book and another sixteen up to his death: in all a total of twenty-nine years. Today's readers may therefore expect some information on this ample segment of his life.

I aim to satisfy this expectation as best I can with this new chapter by returning to verified memories, letters, newspaper clippings, documents found among his papers and elsewhere; but aware of its shortcomings in comparison with the previous chapters [of *La Mia Parabola*] I beg the reader to consider my modest contribution no more than a commentary, necessarily less succinct than the rest.

FOR THE COMPLETION of the picture of his artistic life I refer the reader to the chronology of his career. From that it appears that the troubled tour ended in the Colombian capital marking, in a certain sense, the culmination of his parabola. As a matter of fact, his operatic appearances became progressively less frequent and binding from then on, and in the end virtually ceased, to be replaced almost exclusively by concerts in his last years. I will therefore dwell chiefly on his personal life.

The reader of *La Mia Parabola* will not find explicit opinion of a political nature, but has perhaps intuitively perceived on which side, as by some atavistic force, were my father's heart and mind on this matter, already prior to the assassination of his brother-in-law, Giacomo Matteotti. After that tragic event he wrapped himself in a pained and disdainful silence worthy of his immense respect for his departed relative.

The wave of indignation sweeping the country after the crime against Matteotti was so great as to end the days of fascism. It did not happen. Those who could have or should have seized the great historical opportunity to bring it down for once and for all did not want to or couldn't do it. The crisis resulted in a harsh strengthening of the chains of dictatorship. Returning to Italy to be close to his sister, Velia, my father remained absent from the stage for about six months. In August of 1924, he took part in the funeral of his brother-in-law in the cemetery of Fratta Polesine.

He then resumed his artistic wanderings, with his spirit more hostile than ever toward those who had seized power at all levels and who had begun the systematic corruption of minds and moral principles, even defiling culture through the distortion of the arts. Yet he continued to believe in the healthy principles hidden in the soul of the populace, so much so that in October of 1925, he did not refuse the public the service of his own art. After about a quarter of a century's absence he agreed to sing again in his own native city, appearing in two performances in the role of Hamlet, his favorite role. The audience gathered from everywhere, rewarding him with intense, warm enthusiasm, and his grateful admirers wanted to commemorate the event with a plaque in the Teatro Verdi. The "authorities" however, could not tolerate that an artist so well liked by the public should not allow himself to be linked to the "regime." Already by August 1926 a band of Blackshirts had destroyed the plaque with hammer blows; I will describe this act of vandalism further on. That was the end. My father continued to reject attractive contracts from Italian theaters and repeated requests to sing at benefits, disgusted with the provocations and political compromises they involved.

From that time on his voice would be heard only outside of Italy, just as he lived most of the time outside Italy. He chose to live in France. When he was free of professional commitment, he would roam through Paris, where he always lived in hotels, in the Provence and the Côte d'Azur (Antibes, Cannes, Juan-les-Pins, etc.), and ended by taking up residence in Nice. In 1933 he allowed himself a long trip in Spain and a prolonged sojourn with friends in Great Britain, during which he gave a private concert and made his last recordings, which remained unissued. But even his artistic activities abroad were bristling with pitfalls.

In August 1926, the Royal Italian Ambassador in Buenos Aires confidentially forwarded to the Ministries for Foreign and Internal Affairs in Rome numerous rumors, unsupported by any documentary evidence. These "confidential" rumors surfaced in the domestic fascist papers. Titta Ruffo was denounced as a "distinguished scoundrel" and was accused of financing antifascist newspapers and having inspired some outrageous lampoon of the memory of the Queen Mother, Margherita of Savoia, that appeared in the Buenos Aires newspaper, *Italia del Popolo*. Reprisal came quickly: the aforementoned commemorative plaque flew to pieces. I remember how mortified my father was at the shabbiness and stupidity of the methods employed to injure him! Even some segments of the theatrical hangers-on conspired with the "regime" to prematurely eliminate from the marketplace those singers who were disturbing competitors.

On September 26, 1926, the Minister for Foreign Affairs, Dino Grandi, received a letter from the Secretary General of the National Theater Guild, reading, in part: ". . . *the Milanese atmosphere and especially our syndicate, are much aroused and have voted a strong Order of the Day. Because Ruffo, who recently returned from Argentina is to sail on the 6th to New York, I ask you officially to revoke his passport which would make it possible, here at home, to give him the lesson he deserves.*"

The "regime" could not stifle expressions of dissent in the

theaters abroad which were open to my father, but did not cease to use this form of molestation. Cries, such as "Down with Fascism! Viva Matteotti! Long Live Liberty!" uttered in the semi-darkness of a theater were countered by zealous signaling and intimidating actions by gangs around the villa in Rome, and by the revocation, effective or threatened, of his passport. The "regime" then exerted every possible pressure, at my father's expense, on his fellow countrymen who had any power in theaters abroad; these pressures were so effective that in 1929 they brought about the sudden cessation of every connection with the Metropolitan in New York, the theater dominated by the presence of Gatti-Casazza and the strong presence of Italians faithful to the "Roman salute."

The act of aggression in Marseille whose victim he was on February 18, 1931, should also be remembered. Its object was to prevent him from appearing in public in a city which had a large number of antifascists. But Father did not let himself be intimidated by the anonymous letters and phone calls prior to the aggression, nor the blows and punches he received on the threshold of the theater as he was about to enter to prepare for the performance, not even by the faithless behavior of the impresario who was a party to the plot. Hiding the painful bruises on his head with hair and makeup, he wanted to face his audience. He was received with yells and insults by *agents provocateurs*, blunted by the reaction of the numerous exiles present in the theater; but in spite of the considerable uproar instigated to silence his voice, he honored his contract and finished the performance of *Il barbiere di Siviglia* for which he was engaged.

A macabre trick was played on him in 1932: the announcement of his sudden death in Madrid, invented and spread by a branch office of the Italian press. The hatred for his dignified and immovable demeanor regarding the "regime" did not abate following his definite retirement from the stage. On the morning of October 16, 1937, in Rome, where he came for a family visit, he was taken from the house by two detectives; they seized his passport and after formalities at the police station he was sent to the Regina Coeli prison. There he was photographed and fingerprinted for the card index of criminal records. They confiscated his money, cuff-links, collar buttons, suspenders and shoelaces and threw him in a cell. "I found myself in a state of humiliating dismay," he later recalled, "forced to hold up my pants by hand, while my collar would stand open because of the missing button."

The arrest was due to two approximately identical denunciations: one from a certain Dr. Ubaldo Pera, dated October 10, on which could be read in Mussolini's handwriting: "Lock him up, M.," the other from the impresario Walter Mocchi, deposited on October 17. Here is the second one in its entirety.

In the year 1937 on the 17th day of the month of October in the Political Bureau of the Royal Police Station of Rome, before the undersigned official appeared Walter Mocchi, son of the late Luigi and Laura Nazzaro, born in Torino on September 27, 1871, residing here at 11 Piazza di Piscinula, who responded to questions as follows:

I have known the baritone Titta Ruffo for many years having had him under contract for various years at the Teatro Colón in Buenos Aires and other theaters of my concern. On the afternoon of October 7th I was on a train from Livorno to Rome, due to arrive in this city at 9:00 p.m. As I boarded the train and went through the corridors in search of a seat, I saw in one of the second class compartments the aforementioned Titta Ruffo in an animated discussion with passengers, unknown to me. I knocked on the window to greet him and he signaled me to wait. I then took a seat in the compartment of another carriage where I stayed for about an hour.

Around 7 p.m. stepping out in the corridor I met Titta Ruffo. After the usual greetings and after having spoken about the book he had just published I mentioned to him the formation of a motion picture company created under the presidency of Vittorio Mussolini, which proposed to produce operatic films. I stated moreover that production would begin with Rigoletto and therefore be a good opportunity for him to appear again.

To this he answered that he had already received a proposal from parties in Florence interested in the company to which he had given his firm refusal inasmuch as first of all he did not want to sing any more, and secondly and mainly because he did not want to have contact with the kind of people with whom he was incompatible. This circumstance gave Titta Ruffo the opportunity to show his political sentiments of pure aversion towards the Regime, which I had already noticed in conversations some years before in discussions of political matters in a hotel in Buenos Aires and again in Paris, on the occasion of a film which was to be made with him.

I thought it opportune at the time to point out the innumerable accomplishments of the Regime, the preeminent position in the world of the Fascist Government of Italy and other things, including education, both moral and physical, given to the Fascist youth. At this point Titta sprang up and censured the education of youth, and I can precisely quote his words as follows: "These youths are being raised as cannon fodder, ready for servility, without a sense of dignity, etc., etc." Then I pointed out to him that this youth, thus educated, in seven months had vindicated the disgrace of Adua [Abyssinia, now Ethiopia] and created an Empire; he brusquely interrupted the conversation and we parted practically without greetings.

I cannot state precisely whether on this occasion Titta Ruffo uttered the phrase "Country of abuses and insolence"; but the nature of the conversation as well as the tone in which Ruffo spoke of the Regime and the bitterness he had shown clearly implied that.

I do not recall if there were people in the corridor who could have overheard Titta Ruffo's discourse, except those passengers who passed through the corridor.

As soon as I finished my discussion with Titta Ruffo I returned to my own compartment and did not see him again. I do not know whether he had spoken to or met with other people.

Read, confirmed and signed by Walter Mocchi— Valente Donato, police commissioner.

The event became known to foreign journalists. The news provoked a sensation. Its effect wasn't slow in coming: after three days came the order of release, but, this time, the passport was not restored. Now he could no longer show that he had engagements outside Italy. Deprived of the status of an Italian living abroad and the freedom not to live in a country dominated by a political regime he hated, he was forced to transplant bag and baggage from Nice to Italy. Rendering his existence more bitter, sad, disillusioning, an accumulation of the physical ailments of old age slowly set in, along with legal and fiscal problems inherent in the contracts drawn up in the United States, actions brought by malevolent persons, clouds of financial matters....

A REVIEW OF THE IMPORTANT EVENTS of my father's life cannot ignore a person linked to him with strong emotional bonds, and who comforted him in the solitude of his voluntary exile: a Rumanian immigrant to France, named Olga Isacescu. He had the good fortune to meet her in Nice. Olga was his faithful, devoted secretary, nurse and companion in the last eighteen years of his life, now far from the glories of triumphs and the adulation of his prosperous years. Discreet and unselfish, it was she who typed the manuscript of *La Mia Parabola*. After the death of my father she moved to Milan, although the climate of that city was not suitable for her precarious state of health, to stay near his mortal remains.

And there she lived in the worship of a memory until her death on March 2, 1981.

DEPRIVED OF HIS PASSPORT my father decided to move to the western part of the Ligurian Riviera. He eventually settled in Bordighera and in quiet concentration in that little town wrote the major portion of his autobiography. When the war between Italy and France seemed imminent—the border was closed—fearful of remaining isolated from his family and in order to be closer to Rome he did not hesitate to give up the quiet and the temperate climate of Bordighera so favorable to his health. With advancing years he suffered from an occupational disease, pulmonary emphysema and illness of the respiratory tract, and thus became sensitive to cold.

He then moved to Florence, never imagining that the vicissitudes of the war would make it difficult one day to maintain connections between Florence and Rome, for awhile cut off completely.

In Florence he bewailed the loss of the Riviera climate, but in recompense came out of the isolation in which he had lived until then. In fact, he found the warmth of many friends, fellow artists and the comfort of a constant pilgrimage of visitors—Italian and foreign. It would be impossible for me to remember and cite them all. Confining myself to the world of opera I limit myself to naming only those about whom I am certain: the baritone Bechi, who was always close to him with affectionate devotion; the soprano Lina Cavalieri; the tenor Izquierdo; the baritones Mascherini, Montesanto, Silveri and Tagliabue; the tenors Lauri-Volpi and Di Stefano; the conductor Mugnone. During his years abroad, and after his definitive return to Italy, he never failed to rejoin the family he loved so tenderly. And when he was far away he always wrote many affectionate letters to my mother, to my sister and me; and complained if we did not repay him in equal measure.

On July 26, 1943, the news spread that Mussolini had been arrested; Titta Ruffo showed himself at a window and sang the "Marseillaise," to be joined immediately by a crescendo of voices thus celebrating liberty.

This was, indeed, the very last time that his voice resounded in public.

But the joy over freedom and the rebirth of peace was of short duration. On September 8 German troops invaded Italy, and on the 10th they occupied the capital and in a few days the entire country from the Alps to the so-called "Southern Kingdom."

Then began dark days for father and great new perils. The Nazi-Fascist "authorities" of Florence became arrogant. They began to torment him with invitations to sing on the radio and a refusal could cost him a high price indeed. There were grave moments of anxiety when he was advised to hide; he always found a safe refuge with trusted friends.

His first Florentine lodging was a bright little apartment, on the mezzanine floor of an old palazzo on the banks of the Arno. From the window he could enjoy the views of the nearby Ponte Vecchio. On the nights of August 3 and 4 the Eighth British Army penetrated the Oltrarno quarter of the city, the Germans retreated beyond the line of the river after having blown up all the bridges excepting the Ponte Vecchio. Passage was barred by the ruins of the surrounding palazzi which had been demolished by mines. The inhabitants had been given very short prior notice to evacuate their homes. After living for some time in precarious lodgings, he finally settled for good in an apartment in the Via del Campidoglio 4, near the Piazza della Repubblica.

THE TRVIAL—AND ONLY—experience with films in 1929 only strengthened my father's skepticism about the eventual success of cinematographic versions of opera sufficiently to refuse the most attractive offers of American producers determined to profit from the advent of sound-film, and wanting to exhibit on the screen complete operas such as *Carmen, Barber of Seville, Rigoletto,* and *Faust.*

Nevertheless, and especially after he left the operatic stage, he always longed to venture upon some nonoperatic film, as other famous singers have done, no more photogenic or gifted than he in regard to acting ability: Bechi, Gigli and Schipa, to mention only the Italians. There is evidence of discussions, preliminaries, and exchange of letters concerning numerous movie projects. I limit myself to mentioning a few promoters of such projects: Mario Bonnard, Pittaluga's director, for an eventual *Figaro* based on the Beaumarchais masterpiece, of a *Kean* by the elder Dumas; Jacques Prévert; Jean Renoir for a film based on *Les aventures du roi Pausole* of Louys; Arnoldo dello Sbarba, who was considering a production involving Roberto Rossellini; Vincenzo Tanlongo, who was thinking of a *Mastro Landi* with a screenplay by Giovacchino Forzano (librettist of Puccini's *Gianni Schicchi*).

Unfortunately the wish to appear on the screen also remained unfulfilled, for various reasons. The advent of the sound-film did not coincide with his vocal and physical prime. He was the first to be fully aware of it. His serious professionalism inhibited him from venturing into a cinematographic undertaking guaranteed by the prestige of his name more than by the intrinsic value of cinematic art.

MY FATHER HAD AN INFALLIBLE SENSE of intuition about history. Even when the fortunes of war seemed decided in favor of the aggressors, he never doubted its final outcome. And when the "liberation" formally returned Italy to the rank of democracies he could not rejoice in it. He deplored the lack of profound, authentic renewal of laws and statesmen. "Cunning, servility, provincialism, superficiality, opportunism, subversion, in short, the old ailments of Italy are liable to be repeated, they are not vanquished. The Blackshirts move about more insidiously than before, spread out and well camouflaged," he insisted.

He did propaganda work to gain voters for the Republic. A sympathizer of the partisans of the peace movement, he participated in the congress of this group held in Paris. In the beginning he followed with intense interest the main activities and manifestations of the progressive parties. He kept, however, within himself the spirit of complete freedom. He took no membership card. He did not solicit honors or an appointment for political merit. Disillusioned and embittered, he finally abandoned the political arena too.

On May 14, 1945, he had the great joy of an enthusiastic, warm reception in Pisa by his fellow citizens, on the occasion of the restoration of the commemorative plaque, destroyed by the Fascists, that was dedicated to him twenty years before.

STRUCK DOWN BY AN ATTACK of *angina pectoris,* Titta Ruffo died in Florence, in his own bed, at 2:30 a.m. on July 5, 1953. I was notified by phone in the middle of the night by Olga, her voice broken with grief. In the preceding days there were no warning signs of the possibility of a sudden end from such a cause. In observance of his wish, the body was transported to Milan, to the Monumentale Cemetery, where he rests alongside the remains of the beloved Benedetta.

AFTER SEVERAL YEARS OF ABSENCE, the news of his death suddenly brought back the name of Titta Ruffo to the front pages of the world press. His memory was accorded the most affectionate and universal recognition he could have received. Then began the long posthumous silence, broken every now and then by a radio broadcast of one of his records, by a short newspaper article, or some ceremony inspired by an anniversary date; it would be too long to enumerate all. Particularly warm, affectionate and consistent were those of his native city. On the anniversary of his death a street was named after him and a plaque was affixed to the facade of the house in which he was born. In 1961 a museum was opened in the Teatro Verdi which housed the greater part of his relics: costumes, operatic scores, gifts he received on his benefit nights, photographs, etc. And the tributes were repeated on the tenth anniversary of his death (by Giorgio Gualerzi) and the twentieth (by Gino dell'Ira). I particularly cherish the commemorative ceremonies in Florence (speaker: Eugenio Gara), Moscow (speaker: Aleksandr Less) and Prague (speaker: Antonin Novotny).

In 1966 *La Mia Parabola* was published in Moscow; it

was the first—and has remained until now the only—published translation of his autobiography. The Council of the Accademia di Santa Cecilia, on July 5, 1963, remembering the tenth anniversary of my father's death, proposed to the city of Rome that a street be named after him. The favorable decision of the City Council that followed on November 9, 1965 was fulfilled only a couple of years later. The tablet with the name of Titta Ruffo was placed—without any ceremony—in a new narrow street in the popular quarter of Primavalle, a zone whose thoroughfare the commission in charge of names, curiously enough, had reserved for the hierarchy of the Catholic church and personalities of Italian lyric art. Streets named for Popes, Cardinals, heads of religious orders, etc., are intermixed with streets commemorating singing celebrities of both sexes, Battistini, Caruso, Patti, and many others.

I FEEL OBLIGATED TO MENTION at this point some of the most glaring inaccuracies, inventions, legends, etc., handed down either orally or actually in print, in regard to my father.

(a) The date of his birth is variously given as June 8 or June 10, 1876; this error in dates is particularly evident in the Anglo-Saxon literature and I cannot explain its origins. If my father's own assertions are not enough, I can guarantee that the exact date of his birth was June 9, 1877, as proven by unassailable documentary evidence. The date of his death is also variously given as the 6th as well as the 5th of July, 1953.

(b) It has been written, even in reference works *(A Concise Biographical Dictionary of Singers* by K. J. Kutsch and Leo Riemens, New York, 1969) that he thought of becoming an engineer and began course work towards that end at the University of Rome.

(c) According to an American journalist (Edward J. Smith) who visited him in Florence, at the end of his life Titta Ruffo was obliged to climb long flights of stairs to get to his apartment on the fourth floor, with the imaginable effect on his weakened heart. His last two residences in Florence were, however, on the mezzanine floors!

(d) Titta Ruffo never gave singing lessons; much less did

he think of opening a "School of Singing." Neither did his brother Ettore, who taught for a long time in the United States, ever settle in Hollywood. When a journalist once asked him why he didn't give singing lessons, observing that he could have found plenty of affluent Americans willing to spend money to become his pupils, Titta Ruffo answered: "I never knew how to sing; that's why my voice didn't last beyond my fifties. I have no right to profit from my fame and try to teach something which I did not know how to do."

He always listened attentively and with sympathy to anyone wishing an audition and gave most generously of his time and counsel according to his own judgment, admonishing or dissuading the hopeful singer.

While on this subject, I think it would be of interest to cite part of a letter (dated November 8th, 1945) he sent to a young baritone on the eve of his debut in *Rigoletto*. He writes "Sing calmly! Pay heed to the cantabile passages with the soprano, seeking a mezza voce delivery, not too bright, as some baritones do at times; well accentuate the declamation in the 'Cortigiani' section; and put all paternal feeling into 'Miei signori' and the duet 'Piangi fanciulla,' both of which epitomize the most painful and pathetic melodies in the opera; seek a soulful voice, all the secret is there, and also in the last act, accentuate the declamation in the recitatives and duet which precede Gilda's death. Sing! sing! and sing! with all human feelings. I will not come to the theater because it might make you nervous, but I will be there in my thoughts, with you. Remain calm, as if you were singing at home; your voice is an important one, and you will conquer. This is my wish. I embrace you like a son and God be with you. Titta Ruffo."

(e) Titta Ruffo never sang in *Pagliacci* with Caruso, exchanging roles! Neither did he sing music written for tenor (for example the "Siciliana" from *Cavalleria rusticana*) except as a boy. These are simply legends.

(f) An American journalist has written that Titta Ruffo finished his days reduced to misery, to the point that he had to sell piece by piece his costumes, swords, and objects which were souvenirs of his golden days. Other visitors have attested to Ruffo's poverty in later years. The subject is always treated with dogmatic statements, at times seeking to paint an effective, emphatically dramatic picture. Yes, it is permissible to speak of a "financial parabola" in Titta Ruffo's life; it is enough to compare his sumptuous way of living during his golden period made possible by his large earnings with the forced parsimony, not without renunciation, of the postwar period. But from that to indigence there is a wide gulf! His costumes and theatrical memorabilia have always remained in the custody of the family. Most of them can be seen in the museum in the Teatro Verdi in Pisa. Some relics have been donated by his heirs to other theatrical museums, and some are still retained.

My father was not a shrewd, fortunate administrator of the fruits of his labors and art. He preferred to be paid in a lump sum for almost all of his recordings instead of a percentage. His savings, at one time considerable, were severely reduced by the 1929 Wall Street crash, by the drop of the Argentine peso in the last postwar period, and two great inflationary periods after the wars. In 1936 he sold the villa in Rome, investing the proceeds in real estate; even this new source of income dried up, owing to rent control regulations.

(g) To crown it all, in his book, *Tutti Sulla Mia Barca* (Milan, 1976), Silvio Gigli writes that he was presented with the following string of pearls by Titta Ruffo: "I sang the Verdi *Requiem* and the one by Mozart like nobody else in the world. I knew Pope Pius X and his parents. In a concert on September 22nd, 1905 I sang, and encored, an 'Ave Maria' before the Pontiff, who later received me in private audience...; I had cried out to his face 'down with the priests' and then discussed with him spiritual problems. The next day, in order to be pardoned, I sang a 'Hymn of Praise' to the Madonna at St. Peter's which was recorded on discs."

It is superfluous to add any corrections. Moreover, the same engaging author warns the reader in his foreword to the book frankly, and not very subtly, that his story has a "pinch of fantasy" in it. In recounting his meetings with Titta Ruffo he was obviously carried away.

And now, in conclusion, a last clarification to disperse any hopes fed by inaccurate information.

Some years after the publication of *La Mia Parabola* my father took up his pen again every now and then, for his own pleasure, to try his hand at some fiction. It was nothing more than an attempt to escape the sadnesss of the interminable hours filled only with memories. As he himself asserted in the preface to *La Mia Parabola* he did not nurture "literary ambitions," nor did he ever express to me the intention to release those pages. Therefore no one should expect posthumous publication of any more of Titta Ruffo's writings.

Notes

RUFFO TITTA, JR., and
GIORGIO GUALERZI *(G.)*

CHAPTER 1

[1] According to Giorgio Batini, author of two articles which appeared in *La Nazione* (Florence, 1968), the Titta family came to Pisa in the last century from Gambitelli, a small center in the Apennine Alps. The birth register of the Commune of Pisa gives the author's birth as one o'clock in the afternoon, at number 19 via Carraia, to father Oreste, smith, and mother Amabile Sequenza, a housekeeper; witnessing the act of declaration of birth were a laborer and a painter.

[2] The author's mother, by her own account, was of Spanish origin; her mother and grandmother had great voices but never set foot on the stage, such a thing being inconceivable in those times in a "good" family. The French magazine *Les Oeuvres Libres* published a story entitled "The General's Disappearance" which dealt with the general Marquis Sigüenza who, after having fought in Spain under the banner of Napoleon, left the country with his arms and effects when the Bourbons returned to power, going toward the Italian border. Having crossed it, all traces of him were lost. The baggage of the emigrant consisted of a harp and a piano, instruments which the author's mother remembers having seen in her home from early childhood. Finally, Sigüenza is a Spanish town in the province of Guadalajara (New Castile).

The extent of the conflict between the pious but uncompromising character of the mother and the character of the father Oreste is shown in the following anecdote: one day the cook Cecco took off his apron and left without notice to fight as a volunteer for Greek independence from Turkish rule. When he returned two years later he was reemployed. In the meantime, to keep aiding the Greek patriots financially, he began to market artichokes in oil, sometimes obtaining the assistance of Nella and Settima in the enterprise. But, unfortunately, Amabile surprised him teaching them the "Internationale" (worker's hymn) while he was cleaning his artichokes and dismissed him. The marital disharmony finally ended in a separation; in January 1900 Oreste went to live with another woman, and after the death of Amabile he married her, starting a new family.

The family of artisans which produced Titta Ruffo gave rise to other children with artistic talent. Brother Ettore took a degree from the Academy of St. Cecilia, Rome, in clarinet, composition, and orchestral conducting; in 1905 he conducted 7 performances of *Ballo in maschera* at the Politeama of Pisa; he composed an opera (*Malena*, in three acts, from *The Rumanian Nights* by Mihail Vlacesco, with rhythmic adaptation by A. Colantuoni. Puccio editore, Milano, 1909) and various songs; he gave voice lessons to the baritone Oreste Benedetti; after moving to the United States he taught music and singing there for 35 years; he was also a consultant to the Chicago Opera and the director of the Chicago Musical College.

Sister Fosca had a promising soprano voice (lirico-spinto); she debuted in Rome in 1903 in *Trovatore* at the Teatro Quirino; in 1904 she sang at Amelia (Terni) in *Pagliacci*, and at Pisa in *Pagliacci* and *Trovatore*; in 1905 she sang at Trento in *Trovatore*, *Cavalleria rusticana* and *Pagliacci*, and at Pisa in *Ballo in maschera*, conducted by her brother Ettore; between 1905 and 1907 she was at her brother's side in Russia. She cut three records: in 1907 "Di geloso amor' " from *Trovatore* (see appended discography), in 1908 "Tacea la notte al placido" from *Trovatore* and "Me pellegrina," from *Forza del destino*. Shortly afterward she ended her singing career to get married.

Sister Velia gave evidence of a talent for poetry and storytelling: at eighteen years of age she published two books of verse (*E l'alba*, Pisa, 1908 and *First verses*, Pisa) and at thirty, under the *nom de plume* Andrea Rota, a novel (*L'idolatra,* Treves, Milano, 1920).

[3] The fourth Ruffo... remains in the mind of God forever. Meanwhile, life's vicissitudes have led the third through a career as a business executive, something quite far from the author's dreams, which were expressed by him in an interview given in Budapest and published by the review *Magyar Szinpad* on the 8th of April, 1925. "I have a 15-year-old son. I hope he won't inherit my voice, but will remain free, and not a slave of his profession—that he might live in the country, like a man of the country, to contemplate the blue sky, and bathe in the sun and the silver rays of the moon; in essence, to enjoy the beauty of a simple life. This is a man's true vocation."

[4] To complete the portrait of the son it would be well to add that Oreste Titta was a "freethinker," and close to the libertarian movements. Significant in this regard is the choice of Cafiero for his son's middle name. Though only 30 years of age in 1877 the flaskmaker Carlo Cafiero (1846-1892) was already a prominent figure in early Italian socialism, inspired by anarchism.

[5] Titta Ruffo is therefore his artistic name, though it was exactly the same as that which would have been read on cast lists of the time, where singers gave their last name first and then the given name.

[6] As many as three praiseworthy iron gates forged in the paternal shop may still be seen in Rome: at the Villa Blanc on via Nomentana; inside the Caetani Palace at no. 32 on the street of the same name; inside the Palazzo Mattei at no. 31 via dei Funari.

[7] Via Carraia remains, renamed via Volturno. The house of TR's birth, on the façade of which a commemorative plaque has been affixed, is today no. 31. The change in the name of the street was done deliberately during the Fascist years so as to expunge the old name of a street famous for its population of liberty-loving Pisans.

[8] The Smisoch pastry shop was so called in Pisan dialect. It was located in Stretto village and extant until 1934-35.

[9] This artery has recently undergone a name change and is today called the via Giovanni Giolitti.

According to the research of the attorney Mesiano, Oreste Titta's shop was in the Piazza delle Terme 4, in a building managed by the Orphanage of Sta. Maria degli Angeli. The building which identifies it is still there today at the corner of via Cernaia facing the Planetarium. Oreste Titta remained there until November 1894, and he left it in 1895.

CHAPTER 2

[10] The Alexandrian Giulio Monteverde, a sculptor of the realist school, has remained famous especially for the marble group *Jenner experimenting with vaccination.*

[11] The account of TR's flight from home plays out almost entirely in the vicinity of the Albani foothills, a group of hills which are of volcanic origin southeast of Rome. Rich with vineyards, they are traversed by the Appian Way, at the time the principal highway connecting Rome and Naples. The larger population centers of the Albani hills are also called *Castelli romani* (Roman castles). To get some idea of the effort put forth by the author on his first day of flight, consider that he traveled on foot about 21 kilometers to reach Frascati, 10 more to climb to the Castel Gandolfo and another 3 to descend to Albano: altogether about 34 kilometers with a 400-meter change in altitude.

CHAPTER 3

[12] Called thus are the wineshops utilizing the tufa (of volcanic origin) forming the Albani hills.

CHAPTER 4

[13] The locality is near L'Acqua Acetosa, a source of mineral waters closed today, at the foot of the Villa Glori hills. Once frequented for its sandy shore, the Tiber became dangerous even for expert swimmers because of its very rapid current. Indeed, in the last century a stone plaque had been affixed to the façade of a little house nearby where the following could be read: "S.P.Q.R. - this section of the river is very dangerous."

[14] As many know, *Cavalleria rusticana* had a triumphant première the 17th of May, 1890, at the Teatro Costanzi in Rome, and such was the success, or rather the exaltion of its reception by the public and critics, that it remained at the Costanzi for four years, until the end of May, 1894, by which time it had gone through seven different productions and a total of fifty performances. Putting together the scant available statistics on the contemporaneous appearances of Bellincioni (1864-1950) and Stagno (whose given name was Vincenzo Andreoli: 1836-1897)—the two celebrated "creators" were harmonious and inseparable in life as well as in art—it is not difficult to establish that the performance which the author attended was one of 14 which made up the second production in the fall of 1890. Where it is certain that the very young Ruffo was not mistaken is in his intuition, perhaps confused, but infallible, that the two of them,

and Bellincioni in particular, were actually following the path upon which the modern interpreter would venture in trying to individualize and rediscover dramatic truth. *(G.)*

Certainly the 13-year-old Ruffo could never have imagined that 25 years later Bellincioni, having undertaken a new career as a film director and producer, would be in contact with him for artistic reasons. She wrote to him in fact on February 6, 1916 (having forgot, moreover, that she had sung with him in a concert in Paris in 1905): *"Illustrious colleague: Although I have not had the pleasure of really knowing you, I have had the greatest admiration for you and would like very much to have the pleasure, now that I no longer sing in theaters, of leaving on film a duet with a colleague such as yourself. Please be so good as to tell me what you would accept for such a film. The most that I am able to offer you (I am not speaking of merit) is 8,000 lire. I am making the film, so I would be infinitely appreciative if you could take the lead. I would be grateful for a short reply as soon as possible. Cordial greetings..."* TR's reply was, unfortunately, not positive.

[15] It was therefore around his 14th year that TR had, in a totally casual way, the revelation of an absolutely unique voice, by then already characterized by a power that would be found in no other. Regarding his tenorish timbre, let us not forget that in his prime as an authentic baritone, his voice was also distinctive for its range, so much so that, somewhat later he himself recalls the remark of Cotogni after hearing him in *Amleto* at the Costanzi (March 1909) prompted by his interpolation, in the course of his reprise of the *Brindisi*, of nothing less than a high B-flat, a note certainly "foreign to the baritone register." (See the end of Chapter 19). *(G.)*

[16] Fanfulla of Lodi and Ettore Fieramosca were legendary protagonists on the Italian side in the epic, *The Duel of Barletta* (1503). Of the two, the latter was more popular, immortalized by Massimo D'Azeglio in the novel which inspired at least six successive Italian composers.

[17] The episode is in the context of a major crisis in the building of the Capitale which broke out in 1885, lasted almost a decade, that also involved the banks.

[18] Dante, *The Divine Comedy*, Paradiso, XVII 58-59.

CHAPTER 5

[19] Certain events in the following pages should have preceded this date. These transpositions will be noted throughout this book.

[20] Built in 1890 in an unusual area, it remains today the principal Roman hospital complex.

[21] *La morte civile* (1861). (The Civilized Death.) Then very much in vogue and today completely forgotten, as is the name of its author, Paolo Giacometti (1816-1882), this is a drama of Sicilian ambience and social background with a strong polemical flavor.

CHAPTER 6

[22] Obviously this pertains to the Christmas of 1895, according to the author.

[23] O. Benedetti certainly had to be of the first rank to have been considered a "divine voice" by TR, who "did not remember his equal in the world," who was echoed by no less than Cotogni, who affirmed that he "had never heard a voice so beautiful," and prophesied "a glorious career." In reality, a lack of perseverance in his studies did not permit Benedetti to attain authentic fame. Nevertheless, it did not keep him from successfully taking the stage in good Italian and foreign theaters for around twenty years. *(G.)*

[24] This refers to one of the establishments of Richard Ginori.

[25] From the description he has left us the author appears to realize that Caio Andreoli was one of those teachers who abounded in the 19th century theater, endowed with certain natural abilities, but above all with great experience. He was content to "rehearse scores" (as it was called in theatrical jargon; to "coach") and at the same time to teach singing—besides entertaining useful relations (useful to himself, first, and to his pupils) with impresarios of the second rank, with whom, in a city like Rome, where there were so many small theaters, demands for his services were surely not lacking. *(G.)*

[26] The phrase ending the duet in the second act between the protagonist, blinded by order of the Emperor Justinian, and his daughter Irene. The fact that this selection was familiar to Benedetti, and would be also to the young Titta, demonstrates the persistent popularity, even at the end of the century, of an opera like *Belisario*, afterward neglected and performed at the present time in Italy only as a "novelty." *(G.)*

[27] The Quirino—built of wood in 1871 for the Prince Maffeo Sciarra, between via delle Vergini and via Marco Minghetti, and successively reconstructed of masonry in 1892 and 1898—was the first popular theater in the Roman capital. Destined to be a playhouse, as such it became one of the important centers of Italian theatrical life. From time to time the Quirino was also host to opera seasons of a high level, as the one alluded to by TR certainly was. *(G.)*

[28] In reality during that time Luigi Lucenti—a renowned bass with a long career (we have news of him along a chronological arc which goes from the autumn of 1889 to June 1913)—took part in at least three different Roman productions of *Faust* (two at the Quirino and one at the Nazionale): between March and July of 1895, however, which is prior to the reference to Christmas at the beginning of Chapter 6.

Some time before *La forza del destino* was performed at the Quirino (August 1894) with the notable participation of Carlo Cartica—a tenor famous for his high notes, specifically noted by TR, which permitted him a long and brilliant international career—who would sing the same opera two years later in Rome (June 1896), but at the Nazionale rather than the Quirino. *(G.)*

[29] The long and minute research of Marinelli Roscioni has verified that Benedetti debuted at the Quirino in *Trovatore* the evening of March the 24th, 1894. The *Ernani* at the Teatro Manzoni which is mentioned further on (his *benefit*, as it was called then) is instead on the following July 21st. Therefore, if it is true that the debut of the twenty-year-old Pisan baritone happened "after about a year of study," as TR records, then there is no doubt that the first encounter between TR and Benedetti was quite a bit before the Christmas of 1892, or indeed three

years prior to the date which the author gives at the beginning of this chapter.

[30] Antonio (also called Toto) Cotogni (1831-1918) is considered one of the most beautiful baritone voices of the preceding century, and of the entire history of the lyric theater in general. For about a 40-year period he performed in the greatest Italian and foreign theaters, above all in London and St. Petersburg, in a vast repertoire. Leaving the stage at more than sixty years of age Cotogni devoted himself to teaching, first at the Conservatory of St. Petersburg from 1894 to 1898 (but evidently he found himself in Rome when he happened to hear Benedetti) and then, until his death, at St. Cecilia where his pupils included the baritones Basiola and Franci and the tenor Lauri-Volpi. And it was in those years exactly that TR made the welcome acquaintance of his illustrious predecessor, which, besides, he records with obvious pleasure. (See Chapter 19, last page.) *(G.)*

[31] Inaugurated in 1876 with a brief operatic season, the Teatro Manzoni—situated on via Urbana, on the Esquilino, and predominately a playhouse—followed the Quirino by only five years. Both auditoriums were constructed to satify the growing passion of the Romans for theater, and they acquitted themselves of the task: the Quirino perhaps more so, as noted, and the Manzoni less so, where there was space for debut artists (or those with little experience) such as Benedetti. (In 1886 and 1898 the Nazionale and the Adriano, respectively, were added; the two largest theaters were the Apollo, then substituting for the Costanzi, today the Teatro dell'Opera, and the Argentina, where popular entertainments were given with a certain diligence.) *(G.)*

[32] The soprano in question must have been Penelope Guidi Andreoli, who was virtually unknown beyond her debut. *(G.)*

[33] Another Donizetti opera that would be completely forgotten today were it not for a London revival (February, 1975). Evidently toward the end of the last century it still enjoyed a certain prestige for baritones. The reason may be found in the third act, almost entirely composed of a compelling monologue by the protagonist—naturally, a baritone. *(G.)*

[34] What the author narrates is rather singular since the Roman Alfredo Palombi (1875-1954) was the contemporary of Ettore Titta and was, as a matter of fact, younger by some months. In reality this illustrious student and scholar (expert above all in band instrumentation) afterward received his degree in composition in 1898 and occupied for many years the post of Master of the School of Harmony of St. Cecilia, after winning the open competition for that professorship in 1910. *(G.)*

[35] TR later cut two records of this aria which demonstrate how special it was to him. *(G.)*

[36] Of the two, the less significant was Attilio Ugolini, who from 1880 taught elementary singing. By far the most important figure was Venceslao Persichini, who had just entered his last year of life (in fact he died on the 19th of September, 1897). Even today he is remembered as one of the great singing teachers of the last century. Suffice it to say that Antonio Magini Coletti, Mattia Battistini, and Giuseppe de Luca were his pupils. Leaving out of consideration the serious

(but in part understandable) error of not having immediately recognized the proper register of TR's voice, and then insisting that wrong was right—it is possible that the forbidding conduct of Persichini was negatively influenced either by a conformist, parochial spirit, or, above all, by an irreconcilable contrast between the genteel ways of the old Roman gentleman and the whimsical temperament of the undisciplined young Pisan. *(G.)*

[37] Two years still separated De Luca (1876-1950) from his theatrical debut which arrived in November 1897, that is to say two months after the death of the maestro, at the Politeama di Piacenza in *Faust*. In spite of a happy start, the relative modesty of his vocal means hindered him not a little in ascending to the dramatic heights, and specifically the Verdian heights of the repertory (TR's case was quite different). In fact it was only after about a decade singing lyrical roles that the Roman singer, slowly making room for himself in the crowded baritone ranks, attained those levels to which his great intelligence and extraordinary sensibility gave him every right. It is not by chance then that De Luca will remain on the crest of the wave for around a quarter of a century, spent in great part at the Metroplitan where he became one of the most popular personalities. Exceedingly significant, then, coming from a person of his stature, and from someone in direct competition with him, is De Luca's judgment of the author: "That isn't a voice, that's a miracle. [...] The records don't do him justice. His was the greatest baritone voice I ever heard." [Aida Favia-Artsay, in *The Record Collector*, June 1951, p. 125] *(G.)*

[38] With regard to the Roman Achille Lucidi (1847-1901) it may be added that, very active in his native city as a pianist also, he was the music teacher of Queen Margaret, among others.

[39] Filippo Marchetti (of Bolognola, 1831-1902) was a member of the first generation of post-Verdian composers, along with Boito, Ponchielli and the Brazilian composer Gomes. His *Ruy Blas*, (the best-known of the seven operas he wrote), after decades of good luck, especially in the provinces (the author, for example, performed it during the tour with Cavallaro), fell quickly enough in the public favor and ended by disappearing from all the wall posters. Marchetti, frustrated by the meager success of his last operas, dedicated himself exclusively to teaching after 1880, and he too counted Queen Margaret among his pupils, who confided the direction of the court quintet to him. From 1881 to 1886 he was president of the Academy of St. Cecilia, directing the music school there until his death. *(G.)*

[40] The Alexandrian Virginia Marini (1842-1918) abandoned the theater after a brilliant career of 36 years, and in July 1894 she was called to direct the school of recitation of the Academy of St. Cecilia, a position she held until her death.

[41] The author refers to Antonio Loustalot (or Loustallot, according to the Italian translation), Linda's father in the theatrical work, *La Grâce de Dieu* (1841), by A.E. d'Ennery and G. Lemoine, *drame en cinq actes (mêlé de chant)*, from which was drawn the libretto for the Donizetti opera, where the character in question is known instead only as Antonio. Correspondingly, also for the two preceding titles, the author is already referring not to the lyric operas but to the eponymous theatrical works of Pellico (presumably) and Verga respectively. *(G.)*

[42] Count Enrico San Martino di Valperga (1863-1947) was for half a century a personality of the first rank in the musical life of Rome, Italy, the world. In 1895 he succeeded the deceased Ruggero Bonghi as president of the Academy of St. Cecilia, and held the post until his death. *(G.)*

[43] These *vocalises*, along with *solfèges*, published in Paris in the 1840s and reprinted many times, assured a residual fame to their author, the composer and master of song, Paolo G. G. Concone of Turin (1801-1861). *(G.)*

[Translator's note: the French word for these vocalizations, *vocalises*, has been adapted by English-speaking singers with the final *s* pronounced so that the exercises are "vocal eases."]

[44]The Roman baritone Senatore Paolo Sparapani (1847-1926) had been an excellent singing actor; among others, he is remembered for the *Vascello fantasma* (The Flying Dutchman) and for the *Edmea* of Catalani, which coincided with the Italian debut of the 19-year-old conductor Arturo Toscanini. Esteemed also as a composer (indeed, his *Don Cesare di Bazan* was performed at the Teatro Manzoni of Milan in the same year of 1886), Sparapani, quitting the stage, opened a highly regarded school of singing, which he later transferred to Florence, where he died in 1926. *(G.)*

In the Roman newspaper *The Messenger* on January 26, 1901 the following notice appeared concerning TR: "He is a product of Mme. Giuliani's school, that splendid maestra who has already given so many distinguished singers to Italian art, and who restored Ruffo's baritone voice with great zeal after he had been studying to be a bass for an entire year at the Academy of St. Cecilia." That TR also took lessons from La Giuliani is not corroborated in any other source.

[45] According to the significant testimony of a Tuscan journalist, the iron railing of the American church in via Nazionale, Rome "is entirely constructed by the hands and the talent of the future illustrious singer," as well as a "crown of iron flowers" commissioned for the tomb by the President of the French Republic, Sadi-Carnot, who was assassinated in 1894.

CHAPTER 7

[46] Lelio Casini (1865-1910). On his tomb at Volterra the following may be read: "All those who know art will keep in their hearts forever the echo of his miraculous singing." Rhetoric aside, it is certain that, for as much as he was endowed with means not particularly robust and extensive, Casini, who belonged to a constellation of good baritone voices produced in Pisa in the second half of the last century, made himself respected for the sweetness of his pathos in song, the freshness of his lyrical accents, the mellowness of his classical emission (it was not by chance, as TR will record later, that Casini sang the *Abendsternlied* from *Tannhäuser*, an opera which he had in fact performed with success).

When he met the author, upon whom his teachings certainly had a positive effect, Casini, in spite of being only 32 years old and having begun his career scarcely ten years ago, was already alternating between the stage and the classroom, to which he would at last dedicate himself definitively because of a throat malady. Psychic and mental disturbances caused him to finish his days sadly at the mental hospital in Volterra, where he would die prematurely at the age of forty-five years, leaving his wife Emma Sbisà and his son Piero. *(G.)*

[47] "The greatest tenor of the last generation"—as the author will later (Chapter 20) describe Angelo Masini (1844-1926). In reality it was no accident that he was appreciated by Verdi. As much for the precise qualifications applied to *divi* as for those frankly artistic he was one of the greatest singers ever to appear on the lyric stage in all times and countries: a most authoritative exponent, and in some aspects a unique one, of the so called "*di grazia*" tradition. *(G.)*

[48] A characteristic street of old Milan, spared wartime destruction.

[49] It turns out that that a descendant of Mennini was still conducting business in 1937 on via Pattari 1, at the "Old Mennini Hotel," with a restaurant annex frequented by aspiring singers.

[50] A brief but very precise miniature of the finally too-famous "Galleria," the cross and the delight of singers, real or phony, of the past (near or remote). The definition of "Wall Street of Song" has been well adapted to it—coined by Lauri-Volpi. (Cf. *L'equivoco*, Milano 1938, p. 141.)

[51] Generally better known as "*Cortigiani, vil razza, dannata*," indeed the first words of the stupendous declamation which, without a break in continuity, introduces the aria proper "*Miei signori... perdono, pietade.*" *(G.)*

[52] *Perbacco che voce! Sembra Tamagno.* With its frankly popular ingenuousness this exclamation gives a precise idea, because wedded to reality (in December 1897 with Tamagno alive and still solidly pursuing his career) and not subject to rhetorical exaggerations, of what the great tenor of Turin effectively represented: not only an immensely popular singer, whose pure and simple expression of extraordinary sonorous force went beyond classifications of register, but a downright myth. *(G.)*

[53] The parabola of this singer was singular. At the moment when he met the author (December 1897) Mieli had not been a baritone for at least two years (as such he was active for some time, taking part, prior to Benedetti, in the same production of *Ernani*, among others, performed at the Teatro Manzoni in Rome). After graduating to the higher register, and certain performances here and there, Mieli was awaiting engagement, which would not be late in coming. In fact, a short time afterward, following in the author's footsteps he was signed for the spring season at the Teatro Costanzi, where, in May of 1898, he would sing in *Traviata*. As a tenor, effectively, Mieli would reach a certain fame, taking part, for example, in the Turin première of *Le maschere* (1901) and, still in Turin, in the première of the *Resurrection* of Alfano (1904). And it was always in Turin that—first as Germont in *Traviata*, then as Silvio in *Pagliacci*—that he could be found three years later, become a baritone again in a startling return to his origins. *(G.)*

[54] At issue are recordings performed on "cylinders" (if this was in December 1897), which were never industrially exploited.

CHAPTER 8

[55] An opera composer forgotten today (his *Salambò* was presented at the Pergola in Florence in 1884), the Neapolitan Vincenzo Fornari (1848-1900) evidently alternated between composition and conducting and teaching and the more obscure but no less well-remunerated activity of a rehearsal pianist or coach. *(G.)*

[56] At this time the Roman cav. Carlo D'Ormeville (1840-1924), fifty years old, already boasted of thirty years of intense, profitable, and multiform activity, especially in the world of theater as a dramatic author, a librettist of merit, a journalist and music critic (from 1884 he directed one of the most authoritative specialized periodicals, the *Gazzetta dei Teatri*), agent and impresario in his own right. D'Ormeville was in sum one of the most important personalities of our lyric theater (and would remain so for many years).

[57] Almost certainly the husband of Elvira Repetto, an excellent light lyric soprano, particularly active in Italy and outside it during the 80s and 90s. *(G.)*

[58] Actually this refers to the basso (and not baritone) Ludovico Viviani (not to be confounded with the baritone Gaetano, active in the period between the two wars), who earned himself a certain celebrity during the 70s and the first half of the 80s. But there was also an Orlando Viviani—the editor-in-chief of the *Rivista Teatrale Melodrammatica*—another specialized weekly which had its headquarters at the Vianelli Agency, directed by the former tenor Vittore Deliliers, and which could have confused the author. *(G.)*

[59] This Count Broglio (in reality Luigi Grabinski Broglio), like most of the agents, came to the job after an active career. Indeed, during the 80s and the first half of the 90s he had been a much-appreciated bass-baritone in the principal Italian theaters. Abandoning the stage he was soon dedicated to agent's duties, and at the time of his meeting with the author he had recently (December 1896) taken over the property of the famous C. Cambiaggio and Co. Agency (from the name of its founder, the famous "buffo" Carlo Cambiaggio) which remained his until his death in 1927. *(G.)*

[60] The attorney Vittorio Molco was an active theatrical agent.

[61] The voice of Giuseppe Pacini (1862-1910) was really "one of the most beautiful voices [...] for mellowness, grandeur of volume and homogeneity of the registers" (thus Celletti in *Le grandi voci*, op.cit., col. 593): not only between 1890 and 1910, but from the time his records were handed down where the exceptional extension of his high register and phenomenal lung power were abundantly displayed. An outstanding exponent of the most popular 19th century repertory, the Florentine baritone rapidly became the idol of the "gallery." An instinctive singer and dashing interpreter, Pacini was still appearing in the great Italian and foreign theaters (including La Scala, which contracted him for four seasons between 1894 and 1904) where he did not disdain the contemporary repertory.

It is natural that the author remain particularly impressed, even if his memory betrays him here: as it happens Pacini did not actually sing in Milan in the first months of 1898. *(G.)*

[62] Gustavo Argenti—from the beginning of 1897, head of the theatrical agency which bore his name as well as director of the corresponding periodical, the fortnightly *La Lanterna*—as much as the impresario Rodolfo Bolcioni. Both were baritones, both came up from the performers' ranks. Though Argenti was little more than a simple comprimario, Bolcioni had greater pretensions. It was Argenti then who favored the debut of TR, procuring him contracts either on behalf of Bolcioni or of other impresarios. *(G.)*

[63] Active by this time for many years, Giovanni Giani and Alessandro Arcangeli were in reality both singers of ordinary talent. Giani had scarcely returned to the Costanzi when, between November and December 1897, he took part in *Trovatore*, and as luck would have it, as the Herald in the production of *Lohengrin* which preceded that in which TR would make his debut several months later. Arcangeli occupied a higher level than his colleague, as demonstrated by his presence in the La Scala seasons of 1899-1900 (*Lohengrin* as Telramund and *Anton*), and 1900-1901 (*Bohème* and *Le maschere*), both conducted by Toscanini. *(G.)*

[64] Born in Valencia, Manuel Izquierdo (1871-1951), more famous in Italy as Emanuele Schierdo, belonged to the first wave of Spanish tenors who, by various means, emigrated to Italy toward the end of the century in the wake of Carrion (father and son) and Gayarre, Valero and Viñas, opening the way for the formidable trio of Lázaro-Cortis-Fleta, and in general to the fertile race of Spanish tenors which still endures.

L'Izquierdo in particular was active in Italy and outside it for about twenty years, until the outbreak of the First World War, in an ample repertory of about forty operas (from *Bohème* to *Aida*, from *Rigoletto* to *Otello*). He sang frequently alongside TR, to whom he had ties of close friendship, and with whom he recorded the duet in the fourth act of *Forza del destino* and the *terzetto* at the finale of the first act of *Trovatore* (the Leonora is Fosca Titta, TR's sister). He married the soprano Amelia Sedelmayer, the daughter in her turn of the maestro Abdon Senem-Sedelmayer, who was among the first to direct *Aida* in one of its revivals in Cairo. *(G.)*

[65] Constructed with two rows of boxes and two galleries, for a total of 1600 seats, the Alhambra was one of the minor theaters in a major town of Lombardy, destined as much for operettas as operas of a modest level with second- and third-class singers. *(G.)*

[66] Giuseppe Cavallaro was typical of a vanishing category of private impresario who certainly did not lack artistic and personal merit. The type is well on the way to extinction these days. He was the very same man who two years previously had contributed to the launching of Enrico Caruso in a very similar Sicilian tour, and was therefore undoubtedly gifted with great discernment where voices were concerned (and related business matters besides). As for Mastrojeni, Cavallaro's most aggressive competitor, he was perhaps less competent in this case, but he had the luck to attach his name to a theater, to wit the Teatro Mastrojeni in his city. *(G.)*

He also sought, but without success, to secure the services of TR for a season in "his" theater, as proven by an 1899 letter to Renzo Valcarenghi, an agent (and later partner) in the Ricordi firm.

[67] *Minchia* means *penis* in Sicilian dialect, and may be varied by different suffixes according to its context and the mood of the speaker. It is probably always impolite, but never taken literally. [Tr.]

[68] With many opinions pro and con about theatrical middlemen it cannot be denied that things were worse for debut artists at the end of the last century than they are today. In fact available figures show that Bolcioni, as stipulated in the two-month contract for the services of the twenty-year old TR, received 30% of the 90 lire stipend the singer collected. *(G.)*

CHAPTER 9

[69] Indeed, the right cast to launch a beginner like the young Titta Ruffo. Before all else it guaranteed the proven professionalism of a director like Vittorio Mingardi of Bologna (1860-1918), who was endowed with experience and seriousness of more than incidental value to him. Ten years later Mingardi was named artistic director of La Scala to replace Gatti-Casazza, who had emigrated to the Metropolitan.

As for the company (which boasted such performers as the soprano Lina de Benedetto, the mezzo-soprano Armanda degli Abbati, the bass Francesco Spangher, along with a Wagnerian specialist like the baritone Agostino Gnaccarini), it had as its strong point the Catalan Francisco Viñas (1863-1933) who in scarcely a decade in his dazzling career had reached a solid position in the tenor hierarchy. His beautiful timbre and impeccable technique gave him at least twenty-five years of an uninterrupted series of brilliant exhibitions in Spain, Italy and elsewhere, especially in *Lohengrin*, of which he remains today one of the "historic" interpreters. *(G.)*

[70] In spite of the implications of a happy start for him, the reader should consider the conditions the author confronted in his first public exposure on the evening of April 9, 1898. Scarcely twenty-one years old and deprived of the proper vocal and dramatic preparation, he was not only putting himself to the test in a Wagnerian opera whose music was unusual to his ears, but, among all the singers, his was the first voice to be heard in the vast theater.

[71] In reality, for reasons already decribed, after four years. The author and Benedetti will meet again at least two more times, if not in the same operas at least in the same theaters: at the Costanzi in April, 1910: TR as Figaro, Benedetti as Jachino/Il padrone in *La festa del grano* of Don Giocondo Fino; then at the Verdi of Florence, on December, 1914: TR as Figaro and Hamlet, Benedetti as Count di Luna. *(G.)*

[72] Bini will sing shortly afterward alongside the author as a bass in *Lucia di Lammermoor*, at the Teatro Politeama of Pisa.

[73] An establishment which sprang up in 1864 on a promenade along the sea, the "Pancaldi" was a prime example of the 19th century bathing establishment, right at the center of encounters between the fashionable and artistic elements of the city.

[74] At the end of the century Pisa had actually made itself famous as a spawning ground for baritones. Lelio Casini and Oreste Benedetti and their respectable

careers have already been mentioned. Among the rest the most famous was without doubt Emilio Barbieri (1848-1899), the last specialist in *Belisario*, who, above all during the 80s, was in great demand and came to sing in the major theaters. Cesare Cioni, however, belongs to the following generation—active in the good provincial theaters and in others in major cities and abroad—and the bass (not baritone) comprimario Giovanni Gasperini (not to be confounded with Bindo of the same name, a tenor of some renown in the first decade of the century). *(G.)*

[75] In a strictly statistical sense Gaetani was right. Tommaso Salvini was in fact born in Milan (1829), the second child of Giuseppe, also a famous actor, who was born in Livorno toward the end of the 18th century. A curious fact: while TR was singing in Livorno, on July 31, 1898, precisely, it happened that Tommaso's firstborn, and last of the glorious dynasty, Gustavo (1857-1930), participated along with Lelio Casini in an "Academy of Music and Drama" organized at the Politeama of Pisa for the benefit of the the the local *Filarmonica*.

[76] The last meeting between TR and Cesare Gaetani (1861-1907) presumably took place in the first months of 1906, that is to say during TR's second Russian tour. The suicide of the bizarre Livornese *viveur* concluded a tragically vehement turn of events. For some months Gaetani had cut off relations with the young and promising mezzo-soprano Serena Ronconi (the stage name of Teresa Varese Serena, born at Vignate [Milano] in 1880); informed that she was about to marry someone else, he went to Turin, where Ronconi was under contract, on February 24, 1907. On the very same evening, after her first performance, while she was dining in a restaurant in town in the company of her fiancé and the impresario Crescini, Ronconi came face to face with Gaetani, who shot her with a pistol and wounded her quite seriously (she wasn't active again until the following March 19), afterward turning the gun on himself and fatally shooting himself in the temple.

[77] The successes in Livorni of the debut artist TR were thus publicized in the Pisan weekly *Il Ponte di Pisa* (no. 20, July 24, 1898): "In nearby Livorno, at the Alfieri Arena, our fellow Pisan the young baritone Ruffo Titta has been singing in *Trovatore* for some evenings past, with ever-growing success; the Livornese journals are full of praise for him, and this time the praise is certainly warranted." *(G.)*

[78] The theater was destroyed by aerial bombardment during the Second World War.

[79] The author's debut in Pisa came on the 14th of August in *Trovatore*, which was followed on the 18th of September with *Lucia*. Here the young TR was "simply perfect," impressive for his "powerful voice," which during the sextet gave the impression of "the voice of a hurricane that dominates and subjugates." (*Il Ponte di Pisa*, no. 39, September 25, 1898). "The consensus of our citizens was warmly favorable to him," the same weekly wrote at the conclusion of the season, "predicting a splendid career full of all the satisfactions that art can provide; they are waiting for the chance to applaud him again in the near future as a celebrity." (Op.cit., no. 41, October 9, 1898). In fact he was again applauded, though not yet a celebrity, but decisively poised to become

one, in March 1901 in *Otello* and *Ernani*. However, nearly a quarter of a century would pass before they would see him again, unsurpassable as Hamlet, in October of 1925, when, as it turned out, he definitively took leave of the Italian lyric stage. *(G.)*

[80] Lelio Titta (1861-1939), brother of Oreste, TR's father, and his wife Ines (1865-1934) had two children: Giacinto Titta (1897-1961), Professor of Agriculture at the University of Pisa, and Lida Titta Palmieri.

CHAPTER 10

[81] In reality a theater of modest proportions, with a capacity of not more than 400 spectators: "modernized several times it was brought down during the First World War because of damages it had suffered while serving as quarters for troops" (F. d.N., in the *Enciclopedio dello Spettacolo*, vol. III, col. 237). Otherwise, in the *Annuario del Teatro Lirico* of 1940 it was among the "lesser municipal lyric theaters," counted regularly as the Teatro Municipale (it's exact title) of Catanzaro. *(G.)*

[82] The head of the company was Giuseppe A. Rossellini (1880-1931), the father of the producer Roberto (Roma, 1906-1977) and the composer and music critic Renzo (Roma 1908). A figure rich in human interest (he wrote a novel called *Sic vos non vobis*, Rome, 1928), he carried out, with plans from the engineering firm Sleiter, the construction of the villa which the author built in Rome on via del Sassoferrato 11. Also, Angiolino Bencini, then established in Rome and consolidating his friendship with the author, was born in Calabria.

[83] This singer, who remained in the second rank, actually, was (though unawares) privileged to stand as godfather in less than a year to at least two of the greatest baritones of the (next) century: in November 1897, De Luca in *Faust* at the Politeama di Placenza, and on the October following, Titta Ruffo in *Forza del destino* at the Municipale of Catanzaro. *(G.)*

[84] In fact the tenor was a certain Enea Cavara, who was then replaced by Izquierdo.

[85] The author alludes to the words "*La giovinezza mia...*" with which Marcello takes up and enlarges the music of Musetta's waltz: it is a phrase in E-natural which unfolds on medium-high *tessitura*, with great effect, which evidently encouraged the young baritone to stun his audience by flaunting the miraculous power of his exuberant vocal means. *(G.)*

[86] In reality the first city on the tour was Siracusa; afterward the author becomes inexact in citing the venues and the operas of this Sicilian tour.

[87] The Catanese Rapisardi (1844-1912), a professor of literature at the university, was a poet who in a few years had found himself on the crest of a wave, having consented to a debate with Carducci regarding a satirical allusion in his anticlerical poem *Lucifero*.

[88] Situated in the Piazza Cutelli, it was originally constructed of wood, about 1894, for summer festivals, and given to the impresario Cavallaro to manage.

[89] The eminent criminal lawyer and politician, a native of Termini Imerese, Luigi

Macchi (1871-1930) also wrote articles of penetrating operatic criticism. He witnessed the marriage of Velia (the author's younger sister) when she married, in a civil ceremony, Giacomo Matteotti.

[90] A pugnacious politician, elected deputy for the first time in 1892, Giuseppe de Felice Giuffrida (1859-1920) took an active part in parliamentary life in the socialist ranks during seven legislatures.

[91] Belonging to a famous dynasty of puppeteers, the Catanese Giovanni Grasso (1873-1930) actively shared the verist tastes of the author. He often imposed his will by means of a remarkably fiery temperament that sometimes led him to exaggerate certain brutal aspects of Sicilian reality.

Older by one year, Angelo Musco (1872-1937), also a Catanese, after having taken part in the Grasso's Sicilian company, on his own account began to surpass the master thanks to his greater moderation as an actor and a more acute interpretive intelligence, brought particularly into relief in his Pirandello repertory. *(G.)*

[92] Menotti Delfino (1858-1937), according to Cavallaro's purely euphonic criteria, also suggested to TR, inverted his name with the results already known. Friulian by birth (from Fiumicello in the province of Udine) but of clear Irridentist extraction (his baptismal name derives from the cognomen of the famous martyr of the Risorgimento). At forty Menotti—belonging to the generation of Magini Coletti and Battistini, of Pessina and Ancona, to whom he cannot be considered inferior as a singing actor—was at the apogee of a brilliant career evolving in Italy and abroad. He was particularly appreciated in Russia where he stayed for some years to teach singing at the Conservatory of Odessa (see Chapter 19), followed by comparable appointments in the Conservatory of Boston and of his native Trieste, where for some time he was artistic director of the Teatro Verdi. *(G.)*

[93] Wearing down the singer with the excuse of seeking the best for him (in reality seeking only immediate profit). The history of the lyric theater is literally paved with similar episodes. Fortunately the author possessed resources of power to face up to such tactics. And yet even he will accept the risky proposition of the St. Petersburg impresario to sing in the same day nothing less than a *Rigoletto* and a *Demon*. He will come out of it victorious, but in the manner of a Pyrrhus: with two thousand rubles in his pocket (about five thousand lire in 1906) but "more dead than alive" (c.f. p. 239). Rarely is the art of enduring in harmony with the ambition to prevail at all costs and win "the sacred gold of fame." *(G.)*

[94] City (in the province of Catania) which cultivated the lyric theater from as early as the seventeenth century.

[95] Constructed in 1864 on the grounds of an ancient theater the present hall, dedicated to Bellini, offers three ranks of boxes, an ingenious scenery mechanism and decorations by the painter Giuseppe Spina.

[96] Even if the author repeatedly had such favorite and renowned colleagues in *Barbiere*, *Rigoletto*, and *Hamlet* as the Andalusian Galvany, and the Catalans, Pareto and de Hidalgo, it is certain, however, that with Luisa Tetrazzini (1871-

1940) a duo came into being that was among the most acclaimed of any in the ten years preceding the First World War. Furthermore it is also said that, no less than Caruso and Melba, the gifted Florentine soprano knew how to incarnate *divisma* (mystique) of an Anglo-Saxon (especially American) kind in the most complete accepted meaning of the term. Hence a meeting on stage was inevitable between two outstanding personalities such as the author and Patti's successor. *(G.)*

[97] Considered by many (perhaps not incorrectly) the greatest tenor of the century, Enrico Caruso (1873-1921) is part, along with TR and Eugenia Burzio (1882-1922) of the historic trio of exceptional voices and extraordinary temperaments that will give a vital impulse and an unequalled contribution to the commercial and artistic fortunes of the tendencies asserting themselves in Italian music. Bound by reciprocal ties of comradely collegiality if not deep friendship consolidated over years of artistic association in Europe and South America, Caruso and TR, whose voices were both phonogenic to a maximum degree, have left us in their only record together—the duet in the finale of the second act of *Otello*—a unique example, more in the nature of an athletic performance than one strictly artistic, of the comparison, not to say collision, between two truly titanic voices. *(G.)*

[98] The author must have confused the place, or the time, or both. "A year later," that is in 1920, we see him only in Boston, Chicago and Philadelphia; it turns out that he never sang in New Orleans. In the probable event that he confused it with another city in the south of the United States, the city might be either Savannah, where he stopped briefly three years later during the concert tour of 1923, or else Birmingham, Memphis or Miami, which he visited six years later in the operatic tour of 1926.

[99] Performed for the first time in Venice in July 1898, *La Risurrezione di Lazzaro* is the third of the oratorios composed by the fertile and once highly praised (though little discussed today) Tortonese priest Lorenzo Perosi (1872-1956) during the period of his most intense creative activity. As for the effective presence of the composer on the conductor's podium, serious doubts persist, backed by the fact that the journalists of the time reported the name of a certain maestro Filippo Tarallo. *(G.)*

[100] Particularly distinguished for at least a good twenty years in a largely contemporary repertory that permitted him to display his outstanding resources as a singing actor, the Dalmatian Giuseppe (Josef) Kaschmann (1850-1925), thanks to his talents for intelligent and expressive declamation, and to his being an extremely cultured and refined man, was first noted in the field of oratory, reaping great success in Perosian performances and then, in the last decade of his career, into his seventies, in a repertory of light comedy. *(G.)*

[101] Situated on the via di Sangiuliano, and actually dedicated to Saint Nicholas, this is actually the largest church in Sicily.

[102] More properly Arena Pacini, in the forest of the ex-Capuchins, near the Bellini garden: a typical summer theater, besides opera productions, it is designed to host companies doing operettas and spoken drama with many kinds of staging.

[103] Evidently referring to Dante's "Ahi, Pisa, vituperio delle genti" (*Inferno*, XXXIII, 79).

[104] Abandoning the career of singer after a few appearances in public (the most important were as Valentin in *Faust* at the Costanzi in 1900 and as Count di Luna in *Trovatore* at the Quirino in 1903, where the Leonora was the debut artist Fosca Titta, TR's sister), Amleto Pollastri followed TR for years performing secretarial duties, and working also as a rehearsal pianist.

[105] A popular character in chivalric poetry: Ferraù is the gigantic Saracen of extraordinary strength who challenges the more fearless Christian champions, from which emerges Rinaldo, the bravest. The puppet shows, or "pupi" were in vogue in the nineteenth century and in the first years of the twentieth in Sicily, but in particular at Palermo and Catania, thanks to the famous dynasty of "pupari" (puppeteers), one of whom, of course, was Grasso.

[106] In such a context, expresses great and affectionate admiration.

[107] Musco aside, the most famed of all is Gerolama (called Mimì) Aguglia (born in 1884), a dialectal actress who developed, like her colleagues, in the school of Giovanni Grasso.

CHAPTER 11

[108] The anecdote is inserted in the Caruso biography of Stanley Jackson *(Caruso*, New York 1972), seasoned with many inventions. Jackson imagines TR talking to Caruso while making the sign of the cross, something very alien to his habits; he places him in Naples for his debut; he has Caruso and TR singing together at the Costanzi in Rome. Finally he would have the Neapolitan gangsters (in TR's story) arming TR with a pistol to carry out a bank robbery!

CHAPTER 12

[109] Already Teatro di San Saverio, it was razed by the Brunetti brothers, reconstructed and inaugurated under their name on February 18, 1865; then ceded, because of economic failures, to a certain Lambertini, who rebaptized it the "Eleanora Duse," and inaugurated it on the 12th of June, 1898. Under the same name the theater is still in use today.

[110] Today Teatro Verdi, not to be confounded with the Comunale, now the most important theater of the city.

[111] Roberto Zoppolato, director and proprietor of the Agency of the "Frusta Teatrale" [frusta = whip] of Milan. The impresario who contracted the author was instead a certain G. Mazza.

[112] The merits of the Spoletina Angelica Pandolfini (1871-1959) actually corresponded to the enthusiastic judgment of the author. A singer-actress of historical high standing in the ambit of the first generation of interpreters produced by the "young school," she was, with Storchio, the founder of movement of the intimate, expressive vein, "creating" in 1902 the character of Adriana Lecouvreur. She married seven years later, and survived for half a century after her retirement from the stage, dying at Lenno on Lago di Como. *(G.)*

[113] Elvino Michele Ventura (1873-1931), a lyric tenor with a free and pleasingly timbred voice, spent a brilliant career in Italy and outside it during the first decade of the century, making a name for himself above all, as TR has noted, with the *Iris*, in which he remained one of the first and most worthy "specialists." Retiring from the stage in 1920, he opened a singing school. He died unexpectedly in the vestibule of Carcano where he had gone to hear one of his own pupil's debut. *(G.)*

[114] Nephew of the writer Anton Giulio Barrili (author, among other things, of a biography of Verdi) who introduced him to journalism, the lawyer Breschi, born at Final Pia in 1874, was first the editor of *Secolo XIX* of Genoa, where he wrote theatrical criticism, then he moved on to the *Messagero* of Rome, where he was a director from 1919 to 1931.

[115] The young baritone's growing reputation was evident by the jingling of his purse. From the 150 monthly offered by Bolcioni we have in fact, in the space of two years, moved up to 100 lire per performance; in another couple of months the impresario Ducci will have to pay him no less than ninety per day for the duration of four months. *(G.)*

[116] The maestro Domenico Varola.

[117] This was frequently enough the case, demonstrating that even then things weren't going quite the way some people today might imagine they were going. For the record, the impresario-swindler was called Antonio Comolli. *(G.)*

[118] More than of an aria this is a question of the final concertante of the third act which begins with the words, "O sommo Carlo," intoned by the baritone. *(G.)*

[119] *Mia sposa sarà la mia bandiera* (My wife will be my banner) is the exact title of the popular romance which gave fame to the name of the Roman composer Augusto Rotoli (1847-1904).

[120] Taking part with the company was the vigorous protagonist, the young and quite promising Astigian tenor Angelo Gamba, whose career finished tragically, shattered by the earthquake of Messina, the night of December 28, 1908. *(G.)*

CHAPTER 13

[121] Because of the disagreements provoked by Puccini's decision to compete with Leoncavallo on the very same territory with *Bohème*, it is doubtful that in 1900 Puccini and Tito Ricordi would still be having such friendly relations with the Neapolitan musician that they would be seen strolling with him in the Galleria. This aside, the fact remains that two of the most talked-about musical personalities of the moment are here in question. *(G.)*

In this period the 42-year-old Puccini (1858-1924)—by this time securely riding a wave of successes obtained with *Manon Lescaut* and *Bohème*, which was clinched a few months previously by *Tosca*—already knew of TR, at least by name, since it had been called to his attention by a friend from Lucca who had certainly heard the young baritone at Pisa or Livorno. Indeed, we learn this from a jolly little note from Puccini to this very friend on September 14, 1899:

Dear Ernesto: Titta Ruffo 22 years old! I have forty of them and I am not yet "titta" nor "ruffo," perhaps I will become so as I grow older because one never knows how that's going to finish. I do not know him, either, therefore he hasn't been talked about for Tosca. But I will take your proven judgment into account and make use of him if the occasion arises. Silvia and Elvira return your greetings. This year we'll see each other in Rome where we ought to stay for a good month. I'm very well and you are, too; so what more can we ask? Let's give thanks to the saintly face responsible for today's holiday and I pray you, say hello to my friends and enemies in Lucca for me, a hearty hearty handshake for you. Affectionately yours, Giacomo Puccini.

(TR debuted in the part of Scarpia the 12th of April, 1901, at the Massimo di Palermo, taking the role from Giraldoni on the occasion of its local première.)

Quite different, naturally, will be the attitude of Puccini toward the "celebrated" TR some years later, when in three successive letters dated December 28, 1916, January 11 and September 23, 1917, he will solicit the participation of TR in the première of *Tabarro*. Finally, on March 12, 1918 there is one more letter, written for the same purpose and significant enough, in which Puccini writes to TR:

Dear Titta, my three new operas in one act will probably be given in Rome at the end of April or in the first days of May, all together in one evening. Tabarro *and* Gianni Schicchi *are perfect for your voice and temperament, and I'm asking if you want to sing them. I told you so a year ago and I'm repeating it now. I am told you don't want to sing in Rome, is this true? Please respond right away because time presses for me to make my decision. Affectionate greetings from your G. Puccini.*

But TR was unable to satisfy Puccini's desire, nor for that matter that of Ruggiero Leoncavallo (1857-1919) to have him for the first interpreter of *Majà* at the Costanzi in Rome in 1910.

As for the youngest of the three, Tito Ricordi (1865-1933) was destined a dozen years later to collect the inheritance of "dear Mister Giulio," the friend of Verdi and protector of Puccini, without ever reaching the eminence of such a father.

[122] In reality Luis Ducci, then director of the business of the Teatro Municipal of Santiago, Chile.

[123] An absurd boast, since the career of Adelina Patti (1843-1919)—the celebrated Italian-Spanish diva, without doubt one of the greatest singers of the past (and note the admiration that Verdi always cherished for her), among the select company who "make history" on the basis of what costume they wear—had been launched some forty years previously, to be precise in America (and to be more precise, in New York) where Patti was living and studying singing. *(G.)*

[124] The hotel, today called the "Regina Métropole" advertised thus in the theatrical journals of the time: "Artists of the Teatro alla Scala, before taking up residence in a furnished room, speak to the director of the Hotel Rebecchino

and hear about the special conditions which are accorded each artist! Excellent cuisine, electric light, electric elevator, steam heat."

[125] The name of Mattia Battistini is inexplicably absent, while in exchange that of Antonio Cotogni does figure in, the greatest baritone who still belonged to the preceding generation. As for Victor Maurel of Marseilles (1848-1923), who is qualified to compete for the title of the very best: although endowed with a voice of arguable timbre and resonance, he succeeded, thanks to his impeccable technique and extraordinary expressive faculties, in becoming one of the greatest singing actors of his time, linking his name to such characters as Iago, Tonio and Falstaff, of whom he was the first interpreter in 1887, 1892 and 1893 respectively. Retiring from the stage around 1905 he went to settle in New York where he died in straitened circumstances in 1923, leaving a few records and some writings regarding problems of interpretation and staging (among them a very important study of *Otello*). *(G.)*

[126] A bass of renown, Wulmann had a long and brilliant career. Signed during the 1884-85 season at the Regio di Parma (among others, for *Bella fanciulla di Perth* and *Favorita*), indeed we find him again in December 1910 as Fafner in *Siegfried* at La Scala, where already in December 1904 he had portrayed the King in *Aida*. *(G.)*

[127] A singer of the second rank qualified for clever parts or so-called "characters," Arturo Cerratelli had a good career in Italy and outside it, especially in the South American theaters. *(G.)*

[128] The author wanted to cloak in delicate discretion the identity of this person hiding under the appellatives first of "signora bruna," and then of "Benedetta" (blessed one). The important space dedicated to her in this autobiography and the influence she exerted on the growth of the author's personality, however, legitimizes the reader's curiosity to know her name. I think it would not be irreverent, since by this time all the characters in this book have disappeared, if I will reveal, for the sake of historical fidelity, the identity of "Benedetta," in conformity, furthermore, with what has already been done by the Polish soprano Janina Korolewicz-Wayda (1875-1957) and the United States soprano Grace Moore (1901-1947) in their respective autobiographies, *Life and Art, Memories of a Singer* (ed. Russ., Moscow, 1965) and *You're Only Human Once* (Melbourne, 1944).

"Benedetta" was, then, the mezzosoprano Adelina Fanton, née Fontana, who was born in Venice in 1867 and died in Milan on the 9th of June, 1907. Regarding her career she appeared in *Tannhäuser* at La Scala during the 1891-92 season, probably in the small part of the page, while no trace of her appearances at the Regio di Torino has been found. After having debuted at Urbino as Azucena (season 1891-1893), she sang instead, certainly, in 1893-94 in South American theaters (for example in *Trovatore* and *Carmen*); after that at the Bellini in Catania and the Eretenio of Vicenza; in 1901 in *Nabucco* and *Gioconda* (la Cieca) at the Fenice of Trieste and *Mefistofele* (Elena, or else Marta or Pantalis) in Santiago, Chile. In January 1903 we find Fanton again in *Gioconda* at the Vittorio Emanuele di Torino, then beside the author in *Nabucco* at the Rossini of Venice in the very same year and, probably in 1905, in *Demon* of Rubinstein at the Municipal Theater of Odessa.

[129] Ireos Myrtea—a young soprano of probable Rumanian origin, included in the lists of singers published by agency trade papers of the time—debuted in Santiago in *Faust* alongside TR.

[130] Citations which show the level of culture which the autodidact TR had attained. We note the Flemish painter Peter Paul Rubens (1577-1640); less commonly noted, on the other hand, is the Swiss Böcklin (1827-1901), whose style gains substance from its mythological and allegorical content. *(G.)*

[131] He uses "*gattini*," a term taken from popular Tuscan dialect to signify vomit.

[132] A reference to Dante's "la corata pareve e'l tristo sacco" (*Inferno*, XVIII, 26), where the internal organs appear in a sad sack.

[133] Edoardo Castellano owes the survival of what renown he has among scholars of the history of opera, not so much to the sixteen records he cut between 1901 and 1907—all the same, the notable quality of his lyric tenor explains the high fees he was getting in his day—as for the fact of being Des Grieux in the Italian première of *Manon*, October 19, 1893, at the Carcano of Milan.

[134] An old potion composed of vinegar, essence of garlic, rue and camphor. According to the legend it took its name from a group of thieves who looted plague victims but remained themselves immune to the contagion by virtue of this very medicine, for which they were obliged to reveal the formula in order to save their lives.

[135] This is Arturo Padovani, then director and concertmaster of the Teatro Municipal of Santiago (Chile), older brother of the more famous orchestra conductor and concertmaster, and composer besides, Alfredo (1878-1939), by whom the author was later conducted in Spain in 1916 and in Havana in 1921.

CHAPTER 14

[136] I have not found any date for this performance in Valparaiso in 1900.

[137] The author alludes to the Teatro de la Opera (where in effect he will sing during the summer of 1902) which, after being for some years one of the most important theaters in South America, in the space of just one decade will see itself rapidly supplanted by the new Colón. *(G.)*

[138] Records at the R. Teatro Nuovo (as the Verdi of Pisa came to be called in 1901) also include some performances of *Ernani*. *(G.)*

[139] A Milanese man of letters (1812-1882) remembered for his seven-year labor of translating all the plays of Shakespeare (twelve volumes, 1875-1882).

[140] Of his Iago the Pisan critic Mario Razzi wrote in fact that "it is simply a perfect success, never causing one to complain of any deficiency either of voice or dramatic action, which he has studied lovingly and with happy intuition, developed and delivered without offensive exaggerations and clichés, but rather seriously, consciously, he is giving to the appearance and temperament of the character the imprint and feeling with which the superb and strong conception of Shakespeare formed it." (*Il Ponte di Pisa*, March 3, 1901). In *Ernani* on the other hand, his interpretation was defined as "strong, colored with dramatic

energy and by the robustness of the singing" in such a way that there resulted a Carlo V "resplendent in generosity and noble grandeur" (*op.cit.*, March 31, 1901). *(G.)*

[141] In fact the author sang at Siena prior to the engagement in Pisa.

[142] The Palermitano Mario Sammarco (1868-1930) and the Marseillais Eugenio Giraldoni (1871-1924), an Italian (son of Leone, the famous Verdian baritone, and the no less worthy soprano Carolina Ferni), are paired today, in a historical context, as two of the most illustrious representatives of the baritonal generation immediately preceding that to which Titta Ruffo belongs, having tied their names to, among others, such characters as Gérard and Scarpia, of whom they were respectively the creators. Very different as to their vocal earmarks—the first is clear and decisively tenorish; the second has a rather dark, almost bass-baritone tonality—they had an absolute mastery of technique. The rare incision of their accents and the outstanding ability to color words, the capacity to deepen the psychology of their characters, resources of stagecraft of the first order—all the foregoing made of them two splendid and equally valid models of singing actors of the 19th century mold—precursors of TR. *(G.)*

[143] *Il Ponte di Pisa* (no. 16, April 24, 1901) certainly did not lose any time keeping their own readers informed about the growth of their fellow Pisan's career, having recourse, naturally, to the quotations of others. Thus, by means of *L'Ora* it was learned that in *Rigoletto* (whose last performance, the 25th of April, saw the debut on the conductor's podium of Gino Marinuzzi, not yet twenty years old) "he overcame great difficulties of interpretation," showing "a robust and extensive voice and effective stagecraft." It could be read in the *Giornale di Sicilia* in its turn that the Scarpia of the young baritone "easily passed the most severe test." *(G.)*

[144] According to what Ignazio Ciotti has written, "from 1901 to 1905 the concession of the theater was granted to Comm. Augusto Laganà, an impassioned and competent 'man of the theater'" (*La vita artistica del Teatro Massimo di Palermo*, 1938, p. 13); Ignazio Florio (descendant of Vincenzo (1799-1868), to whom is owed the creation of this worthy Palermo family's fortune) succeeded Laganà from 1906 to 1919, then resumed control from 1923 to 1926. *(G.)*

[145] In fact between the contracts at the Massimo di Palermo (April 1901) and at the Fenice di Venezia (April 1903) two years passed during which the author performed successively at Trieste (Teatro La Fenice), in Egypt (two seasons at Cairo and Alexandria), at Buenos Aires and Montevideo. As for the Venetian *Trovatore*, it's easy to imagine that he was received with real enthusiasm, since right beside TR, a protagonist like the powerful Puerto Rican tenor Antonio Paoli was also in the cast. *(G.)*

[146] *Il santo*—a mystical drama in three acts on the libretto of Count Luigi Sugana (1857-1904), a singular example of Venetian bohemianism, who owed his Goldonian libretto to the *Donne curiose* (Unusual Women) of Wolf-Ferrari—was performed with success on the 7th of May, 1903, and then for five more evenings, under the baton of Rodolfo Ferrari, with tenor Alfredo Cecchi as the protagonist; in contrast to the Saint, TR was playing the part of "Mondo,"

separated into the characters of Publio Valerio and Satan. This was the only opera composed by Ghin (1862-1933), the pupil of Nicolò Ceccon (1826-1903), the Venetian organist, composer and scholar in his own right, and of Antonio Smareglia (1854-1929), a stalwart composer of operas whose output, today almost entirely forgotten, obtained a noteworthy success before the turn of the century in several Italian and middle-European theaters. *(G.)*

CHAPTER 15

[147] The order of events was in reality the reverse. In fact the debut of TR at Covent Garden took place in *Lucia* on the 5th of June, 1903, which on the 1st of July was followed by Rossini's *Figaro*, on both occasions under the baton of the Orvietano Luigi Mancinelli (1848-1921), renowned as a composer (the author himself, some years later, will perform his *Paolo and Francesca* at the Sao Carlos of Lisbon) but above all as a conductor and orchestra director of the modern cast. Three members of the cast were the same in both operas. First of all the Catalan soprano Maria Barrientos (1884-1946), not yet 19 years of age, but already a *maestra di virtuosismo*, who, with Pacini, Huguet, Galvany, Pareto, de Hidalgo and Ottein, was a mainstay of the battle-hardened group of coloraturas of the Spanish school who dominated European and South American theaters uncontested for more than thirty years.

Next there was Alessandro Bonci (1870-1940), then at the zenith of his fame, a *tenore di grazia* who was among the greatest of the century, who, contracted by the Manahattan of New York, knew how to endanger even Caruso's supremacy, to the point of being stolen away by the rival theater and brought to the Metropolitan, and, as if that were not enough, courteously invited to go back to Europe.

Finally, as Bidebent and as Basilio, there was the French bass-baritone Marcel Journet (1867-1933), endowed as much with a beautiful voice as with technical capacity and interpretive talent, who seven years later we will rediscover at the Opéra de Paris in *Hamlet*, alongside the author.

As for the Dalmatian, Antonio Pini-Corsi (1859-1918), from whom TR took over the part of Figaro, he sang practically until his death, first as a baritone primarily of the *brillante* type (Verdi chose him as the first Ford) then as a *buffo* with many resources of color. *(G.)*

[148] The Neapolitan Antonio Scotti (1866-1937) was another of that pleiad of singing actors produced from 1890 to 1910 with whom TR had to settle his accounts. Not yet thirty he became part of the international singing elite, and remained there practically until the end of his career (1933), a favorite of the Covent Garden public and absolutely idolized by the Metropolitan's, where he sang uninterruptedly for 34 seasons (1899-1933, a record). Endowed moreover with notable intelligence and a great flair for business, Scotti not only was the founder of that dynasty of Neapolitan singers who made their fortunes at the Met, but, fortified by the prestige he had acquired, he was made head of his own theatrical organization, the Scotti Grand Opera Company, with which he traveled all over the United States after the First World War. *(G.)*

[149] The Australian Helen Mitchell, for a brief time the wife of Porter Armstrong (1861-1931), much better known as Nellie Melba (a stage name assumed in

honor of her home town of Melbourne), not only was one of the greatest sopranos of her epoch, gifted with one of the most fascinating voices ever heard, but,
with the already cited Adelina Patti and Luisa Tetrazzini (and perhaps others of
that exalted class) made a decisive contribution to the modern *myth of the prima
donna.* An authentic *diva,* according to the most complete meaning of the word
(demonstrated in abundance by her behavior in the incident involving the author), Melba incarnated the excellences as well as the defects of that particular
Anglo-Saxon aspect of the *belle époque* better known as the "Victorian Era," of
which she remains today an undisputed symbol. *(G.)*

[150] The Frenchman André-Charles-Prosper Messager (1853-1929), the pupil of
Saint-Saëns, gained fame for the composition of *opéra-comiques* and operettas
as well as for his work as a conductor in a career which lasted for about a half
century, and saw his name linked to the première of *Louise* (1900) and of *Pelléas
et Mélisande* (1902). When he met the author, Messager was artistic director of
Covent Garden, a post which he held from 1901 to 1906. *(G.)*

[151] He must almost certainly be referring to Neil Forsyth, whose notable theatrical experience led him to take on, in the ambit of the Grand Opera Syndicate
(an organism created in 1897 to manage Covent Garden in a more modern
fashion), duties of great responsibility, which he carried out with the ability of a
"perfect Edwardian diplomat." (H. Rosenthal, *Two Centuries of Opera at Covent
Garden,* London 1958, p. 398). *(G.)*

[152] Five-six, to be exact. The episodes narrated here actually played out in two
distinct phases: in April 1908, contracted by the San Carlo of Naples, the author sang, in order, *Rigoletto, Gioconda,* and *Africana;* in April of the following year, when he returned to the Neapolitan theater, he interpreted, consecutively,
Barbiere, Zazà, and *Amleto* (*Hamlet*). *(G.)*

[153] The author is referring to the four important seasons from October-Novem-
ber which came about at Covent Garden from 1904-1907, during which the
company of the San Carlo of Naples performed. The President of its Board of
Directors was, in fact, Roberto De Sanna, who brilliantly fulfilled his responsibility from 1901 to 1913. The fact is worth noting because it signifies perhaps
the first example of regular collaboration among the greater European theaters.
(G.)

[154] In 1909 the author was 32 years old and Melba was 48; this means that on
the occasion of the London *Rigoletto* the age of the two antagonists was respectively 26 and 42 years. They will sing together later only once, and in *Rigoletto*
no less—February 18, 1914, in Philadelphia!

[155] A tourist center situated on the edge of a wooded plateau dominating the
lake and the city of Como.

[156] The author's interest is kindled for the first time here in the character who
will become, for 25 years—from his debut in February 1907 at the São Carlos
of Lisbon, to the last performance in March, 1934, at Nice, which coincided
with his farewell to the stage—his "warhorse." *(Hamlet* was composed in 1868
by Ambroise Thomas [1811-1896].)

[157] From Hugo to D'Annunzio: a series of names set down one after the other, though representing a variety of epochs and styles, which gives a sufficient idea not so much of the degree of culture the author has attained, as this exceptional autodidact's particular sensibility. *(G.)*

CHAPTER 16

[158] The memories of the author, here as elsewhere superimposing themselves chronologically, might create some understandable perplexity which it would be good to clarify. The return to Brunate came, presumably, in the autumn of 1903 and the succeeding contract was for the Teatro Rossini of Venice for some performances of *Nabucco*, where the author, as he has said, found himself right beside his "Benedetta" as Fenena.

On the other hand the return to Milan to which the author refers is anticipated by about two years; it came at the end of his engagement at the Massimo of Palermo (April 1901), after which, prior to the long engagement in Egypt, there were several performances of *Nabucco* and *Gioconda* at the Teatro la Fenice of Trieste. G.

[159] Then called the Teatro dell'Opera; completely destroyed by fire in 1971.

[160] An epidemic benign illness of tropical and subtropical zones, characterized by fever of brief duration with violent, generalized osteo-articular pains and an eruption followed by desquamation of the skin.

[161] His irritation, justified though it may be, has led the author to exaggerate a little bit in his confrontation with Edoardo Camera, for he is the singer in question. It is a little difficult in fact to think that the voice of the Genoan baritone— who was an excellent Scarpia only a year ago, chosen by Puccini for the première of *Tosca,* and again in March 1903 present at the première in Trieste of the same *Tosca* and then of the *Germania* of Franchetti—was really *finished by this time. (G.)*

[162] At the beginning of the century the Sassarese Alessandro Pomé (1851-1934)— whose name was linked above all to Puccini, for whom he was the first to conduct *Manon Lescaut* at the Regio di Torino—was rightly one of the best-regarded operatic conductors. *(G.)*

[163] Very different was the artistic standard of the two colleagues of TR. The Brescian Virginia Guerrini (1871-1948)—a mezzo-soprano of exceptional vocal means and opulent stage presence, who already enjoyed vast international renown in spite of her youth—particularly favored the part of Dalila, which permitted her to display singing that was expressive, voluptuous and technically impeccable. On a minor level, certainly, but for all that, no stranger to the great theaters, the tenor Carlo Barrera was particularly active during the period 1895 to 1910, in a repertory that included even *Otello*, of which he has left us some discographic testimony, cut in 1908-09. *(G.)*

[164] Inversion also in this case; in fact the author's Cairo debut came on 3 December 1901, not yet in the opera of Saint-Saëns, but rather in *Bohème*, which followed; also in December were *Sansone e Dalila* and *Otello* (protagonist: Barrera, already cited). *(G.)*

[165] Not without significance, even if rare (and perhaps properly so), were the author's incursions into Wagnerian terrain (that developed, however, as regards Egypt, during the second and last seasons, conducted by the maestro Giovanni Zuccani). This was in fact the only time that TR sang the part of Telramund, after having interpreted the Herald five years previously. For Kurwenal, on the other hand, we can cite a pair of South American performances (Colón of Buenos Aires and Municipal of São Paolo) in 1911, and another at the Real of Madrid in 1913 and (perhaps) a last time at the Lirico of Rio de Janeiro in October, 1916.

Without doubt of particular importance are the two performances of Tristan in Cairo because of the presence, as the male protagonist, of Giuseppe Borgatti (1871-1950) of Ferrara. For the virile beauty of his mellow timbre and for his incisive poetic diction, for the chiseling of vigorous accents and his physical handsomeness, he was truly the greatest Wagnerian tenor Italy ever produced and one of the greatest of all times and countries. *(G.)*

[166] In fact "Benedetta" was already contracted to the Teatro Vittorio Emanuele, provisional seat of the customary season of Lenten-carnival, replacing the Regio, which was closed for protracted restorations from 1901 to 1905. With her interpretation of la Cieca she took part in the *Gioconda* of January, 1903, which coincided, then, with the second (and not the first, as it would appear in the author's narrative) Egyptian season of TR. *(G.)*

[167] Indeed, Giovanni Paroli took part in the first performance of *Otello* (February 5, 1887) and of *Falstaff* (February 9, 1893), singing the parts of Cassio and Dr. Cajus, respectively. *(G.)*

[168] Besides the Marseillais Victor Maurel, the principal interpreters of the first *Otello* were the tenor from Turin, Francesco Tamagno (1850-1905), the soprano from Udina, Romilda Pantaleoni (1847-1917), and the Paduan bass, Francesco Navarrini (1855-1923). *(G.)*

CHAPTER 17

[169] Actually Camillo Bonetti represented—with the still more famous Walter Mocchi, of whom in some ways he was the predecessor—without doubt the happiest moment for Italian impresarial activity in South American countries. *(G.)*

[170] The Neapolitan Leopoldo Mugnone (1858-1941), a precocious composer, owes his fame only to his activities as a conductor—certainly among the greatest of the pre-Toscanini generation. He scored triumphs for at least three decades in important European and South American theaters. A vibrant temperament and uncommon sensibility made him particularly suitable for the repertory of the "young school"; he enjoyed two great successes directing the première of *Tosca* and, even earlier, of *Cavalleria rusticana*. (Where the author heard him, scarcely thirteen years old.) After the initial friction between them, he and TR enjoyed an affectionate and lasting friendship. *(G.)*

[171] Hints that are more than sufficient to define the refined art of the Livornese, Mario Ancona (1860-1931), who represented the Edwardian image of an authentic baritonal *grand seigneur* if ever there was one. In the context of his

experience in Russian, Anglo-Saxon and Hispano-American theaters, the only comparable figure remains Mattia Battistini. *(G.)*

[172] In the middle of her splendid forty-year parabola, the Rumanian Hariclea Haricly de Hartulary (1860-1939), whose stage name was Darclée, already for about ten years, and then for almost as many more, constituted one of the major attractions in the world of song (and spoken drama as well). An impeccable vocalist, very versatile, whose interpretations were yet a little cold, in the course of a long and brilliant career (she was at La Scala until 1916) she succeeded in linking her name to at least three important characters which she "created"—Wally, Iris, and Tosca. *(G.)*

[173] For almost twenty years—after the première of *Falstaff* (respectively as Fenton and Nannetta)—the Paduan Edoardo Garbin (1865-1943) and the Triestina (of Bohemian origin) Adelina Stehle (1865-1945) made a splendid couple on many stages in Italy and elsewhere; today the pairing is still considered the most significant in the history of opera. He was famous for ringing high notes and no less for his resources as an actor which made him one of the attractive lovers of the "young school" (memorable as Milio in *Zazà*); she (formerly linked to a Mangiarotti, from whom issued the famous line of Livornese fencers) was most notable as a singing actress with a beautiful vocal line and style, with aplomb onstage, and refined expressive intentions. *(G.)*

[174] Actually, with Alice Cucini, in a career of a little more than ten years (she debuted, in Naples in 1891), we find ourselves in the presence of one of the best mezzo-sopranos that Italy every produced, endowed with an ample voice, sonorous, rich in timbre and color. This is also demonstrated on thirteen records which were cut between 1902 and 1907. *(G.)*

[175] Ultimately, to remove all doubt about the exceptionally high artistic level of the companies of singers which Italian impresarios of the time were used to taking to South America, it would be useful to remember that, among the "others" not mentioned, besides the staunch Romanian bass Ercolani, there figured two tenors of the caliber of the Sicilian Giuseppe Anselmi (1876-1929) and of the Spaniard Julián Biél (1870-1948), whose presence, naturally, excluded that of Giuseppe Borgatti (who debuted in Buenos Aires two years later under the baton of Toscanini). *(G.)*

[176] This woman was a singer, the mezzo-soprano Maria Paolicchi: she was active between the end of the 80s and the beginning of the century, and made it to the major theaters, for example the Costanzi of Rome, where, during the season 1888-89, she sang in several different operas which her husband conducted. *(G.)*

[177] Not coincidentally, Cascart, with Hamlet, Nelusko, Tonio and Figaro, remained the unshakable foundation upon which rested the fame and popularity of TR. *(G.)*

[178] The *Proserpina* to which the author refers is the "lyrical drama in four acts" of Camille Saint-Saëns, performed for the first time at the Opéra-Comique on the 16th of March, 1887. On the 2nd of Janury, 1903, it went on stage at the Zizinia in Alexandria, to be repeated at the Khediviale of Cairo, with Charlotte

Wyns as protagonist (the last Proserpine at the Opéra-Comique in May of 1900), with Borgatti and TR in the respective roles of Sebastiano and Squarrocca.

As for *Fedora*, there was no question of it being a "novelty" for the author, who had sung three performances of it in February, 1902, and again at the Zizinia, during his first Egyptian tour. *(G.)*

CHAPTER 18

[179] This would have been the first (and was perhaps the only) meeting between the author and Arturo Toscanini (1867-1957), already at the apogee of his extraordinary parabola; it was a shame that circumstances didn't permit these two exceptional personalities to work together. *(G.)*

Aside from their origins among the people, the Parmesan musician from Oltretorrente and the Pisan singer from via Carraia had in common their dignified and consistent conduct in confronting fascism.

[180] Taking into account either the author's engagements or the fact that Toscanini left La Scala on the 14th of April, 1903, after the well-known performance of *Ballo in maschera*, it may be presumed that the audition took place in the middle of April during the interval between TR's second Egyptian tour and his consequent engagement by Covent Garden. *(G.)*

[181] Then a coach and singer's accompanist, later a substitute conductor and director of operas, Lorenzo Molajoli was destined to occupy a prominent position in Italian musical life in the years between the two wars as artistic director of the Columbia Records company. His wife Emma, in her turn, had a school for advanced pupils of singing. *(G.)*

[182] Having first attained a degree in naval engineering, the Udinese Giulio Gatti-Casazza (1869-1940) then entered into theatrical life by replacing his father as director of the Teatro Comunale of Ferrara; he did so well that at a mere 29 years of age he was summoned to La Scala, where he headed the company for ten years. In 1908 he went (with Toscanini) to the Metropolitan of New York to assume the position of general manager, which he wielded inflexibly as a true dictator until 1935, writing an important page in the history of America's most important opera theater. *(G.)*

[183] As luck would have it the season 1903-04 would also include the performance of *Dinorah*, where, however, the part of Hoël was given to De Luca, himself debuting at La Scala, who would later figure, along with his ex-classmate, in *Griselda*. (TR and De Luca together in the same opera without at least minimally paralyzing activity in the other theaters, these were luxuries that an artistic director from La Scala could permit himself in those days...) *(G.)*

[184] A musician with a German education, Alberto Franchetti, the Baron from Turin (1860-1942), richly endowed with talent and knowledge, enjoyed a certain popularity at the time, since La Scala had produced *Germania* for him the year before with Caruso and Sammarco, and Toscanini conducting, which was being repeated at the Milanese theater. This opera of his was generally considered better than the one preceding it, *Cristoforo Colombo* (another opera appreciated by Toscanini)—both of which were sung by TR, respectively as Worms and as the protagonist. These were the only works that assured Franchetti that

minimum of fame which remains to him today, to which, on the other hand, he has every right. *(G.)*

[185] The prolific French opera composer—then in great vogue, later largely fallen from favor (except for *Manon* and *Werther*), but for some time newly risen in favor in the Anglo-Saxon countries, where there have been progressive attempts to revive him (at least in recordings)—Jules-Emile Massenet (1842-1912) was no stranger to the predilections of TR, who took two of his characters onstage, the Marchese di Saluzzo in *Griselda* at La Scala on April 10, 1904, and Fra Bonifazio in *Le jongleur de Nôtre-Dame* at the Lirico of Milan on October 18 of the following year. *(G.)*

[186] A valley in the province of Trento, bathed by a small lake of the same name, full of fields, pine forests and orchards.

[187] Brother of the famous tenor Italo, fifteen years older, and brother-in-law of Luisa Tetrazzini, having wed her sister Eva (herself an esteemed soprano), the Parmesan Cleofonte Campanini (1860-1919), belonged to the same generation as Toscanini (from the same town), for whom he substituted at La Scala in the seasons 1903-04 and 1904-05, during which he conducted the premières of *Siberia* and *Madama Butterfly*. A conductor of international rank, Campanini was intensely active outside of Italy, in particular in the United States, becoming artistic director and administrator of the Chicago Opera, where TR sang repeatedly under his baton, and where he died suddenly in 1919. *(G.)*

[188] Duke Uberto Visconti di Modrone (1871-1923), eldest son of Duke Guido (1838-1902), who was responsible for the artistic revival of La Scala after the crisis at the end of the century. He made the most of his difficult inheritance as president (until 1918) of the "Gruppo Esercente l'Impresa del Teatro alla Scala" (as it is called on the contract signed by the aforementioned general manager, Gatti-Casazza). *(G.)*

[189] The "good papa Giulio" would certainly have conducted himself with more firmness, but also with greater tact, a gift for which his son Tito was not noted. *(G.)*

[190] In fact the company of *Rigoletto* saw three tenors succeed each other (Anselmi, Krismer and the Spaniard Ibos), two sopranos (Wermez and Toresella) and two mezzo-sopranos (Giaconia and Monti-Baldini), alongside the sole baritone (TR) and bass, Didur. *(G.)*

[191] Opera seria in three acts, performed at St. Petersburg in 1875 and practically unknown in Italy where only one performance over the radio in the 70s is on record, it is nevertheless the only one of his nine operas which has kept the name of Anton Grigorevich Rubinstein (1829-1894) alive in the West. Much performed in the last years of the last century and the first of this, the title role in *Demon* was a favorite part of some famous Italian baritones such as Battistini, Giraldoni and TR, for the great vocal and dramatic possibilities offered by the part of the protagonist. *(G.)*

[192] To the two telepathic phenomena concerning my progenitors which are narrated by my father in this book, I would like to add the following, also of a paranormal nature, which occurred in Florence in 1944: Lina Cavalieri also

came to live in retirement in that city, in a villa she purchased at Poggio Imperiale. As a singer she had won great fame, not only for her soprano voice, which had been limited in power, resonance and extension, but for her extraordinary beauty, elegance and fascinating stage presence. Born seventy years before in Viterbo, she had debuted with TR in *Fedora* (Paris, 1905). Linked by an old friendship the two colleagues got together frequently. Cavalieri had invited TR and some others to dinner in her villa on the 7th of February. TR, after having accepted with pleasure the evening before, was suddenly struck by a fit of depression, and telephoned her to excuse himself from the invitation: he was upset by the lack of news of his family in Rome; the 8th of February was my birthday, and in short, he preferred to be alone rather than to inflict his melancholy on someone else. The next day, at about the dinner hour, Cavalieri's villa was hit by an aerial bombardment which buried the hostess and her guests under rubble.

[193] A small hydrothermal resort town in the Vicenza province.

[194] That the existence of a rapport between music and color wasn't entirely a deliberate eccentricity on TR's part (he returns to the theory later in this book) is shown by the fact that, at nearly the same time, a musician as respected as Chaliapin was also actively preoccupied with it, though he died before codifying his aims. *(G.)*

[195] An interesting report regarding TR, dated 1911, and from the records of Dr. Giuseppe de Luca, an expert laryngologist of Buenos Aires (who in the course of his long years of professional activity had occasion to examine and treat the throat ailments of a good 445 artists who sang at the Colón), yields the following information: "The vocal cords are long and thick, explaining the exceptional tessitura of this notable artist's voice. His lung capacity is great; he is able to hold a note for 40 seconds. His range is from the LA^1 (108 double vibrations per second) to the DO^4 of the tenor (522 double vibrations per second), which is to say, two and one-half octaves, while the ordinary range of the baritone is from LA^1 to SOL^3 (391 double vibrations per second). In Titta Ruffo I have never found the slightest damage to the vocal organ. Technically perfect, with the proper use of its registers, consequently capable of loud or soft effects in its entire range."

[196] The period considered by the author had to closely coincide with the decade 1906-16, during which, dividing himself uninterruptedly between Russia, Spain and South America (with sporadic performances in Italy) summer did not exist for him.

CHAPTER 19

[197] Neither his London engagement, nor even his debut at La Scala (which will have no sequel in the years to come), though doubtless important milestones, caused such a fuss and so many echoes of approbation around the author's name. This *Zazà*, in fact, preceded by *Siberia* and followed by *Adriana Lecouvreur*, was the decisive stage in TR's career, the basis for his relentless climb to celebrity.

[198] According to the chronology which appears here as an appendix, it is neces-

sary to add *Tosca, Aida, Pagliacci, Otello,* and *Germania,* while no trace is found of *Zazà* and *Ballo in maschera.*

[199] Again, a deviation from the appended chronology. It is correct except that *Trovatore* and *Pagliacci* should be dropped, and *Faust* (TR's debut in the role of Valentin, with the famous Russian tenor Sobinov as protagonist) and *Aida* should be added.

[200] The Aquarium Theater is meant, where the primary Italian company, rich with the names of prestigious artists, performed annually. *(G.)*

[201] In sum, an authentic firmament. Masini has already been mentioned, and Caruso (who was, however, present at St. Petersburg for only one season, that of December 1898 to January of 1899). Almost as famous as Masini, at least in Russia, were the other two tenors: Francesco (called Checco) Marconi (1855-1916), the aggressive rival of the Romagnolo, with a splendid voice and instinctive interpretive gifts, and the Sicilian Giuseppe Anselmi (1876-1929), who had debuted at La Scala in *Rigoletto* contemporaneously with the author, with an enchanting timbre, fiery vibrations and fascinating stage presence, for all that the best-qualified heir of De Lucia in the *"di grazia"* repertory, where he gave no end of trouble to Bonci and even to Caruso. On this terrain, no less important, for vocal bravura and express finesse, was the Italo-Hispanic soprano Olimpia Boronat (1867-1934)—not to be confounded with her sister Elena, another soprano, but less prestigious—who could hold her own against the best coloraturas of her time. The importance of the bass Francesco Navarrini, other than his intrinsic worth, resides in the fact that he was a connecting link between the classic eighteenth-century duo of Maini-Nannetti and the more modern Nazzareno de Angelis. Ultimately these *ad hoc* citations cannot prevent me from pausing a little to consider the extraordinary person that was the Reatino Mattia Battistini (1857-1928), or from adding as a testimony of his celebrity the much-cited definition that would have him "the king of baritones and the baritone of the king." *(G.)*

[202] Another temporal overlapping in the author's memory: he did indeed sing the *Linda* in St. Petersburg (with Galvany), but in March 1906, during the second of the three Russian "tours." *(G.)*

[203] This concerns one of the four performances of *Hamlet* that the author sang at the Costanzi of Rome in March 1909. *(G.)*

CHAPTER 20

[204] In 1905 the thirty-year parabola of the Milanese Edoardo Sonzogno (1836-1920) reached its apogee. Employed in 1874 as a music editor, after a fruitful experience in the fields of journalism and book publishing, he gave an energetic and positive push to Italian opera, introducing into the repertory French operas in the lyrical vein and those Italian works of the "young school" (the competition from which Mascagni emerged triumphant with his *Cavalleria* was Sonzogno's idea). Endowed with a genial and unbiased diligence, in 1894 Sonzogno acquired outright the glorious Teatro della Canobbiana which, restored and transformed into the Teatro Lirico Internazionale, was used during

the twenty-year period preceding the First World War to present operas by "its" composers. *(G.)*

[205] From May 1 to June 15 the following operas were performed under the direction of Cleofonte Campanini: *Adriana Lecouvreur*, *Siberia* (Giordano's Paris debut), *Amico Fritz*, *Fedora*, *Zazà*, *Barbiere di Siviglia*, *Andrea Chénier* and the *Chopin* of Orefice. *(G.)*

[206] Among those already mentioned the names of three very prestigious singers stand out. Above them all, the delicious Portuguese Regina Pacini (1871-1965), by then at the close of her career (two years later she would in fact abandon the stage to marry the Argentine politician Marcelo Torquato de Alvear, the future President of the Republic), but for about the prior fifteen years one of the great coloraturas of her time, founder (with the Catalan Huguet de Arnold) of the famous Spanish school which dominated the international scene from 1890 to 1930. Then there was the Neapolitan Fernando De Lucia (1860-1825), an internationally famous *tenore di grazia*, probably no more than halfway into his career (he sang for just twenty years). Finally, in an entirely different climate of sensations and taste, the Florentine Amedeo Bassi (1872-1949), who had recently ascended to the Olympus of tenors where, in the wake of Borgatti and in the shadow of Caruso, he had set himself (often with TR at his side), and with excellent results, to delineate the specific characteristics of the modern "veristic tenor."

Another Florentine mentioned by the author, though he was inferior in fame and merit to his colleagues, is the bass-baritone Antonio Baldelli (1849-1928), whose comical appearance made him, inside and outside Italy, a much appreciated successor of the great eighteenth-century "buffi." *(G.)*

[207] Victorien Sardou (1831-1909) was a popular and prolific French author of successful comedies and *"drammoni,"* some of which came to be adapted as opera libretti (*Tosca* by Giacosa and Illica for Puccini, *Fedora* by Colautti and *Madame Sans-Gêne* by Simoni for Giordano; *Patri!* and *Théodora* were adapted by Sardou himself respectively for Paladilhe and Leroux). *(G.)*

[208] More than a musical agent, as the author, oddly, defines him, the Frenchman Gabriel Astruc (1864-1938) belongs to the company of great men of the theater considered generally. It was thanks to him that from 1905 to 1914, for two months of the year (the so-called *"Grande Saison de Paris,"* first at the *Théâtre Sarah Bernhardt* and then at the *Théâtre du Châtelet*) Paris could see an authentic musical epic, of which it is possible to cite, among the principal events, the two seasons of Italian opera (organized by Sonzogno) and from 1910, the Metropolitan Opera on tour (directed by Toscanini) and the three seasons of the Ballet Russes of Diaghilev (1909, 1911 and 1912). *(G.)*

[209] The Bohemian violinist and composer Jan Kubelik (1880-1940), seven years into his career by this time, was already in 1905 a famous concert artist, destined to prolong his fame by means of his children, the twins Anita and Mary (1904), both violinists, and Rafael (1914), famous as an orchestra conductor, active mainly in England and in Germany. *(G.)*

[210] François Boucher (1703-1770), Parisian painter of pastoral and mythological scenes.

[211] Truly a bunch of VIPs from an artistic *belle époque*, by now beginning to decline. Figuring in it were famous musicians like Jules Massenet and Camille Saint-Saëns (1835-1921), who had for almost thirty years enjoyed the fame acquired by *Samson et Dalila*; illustrious litterati such as the bohemian poet and playwright Jean Richepin (1849-1926), the Belgian Maurice Maeterlinck (1862-1949), the master of symbolism, but not yet at the peak of his fame like the younger Edmond Rostand (1868-1918), a member of the French Academy at only 34 years of age on the wave of popularity that he had acquired in 1897 with his "heroic comedy" *Cyrano de Bergerac*; and finally the singular figure of a largely self-taught sculptor, the Italian of Russian origin Prince Paolo Troubetzkoi (1863-1938), creator of some of the most representative nineteenth-century works. *(G.)*

[212] There is no reason to doubt that the author had known Tommaso Tittoni (1855-1931), but not in 1907, when Giolitti's *missus dominicus* was Minister of Foreign Affairs; rather during his long stay in Paris as ambassador, or in December 1911 (when TR sang *Rigoletto* and *Hamlet* at the Opéra), or, more probably still, in May of the following year, when Paris hosted a primarily Italian company under the direction of Serafin, to which both Caruso and Chaliapin belonged, which gave memorable performances of *Rigoletto*, *Fanciulla del West* (local debut) and *Barbiere di Siviglia*. *(G.)*

[213] A French noblewoman in spite of her cognomen of evident German origin, Ernestine Stern was also known as a writer under the pseudonym of Maria Star.

[214] After thirteen years of a career (in fact he debuted in 1892 at Foligno) the Roman bass Oreste Luppi (1870-?) was certainly in his prime in terms of vocal and artistic means, already profitably utilized by La Scala during three seasons (from 1899 to 1903), of which there remain traces on various records he made in 1905-06, as a soloist or together with renowned singers of his time. *(G.)*

[215] A palace still in existence, situated on the lungarno Pacinotti. [An address along the Arno River. Tr.]

[216] See note 185. *(G.)*

CHAPTER 21

[217] Second in a family of Vicenzan musicians, Gaetano Coronaro (1852-1908), the pupil of Franco Faccio at the Conservatory of Milan, where he too would teach from 1879 until his death, was also the author of some operas, among them *Un curioso accidente* (Torino, November 1903); the most recent, therefore, in respect to the meeting with TR was therefore his *Enoch Arden*, which he would not see performed either at the Lirico or elsewhere. *(G.)*

[218] With the years the prestige of Arrigo Boito (1842-1918), already noteworthy at the time of *Otello* and *Falstaff*, has grown, and not without reason: first of all he had the conviction to go head to head with one of the most eminent figures in European cultural and artistic life, and then, right or wrong, to regard himself as the trustee of Verdi's last will and testament. *(G.)*

[219] Preferred, yes, but only up to a certain point: as much as it is true that Verdi came to distrust Maurel and his "divismo," considering it "crazy" and thus was

downright fearful that he might be risking the ruin of the production. *(G.)*

[220] The prince Aleksej Cereteli.

[221] In question are the revolutionary uprisings of December 1905, the consequence, a bit slow in coming, of the heavy defeat suffered by the Tsar's empire in the Russo-Japanese War.

[222] As with the operas he sang in Russia, TR is relying exclusively on his memory (see the appended chronology for precise dates), and these facts are not exact. Some of the members of the Cereteli company were Italian certainly: the soprano Emma Carelli, the tenor Giuseppe Armanini and Reno Andreini (father of the Count Cella di Rivara, the "inventor" of the dentrifice *Durban's*), the mezzo-soprano Anna Gramegna, the bass Oreste Carozzi, and the conductor Gino Golisciani. *(G.)*

[223] I have not succeeded in finding a record of TR's performances in other Russian cities besides those mentioned in the appended chronology.

[224] A reference to the noted Portuguese impresario José Pacini, the older brother of the famous soprano, Regina Pacini. (See note 206.)

[225] Since TR fulfilled engagements in Lisbon and Monte Carlo between January and March, 1907, it is evident his memory of various seasons spent in Russia has become confused.

[226] In reality the author went to Lisbon (where he joined Benedetta) because the engagement with the San Carlos preceded that of Monte Carlo. A few lines ahead, then, the destination Lisbon was substituted for the Mediterranean city.

[227] One of the most singular personalities in the history of opera, the Rumanian Raoul Gunsbourg (1859-1955)—creator of the theatrical fortunes of the *Dannazione di Faust*, if not an opera composer himself—in 1892 assumed the direction of the Opéra de Monte Carlo, and held it uninterruptedly for almost 70 years, the surviving "sovereign" of the *belle époque*. *(G.)*

[228] A typical Sicilian gentleman, Francesco Pandolfini (1836-1916) was one of the most classic Verdian baritones, a refined actor no less than an excellent vocalist, whose fame was prolonged by means of his daughter, the already cited soprano Angelica Pandolfini (see note 112) and (a little later) his son Francesco, a tenor active at the beginning of the century. *(G.)*

[229] Regarding Kaschmann, the judgment was obviously referring to *Hamlet*, because in 1907 the activity of the Dalmatian baritone, even if reduced in time and confined to a repertory more adapted to his diminishing resources, proceeded indefatigably. *(G.)*

CHAPTER 22

[230] In the following narration it is understood that the Milanese sojourn follows the tour that detained the author in Russia in the first half of 1906.

[231] Protagonist of a comedy by Edoardo Ferravilla (1846-1916), and considered perhaps the most popular character among those created by the witty dialectal author and great Milanese comic actor.

[232] A large number of objects are kept in the museum of the Teatro Verdi of Pisa, collected with other relics in the room dedicated to TR, which was inaugurated April 8, 1961.

[233] Piero Schiavazzi of Cagliari (1875-1949) and the Neapolitan Emma Carelli (1877-1928), indeed two of the founders of the "verist" interpretive vein, he a tenor, she a soprano: fiery temperaments and vibrant voices, a consuming passion and a technique far from impeccable provoked the premature retirement from the stage of Schiavazzi in 1920 and of Carelli in 1914. However, being of a strong personality, she did not renounce the life of the theater, participating, as Director of the Costanzi already since 1912, in the impresarial activity which was developed by her husband. It was none other than Walter Mocchi (1870-1955) at first a journalist and agitator of socialist beliefs (and later a zealous supporter of Mussolini), who transformed it, from the beginning of the century, into an efficient theatrical organization, and rapidly became, with his wife's help, the most important Italian impresario, for many years the source of strength behind the principal operatic stage of South America. *(G.)*

[234] It is worth citing the date of this exceptional performance of *Rigoletto*—October 2, 1906—because it marks one of the rare occasions that TR and Caruso sang together. *(G.)*

[235] It would be well at this point to recapitulate chronologically the last agonizing phases of the unfortunate relations between the author and "Benedetta."

-Summer 1906: After TR's return from his second Russian tour, there is a brief sojourn in Venice, where she reveals herself as suffering from an incurable illlness, and following this consults a doctor in Milan.

-February 1907: "Benedetta" travels to Lisbon (where the author arrived directly from St. Petersburg) to help him with his difficult debut in *Hamlet*. (See Chapter 21.)

-April 1907: Return of the author to Milan after fulfilling his engagements in Lisbon, Monte Carlo (with its Berlin appendix), and Moscow (with the short appendix of his last Russian tour).

-May 1907: Aggravation of Benedetta's condition, causing her to take refuge in a clinic on the first of June to undergo a surgical intervention, and die of it on June 9, TR's birthday, to be buried the following day in the Monumentale cemetery.

[236] In question is the Roman singer Flora Perini (1881-1968). A student of the Conservatory of St. Cecilia, between 1910 and 1925, she had a noteworthy career as an excellent leading mezzo-soprano, primarily in American theaters (be it the Colón, the Metropolitan, the Chicago Opera), where she often sang beside the author. *(G.)*

[237] On September 26, 1907, at Lazise on the east bank of the Lago di Garda.

CHAPTER 23

[238] Exactly 15 years before, on the 10th of May, 1892, under the direction of Toscanini, who eleven days later held the première of *Pagliacci* (again with Maurel in the part of Tonio). *(G.)*

[239] A little more than a year later (she debuted in Nice in February 1906) the Canadian (?) Lillian Grenville, secularly Goertner (c. 1882-?), had a brilliant initial reception (in the season 1910-1911 she was signed by the Chicago Opera), however a rapid decline followed. *(G.)*

[240] Besides the already-mentioned Sammarco and Giraldoni, the other two are certainly no less important. Younger by a year than the author, in 1907 the Neapolitan Pasquale Amato—beautiful voice, excellent technique and felicitous interpretive resources—had just become part of the company of the best international baritones, by this time right on the verge of crossing the ocean for the Metropolitan, where he would remain for thirteen consecutive seasons.

Belonging in his turn to the generation of Battistini, the Frenchman Maurice Renaud (1861-1933), himself an authentic *grand seigneur* (among other roles, a Hamlet of persuasive vocal and theatrical efficacy), was in many respects a French analog of the great Italian baritone, having in fact established in comparison to the great Faure the very same type of hereditary rapport that existed between Battistini and Cotogni. *(G.)*

[241] A writer and journalist of clearly Irridentist tendency, the Zaratino Arturo Colautti (1851-1914) was also valued as a librettist, collaborating with Giordano for *Fedora* and with Cilèa for *Adriana Lecouvreur* and *Gloria*. *(G.)*

[242] At issue, more precisely, is the Italo-Argentinian Theatrical Society (S.T.I.A.) set up by the impresarios Walter Mocchi and Cesare Ciacchi.

[243] The enthusiasm of the author for the great "matador" of prose is not casual: between him and the Reggiano Ermete Zacconi (1857-1948) a substantial affinity came to be established of tastes, sensibility, and interpretive inclinations, that were a common field of action for the personages of the "verismo" camp. *(G.)*

[244] A singer of historic stature, the Navarrese Sebastian (called Julián) Gayarre (1844-1890), endowed with a singularly enchanting timbre and excellent stylistic and interpretive resources, made his mark during the 1880s as one of the greatest tenors of the world, the protagonist of a myth that would feed on itself after his death and endures in Spain to this day. *(G.)*

[245] These are the truly pejorative and morally squalid aspects of "*divismo*" (of which the great tenor Anselmi, unfortunately, seems to have been a typical exponent), which Toscanini fought from the initial stages of his career, succeeding in sweeping it away (or better, deceiving himself that he had succeeded). *(G.)*

[246] The young Alfonso XIII of Borbone (1886-1941), king from birth (but for sixteen years under the tutelage of his mother), at scarcely two years had married Vittoria Eugenia di Battenberg (1887-1969), who gave him five children (among whom was Don Juan, father of the actual sovereign) and with whom he reigned until the end of April 1931, when he voluntarily abandoned the throne, without yet renouncing the prerogative of the same, taking refuge in Rome, where for nearly two years he sojourned with his family in the villa leased by the author.

[247] Uninterruptedly for six seasons (1907/08-1912/13), and again in the season 1918/1919.

[248] Widow of Alfonso XII, King of Spain (1857-1885), who died while awaiting an heir to the throne, Maria Cristina d'Asburgo-Lorena (1858-1929) then held the regency for Alfonso XIII until 1902.

[249] For *charme*, elegance and wit Isabella (1851-1931) was considered the queen of good Madrid society; princess of Asturias, older sister of Alfonso XII and therefore aunt of the King, she bore the title "Infanta" which in the Spanish monarchy came to be attributed to the children of the King and consorts of the "Infanti."

[250] Considered the greatest actor of his epoch, the Lucchese Ermete Novelli (1851-1919) boasted an exceptional comic talent which was not accompanied, according to some critics, by an adequate capacity for interpretive insight. *(G.)*

[251] Besides the gift of an extraordinary voice the author had instinctive acting and mimetic ability. He made three records that bear witness: the renditions of the "Monologue" and "The apparition of the specter" from *Hamlet* and the joking "Visiting card to Chaliapin," in which he imitated the Italian of the great Russian bass. However TR, as an actor of spoken drama, did indeed venture to appear in public, in 1915, at the Colón of Buenos Aires, alongside Gustavo Salvini. This happened on the occasion of two benefit performances for the *Anfione e Zeto*, a tragedy inspired by Greek myth by Tommaso (Maso) Salvini, son of Gustavo, with stage music by the Argentine composer Pascual de Rogatis (1882). The author took the part of Anfione.

[252] A very successful Spanish painter, Joaquím Sorolla y Bastida (1863-1923) worked in an impressionist style generally inspired by the popular life of Valencia.

[253] Another superposition of the author's memories, since the operas cited by him belong to at least four of the six seasons at Monte Carlo in which he took part from 1907 to 1912 (the *Linda* in fact appeared in March 1911).

[254] Since the author sang *Cristoforo Colombo* in February 1909—that is, after the inaugural season of the Colón for which the directors of the theater in Buenos Aires had come expressly to request the participation of the by then famous baritone—it is clear that his second meeting with them could only have taken place on the occasion of a performance of *Gioconda* (February) or *Barbiere* (March), the only operas in which TR took part during the 1908 season at Monte Carlo.

[255] That TR's impressions were true is easily demonstrated by a pair of facts—34,50 meters of depth and 35,25 meters of width—which testify to the fact that the stage of the Colón is certainly one of the largest in the world. *(G.)*

[256] The author does not specify the theater in question, even if it is to be presumed he wishes to refer to the Teatro de la Opera, where effectively an important season of 14 operas was produced contemporaneously with the season at the Colón, with a conductor as prestigious as Mugnone and singers like Anselmi, Krusceniski, De Luca, Stracciari, Didur, among others. It is true that an analogous opera season (17 operas), directed by Gaetano Bavagnoli, was put on by the Politeama Argentino, but, given its minor artistic level, it certainly couldn't have been an intimidating rival in competition with the Colón. *(G.)*

[257] Roberto Caamaño writes(in *La historia del Teatro Colón*, (1969, v. II, p.118) "the *Aida* of May 25, 1908, was discussed in all its aspects," since Buenos Aires was "accustomed to see this work [...] with an all-star cast, and the Colón's was not, even if it included some respected artists" (the soprano Crestani, the tenor Bassi, the mezzo-soprano Verger, the baritone Bellantoni, the basses Arimondi and Berardi; the conductor Luigi Mancinelli). *(G.)*

[258] In fact TR took part in 24 operas between 1908 and 1931, during nine seasons (of which four were consecutive, 1908-11) at the Colón. Those not cited include *Lucia, Carmen, Fanciulla del West,* and *Evgeny Onegin*, besides the *Aurora* of the Italo-Argentine composer and director Héctor (Ettore) Panizza (1875-1967), performed in 1908 and 1909. *(G.)*

[259] In truth the performances of *Pagliacci* at the Colón which saw TR engaged in a sort of titanic vocal and interpretive duel with Caruso are mythical. For example Ricardo Turro writes in the essay *Italian opera in the Teatro Colón* (in *The Teatro Colón: Fifty Years of Glory*, Buenos Aires 1958, pp. 111-12): "Our house had the honor to host an extraordinary spectacle, Caruso and Titta Ruffo together" in "an unforgettable performance of *I pagliacci*, which remained stamped in letters of gold upon the annals of opera in Buenos Aires." Further confirmation in its turn is provided by a historian of the caliber of Eduardo Arnosi in the essay "The great singers who were active at the Teatro Colón," which appeared in a special celebratory number of the review *Lyra. (G.)*

[260] See note 303.

[261] We have not been successful in discovering who the "vile scribbler" was. It is a fact that the slander was picked up by the country, then gathered in evidence and let loose in Italy against TR.

[262] The inaugural of the Municipal in São Paolo took place on September 12, 1911: just as the author remembers it, with *Hamlet* (except that the Ofelia was Pareto, the only coloratura soprano of that season, which therefore did not include Barrientos). TR's engagement in Buenos Aires ended on the 23rd of August, and prior to arriving in the Brazilian city he had indeed sung at the Urquiza of Montevideo and the Coliseo of Rosario. *(G.)*

[263] A little town in the province of Cuneo, known in particular for its monumental castle which was then the property of the House of Savoia.

[264] As a part of the political accord among the countries of the Triple Alliance, of which Italy had been a part for thirty years, and the Franco-Russian Entente, cautiously supported by England, this visit, in October 1909, was the only one ever made by a Czar to Italy; it was made by the last of the Romanovs, Czar Nicolas II (1868-1918), who nine years later was the tragic victim, along with the imperial family, of his weakness and his errors. *(G.)*

[265] If we are not mistaken this was the first of the two unique occasions of direct artistic collaboration between Mascagni and TR (the other involved a performance of *Barbiere* directed by the maestro, which the author sang at the Costanzi a few months later, on April 4, 1910). Otherwise, of Mascagni's works he interpreted only *Cavalleria rusticana* at the Opera of Buenos Aires in August 1902,

and perhaps the *Iris* at the Khediviale of Cairo (December 1901). *(G.)*

266 A mezzo-soprano of renown (not to be confounded with the older Ernestina Parsi), the Roman Armida Parsi-Pettinella (1872-1949), and two authoritative "verist" interpreters: the Milanese, but Torinese by adoption, Rinaldo Grassi (1882-1946), with the sparkling timbre of an authentic tenor, but lacking in preparation, was at the peak of his long and brilliant parabola; Maria Farneti (the Forlivese) (1877-1955) was one of Mascagni's favorite singers, with a beautiful voice, excellent technique and a noteworthy sensibility, which put her in the first rank among the pioneering sopranos of the intimate vein, in clear contrast to the line of Bellincioni-Carelli-Burzio. *(G.)*

267 The Pistoiese lexicographer (from Castel Cireglio) Policarpo Petrocchi (1852-1902), author of the *New Universal Dictionary of the Italian Language,* founded on the usages of educated Florentine speech.

268 A very significant figure in European politics of those years, the Piedmontese Giovanni Giolitti (1841-1928) was by then in the last period of his third ministry, and in fact would be dismissed the following December. *(G.)*

269 The members of the House of Savoia cited are: Vittorio Emanuele III (1869-1947) and Elena del Montenegro (1872-1952), the King and Queen of Italy; the brothers Emanuele Filiberto Duke d'Aosta (1869-1931) and Vittorio Emanuele Count of Turin (1870-1946), as well as their stepmother, Princess Maria Letizia Bonaparte, Duchess d'Aosta (1866-1926).

270 This singular episode reveals the irrepressibly genuine frankness of the author, but also, between the lines, a badly concealed repudiation of certain kinds of courtly hypocrisy, as well as a certain coldness in confronting the House of Savoia, understandable in that, during the 30s, when this book was written, he noticed in them a fundamental basis of support for the concerns of the regime to which TR was irreconcilably hostile. *(G.)*

271 At issue is the great opera season of 1911 (from March to July, then again from October to December) organized on the occasion of the International Exposition celebrating the fiftieth anniversary of Rome as the capital of Italy, during which the author sang only eight performances of *Barbiere.* He sang *Hamlet* in Rome two years before, precisely four performances in March of 1909. The disparity suggests other hypotheses, but the most reliable appears to be that father and son saw each other both in 1909 and in 1911, and the author has fused the two memories.

272 Illustrious physician and man of science, as well as senator of Regno, the Pavese Pietro Grocco (1856-1916) divided his time between Florence and Montecatini, where he had been treating Puccini in 1904, but above all, in the last years of his life, Verdi, assisting him even on this deathbed. *(G.)*

273 The cemetery of Montecatini Terme where she still reposes.

274 The author is alluding to the already mentioned long season that detained him in South America from May to October 1911 (and not 1912). *(G.)*

275 At least three years into her career, the Parisian Yvonne Gall (1885-1972)

was furthermore one of the greatest prima donnas of the Opéra and the Opéra-Comique for a quarter of a century, particularly appreciated in the light lyric vein of the French repertory, and when she finally abandoned the stage, she became a distinguished teacher of singing. *(G.)*

[276] More exactly, Jan Mieczislaw de Reszke (1850-1925), who, after his debut as a baritone in 1874 in Italy, where he was known as Giovanni De Reschi, he became, at the beginning of the 80s, perhaps the most sought-after, certainly the most idolized, tenor in London, Paris and New York. The rapport which united these two very different personalities might seem rather singular, since they were as pure opposites by birth and culture, by taste and sensibility, as they could be in 1911: the very celebrated de Reszke, an authentic *grand seigneur* of the stage who with his equals Battistini and Melba had known how to embody to its highest degree the elegance of a *belle époque* already fading—and the no less famous (but of "modern" fame) TR. The existence of such a rapport testifies to the rightful respect for the proud Pisan man of the people on the one hand, and on the other to the noble Pole's acute faculty of perception, who, after having predicted that Caruso would be his successor, likewise was perfectly able to take into account the extraordinary quality residing in the exceptional singer and interpreter, TR. *(G.)*

CHAPTER 24

[277] A great man in all respects, Charles Younger, born in England and moved to Madrid where he met the author, was the exclusive representative to the entire world of the most famous brands of typical Spanish wine. Gifted with a prodigious musical memory, the hearing of a few beats was enough for him to recognize an operatic excerpt or one of classical music. For many years he accompanied TR more as a friend than a secretary.

[278] For thirty years a personality of extreme significance in the musical life of North America, Andreas Dippel (1866-1932) was before all else, for eleven seasons, from 1890 on, a tenor at the Metropolitan, where in 1908, after making himself most welcome thanks to his exceptional vocal and stylistic versatility, he became the administrative director accountable to Gatti-Casazza, then moved on to the Philadelphia-Chicago Opera Company (its exact name) as artistic director (from 1910-1913), and finally became the impresario of his own company, with which he made several tours around the United States. Leaving organized activity, Dippel then dedicated himself to the teaching of singing, retiring to Hollywood where he died. *(G.)*

[279] A very wealthy American financier, an associate of the millionaire Pierpont Morgan, Edward T. Stotesbury belonged to that company of more or less illustrious patrons of the arts who, after having worked hard and well for the diffusion of a high level of opera in the United States, came to be for the most part wiped out by the crash on Wall Street in 1929.

[280] The Venetian Giorgio Polacco (1875-1960), a conductor of vast international experience, in 1912 was called to the Metropolitan as "second conductor" under Toscanini in the Italian repertory, of which he became "first

conductor" in the biennial 1915-1917, and then moved on to the Chicago Opera, where he remained uninterruptedly until 1930, also fulfilling the function of artistic director. *(G.)*

The author alludes to the consequences of frictions that flared up in Rome: in March 1909, during the rehearsal of *Hamlet* at the Costanzi, which provoked a formal challenge to a duel on the part of Polacco, accepted by TR. The dispute, afterward patched up by the seconds, ended with reciprocal testimonies of esteem and a handshake from both sides, but not without leaving some consequences on the relationship.

[281] Advisor to the administration until October 1931 and one of the most active at the Metropolitan, Otto H. Kahn (1867-1934) also had interests then in the Philadelphia-Chicago Opera Company. A singular personage endowed with the liveliest musical interest (he knew how to play three instruments), as well as the intuition of a "talent scout," during his long stay at the top of the Met's managerial hierarchy, during which time he spent two million dollars of his personal fortune, because he was Jewish, was never able to become the owner of his own box seat!

[282] Authentic prima donna in the most complete sense of the word, the American Geraldine Farrar (1882-1967)—admired for her extraordinary personality and fascinating beauty (it was no accident that she also took part in several silent films) more than for her specific vocal quality as a lyric soprano—rapidly became as popular as Caruso. Together they were a harmonious couple that for about fifteen years dominated the stage of the Metropolitan. *(G.)*

[283] Armed with a serious musical preparation and great prestige that grew with the years, William James Henderson (1855-1937), was for more than half a century a musical critic, first with *The New York Times* and then after 1903, the *New York Sun*.

[284] Precisely in Chicago.

[285] Another great sponsor of opera, thanks to a paternal fortune made from the invention and production of an agricultural machine, Harold F. McCormick, president of the Philadelphia-Chicago Opera Company, also launched (in Parma, July 1914) perhaps the first Concorso Internationale di Canto (International Singing Competition), from which emerged Beniamino Gigli, Francesco Merli, Isidoro Fagoaga. Divorced from Edith Rockefeller, daughter of John, the great petroleum magnate, his second marriage was to a certain Ganna Walska, an ambitious woman of the world (but also a failed soprano). *(G.)*

[286] It was *Aida* that inaugurated, on the 23rd of April, 1915, the new theater of the Cuban capital which substituted for the old Tacón, conductor Tullio Serafin, protagonista the Argentine soprano Juanita Capella.

CHAPTER 25

[287] This obviously relates to the First World War (July 1914-November 1918) in which Italy intervened on the 24th of May, 1915.

[288] Alberto I, King of Belgium (1875-1934), husband of Elisabetta di Wittelsbach,

Duchess of Bavaria (1876-1965) and father of Maria José (1906) the Queen of Italy, both promoters and generous patrons of musical events.

[289] Actor of variety shows and motion pictures, Primo Cuttica (1876-1921) reached fame during the war for having "created" in Italy the so-called "military buffoon."

[290] This group of mountains and the sadly famous high plateau were sites of bloody battles on the Italian war front.

[291] A locality at eleven kilometers from Terni, and 437 m elevation.

[292] A verse of the Venosino poet Luigi Tansillo (1510-1568), written in lamentation at having to leave his beloved.

[293] A demon of Dante's *Inferno*. (Canto XXII, 139).

[294] A pupil of "Checco" Marconi, the Roman Vincenzo Tanlongo (1888-1973) had a fast and lucky start (season 1913-14 at the Opera of Boston), but the war brusquely interrupted his chances of a career, which he took up again at the end of the conflict on a more modest level, but one not without interest: in fact Tanlongo figured among the pioneers of radiophonic musical activity, in which he frequently took part, in opera and in concerts, until the beginning of the 1930s.

[295] The author was assigned to 1st Machine-gunners Section of the autonomous Anti-aircraft Defense Group of the 33rd Field Artillery Regiment.

[296] A center in the high Camonica valley in the province of Brescia.

[297] The Capuan Oreste Salomone (1879-1918), killed in the sky over Padua, was the first aviator (on the Italian side in WWI) decorated with the gold medal.

[298] From a musical Neapolitan family, though a native of Taranto, Mario Pasquale Costa (1858-1933), active as a pianist and composer, spent the great part of his life in London and Paris. He is remembered for many arias and salon pieces (which he himself interpreted with his tenor voice) and, above all, quite famous in the first decades of the century, his operetta *Scugnizza* and the pantomime *Histoire d'un Pierrot*. (G.)

[299] An Italian storyteller, endowed with a lively imagination and warm humanity within a genre of romanticized idealism, the Reatino Virgilio Brocchi (1876-1961) was the prolific author of novels and stories.

CHAPTER 26

[300] A little hill with a magnificent forest, situated on the outskirts of Mexico City.

[301] The pseudonym of the Nicaraguan writer Félix Rubén García-Sarmiento (1867-1916), a leading exponent of Hispano-American poetry.

[302] In fact the author did not sing *Tosca* in either of the two postwar seasons (January and December 1920) in which he took part at the Auditorium of Chicago, nor on tour with the company. *(G.)*

[303] *Edipo re*, the last work of Leoncavallo, was performed for the first time in Chicago on December 13, 1920, posthumously. In fact the composer died at Montecatini on August 9, 1919, leaving the opera incomplete, and it was finished by the Neapolitan Giovanni Pennacchio (1878-?). The proposal that TR sing in an eventual revival of the *Medici* or of the *Chatterton* (of which TR had already twice recorded the most famous aria of the tenor protagonist, "*Tu sola a me rimani o poesia*") or sing the new *Majà e Malbruk* having remained nothing more than a wish, Leoncavallo was longing for an opera conceived to the measure of TR's vocal and interpretive qualities, as if to seal with a special bond of art their long, affectionate friendship. Therefore in 1910 he thought of *Prometeo*, to a libretto by Colautti, hoping to get TR to perform it in Rome on the occasion of the gala for the fiftieth anniversary of the capital. From the letters of Leoncavallo to Colautti found among the letters of the author, it is learned however that the results of the extreme zeal of the librettist did not correspond to TR's wishes, not even after cuts and revisions, so that Leoncavallo himself, sharing the opinion of TR, asked him to compensate Colautti according to their agreements, and this was done.

At the demise of the *Prometeo* project (and perhaps also of some other) Leoncavallo moved on to *Edipo re*, based on the libretto by Forzano; but not even a vast and profound knowledge of the suject enabled a scholar like Mario Morini to ascertain exactly what happened and why; in the lack of documentation and more enlightening evidence, the *pasticcio* [mess] may be explained solely on the basis of Leoncavallo's well-known confused work methods.

Edipo re is a one-act opera, that lasts around sixty minutes, during which the protagonist is almost always on stage.

[304] An authentic man of the theater, the Florentine Giovacchino Forzano (1884-1970) distinguished himself both as a pioneer of modern operatic management (he was the valued collaborator of Toscanini at La Scala), and as an original librettist, for as such he satisfied the demands of Mascagni (*Lodoletta* and *Il piccolo Marat*), Puccini (*Suor Angelica* and *Gianni Schicchi*), Leoncavallo (*La reginetta delle rose*), Franchetti (*Notte di leggenda* and *Glauco*) and Giordano (*Il re*) among others. *(G.)*

[305] The author, evidently, took at face value the insistence of the same lady that she be called Bertha Rambaud. In reality, from the marriage certificate, it turns out that in Milan, January 20, 1895, Leoncavallo married the 32-year-old Marie-Rose Jean, a native of Carpentras. *(G.)*

[306] It was on the morning of December 19, 1919 when the "beloved Campanini" severed his connection with the city of Chicago to which his name will always be bound by fame—as an expert conductor and indefatigable theatrical organizer, who did so much for the diffusion of Italian opera and the reception of Italian interpretive artists in the United States. *(G.)*

[307] The author is only wrong in the following sense: the Sicilian Gino Marinuzzi (1882-1945), whom we have already encountered at the debut of TR (see note 156)—the most able conductor and director, as well as composer of a pair of operas (*Jacquerie* and *Palla de' Mozzi*), who succeeded Campanini in the artistic direction of the season of 1919-20 and was confirmed for the following

season—already had quit in January of 1921 as a consequence of serious frictions with the ambitious and intolerable Ganna Walska (see Ronald Davis, *Opera in Chicago*, 1966, pp. 131-2), leaving the post to Mary Garden. *(G.)*

[308] The least that can be done is to stress the way the author's memory has again caused an overlapping of events in time, particularly important since it also involves Caruso. The recording session of the famous duet from *Otello* (and also the duet from the first act of *Gioconda* that remained unpublished) took place in fact on the 8th of January in 1914, almost seven years before the time that the author was in New York, engaged with the Chicago Grand Opera Association, recently the heir of the Philadelphia-Chicago Opera Company.

This discographic "duet" was described by a play on words as a "duel" (in Italian as well as English). Commenting on it in her book *Caruso on Records* (Valhalla, N.Y., 1965) Aida Favia-Artsay notes that it is often called "the battle of the Titans."

[309] This isn't completely exact. The disengagement of the McCormicks (Edith and Harold), who were replaced in their functions by Samuel Insull, a benefactor of Jewish origin, in fact coincided, in the spring of 1922, with the dismissal of Mary Garden in the capacity of Director General of the organization. The ostracism lamented by the author (who will still return to Chicago in January of 1926, but as a "guest" for a single performance of *Otello*) resulted, however, from the residency of Giorgio Polacco as musical director of the newborn Chicago Civic Opera. For their part the McCormicks continued to be part of the Board of Trustees of the new organization, and even in 1934 Harold, an old man, accepted the nomination for president, be it only honorary, of the Board of the Chicago Grand Opera Company, the offspring of the scarcely more than ten-year-old Chicago Civic Opera.

As for the Scottish Mary Garden (1874-1967)—as a singer and actress among the greatest in history, and an exquisite interpreter of the French repertory above all—her strong personality put her at risk on the battlefields of theatrical organization (no less arduous than those of the stage) while she was Director General of the Opera of Chicago with full artistic and financial responsibility. The experience of the season 1922-23, negative on a purely economic basis, induced her to resign and continue her career as a singer, primarily in Chicago, where critics and public alike remained faithful until her retirement from the stage in 1931. *(G.)*

[310] Evidently the author was present at the performance of *La Juive* on the 15th of November, 1920, with which the Metropolitan season was inaugurated. *(G.)*

[311] Again a question of overlapping in the author's memory of events; particularly of his debut as Gounod's Mephistopheles, which took place in Budapest at the Popular Opera, but eight years before the date that is given, which is to say, in the spring of 1913.

Instances of fellow baritones taking the part of Mephistopheles are not lacking, beginning with Maurel himself and, even before, with the celebrated Jean-Baptiste Faure (1830-1914), who preferred the diabolical personality to that of Valentin so much that he made of him one of his favorite (and most highly acclaimed) "warhorses." *(G.)*

[312] Adelmo della Casa, an industrialist and hotel owner in Italy.

[313] As luck would have it, it fell to the lot of Caruso's great predecessor, De Lucia, 60 years old by this time, to carry the last melodic message to the man who had broken the hearts of Neapolitans. *(G.)*

[314] In effect the activity of the author at the Metropolitan was more in the nature of guest appearances than that of a stable presence, which was assured, where baritones were concerned, besides the veteran Scotti, by his contemporary De Luca and the younger Danise, to whom would be added, in the twenties, the even younger Basiola and Tibbett.

Contracted initially for the 1921-22 season and engaged for seven consecutive seasons, TR took part in only 46 performances all told (with a maximum of 9 in the season 1922-23), to which we need to add the 8 of the tour (4 at the Academy of Music and the rest in Philadelphia), for a total of 54. Of these 12 (10+2) and 11 (10+1) respectively were of *Barbiere* (his debut opera). *Pagliacci*, *Ernani*, *Aida*, *Andrea Chénier*, *Gioconda* and *Cena delle beffe* (first American performance) were the other operas TR sang at the Metropolitan. To demonstrate the little affection that Gatti-Casazza felt for him, he was denied the possibility of interpreting, not just *Hamlet* or *Demon* or *Edipo re*, operas which needed to be readied purposely for him, but not even *Rigoletto* and *Africaine*, which were already a part of the Met's repertory, with De Luca and Danise (and even Basiola) being regularly cast for them. *(G.)*

[315] John H. Duval gathered his own experiences as a coach of famous singers—a profession he practiced brilliantly for many years in New York—in a book (*Svengali's Secrets and Memoirs of the Golden Age*, New York, 1958) in which there is a chapter devoted to TR.

[316] The earrings which adorned the Great Chief of the Indian tribe, Aimoré. This pertains to a character of the second rank (which is why it was assigned to Maurel when he was 22 years old, while the part of the first baritone belonged to Enrico Storti) who appears only in the third of the four acts into which *Il Guarany* is divided, the first Italian opera (and also the most famous) of the eight composed by the Brazilian Antonio Carlos Gomes (1836-1896). Peformed at La Scala on March 19, 1870, the opera enjoyed great popularity in the last thirty years of the century, but today is nearly forgotten (as is the composer.) *(G.)*

[317] That this judgment of the author about the relations between Verdi and Maurel should be taken with a certain caution has already been said (see note 219), but it is well to stress it again to avoid hagiographic exaggerations. *(G.)*

CHAPTER 27

[318] Belonging to this group of audacious and prosperous Italian impresarios who were active primarily outside the country, Bracale operated primarily in the theaters of Central and South America (the southern zone excluded, with the exception of Chile, which was more pertinent to the group of Mocchi and Co.). He was successful in repeatedly signing not a few famous singers such as Schipa and Galli-Curci, Caruso and Storchio, Lázaro and Barrientos, Cortis

and Besanzoni, Stracciari and naturally, TR. The financier associated with Bracale was called Enrique A. Ortega.

[319] The author took part only in thirty-one performances of eight operas (*Bohème*, *Aida* and *Rigoletto*, besides those cited), distributed over five months of touring, during which the Bracale company went successively to Cuba, Puerto Rico, Venezuela and Colombia.

[320] A revolt was nourished by the grave economic crisis which struck the island at the beginning of the twenties after a crash in the price of sugar, and gave rise to the dictatorship instituted by Gerardo Machado y Morales (1871-1939), elected president the following year.

[321] For the exceptional duration of his government, perhaps the most typical exponent of a prolific dynasty of Central and South American "*caudillos*," Juan Vicente Gomez (1857-1935) from 1908 to his death exercised an undisputed dictatorship over Venezuela.

[322] The author is persecuted by the memory of "Benedetta" whose death, nineteen years before, overtook her after she had undergone an analogous surgical intervention.

[323] With the impresario Bracale and the orchestra conductor (who was an obscure *routinier* by the name of Guglielmo Soriente) a pair of serious professionals also played a part: the Roman Angelo Pintucci (1880-1962), a lyric tenor with an agreeably extended range, and even more famous than his colleague, the Milanese (from Melegnano) Vincenzo Bettoni (1881-1954), renowned above all as a "buffo," whose resources as an actor and interpreter were overflowing, so that for many years he would play, among other parts, a legendary Rossinian Mustafà. *(G.)*

[324] Published in Italy in 1937, in the heyday of the fascist regime, the autobiography of TR is a little quiet about the allusion to a second "grave report" from Rome. Otherwise the author would not have been able to proceed without risking the rigors of censorship. The "report" regarded, in fact, the tragic loss of his brother-in-law, the husband of his younger sister Velia.

Elected deputy in 1919 for the committee of Ferrara and Rovigo, and Secretary General of the Socialist Party in 1924 at only 39 years of age, Matteotti was the most courageous and uncompromising adversary of fascism, who came to denounce abuses and acts of violence on all sides until his discourse in the Camera on May 30, 1924, in which he asked for the annulment *en bloc* of the elections, cost him his life. On the afternoon of the 10th of June, while he was going on foot to the Camera to give another discourse, he was attacked and abducted by fascist hoodlums who stabbed him inside the automobile which was used for the crime. The body was found in a woods called the Quartarella, twenty-five kilometers from Rome, but not until the following August 15.

Giacomo Matteotti and Velia Titta, who knew each other casually during country holidays in the mountains in the summer of 1912, were engaged the following year, and united in matrimony on the 8th of January, 1916. If the statements of Matteotti's widow in the tragic summer of 1924, and of Vera Modigliani, the wife of the Hon. Modigliani, reported in *Esilio* (Milano, 1946) are correct, the author did not favor the marriage; on the contrary, full of dire forethought, he had tried to dissuade his sister with these words: "Don't marry your San Sebastiano! I see him tied to tree and shot full of arrows!"

[325] This is not exact, since the author sang *Rigoletto* again on two other occasions, at the Operház of Budapest and at the Volksoper of Berlin, both in April of 1925. *(G.)*

EPILOGUE

Translated by Andrew Farkas. Originally published in his *Titta Ruffo: An Anthology* (Greenwood Press, 1984). The volume may now serve as an appendix to Ruffo's autobiography.

Roles and Repertory

Escamillo	*Carmen*/George Bizet Padua, 1899 - Havana, 1923
Alfio	*Cavalleria rusticana*/Pietro Mascagni Bologna, 1899 - Buenos Aires, 1902
Tonio	*Pagliacci*/Ruggero Leoncavallo Bologna, 1899 - New York, 1929
Giorgio Germont	*La traviata*/Giuseppe Verdi Genoa, 1900 - Miami, 1926
Don Carlo	*Ernani*/Giuseppe Verdi Ferrara, 1900 - New York, 1928
Nelusko	*L'africaine*/Jakob Meyerbeer Santiago (Chile), 1900 - San Paolo, 1915
Carlo Gérard	*Andrea Chénier*/Umberto Giordano Santiago (Chile), 1900 - New York, 1928
Toni	*La Salinara*/Domenico Brescia Santiago (Chile), 1900
Iago	*Otello*/Giuseppe Verdi Santiago (Chile), 1900 - Buenos Aires, 1928
Scarpia	*Tosca*/Giacomo Puccini Palermo, 1901 - Buenos Aires, 1931
Nabucco	*Nabucco*/Giuseppe Verdi Trieste, 1901 - Venice, 1903
High Priest	*Samson et Dalila*/Camille Saint-Saëns Cairo, 1901 - Alexandria (Egypt), 1902
De Siriex	*Fedora*/Umberto Giordano Cairo, 1901 - Monte Carlo, 1910
Kyoto	*Iris*/Pietro Mascagni Cairo, 1901
Amonasro	*Aida*/Giuseppe Verdi Alexandria (Egypt), 1902 - New York, 1929
Cascart	*Zazà*/Ruggero Leoncavallo Buenos Aires, 1902 - Naples, 1910
Squarrocca	*Proserpina*/Camille Saint-Saëns Alexandria (Egypt), 1903
Kurwenal	*Tristan und Isolde*/Richard Wagner Cairo, 1903 - Madrid, 1913
Publio/Satana	*Il santo*/Francesco Ghin Venice, 1903

Figaro	*Il barbiere di Siviglia*/Gioacchino Rossini London, 1903 - Marseille, 1931
Carlo Worms	*Germania*/Alberto Franchetti Milan, 1904 - Odessa, 1905
Marchese di Saluzzo	*Griselda*/Jules Massenet Milan, 1904
Gléby	*Siberia*/Umberto Giordano Milan, 1904 - Paris, 1905
Michonnet	*Adriana Lecouvreur*/Francesco Chilea Milan, 1904
Il Demon	*Il Demon*/Anton G. Rubinstein Odessa, 1905 - Buenos Aires, 1909
Frère Boniface	*Le jongleur de Notre-Dame*/Jules Massenet Milan, 1905
Antonio	*Linda di Chamounix*/Gaetano Donizetti St. Petersburg, 1906 - Monte Carlo, 1911
Hamlet	*Hamlet*/Ambroise Thomas Lisbon, 1907 - Buenos Aires, 1931
Doctor Malatesta	*Don Pasquale*/Gaetano Donizetti Monte Carlo, 1907 - Rio de Janeiro, 1911
Gianciotto	*Paolo e Francesca*/Luigi Mancinelli Lisbon, 1908
Don Giovanni	*Don Giovanni*/Wolfgang Amadeus Mozart Buenos Aires, 1908 - Philadelphia, 1914
Ignacio dal Puente	*Aurora*/Héctor Panizza Buenos Aires, 1908
Cristoforo Colombo	*Cristoforo Colombo*/Alberto Franchetti Monte Carlo, 1909 - Philadelphia, 1914
Athanaël	*Thaïs*/Jules Massenet Buenos Aires, 1911 - Chicago, 1913
Rodrigo	*Don Carlo*/Giuseppe Verdi Buenos Aires, 1911 - Madrid, 1913
Jack Rance	*La Fanciulla del West*/Giacomo Puccini Buenos Aires, 1911 - San Paolo, 1915
Evgeny Onegin	*Evgeny Onegin*/Piotr Ilich Tchaikovsky Buenos Aires, 1911
Méphistophélès	*Faust*/Charles Gounod Budapest, 1913

Boris Godunov	*Boris Godunov*/Modest Mussorgsky Buenos Aires, 1916
Falstaff	*Falstaff*/Giuseppe Verdi Buenos Aires, 1916 - Madrid, 1919
Oedipus	*Oedipus Rex*/Ruggero Leoncavallo Chicago, 1920 - New York, 1921
Neri Chiaramantesi	*La cena delle beffe*/Umberto Giordano Barcelona, 1925 - Philadelphia, 1927

Repertory of Sacred Music

Christ	*La resurrezione di Lazzaro*/Lorenzo Perosi Catania, 1899 Messa/Luigi Barrella Salerno, 1899 L'Immacolata/Guglielmo Mattioli Bergamo, 1904

Operatic roles:	Operas performed:		Composers:
55			26
	Italian	37	
	French	10	
	German	3	
	Slavic	3	
	Total	53	

Total number of performances: approximately 1500

Chronology

1898

April 9	**Rome** Costanzi	*Lohengrin* (14) (debut in the role of Herald) L. de Benedetto, A. Degli Abbati, F. Viñas, A. Gnaccarini/O. Benedetti, F. Spangher Conductor: V. Mingardi
May 19		*Lucia di Lammermoor* (1) (debut in the role of Lord E. Ashton) A. Padovani, F. Granados, F. Spangher. Conductor: T. de Angelis
July 16	**Livorno** Alfieri	*Il trovatore* (7) (debut in the role of Conte di Luna) M. Grippa, G. Pignani, F. Nieddu. Conductor: A. Torri
July 28		*Lucia di Lammermoor* (6) L. Longoni, F. Nieddu, C. di Ciolo Conductor: A. Torri
August 6		*Rigoletto* (2) (debut in the lead) L. Longoni, C. Dani. Conductor: A. Torri
August	Bagni Pancaldi	Concert: arias from *Macbeth* and *I Puritani*
August 14	**Pisa** Politeama Pisano	*Il trovatore* (2)* M. Grippa, G. Pignani, G. Cesarani/C. Dani, C. di Ciolo. Conductor: A. Torri *In the season benefit, celebrated with this opera, TR sings a selection from *Macbeth*, the romanza: "Son lontano" of Ubaldo Ceccarelli and the song "Luce mia" by his brother Ettore.
September 18		*Lucia di Lammermoor* (3) D. Tanini/L. Longoni, C. Dani, A. Bini/ C. di Ciolo. Conductor: A. Torri
September 25		Concert: *Lucia di Lammermoor*, Act III, Scene I. A. Bini
December 22	**Catanzaro** Comunale	*La forza del destino* (debut in the role of Don Carlo di Vargas) E. Adaberto, E. Cavara, G. Rebonato, R. de Falco. Conductor: A. Doncich

1899

January 11	**Catanzaro** Comunale	*Ruy Blas* (debut in the role of Don Sallustio) T. Chelotti, E. Marenzi, E. Cavara Conductor: A. Doncich
January 25		*La bohème* (debut in the role of Marcello) E. Adaberto, E. Marenzi, M. Izquierdo Conductor: A. Doncich
February 20	**Siracusa** Massimo	*La bohème* E. Adaberto, E. Marenzi, E. Cavara Conductor: A. Doncich
March 15		*Rigoletto* E. Adaberto, T. Farelli, A. Sarcoli, A.Venturini Conductor: A. Doncich
April 7	**Acireale** Bellini	*Manon Lescaut* (debut in the role of Lescaut) T. Chelotti, E. Cavara, Conductor: A Doncich
May		*La bohème* E. Adaberto, T. Chelotti, A. Sarcoli Conductor: A. Doncich
May		*Un ballo in maschera* (debut in the role of Renato) E. Adaberto, T. Farelli, A. Dianni Conductor: A. Doncich
May		*Rigoletto* E. Adaberto, T. Farelli, A. Sarcoli, A.Venturini Conductor: A. Doncich
May 15	**Catania** Nazionale	*La bohème* (3) E. Adaberto, A. Scalera/T. Chelotti, A. Sarcoli Conductors: A. Doncich/C. Salibra
May 26		*Rigoletto* E. Adaberto, T. Farelli, A. Sarcoli, A. Venturini Conductor: A. Doncich
June 6		*Un ballo in maschera* E. Adaberto, T. Farelli, A. Dianni Conductors: A. Doncich/P. Monaco
July 20	Benedictine Church	*La risurrezione di Lazzaro* (oratorio) (2) (local première and debut in the role of Cristo) A. Antinori, M. Pozzi, A. Sarcoli Conductor: F. Tarallo
July 25	Nazionale	*La Gioconda* (8) (debut in the role of Barnaba) A. Giuliani/A. Antinori, M.Pozzi, A. Sarcoli, A. Fabbro. Conductors: G. Serrao/F. Tarallo
August 18	**Siracusa** Massimo	*La Gioconda* A. Giuliani, M. Pozzi, A. Sarcoli, A. Fabbro, Conductor: G. Serrao

August 20		*La favorita* (2) (debut in the role of Alfonso XI) M. Pozzi, A. Sarcoli. Conductor: F. Tarallo
August 25	**Catania** Nazionale	*La Gioconda* (2) A. Giuliani, M. Pozzi, A. Sarcoli, A. Fabbro. Conductors: P. Serrao/F. Tarallo
September 13	**Salerno** Municipale	*La bohème* G. Tosi, J. Massa, A. Sarcoli Conductor: C. Sebastiani
September		*Faust* (debut in the role of Valentin)
September 23	Duomo	"Messa" of Luigi Barella (2) (world première and debut) J. Massa, A. Sarcoli
September 23	Municipale	*Rigoletto* J. Massa, G. del Prato, A. Sarcoli, G. Berenzone Conductor: C. Sebastiani
September		*La Gioconda* J. Massa, G. del Prato, A. Sarcoli Conductor: C. Sebastiani
November 7	**Padua** Garibaldi	*Carmen* (3) (debut in the role of Escamillo) E. Bruno, A. Matassini Conductor: S. Boscarini
December 24	**Bologna** Duse [8]	*Cavalleria rusticana* (debut in the role of Alfio) A. Busi, O. Frosini. Conductor: A. Siragusa *Pagliacci* (debut in the role of Tonio) P. Drudi, O. Frosini. Conductor: A. Siragusa

1900

January 6	**Bologna** Duse	*Carmen* (1) Z. Montalcino, O. Frosini Conductor: A. Siragusa
January 21	**Genoa** Carlo Felice	*La traviata* (2) (debut in the role of Giorgio Germont) A. Pandolfini, E. Ventura Conductor: O. Anselmi
February 14		*Rigoletto* (1) A. Occhiolini, G. Marchi, A. Stampanoni, R. Ercolani. Conductor: O. Anselmi
March 10	**Parma** Regio	*Il trovatore* (5) I. Paoli, E. Ghibaudo, V. Bieletto, F. Fabbro Conductor: A. Franzoni
May 9	**Ferrara** Tosi-Borghi	*Ernani* (8) (debut in the role of Don Carlo) M. Pizzagalli, A. Gamba, A. Brondi Conductor: D. Varola

June 3	**Lucerne** Kursaal	*Rigoletto* G. Raschke-Lucignani, C. Dani, A. Dadò Conductor: A. Fumagalli
July 28	**Santiago** (Chile) Municipal	*L'africaine* (debut in the role of Nelusko) N. Mazzi, G. Piccoletti, M. Izquierdo, A. Venturini, P. Wulmann Conductor: Arturo Padovani
July 29		*Rigoletto* G. Piccoletti, M. Pozzi, E. Castellano Conductor: A. Padovani
August 8		*Il trovatore* N. Mazzi, M. Pozzi, M. Izquierdo, A. Venturini Conductor: A. Padovani
August 13	**Valparaiso** Victoria	*L'africaine* N. Mazzi, G. Piccoletti, M. Izquierdo, P. Wulmann. Conductor: A. Padovani
August 23	**Santiago** Municipal	*La forza del destino* N. Mazzi, M. Pozzi, M. Izquierdo, A. Cerratelli, P. Wulmann. Conductor: A. Padovani
August 27	**Valparaiso** Victoria	*Il trovatore* N. Mazzi, M. Pozzi, M. Izquierdo, F. Cervi. Conductor: A. Padovani
August 29		*La Gioconda* N. Mazzi, M. Pozzi, E. Castellano, P. Wulmann Conductor: A. Padovani
September 1	**Santiago** Municipal	*La Gioconda* N. Mazzi, M. Pozzi, E. Castellano, P. Wulmann Conductor: A. Padovani
September 5		*Andrea Chénier* (debut in the role of Carlo Gérard) E. Miotti, E. Castellano Conductor: A. Padovani
September 22		*Ruy Blas* N. Mazzi, M. Pozzi, M. Izquierdo Conductor: A. Padovani
September 29		*Un ballo in maschera* N. Mazzi, G. Piccoletti, M. Pozzi, M. Izquierdo Conductor: A. Padovani
October 1	**Valparaiso** Victoria	*Ruy Blas* N. Mazzi, M. Pozzi, M. Izquierdo Conductor: A. Padovani
October 9	**Santiago** Municipal	*Faust* I. Myrtea, E. Castellano, P. Wulmann Conductor: A. Padovani

October 11		*La salinara* (world première, debut in the role of Toni) N. Mazzi, M. Pozzi, M. Izquierdo Conductor: A. Padovani
October 12		*Cavalleria rusticana* N. Mazzi, M. Izquierdo. Conductor: A. Padovani
October 19		*Otello* (1) (debut in the role of Iago) N. Mazzi, M. Izquierdo. Conductor: A. Padovani
October 23	**Valparaiso** Victoria	*Andrea Chénier* E. Miotti, M. Izquierdo. Conductor: A. Padovani
October 28		*Otello* N. Mazzi, M. Izquierdo. Conductor: A. Padovani
November 13	**Talca** Municipal	*La Gioconda* N. Mazzi, M. Pozzi, M. Izquierdo, P. Wulmann Conductor: A. Padovani
November 19	**Concepción** Concepción	*L'africaine* N. Mazzi, M. Pozzi, M. Izquierdo, P. Wulmann Conductor: A. Padovani
November 20		*La Gioconda* N. Mazzi, M. Pozzi, E. Castellano, P. Wulmann Conductor: A. Padovani

1901

January 21	**Siena** T. dei Rinnovati	*Ernani* (10) E. Canovas, F. de Grandi. Conductor: U. Zanetti
March 2	**Pisa** R. Teatro Nuovo	*Otello* (20) M. Maragliano/M. Sirti, E. Galli, U. Ceccarelli Conductor: R. Bracale
March 19		*Ernani* (3) A. Stinco Palermini, M. Izquierdo, U. Ceccarelli Conductor: R. Bracale
April 2		Concert for scholastic charity M. Sirti, U. Ceccarelli. Piano accompaniment: M. Rosselli Nissim
March	**Livorno** Goldoni	Concert commemorating the death of Verdi: *Ernani* Act III, Finale.* A. Stinco Palermini, E. Galli, U. Ceccarelli

*For the occasion the verse of F.M. Piave: "A Carlo Magno—sia gloria e onor" was changed as follows (!): "Al sommo Verdi—sia gloria e onor."

| April 12 | **Palermo** Massimo [16] | *Tosca* (debut in the role of Scarpia) E. Bianchini Cappelli, G. Anselmi Conductor: R. Ferrari |

April 13		*Rigoletto* B. Morello, G. Giaconia, E. Ventura, G. Tisci-Rubini. Conductor: R. Ferrari
September 1	**Trieste** La Fenice	*Nabucco* (debut) I. de Frate, A. Fanton, A. Zennaro, C. Thos Conductor: E. Perosio
September 14		*La Gioconda* (7) I. de Frate, C. Pagnoni, A. Fanton, A. Maurini, C. Thos. Conductor: G. Gialdini
December 3	**Cairo** Khediviale	*La bohème* A. Pandolfini, A. Barone, E. Garbin, Conductor: A. Pomé
December 9		*Samson et Dalila* (debut in the role of High Priest) V. Guerrini, C. Barrera Conductor: A. Pomé
December 15		*Otello* (1) A. Carrera, C. Barrera. Conductor: A. Pomé
December 16		*Fedora* (debut in the role of De Siriex) A. Pandolfini, A. Fusco, F. Giraud Conductor: A. Pomé
December		*Iris* (debut in the role of Kyoto) A. Pandolfini, F. Giraud, A. Anceschi, G. Tisci-Rubini. Conductor: A. Pomé

1902

January 28	**Alexandria** (Egypt) Zizinia	*Aida* (6) A. Carrera, V. Guerrini, C. Barrera, G. Tisci-Rubini. Conductor: A. Pomé
February 5		*Fedora* (3) A. Pandolfini, A. Barone, F. Giraud, Conductor: A. Pomé
February 12		*Samson et Dalila* (7) V. Guerrini, C. Barrera. Conductor: A. Pomé
February 14		*La bohème* A. Pandolfini, A. Barone, F. Giraud Conductor: A. Pomé
May 21	**Buenos Aires** T. de la Òpera	*Aida* (4) M. de Lerma, A. Cucini. J. Biel, M. Boudouresque. Conductor: L. Mugnone
June 9		*L'africaine* (2) M. de Lerma, I. Timroth, J. Biel, R. Ercolani Conductor: L. Mugnone

July 17		*Il trovatore* (1) H. Darclée, A. Cucini, J. Biel, R. Ercolani Conductor: L. Mugnone
August 9		*Zazà* (2) (national première, debut in the role of Cascart) H. Darclee, E. Garbin, M. Boudouresque. Conductor: L. Mugnone
August 13		*Cavalleria rusticana* (1) H. Darclée, E. Garbin. Conductor: L. Mugnone
August 19	**Montevideo** Solís	*Aida* M. de Lerma, A. Cucini, J. Biel, M. Boudouresque. Conductor: L. Mugnone
August 29		*Il trovatore* H. Darclée, A. Cucini, J. Biel
August 31		*Zazà* (local première) H. Darclée, E. Garbin
October 2	**Salsomaggiore** Ferrario	Concert for the earthquake victims of Sicily. Operatic selections. M. Franchilucci, A. Dianni
December	**Alexandria** (Egypt) Zizinia	*La bohème* A. Stehle, C. Rommel, E. Garbin Conductor: G. Zuccani
December 11		*Manon Lescaut* A. Santarelli, G. Borgatti, C. Walter Conductor: G. Zuccani
December 18		*Carmen* C. Wyns, G. Borgatti Conductor: G. Zuccani

1903

January 3	**Alexandria** (Egypt)	*Proserpina* (national première and debut in the role of Squarrocca) C. Wyns, E. Trentini, G. Borgatti, C. Walter. Conductor: G. Zuccani
January 12		*Manon* (debut in the role of Lescaut) A. Santarelli, E. Garbin, C. Walter Conductor: G. Zuccani
January 22	**Cairo** Khediviale	*Manon Lescaut* A. Santarelli, G. Borgatti, C. Walter Conductor: G. Zuccani
January 24		*Manon* (?)
January 28		*Carmen* C. Wyns, C. Rommel, G. Borgatti Conductor: G. Zuccani

January 31   *Prosperina* (local première)
C. Wyns, E. Trentini, G. Borgatti, C. Walter
Conductor: G. Zuccani

February 26   *La bohème*
C. Wyns, C. Rommel, E. Garbin
Conductor: G. Zuccani

March 14   *Tristan und Isolde* (2) (debut in the role of
Kurwenal) G. Borgatti. Conductor: G. Zuccani

April 18   **Venice**   *Il trovatore* (10)
          La Fenice   R. Calligaris Marti, M. Julia, A. Paoli,
T. Montico. Conductor: R. Ferrari

May 7   *Il santo* (6) (world première and debut in
the role of Publio/Satana) E. Canovas,
S. Ronconi, A. Cecchi. Conductor: R. Ferrari

June 5   **London**   *Lucia di Lammermoor* (1)
          Covent Garden   E. Wedekind, A. Bonci, M. Journet,
Conductor: L. Mancinelli

June 24   33 Grosvenor   Vocal and instrumental concert for
          Square   Sir Philip Livine: Prologue to *Pagliacci;* romanza
from *Dinorah.* M. Garden, F. Lambert
Piano accompaniment: L. Ronald, W. Backhaus

July 1   Covent Garden   *Il barbiere di Siviglia* (1) (debut in the role
of Figaro) M. Barrientos, A. Bonci,
M. Journet, C. Gilibert.
Conductor: L. Mancinelli

November 4   **Venice**   *Nabucco* (6)*
          Rossini   P. Roluti, A. Fanton, L. Penso-Boldrini,
A. Masini, O. Carozzi. Conductor: F. Tanara

                                     *In this benefit, celebrated on November 10, after Act II, TR
sings: "Eri tu che macchiavi quell'anima" from Un ballo in
maschera.

1904

January 7   **Milan**   *Rigoletto* (16)
          Scala   G. Wermez/F. Toresella, G. Giaconia/I.
Monti-Baldini, G. Anselmi/G. Ibos/G. Krismer,
A. Didur/S. Cirotto. Conductor: C. Campanini

January 30   *Germania* (9) (debut in the role of Carlo Worms)
C. Pasini, E. Trentini, F. Viñas/G. Zenatello,
A. Pini-Corsi, A. Didur
Conductor: C. Campanini

April 10   *Griselda* (2) (debut in the role of
Marchese di Saluzzo) C. Pasini, I. Monti-Baldini,
G. Bazelli, G. de Luca. Conductor: C. Campanini

April	La Famiglia Artistica Milanese*	Concert: Prologue to *Pagliacci* E. Oddone, G. Borgatti Piano accompaniment: H. Panizza

*Celebrating the thirtieth anniversary and inaugurating the new residence of the society. F. Cilea and A. Colautti were present.

April 20	**Florence** La Pergola	*Rigoletto* (3) M. Galvany, A. Colombo, I. Cristalli, O. Banti/E. Vannuccini. Conductor: S. Boscarini

October 6	**Milan** Lirico Internazionale	*Siberia* (6) (debut in the role of Gléby) E. Carelli/A. Revy, A. Franceschini, A. Sabellicoy Conductor: L. Mugnone

October 22		*Zazà* E. Carelli, E. Vecla, E. Leliva Conductors: L. Mugnone/R. Capocci

October 25		*Adriana Lecouvreur* (4) (debut in the role of Michonnet) S. Krusceniski, N. Frascani, P. Zeni, E. Sottolana. Conductor: L. Mugnone

December 4	**Bergamo** Donizetti	*L'Immacolata* (oratorio) (3) (debut) P. Sassi, A. Alemanni, A. Bendinelli, E. Brancaleoni. Conductor: G. Mattioli

1905

January 8	**Odessa** Municipale	*Rigoletto* A. Gonzaga, G. Giaconia, A. Dianni/G. Anselmi, G. Gravina. Conductor: A. Bernardi

January 11		*Tosca* (5) A. Santarelli, R. de Rosa/A. Dianni/G. Anselmi Conductor: I.V. Pribic

January 12		*Il trovatore* Ristori/M. Santoliva, M. Verger, M. Gilion Conductor: I.V. Pribic

January 20		*Aida* M. Santoliva/Ristori, M. Verger, M. Gilion, A. Sabellico. Conductor: I.V. Pribic

January 31		*Demon* (debut) J. Korolewicz-Wayda, M. Gilion, A. Sabellico/O. Villani. Conductor: A. Bernardi

February 11		*Pagliacci* J. Korolewicz-Wayda, A. Dianni Conductor: A. Bernardi

February 17		*Il barbiere di Siviglia* A. Gonzaga, G. Anselmi, A. Sabellico, E. Coletti. Conductor: A. Bernardi

February 21		*Otello* J. Korolewicz-Wayda, M. Gilion Conductor: A. Bernardi
March 4		*Germania* (national première) A. Santareli, A. Gonzaga, M. Gilion, G. Gravina. Conductor: A. Bernardi
March 20	**St. Petersburg** New Conservatory	*Rigoletto* (11) M. van der Brandt, E. de Cisneros, L. Sobinov, A. Sabellico. Conductor: E.D. Esposito
March 21		*Il trovatore* T. Chelotti, E. de Cisneros, A. Paoli, Conductor: E.D. Esposito
March 24		*Faust* M. van der Brandt, L. Sobinov, A. Sabellico Conductor: E.D. Esposito
March 26		*Demon* Sardgevi, L.M. Sibiriakov Conductor: E.D. Esposito
March 27		*Aida* T. Chelotti, E. de Cisneros, A. Paoli, A. Sabellico Conductor: E.D. Esposito
April 11		*Otello* A. Paoli. Conductor: E.D. Esposito
April 16		*Il barbiere di Siviglia* A. Gonzaga. Conductor: E.D. Esposito
April 19		*La traviata* L. Sobinov. Conductor: E.D. Esposito
April		*Pagliacci* Conductor: E.D. Esposito

1905

May 4	**Paris** Sarah Bernhardt	*Siberia* (national première) A. Pinto, A. Bassi. Conductor: C. Campanini
May 13, 15, 16, 18, 19		*Fedora* (5) (national première) L. Cavalieri, A. Barone, E. Caruso Conductors: C. Campanini/R. Ferrari
May 22	?	Instrumental and vocal concert organized by the journal "Le Figaro": *Pagliacci,* Prologue Violinist: P. Sarasate
May 30	Sarah Bernhardt	*Il barbiere di Siviglia* R. Pacini, A. Masini, O. Luppi, A. Baldelli Conductor: R. Ferrari

June 2	Palais Comtesse Château	Instrumental and vocal concert: Songs; *Pagliacci,* Prologue; romanza, *Chatterton* Piano accompaniment: Schwab, violinist: J. Kubelik
June 5	?	Concert: aria from *Dinorah,* Cavatina from *Il barbiere di Siviglia,* duet from *Rigoletto* with L. Cavalieri
June 8	Palais du Trocadéro	Concert for the thirtieth anniversary of the theater: aria from *Siberia,* Act II of *La traviata.* G. Bellincioni, A. Bendinelli Conductor: E. Mangin
October 18	**Milan** Lirico Internazionale	*Le jongleur de Notre-Lame* (national première and debut in the role of Frère Boniface) (5) E. Leliva, V. Mentasti, U. Cocchi, S. Massocci Conductor: R. Ferrari
December	**Moscow** Imperiale	*Il barbiere di Siviglia*
December		*Demon*
December 15	**St. Petersburg** New Conservatory	*Rigoletto*
December 19		*Demon*
December 20		*Tosca*
December 31		*La Gioconda*

1906

January	?	Benefit concert
March 5	**St. Petersburg** New Conservatory	*Tosca* E. Carelli, A. Giorgini
March 8		*Linda di Chamounix* (debut in the role of Antonio) M. Galvany, G. Fabbri, A. Giorgini, A. Sabellico. Conductor: G. Golisciani
March 13		*Il barbiere di Siviglia*
March 16	**Moscow** Imperial	*Rigoletto* M. Galvany, A. Gramegna, R. Andreini/G. Armanini. Conductor: G. Golisciani
March 25	**St. Petersburg** New Conservatory	*La Gioconda* E. Carelli, G. Armanini
March 26	Salon of the 1st Corps of Cadets	Concert for Russian revolutionaries: F. Titta

March 26	New Conservatory	*Linda di Chamounix* R. Andreini
March 28		*Zazà* E. Carelli, G. Armanini
April 3		*Il barbiere di Siviglia*
April 16	**Khar'kov** Municipale	*Il barbiere di Siviglia* M. Galvany, G. Gasparri Conductor: A. Bernardi
April 19		*Demon* J. Korolewicz-Wayda, G. Gasparri Conductor: A. Bernardi
April 21		*Faust* J. Korolewicz-Wayda. Conductor: A. Bernardi
April 22		*La traviata* M. Galvany. Conductor: A. Bernardi
April 23		*Il trovatore* J. Korolewicz-Wayda. Conductor: A. Bernardi
April		*Rigoletto*
April	**Kiev** Solozov	*Demon* J. Korolewicz-Wayda, Machin Conductor: A. Margulian
April		*Il trovatore* Conductor: A. Margulian
April 28		*Il barbiere di Siviglia* M. Galvany. Conductor: A. Margulian
April 28		*Rigoletto* M. Galvany, A.J. Dobrovolsikaja, G. Gasparri/ V. Coppola, Seghievic. Conductor: A. Margulian
May		*La traviata*
May		*Ernani*
May 3	**Odessa** Sibiriak?	Benefit concert: *La traviata*, Act III M. Galvany
May 13	Municipale	*Il barbiere di Siviglia* M. Galvany, Askocienski. Conductor: I.V. Pribic
May		*Rigoletto* M. Galvany, Kovielkova, Askocienski, Nezdikov. Conductor: I.V. Pribic
June		*Demon* J. Korolewicz-Wayda. Conductor: I.V. Pribic

September 5	**Milan** Lirico Internazionale	*Zazà* (12) E. Carelli, P. Schiavazzi. Conductor: G. Baroni
October 6	**Vienna** Hofoper	*Rigoletto* (1) S. Kurz, H. Kittel, E. Caruso, W. Hesch Conductor: F. Spetrino
November	**St. Petersburg** Aquarium	*La Gioconda* L. Berlendi, M.I. Dolina, L.M. Klementiev
November 19	Nikolai I Orphanage	Benefit Concert
November	Opera Nuova	*Rigoletto* V.P. Antonova. A.J. Dobrovolsikaja, L.M. Klementiev, Seghievic
November 22	Aquarium	*Il barbiere di Siviglia* M. Galvany, M. Riera
November 23	New Conservatory	*Rigoletto* M. Galvany/M.D. Turkianinova, G.I. Nikitina, R. Saianov, Zhuchov
November 29	**St. Petersburg** Aquarium	*Demon*
November 30		*Il trovatore* L. Berlendi/F. Titta, Jakarova, L.M. Klementiev
December 7	New Conservatory	*Pagliacci* and *Ernani*, Act III Dolina, L.M. Klementiev
December 16	Aquarium	*L'africaine*
December		*Demon* M.M. Gushkina, N.A. Polsciakov Conductor: Sierk
December 25	**Moscow** Imperiale [7]	*Rigoletto**
December		*Il barbiere di Siviglia**
December 27		*Demon**
December		*Zazà**

*possible performers: H. Darclée, O. Boronat, S. Arnoldson—
C. Pagnoni, L. Hotkovska —A. Paoli, G. Anselmi, F.
Marconi, U. Colombini—G. Tansini, G. Bossè. Conductor: E.
Plotnikov

| December | | Concert: F. Titta |

1907

January 14	**St. Petersburg** New Conservatory	Benefit Concert
January 15		*Tosca* L. Berlendi, L.M. Klementiev
January 21	Technical School	Concert for famine victims
January	New Conservatory	*Pagliacci*
January 24	**Lisbon** São Carlos	*Hamlet* (6) (debut) E. Clasenti, A. Torretta, G. Grino Conductor: L. Mancinelli
February 2		*Rigoletto* (1) E. Clasenti, A. Torretta, P. Schiavazzi, A. Brondi. Conductor: V. Lombardi
February 12	**Monte Carlo** Grand-Théâtre	*Un ballo in maschera*, Acts III and IV (1) L. de Benedetto, S. Kurz, N. Zerola Conductor: A. Pomé
February 16	**Monte Carlo** Grand-Théâtre	*Don Pasquale* (3) (debut in the role of Dr. Malatesta) R. Storchio, L. Sobinov, A. Pini Corsi. Conductor: A. Pomé
March 1		Concert: *Hamlet*, Drinking Song; *Dinorah* romanza
March 8		Concert: *Un ballo in maschera*, aria; *Stornello* by Billi
March 14		*Il barbiere di Siviglia* (3)* R. Storchio, F. De Lucia, F. Chaliapin, A. Pini-Corsi. Conductor: A. Pomé *The first performance was a benefit for charitable works in the principality.
April 5	**Moscow** Solodovnikov	*Rigoletto* O. Boronat
April 13	**Berlin** Königliches Opernhaus	*Il barbiere di Siviglia* Act II* (1) R. Storchio, F. De Lucia, F. Chaliapin, A. Pini Corsi. Conductor: A. Pomé *The company of the Grand-Théâtre di Monte Carlo; presented *Samson et Dalila*, Act II, and *Hérodiade*, Act III, prepared by the same company.
October 16	**Milan** Lirico Internazionale	*Hamlet* (8) L. Grenville, M. Grassé, G. Quinzi-Tapergi, Conductor: E. Perosio

November 2	**Bucarest** National [12]	*Rigoletto* B. Morello, T. di Angelo, G. Armanini, J. Torres de Luna. Conductor: F. Spetrino
November 5		*Ernani* T. Poli-Randaccio, A. Angioletti, J. Torres de Luna. Conductor: F. Spetrino
November 7		*Il barbiere di Siviglia* B. Morello, G. Armanini, J. Torres de Luna Conductor: F. Spetrino
November 9		*Un ballo in maschera* T. Poli-Randaccio, T. di Angelo, A. Angioletti Conductor: F. Spetrino
November 12		*Il trovatore* T. Poli-Randaccio, T. di Angelo, A. Angioletti Conductor: F. Spetrino
December 3	**Warsaw** Wielki	*Rigoletto* (2) W. Stajewska, H. Oleska, Lowczynski, A. Ostrowski. Conductor: A. Vigna
December 10		*Hamlet* (2) W. Stajewska, H. Oleska, A. Ostrowski Conductor: A. Vigna
December 13	Filharmoji	Concert: opera selections, Tuscan verse Conductor: A. Vigna
December 14	Wielki	*Demon* (3) J. Korolewicz-Wayda, H. Oleska, A. Ostrowski. Conductor: E.N. Reznicek
December 17		*Pagliacci* (1) J. Korolewicz-Wayda, W. Alberti Conductor: A. Vigna

1908

January 7	**Madrid** Real	*Rigoletto* G. Pareto, M. de Marsan, G. Anselmi, F. Navarrini. Conductor: R. Villa
January 13	Palacio Real	Concert: arias from *Favorita, Faust, Il barbiere* *di Siviglia;* Tosti, "Donna vorrei morir"; stornelli toscani (Tuscan verse). G. Pareto, Piano accompaniment: I.M. Guervós
January 14	Real	*Tosca* E. Bianchini Cappelli, G. Anselmi Conductor: R. Villa

January 22		*Hamlet* M. Solís, L. Hotkovska, F. Navarrini, Conductor: G. Golisciani
February 4	**Monte Carlo** Grand-Théâtre	*La Gioconda* (3) F. Litvinne, M. Talaisi, G. Bailac, G. Anselmi, J. Nivette. Conductor: A. Pomé
February	**Valencia*** Principal	*Hamlet* A. Alabau, C. Mas, Landerer Conductor: J. Tolosa

*Combined three times with *Il barbiere di Siviglia,* Act I, E. Parea; one time with *Rigoletto,* Act III.

February 29	**Lisbon** São Carlos	*Paolo e Francesca**(4) (national première and debut in the role of Gianciotto) G. Piccoletti, G. Krismer Conductor: L. Mancinelli

* One performance of *Hamlet* and one of *Rigoletto* were given as benefit, respectively, for the Hospital and the Press Association.

March 9		*Hamlet* (4) E. Clasenti, E. Mantelli, O. Luppi Conductor: L. Mancinelli
March 22	**Valencia** Principal	*Rigoletto* G. Rubio, D. Eguileor. Conductor: A. Baratta
March 23		*Il barbiere di Siviglia* Salas, L. Iribarne, Cajal, A. Leoni Conductor: A. Baratta
March 26	**Monte Carlo** Grand-Théâtre	*Il barbiere di Siviglia* (2) S. Kurz, D. Smirnov, F. Chaliapin, A. Pini Corsi. Conductor: A. Pomé
April 2	**Naples** San Carlo	*La Gioconda* (2) T. Burchi, T. di Angelo, B. Wheeler, G. Taccani, A. Perellò de Segurola. Conductor: G. Papi
April 6		*L'africaine* (3) S. Krusceniski, E. Scafidi, F. Viñas, A. Perellò de Segurola, G. Tisci-Rubini Conductor: E. Mascheroni
April 10		*Rigoletto* (1) E. Scafidi, T. di Angelo, G. Armanini, G. Berenzone. Conductor: G. Papi
April 17	**Barcelona** Liceo	*Hamlet* G. Pareto, M. Pozzi, S. Cirotto. Conductor: E. Vitale
April 22		*Tosca* L. Pasini-Vitale, F. Fazzini. Conductor: E. Vitale

May 30	**Buenos Aires** Colón	*Hamlet* (6) E. Clasenti, G. Fabbri, L. Nicoletti-Kormann, Conductor: L. Mancinelli
June 14		*Rigoletto* (5) (prima teatrale) E. Clasenti, T. Ferraris, A. Bassi/M. Polverosi, L. Nicoletti Kormann, Conductor: A. Vigna
June 16		*Tosca* (2) A. Pinto/L. Crestani, A. Bassi Conductor: A. Vigna
June 24		*La Gioconda* (5) A. Pinto, T. Ferraris, G. Fabbri, M. Polverosi, V. Arimondi. Conductor: A. Vigna
July 4		*Paolo e Francesca* (3) (national première) M. Farneti, A. Bassi, G. Bonfanti Conductor: L. Mancinelli
July 9	**La Plata** Argentino	*Rigoletto* (1)* E. Clasenti, T. Ferraris, M. Polverosi, L. Nicoletti Kormann, Conductor: G. Falconi *Gala performance with the company of the Colón to celebrate the national holiday.
July 18	**Buenos Aires** Colón	*Otello* (7) M. Farneti, A. Paoli Conductor: L. Mancinelli
July 28		*Il barbiere di Siviglia* (6) E. Clasenti, M. Polverosi, F. Chaliapin, A. Pini-Corsi. Conductor: L. Mancinelli
August 5		*Pagliacci* (4) E. Reussi, A. Bassi, F. Sarmiento Conductor: A. Vigna
August 18		*Don Giovanni* (3) (debut) A. Pinto, M. Farneti, E. Clasenti, M. Polverosi, F. Chaliapin, A. Pini-Corsi Conductor: L. Mancinelli
September 6		*Aurora* (3) (world première and debut in the role of Don Ignazio Dal Puente) M. Farneti, E. Clasenti, A. Bassi, Conductor: H. Panizza
September 10	Salon La Argentina	Concert: Stornelli toscani (Tuscan verse)
September 14	**Montevideo** Solís	*Pagliacci* and *Hamlet,* Act IV A. Galli-Curci, M. Izquierdo, G. La Puma Conductor: E. Vitale
December 16	**Madrid** Real	*Hamlet* A. Alabau/G. Pareto, G. Lucacewska, A. Parsi Pettinella, M. Gaudio Conductor: R. Villa

| December 30 | | *Il barbiere di Siviglia*
G. Pareto, E. Parea, M. Gaudio, M.
Verdaguer. Conductor: R. Villa |

1909

January 7	Palacio Real	Concert: Prologue to *Pagliacci*; duet from *Don Giovanni*; "La mia dama" of Ferradini, songs; G. Pareto Piano accompaniment: I.M. Guervós
January 12	Real	*Linda di Chamounix* R. Storchio, G. Lukacewska, E. Perea, F. Meana. Conductor: P. Urrutia
January 14		*Il barbiere di Siviglia*, Act II* G. Pareto, E. Parea, M. Gaudio, M. Verdaguer. Conductor: R. Villa *Performed in the context of a mixed musical revue in which TR sang two *stornelli toscani* and, in chorus with the principal singers, the "*Lamentazione*" of Gounod's *Gallia*.
January 24		*Rigoletto* G. Pareto, G. Lukacewska, I. Gistalli, A. Vidal Conductor: R. Villa
January		Concert for the victims of the 1908 earthquake in Sicily and Calabria
January 29		Concert for the Press Association: *Il barbiere di Siviglia,* Acts II and III G. Pareto, E. Perea, M. Gaudio, M. Verdaguer Conductor: R. Villa
February 9	**Monte Carlo** Grand-Théâtre	*Cristoforo Colombo* (3) (debut) Y. Dubel, G. de Tura, J. Vallier Conductor: A. Pomé
February 18		*Rigoletto* (3) F. Hempel, I. de Kowska, D. Smirnov, V. Marvini. Conductor: A. Pomé
February 27		*Il barbiere di Siviglia* (2) E. de Hidalgo, D. Smirnov, F. Chaliapin, A. Pini-Corsi. Conductor: A. Pomé
February	**Nice** Vaisseau amiral "Patrie"	Concert
March 2	**Monte Carlo** Grand-Théâtre	*La Gioconda* (2) F. Litvinne J. Spennert, I. de Kowska, G. Anselmi, J. Vallier. Conductor: A. Pomé
March	**Valencia** Principal	*Rigoletto* L. Garcia-Rubio, E. Eguileor Conductor: A. Baratta

March 13	**Rome** Costanzi	*Hamlet* (4) G. Pareto, E. Ceresoli Salvatori, B. Berardi. Conductor: G. Polacco
March 21		*La Gioconda* (4) G. Russ, E. Ceresoli Salvatori, M. Claessens, J. Palet, A. Masini-Pieralli Conductor: G. Polacco
April 11	**Naples** San Carlo	*Hamlet* (2) G. Pareto, N. Frascani, A. Ricceri Conductor: G. Zuccani
April 13		*Il barbiere di Siviglia* (3) G. Pareto, E. Perea, A. Ricceri, P. Poggi Conductor: G. Zuccani
May 23	**Buenos Aires** Colón	*La Gioconda* (5) E. Burzio, E. Petri, M. Claessens, F. Constantino, C. Walter. Conductor: G. Baroni
May 25		*Rigoletto* (5) G. Pareto, E. Lucci, A. Bonci, M. Gaudio Conductor: L. Mancinelli
		Il barbiere di Siviglia (7) G. Pareto, A. Bonci, M. Gaudio, A. Pini-Corsi Conductor: L. Mancinelli
June 29		*Hamlet* (8) G. Pareto, E. Petri, C. Walter Conductor: L. Mancinelli
July 6		*Aurora* (3) H. Darclée, G. Grazioli, F. Constantino Conductor: G. Baroni
July 26	Odeón	Concert in honor of H. Theodorini: *Don Giovanni,* duet and Serenade; Italian songs. F. Dereyne. Piano accompaniment: E. Drangosh, A. Pollastri
July		Daytime entertainment for the Society of the Sisters of Mercy: singers, actors, instrumental soloists, orchestra. Italian songs. G. Pareto, G. de Luca
August 17	Colón	*Pagliacci* (2) F. Dereyne, A. Rosanov, G. Novelli Conductor: G. Baroni
August 18	Odeón	Concert for the "Colegio Taller": A. Leander Flodin, A. Bonci, R. Oltman Conductor: E. Drangosch
August 31	Colón	*Demon* (2) (national première) H. Darclée, F. Constantino, M. Gaudio Conductor: G. Baroni

?	**Montevideo** Urquiza	*Rigoletto* G. Pareto, E. Tucci, A. Bonci, M. Gaudio Conductor: L. Mancinelli
October 24	**Racconigi** Castello Reale	Concert in honor of Tzar Nikolai II: *Hamlet,* Drinking Song; *Rigoletto,* Quartet. F. Farneti, A. Parsi-Pettinella, R. Grassi Piano accompaniment: P. Mascagni
December 30	**Paris** Palais Stern	Concert

1910

January 4	**Madrid** Real	*Hamlet* G. Finzi-Magrini, E. Petri/F. Perini; A. Ricceri. Conductor: R. Villa
January 14	Palacio Real	Concert with the participation of the Rosen Quartet: *Chatterton,* aria; Italian songs. Piano accompaniment: I.M. Guervós
January 20	Real	*Rigoletto* G. Finzi-Magrini, F. Perini, G. Taccani, A. Ricceri. Conductor: G. Marinuzzi
January 23		*La Gioconda* T. Poli-Randaccio, E. Petri, F. Perini, G. Taccani, A. Ricceri. Conductor: G. Marinuzzi
January 24		Concert for the Press Association
February 8	**Monte Carlo** Grand-Théâtre	*Il barbiere di Siviglia* E. de Hidalgo, D. Smirnov, F. Chaliapin, V. Chalmin. Conductor: A. Pomé
February 15		*Otello* (3) L. Edvina/J. Spennerx, C. Rousselière Conductor: A. Pomé
February 26		*Rigoletto* (4) G. Pareto, Mati, D. Smirnov, R. Marvini Conductor: A. Pomé
March 10		*La traviata* (3) A. Zeppilli, D. Smirnov. Conductor: A. Pomé
March 15		*Fedora* (national première) (3) M. Chénal, J. Spennert, D. Smirnov Conductor: A. Pomé
April 4	**Rome** Costanzi	*Il barbiere di Siviglia* (1) R. Pinkert, U. Macnez, C. Walter, P. Malatesta. Conductor: P. Mascagni
April 7	**Naples** San Carlo	*Il barbiere di Siviglia* (1) S. Michelini, M. Polverosi, V. Arimondi, P. Poggi. Conductor: C. Campanini

April 12	Circolo artistico	Concert: T. di Angelo, A. Agostinelli, M. Polverosi. Piano accompaniment: U. Mazzone
April 13	San Carlo	*Zazà* (local première) (1) A. Agostinelli, R. Andreini Conductor: E. Perosio
May 25	**Buenos Aires** Colón	*Rigoletto* (5) G. Pareto, F. Perini, G. Anselmi, S. Cirotto. Conductor: E. Vitale
June 4		*La Gioconda* (2) E. Mazzoleni, F. Perini, A. Cucini, G. Taccani, G. Cirino. Conductor: E. Vitale
June 12		*Il barbiere di Siviglia* (6) G. Pareto, G. Anselmi, A. Didur/G. Cirino, C. Paterna. Conductor: E. Vitale
June 21		*Cristoforo Colombo* (4) E. Mazzoleni, A. Pintucci, G. Cirino Conductor: E. Vitale
June	Palacio de Castellis	Concert in honor of the Infanta Isabella of Spain
June	Palacio Mihanovich	Concert in honor of the President of Chile
July 14	Colón	*Hamlet* (8) G. Pareto/E. Clasenti, F. Perini, G. Cirino Conductor: E. Vitale
July 30	Avenida	Concert in honor of the Spanish actor Riccardo de la Vega and other actors: M. Gay
August 14	Coliseo	Concert: A. Agostinelli
September 1	Colón	*Pagliacci* (1) A. Agostinelli, C. Rousselière, R. Rasponi Conductor: E. Vitale (in *Rigoletto,* Act III, G. Pareto)
September 7	**Montevideo** Urquiza	*Il barbiere di Siviglia* G. Pareto/A. Galli-Curci, F. Carpi, G. Cirino, G. La Puma. Conductor: E. Vitale
September 8		*Rigoletto* G. Pareto, F. Perini, F. Carpi, C. Paterna Conductor: E. Vitale
September 13	**Montevideo** Urquiza	*Pagliacci* and *Hamlet,* last act A. Galli-Curci, M. Izquierdo. Conductor: E. Vitale
September 17		*Hamlet* G. Pareto, F. Perini, G. Cirino Conductor: E. Vitale

1911

February 2	**Naples** San Carlo	*L'africaine* (2) E. Mazzoleni, E. Scafidi, M. Gilion, L. Contini, O. Luppi. Conductor: I. Nini Bellucci
February 6		*Tosca* (1) A. Karola, A. Giorgini. Conductor: I. Nini Belluci
February 8		*Il barbiere di Siviglia* (2) S. Michelini, E. Perea, L. Contini, V. Trevisan Conductor: V. Gui
March 9	**Monte Carlo** Grand-Théâtre	*Il barbiere di Siviglia* (3) E. de Hidalgo, A. Giorgini/F. Carpi, F. Chaliapin, V. Chalmin. Conductor: A. Pomé
March 21		*Linda di Chamounix* (2) E. de Hidalgo, N. Lollini, A. Giorgini Conductor: A. Pomé
March 28		*La Gioconda* (2) F. Litvinne, M. Borga, C. Croiza, F. Carpi, R. Marvini. Conductor: A. Pomé
April 3	**Naples** San Carlo	*La Gioconda* (2) E. Mazzoleni, E. Petri, M. Verger, R. Grassi/ G. Genzardi, G. Luppi. Conductor: V. Gui
April 7	Politeama Giacosa	Concert
April 8	San Carlo	*Aida* (1) E. Mazzoleni, E. Petri, N. Fusati, O. Luppi Conductor: V. Gui
April 16	**Rome** Costanzi	*Il barbiere di Siviglia* (4) G. Pareto, U. Macnez, N. de Angelis, G. Kaschmann. Conductors: L. Mancinelli, T. de Angelis
May 24	**Buenos Aires** Colón	*Thaïs* (2) (debut in the role of Athanaël) A. Agostinelli, A. Bada, V. Bettoni Conductor: E. Vitale
May 25		*Lucia di Lammermoor* (6) M. Barrientos, F. Constantino, N. de Angelis Conductor: E. Vitale
June 1		*Rigoletto* (6) M. Barrientos, F. Perini, F. Constantino. P. Ludikar. Conductor: E. Vitale
June 25		*Il barbiere di Siviglia* (6) M. Barrientos, A. Bonci, N. de Angelis, C. Paterna. Conductor: E. Vitale

July 7		*Don Carlo* (5) (debut in the role of Marchese di Posa) A. Agostinelli, L. Garibaldi, F. Constantino, N. de Angelis, P. Ludikar Conductor: E. Vitale
July 25		*La fanciulla del West* (4) (debut in the role of Jack Rance) A. Agostinelli, E. Ferrari-Fontana Conductor: E. Vitale
August 10		*Tristan und Isolde* (2) L. Pasini-Vitale, L. Garibaldi, E. Ferrari-Fontana, N. de Angelis. Conductor: E. Vitale
August 20		*Evgeny Onegin* (2) (national première and debut in the role of Onegin) L. Pasini-Vitale, F. Anitúa, A. Pintucci, P. Ludikar Conductor: E. Vitale
August 25	**Montevideo** Urquiza	*Il barbiere di Siviglia* M. Barrientos, A. Bonci, N. de Angelis, C. Paterna. Conductor: E. Vitale
August 26		*La fanciulla del West* (national première) A. Agostinelli, E. Ferrari-Fontana Conductor: E. Vitale
August 30		*Rigoletto* M. Barrientos, F. Perini, F. Constantino, P. Ludikar. Conductor: E. Vitale
September 2	**Rosario di Santa Fe** Colón	*Il barbiere di Siviglia* M. Barrientos, A. Bonci, P. Ludikar, C. Paterna. Conductor: E. Vitale
September 3		*Rigoletto* M. Barrientos, F. Perini, A. Pintucci, P. Ludikar. Conductor: E. Vitale
September 5		*Hamlet* A. Gonzaga, F. Perini, P. Ludikar Conductor: E. Vitale
September 12	**São Paolo** Municipal*	*Hamlet* (2) (inaugural opera) G. Pareto, F. Perini, P. Ludikar Conductor: E. Vitale
		*Inaugural season of the theater
September 17		*La bohème* (3) A. Agostinelli, R. Garavaglia, A. Bonci, V. Bettoni, P. Ludikar. Conductor: E. Vitale
September 19		*Tristan und Isolde* (2) L. Pasini-Vitale, F. Perini, E. Ferrari-Fontana, P. Ludikar. Conductor: E. Vitale
September 24		*Il barbiere di Siviglia* (3) G. Pareto, A. Bonci, P. Ludikar, C. Paterna Conductor: E. Vitale

September 26		*Rigoletto* (1) G. Pareto, F. Perini, A. Bonci, P. Ludikar Conductor: E. Vitale
September 29		*Don Pasquale* (1) A. Agostinelli, A. Bonci, C. Paterna Conductor: E. Vitale
October 3	**Rio de Janeiro** Lyrico [7]	*Rigoletto* G. Pareto, F. Perini, A. Bonci, P. Ludikar Conductor: E. Vitale
October 5		*Hamlet* G. Pareto, F. Perini, P. Ludikar Conductor: E. Vitale
October 7		*Il barbiere di Siviglia* G. Pareto, A. Bonci, P. Ludikar, C. Paterna Conductor: E. Vitale
October 10		*Don Pasquale* A. Agostinelli, A. Bonci, C. Paterna
November 18	**Rome** Costanzi	*Il barbiere di Siviglia* (4) E. de Hidalgo, F. Carpi, N. de Angelis, G. Schottler. Conductor: L. Mancinelli
December 18	**Paris** Opéra	*Rigoletto* Y. Gall, L. Charny, R. Lassalle, M. Journet Conductor: P. Vidal
December 20	Trocadéro	Concert
December 22	Opéra	*Hamlet* (2) J. Campredon/Y. Gall, K. Lapeyrette, M. Journet. Conductor: P. Vidal

1912

January 20	**Madrid** Real	*Il barbiere di Siviglia* P. Sanz, U. Macnez, A. Masini-Pieralli, M. Verdaguer. Conductor: G. Marinuzzi
January 30		*L'africaine* M. de Lerma, E. Fiorin, F. Viñas, A. Masini-Pieralli, R. Villa
February 17		*Pagliacci* G. Baldassarre Tedeschi, M. Izquierdo, C. Patino. Conductor: G. Marinuzzi
February		Concert for the wounded of Campagna del Rif
February 13	**Florence** Verdi	*Il barbiere di Siviglia* (2) E. Gomez, G. Vogliotti, E. Benazzo, C. Rossi Conductor: A. Alvisi

February 24	**Monte Carlo** Grand-Théâtre [5]	*Il barbiere di Siviglia* E. de Hidalgo, M. Polverosi, F. Chaliapin, V. Chalmin. Conductor: A. Pomé
March 2		*Don Carlo* (2) J. Lambert-Villaume, C. Mattei, C. Roussellière, F. Chaliapin Conductor: A. Pomé
March 26	**Budapest** Népopera	*Il barbiere di Siviglia* (2) E. Sándor, D. Arányi, R. Kornai, F. Hegedüs Conductor: E. Ábrányi
March 29		*Rigoletto* (1) E. Sándor, D. Bársony, D. Arányi, R. Kornai, Conductor: A. Szikla
April 1		*Hamlet* (1) E. Sándor, A. Fodor, F. Székelyhidy, B. Venczell, R. Kornai. Conductor: E. Ábrányi
April 21	**Venice** La Fenice	*Il barbiere di Siviglia* (4) E. de Hidalgo, E. Perea, F. Navarrini, G. Kaschmann. Conductor: R. Ferrari
May 12, 23, 30	**Paris** Opéra	*Rigoletto* (3) A. Nezhdanova, N. Lollini, E. Caruso, J. Torres de Luna. Conductor: L. Jéhin/A. Pomé
May 16, 21, 28		*La fanciulla del West* (3) (national première) C. Melis/T. Poli Randaccio, E. Caruso Conductor: T. Serafin
May 19		*Il barbiere di Siviglia* E. de Hidalgo, D. Smirnov, F. Chaliapin, V. Chalmin. Conductor: A. Pomé
May 31	House of Madame Moore	Concert: C. Croiza, D. Smirnov, Neapolitan songs. Piano accompaniment: Samonelsen
May 31	House of Lord and Lady Michelham 31, rue Nitot	Benefit Concert C. Melis, E. Caruso
August 11, 15	**Deauville** Casino	*Il barbiere di Siviglia* (2) M. Barrientos, L. David, F. Chaliapin
November 4	**Philadelphia** Metropolitan	*Rigoletto* A. Gluck/A. Zepilli, M. Keyes, O. Harrold, H. Scott. Conductors: C. Campanini/E. Perosio
November 6		*Un ballo in maschera* C. Gagliardi, J. Dufau, M. Gay, G. Zenatello Conductor: E. Perosio

November 13		*Hamlet* A. Zeppilli, E. de Cisneros, H. Huberdeau Conductor: C. Campanini
November 21		*Il trovatore* C. Gagliardi, M. Gay, G. Zenatello, C. Nicolay. Conductor: C. Campanini
November 19	**New York** Metropolitan	*Hamlet* A. Zeppilli, E. de Cisneros, G. Huberdeau Conductor: C. Campanini
November 25	Carnegie Hall	Vocal Concert with Instrumental Accompaniments. *Pagliacci,* Prologue; *Chatterton; Il barbiere di Siviglia,* Cavatina; *Don Giovanni*, Serenade. H. Stanley Conductor: E. Perosio
November 29	**Chicago** Auditorium	*Rigoletto* (2) A. Zeppilli/J. Dufau, O. Harrold, G. Huberdeau/ H. Scott. Conductor: C. Campanini
December 3		*Hamlet* (1) A. Zeppilli, E. de Cisneros, G. Huberdeau, Conductor: C. Campanini
December 5		*Pagliacci* (2) A. Zeppilli, I. Caileja/G. Zenatello Conductor: E. Perosio
December 15	**New York** Hippodrome	Concert M. Teyte

1913

January 7	**Barcelona** Liceo	*Il barbiere di Siviglia* (1) E. de Hidalgo, M. Polverosi, L. Rossato Conductor: Giulio Falconi
January 10		*Rigoletto* (1) M. Llopart, M. Blanco Sadun, M. Polverosi, E. Sesona. Conductor: G. Falconi
January 14		*Pagliacci* (2) M. Llopart, L. Colazza, A. Pacini Conductor: G. Falconi
January 16	**Madrid** Real [16]	*Tristan und Isolde* C. Gagliardi, V. Guerrini, F. Viñas, O. Luppi Conductor: G. Zuccani
January 21		*Don Carlo* C. Gagliardi, V. Guerrini, J. Palet, A. Masini Pieralli. Conductor: G. Zuccani

January 26		*Pagliacci* M. Moscicka, J. Palet, C. Patino Conductor: G. Zuccani
February 1		*Rigoletto* A. Gonzaga, R. Cesaretti, G. Rotondi/J. Palet, A. Vidal. Conductor: G. Zuccani
February 19		*Hamlet* A. Gonzaga, V. Guerrini, O. Luppi Conductor: G. Zuccani
March 1		*Il trovatore* C. Gagliardi, Buisan, F. Buroni, A. Vidal Conductor: G. Zuccani
March		Concert for the Press Association
March 12	**Valencia** Principal	*Pagliacci* (1)* C. Crevet, F. Buroni, C. Patino Conductor: G. Zuccani

*Before the performance the orchestra played the Overture to *Der fliegende Holländer*; at the end TR sang arias and songs.

March 14		*Hamlet* (1) A. Gonzaga, V. Guerrini, O. Luppi Conductor: R. Villa
April 11	**Budapest** Népopera	*Il trovatore* (1) M. Jávor, I. Durigo, P. Seidler Conductor: F. Reiner
April 15		*Hamlet* (3) A. Adler, M. Basilides, S. Bihari Conductor: F. Reiner
April 18		*Il barbiere di Siviglia* (2) A. Adler, A. Tedeschi, S. Bihari, E. Mátrai Conductor: F. Reiner
April 22		*Faust* (1) (debut in the role of Méphistophélès) A. Adler, M. Basilides, P. Seidler, J. Gábor Conductor: F. Reiner
April 28		*Rigoletto* (1) M. Jávor, M. Basilides, F. Kurt, S. Bihari Conductor: F. Reiner
June 1	**Paris** Champs-Elysées	Benefit Concert: *Il barbiere di Siviglia,* Act II L. Lipkowska, F. Carpi. Conductor: L. Camilieri
August 12	**San Sebastián** Gran Teatro Circo	*Pagliacci* (3)* L. Cavalieri, G. Ibos/G. Gaudenzi

*Special performance in the celebration square of the first centenary of the city's liberation from French occupation.

November 5	**Philadelphia** Metropolitan	*Il barbiere di Siviglia* (1) J. Dufau, A. Giorgini, H. Scott, V. Trevisan Conductor: G. Sturani
November 7	**Baltimore** Ford's Grand Opera (?)	Rigoletto (1) A. Zeppilli, M. Keyes, A. Giorgini, H. Scott Conductor: C. Campanini
November 10	**Philadelphia** Metropolitan	*Rigoletto* (1) A. Zeppilli, A. Giorgini. Conductor: E. Perosio
November 13		*Pagliacci* (1) J. Osborn-Hannah, A. Bassi, A. Crabbé Conductor: G. Sturani
November 17		*La Gioconda* (1) C. White, J. Claussen, A. Bassi, H. Scott Conductor: G. Sturani
November 20		*Cristoforo Colombo* (2) (national première) R. Raisa, A. Bassi, G. Huberdeau Conductor: C. Campanini
November 25	**Milwaukee** Auditorium	*La Gioconda* (1) C. White, J. Claussen, A. Giorgini, H. Scott Conductor: G. Sturani
December 1	**Chicago** Auditorium	*Rigoletto* A. Zeppilli/J. Dufau, M. Keyes, A. Giorgini, G. Huberdeau/H. Scott.Conductor: E. Perosio
December 4		*Cristoforo Colombo* (2) R. Raisa, A. Bassi, G. Huberdeau Conductor: C. Campanini
December 15		*Il barbiere di Siviglia* (1) J Dufau, A. Giorgini, H. Scott, V. Trevisan Conductor: C. Campanini
December 18		*Don Giovanni* (1) M. Dorda, J. Dufau, C. White, A. Giorgini, G. Huberdeau. Conductor: C. Campanini
December 19		*Pagliacci* (2) J. Osborn-Hannah, A. Bassi Conductor: C. Campanini
December 26		*Thaïs* (2) M. Garden, C. Dalmorès, G. Huberdeau Conductor: C. Campanini

1914

January 4	**New York** Hippodrome	Concert. Violinist: W.M. Rummel, Piano accompaniment: A. Rosenstein, Mona Krog. Conductor: N. Franko

January 9	**Washington** The Vanderbilt House	Private Concert
January 11	**Boston** ?	Concert
January 16	**Detroit** Armory	Concert
January 19	**Columbus** ?	Concert
January 21	**Cincinnati** Music Hall	Concert: L. Tetrazzini
January 23	**Minneapolis** Armory	Concert: L. Tetrazzini
January 26	**Toledo** ?	Concert
January 28	**Toronto*** Massen Hall	Concert: L. Tetrazzini *This is the only appearance in Canada.
January 30	**Buffalo** Broadway	Concert: L. Tetrazzini
February 1	**New York** Hippodrome	Concert
February 2	**Philadelphia** Metropolitan	*Pagliacci* A. Zeppilli, A. Bassi, A. Crabbé Conductor: C. Campanini
February 5	**Boston**	Concert: Arias from *Don Carlo* and *Dinorah;* songs. L. Tetrazzini Piano accompaniment: Y. Nat
February 16	**Chicago**	Concert: L. Tetrazzini
February 18	**Philadelphia** Metropolitan	*Rigoletto* N. Melba, M. Keyes, A. Giorgini, H. Scott Conductor: C. Campanini
February 21		*Don Giovanni* R. Raisa, C. White, A. Zeppilli, A. Giorgini, G. Huberdeau, A. Hinkley Conductor: C. Campanini
February 23		*Cristoforo Colombo* R. Raisa, A. Bassi, G. Huberdeau Conductor: C. Campanini
February 28		*Hamlet* A. Zeppilli, J. Claussen, G. Huberdeau Conductor: C. Campanini

March 4	**Dallas** (?) Coliseum	*Rigoletto* F. Macbeth, M. Keyes, A. Giorgini, H. Scott Conductor: C. Campanini
March 7		*Pagliacci* J. Osborn-Hannah, O. Marák, A. Crabbé Conductor: C. Campanini
March 10	**Los Angeles** Philharmonic Auditorium	*Rigoletto* F. Macbeth, M. Keyes, A. Giorgini, H. Scott Conductor: C. Campanini
March 14		*Hamlet* A. Zeppilli, J. Claussen. Conductor: G. Sturani
March 30	**Seattle** (?) Orpheum	*Pagliacci* J. Osborn-Hannah, A. Bassi, A. Crabbé Conductor: G. Sturani
April 2	**Portland** Orpheum	*Pagliacci* J. Osborn-Hannah, A. Bassi, A. Crabbé Conductor: G. Sturani
April 8	**Denver** Auditorium	*Pagliacci* J. Osborn-Hannah, A. Bassi, F. Federici Conductor: C. Campanini
April 11	**Kansas City** Convention Hall	*Rigoletto* F. Macbeth, M. Keyes, A. Giorgini, H. Scott. Conductor: C. Campanini
April 17	**Saint Louis** Odeon	*Pagliacci* A. Zeppilli, O. Marák
April 20	**Saint Paul** Auditorium	*Rigoletto* F. Macbeth, B. Wheeler, M. Keyes, A. Giorgini, G. Huberdeau. Conductor: C. Campanini
April 22		*Pagliacci* A. Zeppilli, A. Bassi. Conductor: G. Sturani
April 27	**New York** Saint Denis	Concert: A. Fitziu
May 1	**Paterson** Regent	Vocal and Instrumental Concert Arias of *Patrie* by Paladilhe. L. May Piano accompaniment: R. Gruen, violinist: R. Bochco
June 8	**Savona** Wanda	*Rigoletto* (1) A. Pinto, U. Macnez
August 15, 23	**Ostend** Kursaal	Concerts (2)

October 16	**Milan** Carcano*	*Il barbiere di Siviglia* (1) A. Galli-Curci, E. Perea, A. Masini-Pieralli, A. Pini-Corsi. Conductor: L. Mancinelli
		*For unemployed opera singers and the Verdi Association of mutual aid.
October 29	**Bologna** Corso	*Il barbiere di Siviglia* (2) A. Galli-Curci, A. Salvaneschi, A. Masini-Pieralli, A. Pini-Corsi. Conductor: G. Bavagnoli
December 17	**Florence** Verdi	*Hamlet* (4) E. Angelini Borelli, A. Gramegna, G. La Puma Conductor: E. Mascheroni
December 27		*Il barbiere di Siviglia* (2) E. Angelini Borelli, G. Paganelli, O. Carozzi, G. La Puma. Conductor: A. Alvisi

1915

January 5	**Genoa** Politeama Genovese	*Pagliacci* (2) E. Rago/M. Llacer, G. Gaudenzi, M. Aineto Conductor: G. Baroni
February 2		*Hamlet* (3) B. Morello, L. Garibaldi, L. Manfrini Conductor: G. Baroni
April 22	**Havana** Nacional [15]	*Aida* J. Capella, R. Alvarez/M. Gay, J. Palet, M. Gaudio. Conductor: T. Serafin
April 24		*Pagliacci* C. Muzio, G. Zenatello/J. Palet Conductor: A. Bovi
April 29		*Rigoletto* B. de Pasquali, M. Polverosi, M. Gaudio Conductor: T. Serafin
May 1		*Il barbiere di Siviglia* B. de Pasquali, M. Polverosi, M. Gaudio, G. La Puma. Conductor: T. Serafin
May 6		*Otello* C. Muzio, G. Zenatello. Conductor: T. Serafin
May 9		*Un ballo in maschera* J. Capella, R. Alvarez, J. Palet
May 11		*La bohème* C. Muzio, A. Giana, G. Zenatello Conductors: T. Serafin/A. Bovi
May 13		*Carmen* M. Gay, C. Muzio, G. Zenatello Conductor: T. Serafin

May 22		*La Gioconda* E. Rakowska, R. Alvarez, E. Lucci, J. Palet, M. Gaudio
May	**Matanzas** Sauto	*Pagliacci* C. Muzio, J. Palet. Conductor: A. Bovi
		Il barbiere di Siviglia B. de Pasquali, M. Gaudio, G. La Puma Conductor: T. Serafin
		La bohème C. Muzio, A. Giana, G. Zenatello Conductor: A. Bovi
June 1, 3	**New York** Manhattan	Concerts (2)
July 6	**Buenos Aires** Colón	*L'africaine* (3) R. Raisa, M. Melsa/H. Spani, B. de Muro, G. Cirino, T. Dentale. Conductor: G. Marinuzzi
July 7		*Il barbiere di Siviglia* (5) A. Galli-Curci, A. Tedeschi, G. Cirino, G. Niola Conductor: G. Marinuzzi
July 26		*Rigoletto* (2) A. Galli-Curci, F. Perini, H. Lázaro, B. Berardi Conductor: G. Marinuzzi
July 30		*Hamlet* (4) A. Galli-Curci, N. Frascani, B. Berardi Conductor: G. Marinuzzi
August 2	?	Concert. Conductor: G. Marinuzzi
August 4	Colón	*Pagliacci,* Act I* H. Spani, E. Caruso, E. Caronna Conductor: G. Marinuzzi *In the context of a concert for the Press Association
August 8	**Rosario di Santa Fe** Opera	*Il barbiere di Siviglia* A. Galli-Curci, A. Tedeschi, G. Cirino, G. Niola. Conductor: G. Marinuzzi
August 11	**Buenos Aires** Colón	*Carmen,* Act II* G. Vix, B. de Muro. Conductor: G. Sturani *In the context of a concert for the Red Cross
August 13		*Carmen* and *Pagliacci,* Prologue N. Frascani, B. de Muro. Conductor: C. Sturani
August 15	**Montevideo** Solís	*Il barbiere di Siviglia* A. Galli-Curci, A. Tedeschi, G. Cirino, G.Niola. Conductor: G. Sturani

August 16	Urquiza	*Pagliacci* M. Roggero, E. Caruso, L. Nardi, E. Caronna. Conductor: G.Marinuzzi
August 18	**Buenos Aires** Colón	*Anfione e Zeto* (2) (in the role of Anfione) G. Salvini and other actors. Conductor: P. de Rogatis, author of the music and the play
August 21	**Montevideo** Solís	*Hamlet* A. Galli-Curci, N. Frascani, L. Nardi, G. Niola
August 23	Urquiza	*L'africaine* R. Raisa, B. de Muro, G. Cirino
August 26	Solís	*Rigoletto* A. Galli-Curci, H. Lázaro
August 27		Concerto R. Raisa
September 4	**Rio de Janeiro** Municipal	*Hamlet* (1) A. Galli-Curci, N. Frascani, G. Cirino Conductor: G. Marinuzzi
September 8		*Rigoletto* (1) A. Galli-Curci, F. Perini, H. Lázaro, B. Berardi. Conductor: G. Marinuzzi
September 11		*Pagliacci* (1) A. Giacomucci, J. Martins, E. Caronna Conductor: G. Sturani
September 13		*L'africaine* (1) R. Raisa, A. Galli-Curci, B. de Muro, G. Cirino, B. Berardi. Conductor: G. Marinuzzi
September 16		*Il barbiere di Siviglia (1)* A. Galli-Curci, A. Tedeschi, G. Cirino, C. Niola. Conductor: G. Marinuzzi
September 18		*Tosca* (1) G. Dalla Rizza, H. Lázaro Conductor: G. Marinuzzi
September 21	**São Paolo** Municipal	*Rigoletto* (1) A. Galli-Curci, N. Frascani, H. Lázaro, B. Berardi. Conductor: G. Marinuzzi
September 23		*L'africaine* (1) R. Raisa, A. Giacomucci, B. de Muro, G. Cirino, B. Berardi. Conductor: G. Marinuzzi
September 26		*Il barbiere di Siviglia* (1) A. Galli-Curci, A. Tedeschi, G. Cirino, G. Niola. Conductor: G. Marinuzzi

September 28		*Pagliacci* (1) A. Giacomucci, J. Martins, E. Caronna Conductor: G. Sturani
October 1		*La fanciulla del West* (1) G. Dalla Rizza, B. de Muro Conductor: G. Marinuzzi
October 4		*Hamlet* (1) A. Galli-Curci, N. Frascani, B. Berardi Conductor: G. Marinuzzi

1916

February 11	**Barcelona** Liceo [4]	*Hamlet* G. Pareto, N. Frascani, L. Manfrini Conductor: Alfredo Padovani
February 13		*Pagliacci* P. Barti/A. Agostinelli, E. Cunego, P. del Grillo Conductor: A. Padovani
February 16		*Rigoletto* G. Pareto, E. Lucci, G. Broccardi, L. Nicoletti Kormann. Conductor: A. Padovani
February 18	**Madrid** Palacio Real	Concert: *Hamlet,* Drinking Song; Italian and Spanish songs. G. Vix, J. Palet Piano accompaniment: I.M. Guervós
February 20	**Barcelona** Liceo	*Il barbiere di Siviglia* G. Pareto, C. Hackett, L. Nicoletti Kormann Conductor: A. Padovani
February 23		*Pagliacci* P. Barti, E. Cunego, R. Rasponi Conductor: A. Padovani
February 27	**Valencia** Principal	*Hamlet* (4) G. Pareto, A. Agostinelli L. Nicoletti Kormann. Conductor: A. Padovani
March 2		*Il barbiere di Siviglia* R. D'Ory, L. Nicoletti Kormann Conductor: A. Padovani
March 12	**Madrid** Zarzuela	*Pagliacci* A. Agostinelli, J. Elìas. Conductor: A. Padovani
March 15		*Il barbiere di Siviglia* R. D'Ory, Kasadei/C. Hackett, L. Nicoletti Kormann, F. Puiggener. Conductor: A. Padovani
March 18		*Hamlet* R. D'Ory, N. Frascani, L. Nicoletti Kormann, Conductor: A. Padovani

May 20	**Buenos Aires** Colón*	*Boris Godunov* (2) (debut) A. Agostinelli, P. Navia, A. Algos, M. Gaudio Conductor: G. Baroni

*During the season, in specially arranged performances, TR sings the Prologue to *Pagliacci* on June 29 and Neapolitan songs on August 6.

June 3		*Andrea Chénier* (3) G. Dalla Rizza, E. di Giovanni Conductor: G. Baroni
June 11		*Rigoletto* (4) M. Capsir/E. Clasenti, E. Barsanti, P. Navia, M. Journet. Conductor: G. Baroni
June 29		*Hamlet* (4) M. Barrientos/M. Capsir, J. Royer, M. Journet Conductor: G. Baroni
July 3		*Pagliacci* (3) A. Agostinelli/N. Vallin Pardo, G. Crimi, A. Bettazoni. Conductor: G. Baroni
July 6	**Tucumán** Odeón*	*Rigoletto* E. Soler Santangelo, A. Frabetti, N. del Ry, C. Melocchi. Conductor: G. Baroni

*In a brief tour outside the capital to celebrate the centenary of national independence TR appears in nine performances altogether.

July 9		*Andrea Chénier* A. Agostinelli, V. Cacioppo, E. di Giovanni Conductor: G. Baroni
July 14	**Cordova** Rivera Indarte	*Andrea Chénier* A. Agostinelli, E. di Giovanni Conductor: G. Baroni
July 16		*Rigoletto* E. Soler Santangelo, A. Frabetti, N. del Ry, C. Melocchi. Conductor: G. Baroni
July 27	**Buenos Aires** Colón	*Falstaff* (3) (debut) R. Raisa, N. Vallin Pardo, E. Casazza/G. Bertazzoli, T. Schipa, A. Crabbé, M. Gaudio Conductor: G. Baroni
August 2		*Il barbiere di Siviglia* (3) M. Barrientos, T. Schipa, M. Gaudio, G. Niola. Conductor: G. Baroni
August 14	Coliseo	*Pagliacci* (1)* V. Cacioppo, E. Bergamaschi Conductor: A. de Angelis

*Performance for the Italian War Committee

August 16	**Montevideo** Solís	*Hamlet* E. Clasenti, J. Royer, M. Journet
August 18		*Falstaff* R. Raisa, N. Vallin Pardo, T. Schipa, A. Crabbé
August 21		*Il barbiere di Siviglia* M. Barrientos, T. Schipa, M. Gaudio
August 24		*Rigoletto* M. Barrientos, T. Schipa
August 27		Vocal and Orchestral Concert* R. Raisa, L. Lafitte, A. Crabbé, G. Martinelli Piano accompaniment: A. Messager *For the Allied Red Cross
November 20	**Nice** Eldorado	*Pagliacci* (1)* F. Dereyne, T. Salignac. Conductor: H. Cas *Performance for the Military Auxiliary Hospital no. 207

1917

April 27	**Paris** 27 Opéra- Comique	*Pagliacci* (1)* B. Lamare, C. Fontaine, F. Bellet Conductor: P. Vidal *For military tuberculosis victims; TR also sings Italian arias with piano accompaniment by A. Vigna
April 28	Opéra	*Hamlet** *For indigent French artists
November 2	**Aquilea** Basilica	*Requiem Mass* (?)* *Organized by the Third Army Command in suffrage for those fallen in battle

1918

December 17	**Madrid** Real [8]	*La bohème* E. Mazzoleni, P. Barti, G. Taccani, L. Nicoletti Kormann. Conductor: G. Falconi
December 22		*Il barbiere di Siviglia* J. Dufau, U. Macnez, V. Bettoni, G. Azzolini Conductor: G. Falconi
December 26		*Andrea Chénier* (national première) M. Roggero, B. DeMuro. Conductor: G. Falconi
December	?	Benefit concert

1919

January 6	**Madrid** Real	*Falstaff* E. Mazzoleni, P. Barti, M. Gay, M. Capuana, G. Taccani, G. Giardini, V. Bettoni Conductor: G. Falconi
March 3	**Trieste** Verdi	Concert for civil assistance: *Rigoletto*, Act III, last scene; selections from *Cristoforo Colombo;* "Il canto del tricolore a Trieste" by L. Mancinelli. L. Tetrazzini Conductor: L. Mancinelli
April 29	**Mexico City** [12] Esperanza Iris	*Pagliacci* (3) E. Mason, J. Palet, S. Civai, J. Mojica, L. Oliviero. Conductor: G. Polacco
May 3		*Il barbiere di Siviglia* (1) C. Escobar de Castro, A. Bonci, V. Trevisan, V. Lazzari. Conductor: G. Polacco
May 7		*Rigoletto* (4) E. Mason, F. Perini, J. Palet, V. Lazzari Conductor: G. Polacco
May 21		*Hamlet* (2) C. Escobar de Castro, F. Perini, V. Lazzari Conductor: G. Polacco
May 24		*Andrea Chénier* L. Lawrence, A. Bonci. Conductor: G. Sturani
June 8		*Un ballo in maschera* (1) R. Raisa, F. Perini, J. Palet Conductor: G. Polacco
June 10		*Otello* (1) E. Mason, F. Castellani. Conductor: G. Polacco

1920

January 5	**Chicago** Auditorium	*Pagliacci* (1) M. Sharlow, F. Lamont Conductor: G. Marinuzzi
January 10		*Rigoletto* (1) F. Macbeth, M. Claessens. T. Schipa, V. Arimondi Conductor: G. Marinuzzi
January 15		*Hamlet* (1) F. Macbeth, C. Van Gordon, V. Lazzari Conductor: M. Charlier
January 18		Concert: Y. Gall

January 28	**New York** Lexington	*Pagliacci* (1) M. Santillan/A. Fitziu, F. Lamont, D. Defrère Conductor: G. Marinuzzi
February 1	Hippodrome	Concert: *Hamlet,* Drinking Song Y. Gall. Conductor: G. Marinuzzi
February 13	Lexington	*Hamlet* (1) F. Macbeth, C. Van Gordon, V. Lazzari Conductor: M. Charlier
February 20		*Rigoletto* (1) A. Galli-Curci/L. Lipkovska, M. Claessens, T. Schipa, E. Cotreuil. Conductor: G. Marinuzzi
February 27	Hotel Commodore	Concert: C. Van Gordon, I. Patterson Pianist: A. Rubinstein
March 1, April 9	**Philadelphia** Metropolitan	Concert: *Hamlet,* Drinking Song; French, Italian and Spanish songs; "Somewhere a Voice is Calling." Piano accompaniment: E.I. Polak, cello: L. Orrell
March 6	**Boston** Boston Opera	*Pagliacci* A. Fitziu, F. Lamont. Conductor: G. Marinuzzi
March 10		*Rigoletto* F. Macbeth, M. Claessens, T. Schipa, E. Cotreuil. Conductor: G. Marinuzzi
March 18	**Pittsburgh** Syria Mosque	*Pagliacci* A. Fitziu, F. Lamont
March 20	**Cincinnati** Music Hall	*Pagliacci* A. Fitziu, F. Lamont, D. Defrère Conductor: G. Marinuzzi
March 24	**Detroit** Orchestra Hall	*Rigoletto* F. Macbeth, F. Lamont
March 27	**Cleveland** Masonic Hall	*Pagliacci* M. Santillan, F. Lamont
March April May	**Atlantic City** **Boston** **Chicago** **Philadelphia** **Newark** **Syracuse**	Concerts
May 1	**New York** Hippodrome	Concert: A. Fitziu. Pianist: A. Rubinstein
May 8	**Springfield** (Mass.) Auditorium	Concert in the context of the XVIII Civic Music Festival. Chicago Symphony Orchestra. Conductor: F. Stock

May 25	**Evanston** (Illinois) Northwestern University	Concert in the context of Northshore Music Festival. Chicago Symphony Orchestra. Conductor: F. Stock
October 18	**Milwaukee** Auditorium	*Pagliacci* (1) M. Craft, F. Lamont, D. Defrère
October 20	**Springfield** (Illinois) State Arsenal	*Pagliacci* (1) M. Craft, F. Lamont/J. Mojica Conductor: P. Cimini
October 22	**Des Moines** Coliseum	*Pagliacci* M. Craft, F. Lamont. Conductor: P. Cimini
October 25	**Sioux City** (Iowa) ?	*Pagliacci* (2) M. Craft, F. Lamont/L. Oliviero, D. Defrère. Conductor: P. Cimini
October 27	**Sioux Falls** (S. Dakota) ?	*Pagliacci* (1) M. Craft, F. Lamont. Conductor: P. Cimini
October 29	**Saint Paul** (Minn.)	*Rigoletto* M. Craft, D. Francis, J. Hislop, C. Nicolay Conductor: P. Cimini
November 24	**Chicago** Auditorium	*Andrea Chénier* (2) R. Raisa, E. Johnson. Conductor: G. Marinuzzi
November 28		*Rigoletto* (1) F. Macbeth, C. Pascova, J. Hislop, V. Lazzari Conductor: G. Marinuzzi
December 13		*Oedipus Rex* (3) (world première and debut) D. Francis, A. Paillard, D. Defrère, T. Dentale Conductor: G. Marinuzzi
December 29		*Otello* (1) R. Raisa, C. Marshall. Conductor: P. Cimini

1921

January 19	**Havana** Nacional	*Otello* O. Nieto, M. Salazar. Conductor: A. Padovani
January 22		*Hamlet* A. Ottein, N. Lollini, R. Díaz, V. Bettoni Conductor: A. Padovani
January 24		*Pagliacci* O. Nieto, M. Salazar. Conductor: A. Padovani
January 29	**New York** Manhattan	*Rigoletto* F. Macbeth, T. Schipa Conductor: G. Marinuzzi

February 1		*Otello* (3) R. Raisa, M. Claessens, C. Marshall, V. Lazzari/T. Dentale. Conductor: P. Cimini
February 13	Hippodrome	Concert: Cleveland Symphony Orchestra, M. Piastro. Conductor: N. Sokolov
February 18	Hotel Biltmore	Concert, "Friday Morning Musicals": L. May Piano accompaniment: C.G. Spross Violinist: R. Vidas
February 19	Manhattan	*Pagliacci* (2) A. Zeppilli/M. Maxwell, E. Johnson, D. Defrère. Conductor: P. Cimini
February 21		*Oedipus Rex* (local première) D. Francis, A. Paillard, D. Defrère, T. Dentale Conductor: G. Marinuzzi
February	**Philadelphia** Metropolitan	Concert
March 1	**New York** Manhattan	*Il barbiere di Siviglia* F. Macbeth, T. Schipa, V. Lazzari, V. Trevisan. Conductor: G. Marinuzzi
March 5		*Hamlet* F. Macbeth, C. Van Gordon, J. Mojica, T. Dentale, V. Lazzari. Conductor: P. Cimini
March 9	**Baltimore** Lyric	*Otello* R. Raisa, C. Marshall/J. Mohica, V. Lazzari Conductor: P. Cimini
March 12	**Pittsburgh** Syria Mosque	*Rigoletto* M. Craft, A. Bonci, V. Lazzari Conductor: P. Cimini
April 24	**New York** Hippodrome	Vocal Concert: Arias from *Cristoforo Colombo* and *Il barbiere di Siviglia*; songs. L. Tetrazzini Piano accompaniment: C.G. Spross
October 30	**Kansas City** Shubert	Concert in honor of General Armando Diaz: Selections from Verdi; *Il barbiere di Siviglia*, Cavatina; songs Piano accompaniment: S. Alberti

1922

January 19	**New York** Metropolitan	*Il barbiere di Siviglia* (2) C. Chase/A. Ottein, M. Chamlee, J. Mardones/ A. Didur, P. Malatesta. Conductor: G. Papi
January 28		*Ernani* R. Ponselle, G. Martinelli, J. Mardones Conductor: G. Papi

January 31	Academy of Music	*Il barbiere di Siviglia* A. Galli-Curci, O. Harrold, A. Didur, P. Ananian. Conductor: G. Papi
February 2	Metropolitan	*Pagliacci* (1) F. Easton, M. Kingston, M. Laurenti Conductor: R. Moranzoni
February 19	Hippodrome	Concert: F. Hempel
May 5	**London** Queen's Hall	Concert: *Hamlet,* Drinking Song; *Il barbiere di Siviglia,* Cavatina; *Pagliacci,* Prologue; other operatic selections; songs. M. Namara. Piano accompaniment: C. Raybould Pianist: B. Moiseiwitsch
May 14	Albert Hall	Concert: Selections of Verdi, Massenet, Paladilhe, Donizetti, songs. M. Namara Piano accompaniment: C. Raybould. Pianist: B. Moiseiwitsch
May 17	?	Private Concert
September 24	Albert Hall	Vocal and Instrumental Concert: Arias from *Roi de Lahore, Patrie, Don Carlo.* M. Namara Piano accompaniment: C. Raybould. Violin: M. Bratsa
October 22	**Boston** Symphony Hall	Concert: Y. D'Arle
October 29	**New York** Hippodrome	Benefit Concert for the Bronx Hospital Y. D'Arle. Piano accompaniment: A. Sciarrett
November 2	**Pittsburgh** Syria Mosque (?)	Concert
November 7	**Philadelphia** Metropolitan	Concert
December 16	**New York** Metropolitan	*Ernani* (4) R. Ponselle, G. Martinelli, J. Mardones Conductor: G. Papi
December 19	Academy of Music	*Pagliacci* (1) E. Rethberg, M. Kingston, G. Schützendorf Conductor: R. Moranzoni

1923

January 3	**New York** Metropolitan	*Pagliacci* (2) E. Rethberg, E. Johnson, V. Reschiglian Conductor: G. Papi
January 18		*Aida* (1) E. Rethberg, J. Gordon, G. Martinelli, J. Mardones. Conductor: R. Moranzoni

January 29		*Il barbiere di Siviglia* (2) A. Galli-Curci, M. Chamlee, A. Didur, P. Malatesta. Conductor: C. Papi
February	**Chicago** ?	Vocal and Instrumental Concert: Y. D'Arle Piano Accompaniment: F. Renk
March 9	**Los Angeles** Philharmonic Auditorium	Concert
April	**San Francisco** Exposition Auditorium	Concerts (2)
Mar/Apr	**Seattle** Arena	Concert
Mar/Apr	**Portland** Auditorium	Concert
Mar/Apr	**Savannah** Auditorium	Concert
April 24	**Havana** Nacional	*II barbiere di Siviglia* J. Lucchese, T. Schipa, P. Ludikar, N. Cervi Conductor: C. Peroni
April 26		*Otello* A. Fitziu, A. Paoli. Conductor: C. Peroni
May 3		*Aida* M. Rappold, S. de Mette, G. Martinelli, N. Cervi, P. di Biasi. Conductor: C. Peroni
May 6		*Hamlet* J. Lucchese, S. de Mette, P. Ludikar Conductor: C. Peroni
May 12		*Carmen* M. Kusnetsov, Y. D'Arle, G. Martinelli Conductor: C. Peroni
May 14		*La bohème* L. Bori, Y. D'Arle, G. Martinelli, P. di Biasi Conductor: C. Peroni
May 15		*Pagliacci* L. Bori, G. Martinelli. Conductor: C. Peroni
May 23		Concert Piano accompaniment: A. Bovi
December 17	**New York** Metropolitan	*Andrea Chénier* (1) R. Ponselle, B. Gigli Conductor: R. Moranzoni

December 25	Academy of Music	*Ernani* (1) R. Ponselle, G. Martinelli, J. Mardones Conductor: G. Papi
December 28	Metropolitan	*Ernani* (1) R. Ponselle, G. Martinelli, J. Mardones Conductor: G. Papi

1924

January 3	**New York** Metropolitan	*Pagliacci* (1) L. Bori, M. Fleta, L. Tibbett Conductor: G. Papi
January 15	**Havana** Nacional	*Andrea Chénier* (1) O. Carrara, A. Cortis. Conductor: G. Soriente
January 17		*Tosca* (1) O. Carrera, A. Cortis. Conductor: G. Soriente
January 24	Sala Payret	Vocal and Instrumental Concert of the "Pro Arte Musical": *L'africaine,* Adamastor; *Don Giovanni,* duet; other operatic selections; Y. D'Arle. Piano accompaniment: V. Lanz
January 26	**Cienfuegos** Terry	*Hamlet* (1) P. Garavelli, A. Salori, V. Bettoni Conductor: G. Soriente
January 28		*La bohème* (1) O. Carrara, P. Garavelli, A. Cortis Conductor: G. Soriente
January 31	**Camagüey** ?	*Hamlet* (1) P. Garavellis A. Salori, V. Bettoni Conductor: G. Soriente
February 3	**Santiago** (Cuba) Oriente	*Hamlet* (1) P. Garavelli, A. Salori, V. Bettoni Conductor: G. Soriente
January 15	**San Juan** (Puerto Rico) Municipal	*Hamlet* (1) P. Garavelli, A. Salori, V. Bettoni Conductor: G. Soriente
February 17		*Il barbiere di Siviglia* (1) P. Garavelli, A. Pintucci, V. Bettoni, V. Baldo Conductor: G. Soriente
February 20		*Pagliacci* (1) Y. D'Arle, A. Cortis, G. Puliti Conductor: G. Soriente
February 22	**Ponce** Broadway	*Hamlet* (1) P. Garavelli, A. Salori, V. Bettoni Conductor: G. Soriente

February 25		*La bohème* (1) O. Carrara, P. Garavelli, A. Cortis Conductor: G. Soriente
February 27	**San Juan** (Puerto Rico) Municipal	*La bohème* (1) O. Carrara, P. Garavelli, A. Cortis Conductor: G. Soriente
March 8	**Caracas** Municipal	*Hamlet* (1) P. Garavelli, A. Salori, V. Bettoni Conductor: G. Soriente
March 11		*Andrea Chénier* (1) O. Carrara, A. Cortis. Conductor: G. Soriente
March 13		*Il barbiere di Siviglia* (1) P. Garavelli, A. Pintucci, V. Bettoni, V. Baldo Conductor: G. Soriente
March 16		*Tosca* (1) O. Carrara, A. Cortis. Conductor: G. Soriente
March 20		*Pagliacci* (2) Y. D'Arle, A. Cortis, G. Puliti Conductor: G. Soriente
April 14	**Cartagena** Municipal	*Tosca* (1) O. Carrara, A. Cortis. Conductor: G. Soriente
		Hamlet (2) P. Garavelli, A. Salori, V. Bettoni Conductor: G. Soriente
April 15	Governor's Palace	Concert
April 20	**Barranquilla** Cisneros	*Hamlet* (1) P. Garavelli, A. Salori, V. Bettoni Conductor: G. Soriente
April 24		*Pagliacci* Y. D'Arle, A. Cortis. Conductor: G. Soriente
May 10	**Bogotá** Colón	*Hamlet* (1) P. Garavelli, A. Salori, V. Bettoni Conductor: G. Soriente
May 15		*Pagliacci* (2) Y. D'Arle, A. Cortis, G. Puliti. Conductor: G. Soriente
May 17		*Tosca* (1) O. Carrara, A. Cortis. Conductor: G. Soriente
May 22		*Il barbiere di Siviglia* (3) P. Garavelli, A. Pintucci, V. Bettoni, V. Baldo Conductor: G. Soriente

May 25		*Aida* (2) O. Carrara, A. Salori, A. Cortis, V. Bettoni Conductor: G. Soriente
June 3		*Rigoletto* (2) P. Garavelli, A. Salori, A. Pintucci, V. Bettoni Conductor: G. Soriente
December 15	New York Metropolitan	*Andrea Chènier* (1)* R. Ponselle, B. Gigli. Conductor: T. Serafin *Special performance for Italian Hospital
December 23	Academy of Music	*La Gioconda* (1) F. Easton, J. Gordon, M. Alcock, B. Gigli Conductor: T. Serafin

1925

January 2	New York Metropolitan	*Aida* (1) R. Ponselle, J. Gordon, M. Fleta, J. Martones Conductor: G. Bamboschek
January 9		*La Gioconda* (1) R. Ponselle, J. Gordon, M. Alcock, B. Gigli, J. Mardones. Conductor: T. Serafin
January 12		*Il barbiere di Siviglia* (1) A. Galli-Curci, R. Errólle, A. Didur, P. Malatesta. Conductor: G. Papi
April 4	Budapest Városi Szinház	*Il barbiere di Siviglia* (1) E. Sándor, J. Somló, B. Venczell, F. Hegedüs Conductor: D. Márkus
April 9		*Hamlet* (1) E. Sándor, M. Basilides, B. Venczell Conductor: R. Máder
April 13		*Rigoletto* (1) E. Sándor, R. Marschalkó, K. Pataky, M. Székely. Conductor: D. Márkus
April 17	Berlin	Vocal and Instrumental Concert: *Pagliacci*, Prologue; *Hamlet*, Drinking Song; *L'africaine*, All'erta marinar; Italian and Spanish songs. Piano accompaniment. F. Lindemann, cellist: G. Urack
April 22	Grosses Volksoper im Theater des Westens	*Rigoletto* (1) S. Yergin, P. Raitchev Conductor: I. Dobrowen
May 5	Budapest Városi Szinház	*Tosca* R. Walter, J. Halmos Conductor: E. Ábrányi

May 8		*Pagliacci**
		T. Köszegi, K. Ocskay, J. Balla
		Conductor: E. Ábrányi
		*Between Acts I and II TR sings Italian songs.
October 11	**Pisa**	*Hamlet* (2) (local première)
	Verdi*	A. Bucciantini, F. Perini, N. Marotta
		Conductor: E. Mascheroni
		*Special benefit performance
November 7	**Barcelona**	*La cena delle beffe* (national première
	Liceo	and debut in the role of Neri Chiaramantesi)
		H. Spani, C. Folco Bottaro
		Conductor: F. Paolantonio
November 11		*Tosca*
		O. Carrara, M. Fleta
		Conductor: F. Paolantonio
December 11	**New York**	*La Gioconda* (1)
	Metropolitan	R. Ponselle, J. Gordon, M. Alcock,
		B. Gigli, J. Mardones. Conductor: G. Setti
December 16		*Andrea Chénier* (1)
		R Ponselle, B. Gigli. Conductor: G. Bamboschek
December 18		*Pagliacci* (2)
		Q. Mario, E. Johnson/A. Tokatyan,
		L. Tibbett/M. Picco. Conductor: G. Papi

1926

January 2	**New York**	*La cena delle beffe* (2) (national première)
	Metropolitan	F. Alda, B. Gigli. Conductor: T. Serafin
January 5	**Philadelphia**	*La cena delle beffe* (1) (city première)
	Metropolitan	F. Alda, B. Gigli. Conductor: T. Serafin
February 13	**Washington**	*Rigoletto*
	?	E. Mason, C. Hackett
January 27	**Chicago**	*Otello* (1)
	Auditorium	A. Fitziu, C. Marshall. Conductor: R. Moranzoni
January 30	**Boston**	*Un ballo in maschera*
	Boston Opera	R. Raisa, C. Van Gordon,
		C. Marshall. Conductor: G. Polacco
February 16	**Cleveland**	*Tosca* (1)
	Keith Palace	C. Muzio, C. Hackett. Conductor: R. Moranzoni
February 19		*Otello* (1)
		R. Raisa, C. Marshall, A. Kipnis
		Conductor: R. Moranzoni

March 3	**Birmingham** Municipal Auditorium	*La traviata* (1) C. Muzio, C. Hackett. Conductor: R. Moranzoni
March 5	**Memphis** Auditorium	*La traviata* (1) C. Muzio, A. Cortis, C. Hackett Conductor: R. Moranzoni
March 10	**Miami** Coral Gables Stadium	*La traviata* (1) C. Muzio, A. Cortis. Conductor: R. Moranzoni
May 29	**Buenos Aires** Colón	*Hamlet* (5) G. Pareto/N. Morgana, F. Anitúa/A. Buades, E. Pinza. Conductor: G. Marinuzzi
June 6		*Andrea Chénier* (1) C. Muzio. G. Lauri-Volpi. Conductor: G. Santini
June 18		*Pagliacci* (3) R. Pampanini, A. Pertile, G. Vanelli Conductor: G. Santini
July 5		*Tosca* (2) C. Muzio, G. Lauri-Volpi. Conductor: G. Santini
July 8	Coliseo	Benefit Concert
July 14	Colón	*Il barbiere di Siviglia* (3)* G. Pareto/N. Morgana, R. D'Alessio, E. Pinza/ T. Pasero, G. Azzolini. Conductor: G. Santini

*The gala première performance is for the charitable works of the French colony.

August 5		*La bohème* (1) I. Marengo, A. Morelli, A. Pertile, R. Rasponi, E. Pinza. Conductor: G. Marinuzzi
August 17	**Rio de Janeiro** Lyrico	*Hamlet* G. Pareto, A. Buades. E. Pinza, L. Nardi Conductor: G. Marinuzzi
August 22		*Tosca* (2) C. Muzio, G. Lauri-Volpi. Conductor: G. Santini
August 25 (?)		*Il barbiere di Siviglia* G. Pareto, R. D'Alessio, E. Pinza, G. Azzolini Conductor: G. Santini
November 16	**New York** WEAF Studios	Vocal and Orchestral Radio Concert: *Pagliacci,* Prologue; songs. Conductor: R. Graham
December 10	Metropolitan	*La cena delle beffe* (2) F. Alda, E. Dalossy, B. Gigli, A. Badà Conductor: T. Serafin

December 14	**Philadelphia** Academy of Music	*Andrea Chénier* (1) E. Rethberg, G. Lauri-Volpi Conductor: T. Serafin
December 23	**New York** Metropolitan	*La Gioconda* (1) R. Ponselle, C. Van Gordon, M. Alcock, B. Gigli, E. Pinza. Conductor: T. Serafin
December 26		Benefit Concert: Selections from *Patrie* and *Rigoletto* M. Talley, M. Alcock, B. Gigli Conductor: G. Bamboschek

1927

January 5	**New York** Metropolitan	*Pagliacci* (2) Q. Mario, G. Martinelli/V. Fullin, G. Cehanovsky/L. Tibbett Conductor: V. Bellezza
January 8	Mecca Temple	Concert*
		*Organized by the Committee for Special Aid of the union of Jewish-American typesetters
January 11	**Philadelphia** Academy of Music	*La cena delle beffe* (1) F. Alda, B. Gigli. Conductor: T. Serafin
January 18	**Pittsburgh** Syria Mosque	*Pagliacci* (2) F. Campiña, J. de Gaviria. Conductor: P. Paci
January 22		*Tosca* (1) F. Campiña, J. de Gaviria. Conductor: P. Paci
January 29	**Philadelphia** Metropolitan	*Otello* M. Cianci, F. de Angelis. Conductor: P. Paci
February 6	**Cleveland** WTAM Studios (and affiliates)	Radio Concert: *Pagliacci,* Prologue; *Il barbiere di Siviglia,* Cavatina; *Patrie* by Paladilhe; songs. Conductor: L. Edlina Piano accomaniment: R. Gruen
May 31	**Paris** Opéra	Concert
June 10	Opéra-Comique	*Tosca* (1) C. Victrix, A. Villabella Conductor: A. Messager
July 14	Salon des Ambassadeurs	Benefit Concert promoted by the President of the French Republic
August 23	**Deauville** Casino	*La bohéme* (2) E. Norena, Y. d'Arle, E. DiMazzei, P. Lanteri

August 26	**Ostend** Kursaal	Concert
September 15	**Berlin** Philharmonic	Vocal and Instrumental Concert: *Patrie* by Paladilhe; *L'africaine,* All'erta marinar; Italian and Spanish songs. Piano accompaniment: M. Raucheisen, violinist: F. Arányi
November 16	**Philadelphia** Metropolitan	*Hamlet* P. Garavelli, R. Toniolo, M. Fattori Conductor: W. Grigaitis
November 30		*Otello* M. Micketa, F. de Angelis Conductor: A. Rodzinski
December 5	**New York** Metropolitan	*Andrea Chénier* (2)* F. Easton/R. Ponselle, B. Gigli Conductor: T. Serafin
		*The second performance, January 7, 1928, with Rosa Ponselle, is for the Italian Hospital.
December 14		*Aida* (1) G. Stückgold, L. Homer, G. Martinelli, E. Pinza. Conductor: T. Serafin
December 16		*Pagliacci* (1) Q. Mario, G. Martinelli, E. Marshall Conductor: V. Bellezza
December 29		*La Gioconda* (1) R. Ponselle, L. Homer, A. Alcock, B. Gigli, L. Rothier. Conductor: T. Serafin

1928

January 2	**New York** Metropolitan	*Il barbiere di Siviglia* (3) A. Galli-Curci, M. Chamlee, E. Pinza/ L. Rothier, P. Malatesta Conductor: V. Bellezza
January 9	WEAF Studios	Radio Concert: *Pagliacci,* Prologue; Italian and Spanish songs Conductor: R. Graham
February 8	**Philadelphia** Metropolitan	*Tosca* (1) M. Sharlow, G. Zenatello Conductor: A. Rodzinski
February 22	**New York** Carnegie Hall	Concert spettacolo: *Dinorah,* Sei vendicata; *L'africaine,* Adamastor; *Il barbiere di Siviglia,* Cavatina; songs. Violinist: M. Corti

February 29	**Philadelphia** Metropolitan	*Andrea Chénier* M. Sharlow, G. Zenatello Conductor: A. Rodzinski
April 27	**Budapest** Városi Szinház	*Tosca* (1) E. Rakowska, J. Halmos. Conductor: D. Márkus Followed by a concert
April 30		*Il barbiere di Siviglia* (1) I. Zoltán, M. Szedö, E. Pajor, J. Vermes, Medveczky. Conductor: D. Márkus With concert after Act II
May 7	**Paris** Champs-Elysées	Concert
September 5	**Santiago** (Chile) Municipal	*Hamlet* (1) L. Pasini, E. Casazza, M. Gaudio Conductor: G. Falconi
September 9		*Il barbiere di Siviglia* (1) L. Pasini, D. Borgioli, M. Gaudio Conductor: G. Falconi
September 16		*Tosca* (1) G. Cobelli, A. Cortis. Conductor: G. Falconi
September 21		*Otello* (1) G. Cobelli, R. Zanelli. Conductor: G. Falconi
September 23		*Tosca* G. Corbelli, A. Cortis. Conductor: G. Falconi
September 26		*Tosca* G. Cobelli, F. Tafuro. Conductor: G. Falconi
September 27	**Valparaiso** La Victoria	*Otello* (1) G. Cobelli, R. Zanelli. Conductor: G. Falconi
September 30		*Hamlet* L. Pasini, E. Casazza, M. Gaudio, Mansueto. Conductor: G. Falconi
October 3		*Tosca* (1) F. Cristoforeanu, F. Tafuro Conductor: G. Falconi
October 14	**Buenos Aires** Colón	*Hamlet,* Act I and Drinking Song* L. Romelli, E. Casazza, J. Lanskoy Conductor: A. de Angelis
October 18		*Il barbiere di Siviglia,* Acts II and III* B. Sayão, C. Rodriguez, J. Lanskoy, A. Pacini. Conductor: C.A. Stiattesi

*Performance in honor of the foreign ambassadors on the occasion of the President of the Republic, H. Irigoyen, taking office.

October 23		*Otello* (1) I. Alfani-Tellini, R. Zanelli. Conductor: A. de Angelis
October 27		*Hamlet* (1) R. Romelli, E. Casazza, J. Lanskoy Conductor: A. de Angelis
October 31	**Montevideo** Solís	Vocal Concert: *L'africaine,* Adamastor; selections from *Falstaff; Panurge,* Chanson de la Touraine; "Until" by Sanderson; songs
November 6	**Rio de Janeiro** Palacio	Vocal Concert: *Patrie,* selection; *Hamlet,* Drinking Song; Spanish and Italian songs
December 8	**New York** Metropolitan	*Andrea Chénier* (1) R. Ponselle, G. Martinelli. Conductor: T. Serafin
December 17		*Ernani* (1) R. Ponselle, G. Martinelli, E. Pinza Conductor: V. Bellezza

1929

January 1	**New York** Metropolitan	*Il barbiere di Siviglia* (2) A. Galli-Curci, A. Tokatyan, E. Pinza/L. Rothier, P. Malatesta Conductors: V. Bellezza and G. Bamboschek
January 21		*Pagliacci* (1) N. Guilford, E. Johnson, E. Marshall Conductor: G. Bamboschek
January 29	**Philadelphia** ?	*Il barbiere di Siviglia* (1) A. Galli-Curci, A. Tokatyan, E. Pinza, P. Malatesta. Conductor: G. Bamboschek
February 1	**New York** Metropolitan	*Aida* (2) M. Müller/L. Corona, K. Branzell, G. Martinelli/G. Lauri Volpi, P. Ludikar, Conductor: T. Serafin
March 3	**Sam H. Harris** Cinema	*Il barbiere di Siviglia,* Cavatina, First projection anywhere of the "Metro-Movietone,"* sound film; part of the MGM film "Madame X." *"Metro-Movietone" filmed only the Credo from *Otello* and from *L'africaine,* All'erta marinar.
March 22	**Paris** Salle Gaveau	Concert: arias from *Le Nozze di Figaro, Patrie,* *Demon, Panurge, Falstaff; Il barbiere di* *Siviglia;* duets from *Don Giovanni* and *Thaïs;* Tarantella by Rossini; aria by B. Marcello; Spanish songs. The concert was closed by a recitation by TR of Hamlet's Monologue and the Curse of King Lear.

March 24	Salle Pleyel	Concert
August 24	**Ostend** Kursaal	Concert: *Il barbiere di Siviglia*, Cavatina; *L'africaine*, aria

1930

February 25	**Vienna** Grosser Konzerthaus	Concert: *Dinorah*, aria; *Il barbiere di Siviglia*, Cavatina; *L'africaine*, Adamastor; songs. Piano accompaniment: P. Sirota. Pianist: J. McGown Clark
March 1	**Paris** Salle Pleyel	Concert: *Dinorah*, aria; *L'africaine*, Adamastor; *Il barbiere di Siviglia*, Cavatina; Neapolitan and Spanish songs. Piano accompaniment: P. Sirota. Pianist: M. Roesgen-Champion
March 7	**Brussels** Palais des Beaux-Arts	Concert with Voice and Harpsichord *Dinorah*, aria; *L'africaine*, All'erta marinar; *Il barbiere di Siviglia*, Cavatina; Spanish and Italian songs. Piano accompaniment: P. Sirota. Harpsichord: G. Mombaerts
March 18	**Warsaw** Filharmonji	Vocal Concert: *Dinorah*, aria; *L'africaine*, aria; *Il Barbiere di Siviglia*, Cavatina Piano accompaniment: P. Sirota
March 25	**Bucarest** Opera Româna	*Il barbiere di Siviglia* (1) Metaxas, Oprisan, G. Niculescu-Basu, Chicideanu
June 17	**Athens** Olympia	*Il barbiere di Siviglia* L. Perpinia, M. Tomakos, M. Blakopoilos, G. Moillas. Conductor: A. Kiparissis
September 19, 21	**Stockholm** State Theater	Concerts (2): *Il barbiere di Siviglia*, Cavatina; selections from *Dinorah* and *Hamlet*; Italian songs Piano accompaniment: V. Kosti
October 1	**Copenhagen** Odd Fellow Palaeet	Vocal and Piano Concert Piano accompaniment: V. Kosti
December 11	**Amsterdam** Concertgebouw	Concert: *L'africaine*, aria; *Il barbiere di Siviglia*, Cavatina; Songs Piano accompaniment: P. Sirota. Pianist: A. Kitain
December 15	**L'Aia** Gebouw v. K. e W.	Concert (as above)

1931

January 8, 18	**Nice** Casino de la Jetée-Promenade	Concerts (2)
February 4	**Cannes** Casino Municipal	*Tosca*
February 9	**Nice** Casino de la Jetée-Promenade	Concert
February 11	**Pau** Nouveau Casino Municipal	Concert
February 14	**Cannes** Casino Municipal	*Hamlet* (1) M. Gallyot, I. Gregoire Conductor: J. Spaandermann
February 18	**Marseille** Casino Municipal	*Il barbiere di Siviglia* (1) M. Gentile, L. Cecil, E. Billot, Euryale, Conductor: F. Melli
May 25	**Buenos Aires** Colón	*Hamlet* (3) I. Marengo, Y. Alard, E. Pinza Conductor: F. Calusio
June 14	Concert:	Spanish and Italian songs. Piano accompaniment: L. Ricci. Pianist: R. Spivak
June 23		*Tosca* (5) G. Cobelli, G. Thill. Conductor: F. Calusio
December 4	**Geneva** Victoria Hall	Concert Piano accompaniment: P. Sirota
December 11	**Amsterdam** Concertgebouw	Concert: *L'africaine,* aria; *Pagliacci,* Prologue; *Il barbiere di Siviglia,* Cavatina; songs. Piano accompaniment: P. Sirota

1932

| January 7 | **Paris** Salle Pleyel | Concert: *Il barbiere di Siviglia,* Cavatina and duet; B. Marcello, Quella fiamma; *Le Nozze di Figaro,* aria; *Don Giovanni,* Serenade and duet; *Pagliacci,* Un nido di memorie; songs. B. Sayão. Piano accompaniment: M.M. Foa |

January 20, 26	**Madrid** Avenida	Concerts (2): Spanish and Italian songs. *Il barbiere di Siviglia,* Cavatina; arias from *Hamlet, L'africaine, Don Giovanni, Falstaff*
February 16	**Barcelona** Palau de la musica catalana	Concert: Spanish and Italian songs; *Il barbiere di Siviglia,* Cavatina; *Don Giovanni* and *Thaïs,* duets. G. Fisher Piano accompaniment: P. Sirota
March	**Paris** Salle Gaveau	Concert M. Nugent, L. Tragin
December 27	**New York** Radio City Music Hall	Grand Opening *Carmen,* selections (1) C. Glade, A. Lindi. Conductor: D. Defrère

1933

November 21	**London** Palace of Lady Kleinwort 30 Curzon Street	Musical Concert for the Messrs. Van Gelder Operatic arias; *Don Giovanni,* duet. M. Salvi, A. Grüninger Piano accompaniment: F. Longas. Pianist: A. Grande

1934

February 25	**Nice** Casino de la Jetée-Promenade	Concert: operatic arias and songs
March 8	Eldorado	Grand Concert of Entertainment for the Press N. Vallin-Pardo
March 10	Casino de la Jetée-Promenade	*Hamlet,* Acts I, scene II and III M. Germain, S. Joris, A. Philippe Conductor: H. Mario

Acknowledgments

I want to give especially warm thanks to Thomas G. Kaufman, operatic expert, for the valuable information he was able to gather regarding Titta Ruffo's career. I have also received, directly or indirectly, useful data that helped me complete this chronology from Antonio Altamirano, Eduardo Arnosi, Gino dell'Ira, Juan Dzazopulos, Giovanni Idonea, Veli-Jussi Koskinen, Lim M. Lai, Antonio Massísimo, Vincenzo Mesiano, Mario Moreau, Jean-Pierre Mouchon, Carlo Marinelli Rosconi, Charles Mintzer, Horacio Sanguinetti, and Péter Pál Várnai.

Index to the Chronology

Ábrányi, Emil *(conductor)*, 1912, 1925
Adaberto, Ester *(soprano)*, 1898, 1899
Adler, Adelina *(soprano)*, 1913
Adriana Lecouvreur (F. Cilea), 1904
Africaine (L') (J. Meyerbeer), 1900, 1902, 1906, 1908, 1911, 1912, 1915
Agostinelli, Adelina *(soprano)*, 1910, 1911, 1916
Aida (G. Verdi), 1900, 1902, 1905, 1911, 1915, 1916, 1923, 1924, 1925, 1927, 1929
Aineto, Marino *(baritone)*, 1915
Alabau, Amparo *(soprano)*, 1908
Alard, Yvonne *(mezzosoprano)*, 1931
Alberti, Sol *(accompanist, piano)*, 1921
Alberti, Werner *(tenor)*, 1907
Alcock, Merle *(mezzosoprano)*, 1924, 1925, 1926, 1927
Alda, Frances *(soprano)*, 1926, 1927
Alemanni, Amedeo *(tenor)*, 1904
Alfani-Tellini, Ines *(soprano)*, 1928
Algos, Angelo *(tenor)*, 1916
Alvarez, Regina *(mezzosoprano)*, 1915
Alvisi, Adolfo *(conductor)*, 1912, 1914
Ananian, Paolo *(bass)*, 1922
Anceschi, Aristide *(baritone)*, 1901
Andrea Chénier (U. Giordano) 1900, 1916, 1918, 1919, 1920, 1923, 1924, 1925, 1926, 1927, 1928
Andreini, Remo *(tenor)*, 1906, 1910
Anfione e Zeto (Maso Salvini), 1915
Angelini Borelli, Ester *(soprano)*, 1914
Angioletti, Angelo *(tenor)*, 1907
Anitúa, Fanny *(mezzosoprano)*, 1911, 1926
Anselmi, Giuseppe *(tenor)*, 1901, 1904, 1906, 1908, 1909
Anselmi, Oscar *(conductor)*, 1900, 1905, 1910
Antinori, Adele *(mezzosoprano)*, 1899
Antonova, Varvara Petrovna *(soprano)*, 1906
Arányi, Desider *(tenor)*, 1912
Arányi, Francis *(violinist)*, 1927
Arimondi, Vittorio *(bass)*, 1908, 1910, 1920
Armanini, Giuseppe *(tenor)*, 1906, 1907

Arnoldson, Sigrid *(soprano)*, 1906
Askocienski *(tenor)*, 1906
Aurora (H. Panizza), 1908, 1909
Azzolini, Gaetano *(bass)*, 1918, 1926

Backhaus, Wilhelm *(pianista)*, 1903
Badà, Angelo *(tenor)*, 1911, 1926
Bailac, Germaine *(mezzosoprano)*, 1908
Baldassarre Tedeschi, Giuseppina *(mezzosoprano)*, 1912
Baldelli, Antonio *(bass)*, 1905
Baldo, Vittorio *(bass)*, 1924
Balla, I. *(baritone)*, 1925
Ballo in maschera (Un) (G. Verdi), 1899, 1900, 1907, 1912, 1915, 1919, 1925, 1926
Bamboschek, Giuseppe *(conductor)*, 1925, 1926, 1929
Banti, Ottavio *(bass)*, 1904
Baratta, Arturo *(conductor)*, 1908, 1909
Barbiere di Siviglia (Il) (G. Rossini), 1903, 1905, 1906, 1907, 1908, 1909, 1910, 1911, 1912, 1913, 1914, 1915, 1918, 1919, 1921, 1923, 1924, 1925, 1926, 1928, 1929, 1930, 1931
Barella, Luigi *(composer)*, 1899
Barone, Anita *(soprano)*, 1901, 1902, 1905
Baroni, Giuseppe *(conductor)*, 1906, 1909, 1915, 1916
Barrera, Carlos *(tenor)*, 1901, 1902
Barrientos, Maria *(soprano)*, 1903, 1911, 1912, 1916
Barsanti, Emma *(mezzosoprano)*, 1916
Bársony, Dóra *(mezzosoprano)*, 1912
Barti, Perla *(soprano)*, 1916, 1918, 1919
Baselli, Giorgio *(tenor)*, 1904
Basilides, Mária *(mezzosoprano)*, 1913, 1925
Bassi, Amedeo *(tenor)*, 1905, 1908, 1913, 1914
Bavagnoli, Gaetano *(conductor)*, 1914
Bellet, Félix *(baritone)*, 1917
Bellezza, Vincenzo *(conductor)*, 1927, 1928, 1929
Bellincioni, Gemma *(soprano)*, 1905

The Recordings of Titta Ruffo:
A Discography

WILLIAM R. MORAN

Dedicated to the memory of Richard Bonelli (1889-1980):
one of Ruffo's greatest admirers and a true successor

THE RECORDING CAREER of Titta Ruffo covered some thirty years and clearly
defines the parabolic trace of his artistic career which he himself so clearly
recognized. His first group of recordings were made in Paris in the year
1904 for the Pathé Frères Company. These were originally recorded on
wax cylinders, and were sold in that form as well as vertical cut discs, the
latter made from the original master cylinders by a pantograph process.
In their early form the discs came in several sizes, from 8 to 14 inches in
diameter, first single faced, and later coupled in various combinations.
The titles were etched in the centers, and the records played from the
inside to the outer rim, at speeds around 90 revolutions per minute. Cylinders and early discs all bore the master cylinder number (4200 through
4213 and 4260) and all were announced by the artist. In the 'teens and
twenties the same recordings were made available in a new form: The
size was standardized at about 11½ inches, playing speeds were fairly
well established at 80 rpm, the recordings played from the outside in,
and the original spoken announcements were removed. The discs were
still vertical cut ("hill-and-dale"), and special reproducers were required
to play them on most machines. Fortunately for today's listeners, many
of them have been transcribed to Long Playing recordings, although not
all such transcriptions have been made at the proper playing speeds.
Correct playing speeds cannot be given for the Pathé records, as the speeds
varied from copy to copy of the same selection.

From 1907 to 1933 Ruffo recorded for the Gramophone Company
("His Master's Voice") in Milan and London and its affiliated company,
The Victor Talking Machine Co., in New York and Camden, N.J. These

records, issued by each company under its own cataloging numbers, are listed together in Part II of this discography. Through the years, various titles were re-made and substituted. During the period when Ruffo recorded for these two concerns, recording speeds were far from standardized and strangely, no written record was maintained of the turntable speeds used when the records were made. To reproduce these recordings properly, they must be played at the speeds at which they were recorded. The determination of playing speed of each record is a painstaking job requiring much subjective judgement and many hours of study and comparison. The playing speeds given in the discography have been determined by the author from recordings in his personal collection, and are offered as "best judgment" recommendations.

Recordings made in the United States by Victor can be identified by the matrix number letter prefix: B or BVE which indicate 10-inch recordings, the first made by the acoustical process and the latter electrically made. Similarly, C and CVE prefixes indicate 12-inch Victor recordings. All matrix numbers not prefixed as above were made in Europe by the acoustical process, with the exception of the 10-inch electrical recordings made in London in 1933 which have an OB prefix. Those ending in the letters *ai, c, f, i,* and *v* are 12-inch recordings; all others are 10-inches in size.

Exact recording dates for the Victor records, as well as information on unpublished recordings have been obtained from data in the Victor files being compiled at the Stanford Archive of Recorded Sound. The author wishes to express his appreciation to his associate in this work, Mr. Ted Fagan.

Two recordings not of HMV-Victor origin have been included for convenience in Part II: these are from sound films. (See Discography Nos. 30 and 89.)

An asterisk preceding a discography number indicates that there is a note on that recording at the end of this appendix.

THE PRESENT DISCOGRAPHY is a corrected and updated version of the one originally published in the reprint edition of *Titta Ruffo: La Mia Parabola* (New York: Arno Press, 1977) and a further revised edition published in *Titta Ruffo: An Anthology* (Andrew Farkas [Ed.], Westport [CT]/London: Greenwood Press, 1984). Dr. Ruffo Titta, the singer's son, and Mr. E. G. Mathews were most helpful with their comments on the first edition. Alan Kelly corrected a number of errors in recording dates and offered further suggestions which have been incorporated in the present version. The author wishes to express his appreciation to all of them, as well as to Mr. Andrew Farkas.

July, 1995

Part I. Cie. Pathé Frères, Paris, 1904
(All with Piano Accompaniment)

Disco. No.	SF & Master Cyl No.	DF Cat. No. Italy	DF Cat. No. France	DF Cat. No. U.K.	DF Cat. No. U.S.A.	Transcriptions to 78 rpm At 78 rpm	Transcriptions to Lateral Cut Discs Long Playing Discs
1. AMLETO: *O vin discaccia la tristezza* (Thomas) (I)							
	4202	10067	0556	5244	60011	—	TAP 309; Scala 812
2. Il BARBIERE DI SIVIGLIA: *Largo al factotum* (Rossini) (I)							
	4203	10067	0556	5244	60011	—	TAP 309; Scala 812
3. La BOHEME: *O Mimì, tu più non torni* (Puccini) (w. Amedeo Bassi) (I)							
	4260	12569	0559	—	—	—	Scala 812 2582
4. CHATTERTON: *Tu sola a me rimani o poesia* (Leoncavallo) (I)							
	4210	10069	—	—	—	IRCC 3027	TAP 309; Scala 812; HRS 3005
5. DINORAH: *Sei vendicata assai* (Meyerbeer) (I)							
	4212	—	—	—	—	—	—
6. DON CARLO: *Per me giunto* (Verdi) (I)							
	4211	10069	—	—	—	—	TAP 309; TAP 314; Scala 812; HRS 3005
7. FAUST: *Stammi ad udir, Margherita!* (Morte di Valentino) (Gounod) (I)							
	4208	10286	0558	5245	60038	HRS 1085	TAP 309; Scala 812
8. La FAVORITA: *Vien, Leonora* (Donizetti) (I)							
	4204	10068	—	—	—	IRCC 3110	—

9. FEDORA: *La donna russa* (Giordano) (I) 4209	—	—			HRS 3005; Scala 855
HAMLET see: AMLETO					
10. *Mia sposa sarà la mia bandiera* (A. Rotoli) (I) 4213	—	—			—
11. SIBERIA: *O bella mia* (Giordano) (I) 4205	10286	0558	5245	HRS 1085	TAP 309; Scala 855
12. La TRAVIATA: *Di Provenza il mar* (Verdi) (I) 4207	—	—			TAP 309; Scala 812; HRS 3005
13. Il TROVATORE: *Il balen del suo sorriso* (Verdi) (I) 4206	10068	—			TAP 309; HRS 3005
14. ZAZÀ: *Buona Zazà, dei mio buon tempo* (Leoncavallo) (I) 4200	10066	5677			TAP 309; Scala 812
15. ZAZÀ: *Zazà, piccola zingara* (Leoncavallo) (I) 4201	10066	5677			TAP 309; Scala 812

Part II. The Gramophone Co. ("His Master's Voice") Milan and London
The Victor Talking Machine Co., Camden, N.J., and New York

Discog. No. Matrix No.	Date mo/day/yr	SF Victor Cat. No.	DF Victor Cat. No.	SF HMV Cat. No.	DF HMV Cat. No.	Special "78" Rpm Issues	Speed of Original	Transcription to EPs or LPs
16. L'AFRICANA: All'erta, Marinari (Meyerbeer) (I) (Or. Rogers)								
B-15894-1	4/14/15	87223	817	7-52072	DA 164	——	77.43	LM20110; VL 47215
17. L'AFRICANA: Adamastor, re dell'acque profonde (Meyerbeer) (I) (Or. '20 Pasternack; '29 Bourdon)								
C-23947-1,-2	4/20/20	88622	6262	2-052186	DB 406	——	76.00	VIC 1680; LM 20150; VL 47215
CVE-23947-3	2/18/29	——	7153					
CVE-23947-4	3/20/29	——	7153	(42-736)	DB 1397	——	77.43	——
18. AMLETO: Apparizione dello Spettro ("Angels and ministers of grace defend us!") (Shakespeare) (Spoken, in Italian)								
17467u	10/15/12	87381	985	51097	DA 352	——	76.60?	——
*19. AMLETO: Essere o non essere ("To be, or not to be...") (Shakespeare) (Spoken, in Italian)								
17468u	10/15/12	87382	985	51098	DA170	——		——
OB-5470-1	11/24/33	——	985		DA170	——	76.60?	——
20. AMLETO: Nega se puoi la luce (Thomas) (w. Maria Galvany) (I) (Or. Sabaino)								
1312½c	?/07	92500	8055	054180	——		74.23	Rococo R16; ORL 217; Scala 855; COLH 155
21. AMLETO: Spettro infernal, immagin venerata (Thomas) (I) (Or. Sabaino)								
1089½ b	10-11/07*	87153	935	2-52622	DA 170	AGSA 16	74.23	Rococo R16; ORL 217; Scala 855; COLH 155

*i.e., Oct-Nov/07

22. AMLETO: *Spettro santo! ombra vendicatrice* (Thomas) (I) (Or. Sabaino)

Matrix	Date						rpm	Reissues
10897b	10-11/07	87154	935	2-52621	DA 352	AGSA 16	74.23	Rococo R16; ORL 217; Scala 855; COLH 155

*23. AMLETO: *O vin, discaccia la tristezza* (Thomas) (I) (Or. & La Scala Cho. '07 Sabaino; '20 Pasternack)

Matrix	Date						rpm	Reissues
1315c	10-11/07	92037	—	052188	DB569	—	74.23	Rococo R16; COLH 155; ORL 217;
C-24110-1,-2	5,13/20	88619	6266 / 18140	052188	—	—	76.00	VIC 1394; LM 20150; VL 47216

24. AMLETO: *Essere o non essere (Monologo)* (Thomas) (I) (Or. Sabaino)

Matrix	Date						rpm	Reissues
1329c	10-11/07	92042	6403	052189	—	—	74.23	ORL 217; COLH 155

25. AMLETO: *Com il romito fior* (Thomas) (1) (Or. Sabaino)

Matrix	Date						rpm	Reissues
2732f	11/23/08	92064	6403	052248	DB 569	—	79.13	Rococo R16; ORL 217; EB 37; Scala 855; COLH 155

26. ANDREA CHÉNIER: *Son sessant'anni* (Giordano) (I) (Or. Pasternack)

Matrix	Date						rpm	Reissues
B-24621-1,-2	10/11/20	87325	817	7-52173	DA 351	—	76.00	VIC 1680; LM 20150; VL 47216

*27. ANDREA CHÉNIER: *Nemico della patria?!...Un dì m'era di gioia* (Giordano) (I) (Or. '20 Pasternack; '29 Bourdon)

Matrix	Date						rpm	Reissues
C-24622-1,-2	10/11/20	88626	6262	2-052187	DB 242	—	76.00	VIC 1680; VL 47216
CVE-24622-3	2/18/29	—	7153	(42-755)	DB 1397	DB 5386	77.43	17-0047; LM 20110; LCT 1006

28. Un BALLO IN MASCHERA: *Alla vita che t'arride* (Verdi) (I) (Or. Rogers?)

Matrix	Date						rpm	Reissues
B-12622-1	11/17/12	87113	937	7-52036	DA 358	—	76.60	VL 47215

Discog. No.	Matrix No.	Date mo/day/yr	SF Victor Cat. No.	DF Victor Cat. No.	SF HMV Cat. No.	DF HMV Cat. No.	Special "78" Rpm Issues	Speed of Original	Transcription to EPs or LPs
29. Un BALLO IN MASCHERA: *Eri tu che macchiavi quell'anima* (Verdi) (I) (Or. Rogers)									
C-15895-1	4/14/15	88544	6266	2-052170	DB 398	——	77.43	LM 20110; VL 47215
*30. Il BARBIERE DI SIVIGLIA: *Largo al factotum* (Rossini) (I) (Or. '07 & '12 Sabaino: '20 Pasternack: '26 Bourdon)									
791 c	10/06/07	92039	6405	052132	DB 502		77.43	VIC 1680
463ai	9/3/12	88391		052380			76.00	COLH 155
C-23945- 1,-2	4/19/20	88391	6263	2-052184	DB 405		76.00	LM 20110; VL 47216
CVE-23945-3, -4	2/26/26	No. 364-6A	(a-128) - 495 ft.	——	——		74.23	EJS 142;
Sound Film Disc	2/28/29							
31. Il BARBIERE DI SIVIGLIA: *Dunque io son?* (Rossini) (w. Maria Galvany) (I) (Or. Sabaino)									
1328½c	10-11/07	92501	8054	054181	DB 400		74.23	HER 407; TAP 332; Scala 855; VIC 1680
*32. La BOHÈME: *In un coupè...O Mimì, tu più non torni* (Puccini) (w. Beniamino Gigli) (I) (Or. Bourdon)									
CVE-37320-1,-2	12/17/26						AGSB 56	77.43	EJS 111; LM 20150; VL 47215; 49-1422
CVE-37320-3	12/17/26							——	
*33. CARMEN: *Ecco alfin ognun si tace* (Canzone del Toreador, 2nd verse) (Bizet) (I) tw. Chorus) (Or.'08 Sabaino; '23 Bourdon)									
2736f	11/25/08	92065	6406	052249	DB 406	DB 5386	79.13	——
C-27751-1,-2	4/11/23								——
C-27751-3	11/27/23								——
*34. CHATTERTON: *Tu sola a me rimani o poesia* (Leoncavallo) (I) (Or. Sabaino)									
9228e	11/26/08	87155		2-52686	VA 16	——	79.13	Rococo R16

35. *Chitarrata Abruzzese* (Abruzzi Serenade) (R. Mazzola—F. Paolo Tosti) (I) (Mandolin, Bianculli; Guitar, E. Cibelli; Or. Bourdon)
B-31699-1,-2 1/21/25 · 1076 · (7-52332) · DA 769 · — · 76.00 · CL 99-63

36. *Le Credo du Paysan* (Borel—Goublier) (F) (Or. Bourdon)
B-29035-1,-2,-3 11/27/23 · 1070 · (7-52259) · DA 703 · — · 76.00 · ——

37. CRISTOFORO COLOMBO: *Perchè piangete ignavi?...Aman lassù le stelle* (Franchetti) (I) (Or. Rogers)
C-14517-1 2/26/14 · 88486 · 2-052096 · DB 179 · AGSB 28 · 76.00 · LM 20110; VL 47216

38. CRISTOFORO COLOMBO: *Dunque ho sognato?* (Franchetti) (I) (Or. Pasternack)
C-25213-1,-2 4/14/21 · 88668 · 6429 · (2-052226) · DB 179 · AGSB 28 · 76.00 · LM 20110; VL 47216

*39. *Cubanita* (Schipa—Huarte) (Spanish) (Or. Bourdon)
B-31694-1,-2 1/21/25 · 88395 · — · — · — · 76.00 · EJS 223

*40. *Dai canti d'amore* (Canzone) (Ettore Titta) (I) (Or. Sabaino)
464ai 9/3/12 · 15- 1028 · 052382 · — · — · 76.00 · ——

*41. La DANNAZIONE DI FAUST: *Che fai tu qui* (Serenata di Mefistofele) (Berlioz) (I) (Or. Pasternack)
B-27026-1,-2 10/13/22
B-27026-3,-4,-5 10/18/22 · 87369 · 963 · 7-52226 · DA 164 · — · 76.00 · ——

42. *La Danza* (Tarantella) (Rossini) (I) (Or. Bourdon)
B-31695-1,-2 1/21/25 · 87369 · — · — · — · — · ——

43. DEMON: *Do not weep, my child* (Arioso) (Rubinstein) (In Russian) (Or. Pasternack)
B-27023-1,-2,-3,-4 10/12/22 · 87370 · 963 · (7-22010) · — · 77.43 · VIC 1680; LM 20150; VL 47216

44. DINORAH: *Sei vendicata assai* (Meyerbeer) (I) (Or. Rogers)
C-14279-1 1/8/14 · 88366 · 6398 · 2-052088 · DB 178 · AGSB 91 · 76.00 · Rococo R16; TAP 324; VL 47215

Discog. No. Matrix No.	Date mo/day/yr	SF Victor Cat. No.	DF Victor Cat. No.	SF HMV Cat. No.	DF HMV Cat. No.	Special "78" Rpm Issues	Speed of Original	Transcription to EPs or LPs
45. DON CARLO: *Felice ancor io son...Per me giunto* (Verdi) (I) (Or. Sabaino)								
1318c	10-11/07	92038	15-1028	052190	DB 178	—	73.47	—
46. DON GIOVANNI: *Là ci darem la mano* (Mozart) (w. Graziella Pareto) (I) (Or. Sabaino)								
2728f	11/21/08	92505	8053	054229	DB 875	—	79.13	—
47. DON GIOVANNI: *Finch'han dal vino* (Mozart) (I) (Or. Rogers)								
B-14274-1	1/7/14	87174	938	7-52054	DA 357	—	76.00	—
48. DON GIOVANNI: *Deh vieni alla finestra* (Serenata) (Mozart) (I) (Or. '07 Sabaino; '12 Rogers?; '20 Pasternak)								
10914b	10-11/07			2-52625	DA 462	—	73.47	Rococo R16
B-12620-1	11/17/12	87112		7-52037	DA 357	—	76.60	LM20110; VL 47216
B-12620-2,-3	4/19/20	87112	818			—	76.00	
49. I Due Granatieri (Die beiden Grenadiere) (Robert Schumann, Op. 49, No. 1) (I) (Or. Rogers)								
C-15888-1	4/13/15	88527		2-052103	DB 242	—	77.43	—
E canta il grillo (From TIZIANELLO) (V. Billi—E. Bicci): See Discography No. 120 and 121								
50. E la mia dama (Stornello Toscano) (I) (Or. Sabaino)								
9214e	11/21/08	87147		2-52678	DA 169	—	79.13	CL 99-63
51. Elégie (based on Invocation from Les ERINNYES) (Gallet—Massenet) (F) (Or. Bourdon, Vlc. Lennartz)								
C-27750-1	4/11/23					—		—
B-27750-1	4/11/23					—		—
52. ERNANI: *Lo vedremo, o veglio audace* (Verdi) (I) (Or. Pasternack)								
B-25215-1,-2	4/13/21	87336		7-52208	DA 163	—	76.00	VIC 1680; LM 20150; VL 47216
B-25215-3,-4	4/14/21		818			—		

53. ERNANI: *O de' verd'anni miei* (Verdi) (I) (Or. Rogers?)
B-12662-1   11/27/12   —   —   —

54. ERNANI: *Gran Dio! costor sui sepolerali...O de' verd'anni miei* (Verdi) (I) (Or. Pasternack)
C-25212-1,-2   4/13/21   88660   6264   2-052225   DB 398   —   76.00   VIC 1680; LM 20150; VL 47216

*55. *E suonan le campane* (Ettore Titta) (I) (Or. Rogers)
B-14269-1   1/5/14   87138   933   7-52049   DA 356   —   76.00   CL 99-63

56. FALSTAFF: *L'onore! Ladri!* (Verdi) (I) (Or. Pasternack)
C-25217-1,-2   4/15/21   88637   6264   2-052199   DB 402   —   76.00   LM 20110; VL 47215

57. FALSTAFF: *Quand'ero paggio* (Verdi) (I) (Or. Pasternack)
B-27022-1,-2   10/12/22   87360   876   7-52224   DA 396   —   77.43   VIC 1680; LM 20150; VL 47215
B-27022-3,-4   10/13/22

*58. a) FALSTAFF: *Quand'ero paggio* (Verdi) (I); b) *Perjura!* (Miguel Lerda de Tejada) (Spanish) (Pf. P. B. Kahn or G. Moore)
OB-5460-1   11/25/33   —   —   —   —

59. FAUST: *Dio possente* (Gounod) (I) (Or. '06 Sabaino; '15 Rogers; '22 Pasternack)
792c   10/06   92043   6406   052133   —   77.43   Rococo R16; LM 20150
C-15893-1   4/14/15   (88528)   —   2-052104   DB 405   76.60   VIC 1680; VL 47216
C-15893-2,-3   10/18/22   —   6429   —   —   76.00   LM 20110

60. FAUST: *Rammenta i lieti di quando* (Gounod) (I) (Or. Rogers)
B-15889-1   4/13/15   87166   819   7-52070   DA 360   —   77.43   —
B-15889-2   4/14/15

61. FAUST: *Tu, che fai l'addormentata* (Serenata) (Gounod) (I) (Or. Rogers)
B-15890-1   4/13/15   87222   819   7-52071   DA 360   —   77.43   LM 20110; VL 47216
B-15890-2   4/14/15

Discog. No. / Matrix No.	Date mo/day/yr	SF Victor Cat. No.	DF Victor Cat. No.	SF HMV Cat. No.	DF HMV Cat. No.	Special "78" Rpm Issues	Speed of Original	Transcription to EPs or LPs
62. La FAVORITA: Vien, Leonora, a piedi tuoi (Donizetti) (I) (Or. Pitt)								
z6933f	12/24/12	—	—	2-052075	—	AGSB 91	80.00	Rococo R16
63. La FORZA DEL DESTINO: Solenne in quest'ora (Verdi) (w. Beniamino Gigli) (I) (Or. Bourdon)								
CVE-37319-1,-2,-3	12/17/26	—	—	—	—	AGSB 91	77.43	EJS 111
*64. La FORZA DEL DESTINO: Urna fatale del mio destino! (Verdi) (I) (Or. Rogers)								
B-15892-1	4/14/15	—	—	—	—	HRS 2015	77.43	Rococo R16 AGSA 10
65. La FORZA DEL DESTINO: Le minaccie, i fieri accenti (Verdi) (w. Emanuele Ischierdo) (I) (Or. Sabaino)								
550i	10/06	92504	—	054102	DB 177	—	73.47	EB 37
66. La GIOCONDA: Enzo Grimaldo, Principe di Santafior, che pensi? (Ponchielli) (w. Enrico Caruso) (I) (Or. Rogers)								
C-14273-1	1/8/14	—	—	—	—	—	—	—
67. La GIOCONDA: Enzo Grimaldo, Principe di Santafior, che pensi? (Ponchielli) (w. Beniamino Gigli) (I) (Or. Bourdon)								
CVE-37321-1	12/17/26	—	—	—	—	AGSB 49	77.43	EJS 111 17-0028; LCT 1004; LM 20150
CVE-37321-2	12/17/26	—	—	—	—	—		
68. La GIOCONDA: O monumento! (Ponchielli) (I) (Or. Sabaino)								
459ai	9/2/12	88396	6398	052376	DB 180	—	79.13	LCT 6701; CSLP 501; VIC 1680
69. La GIOCONDA: Ah! Pescator, affonda l'esca (Barcarola) (Ponchielli) (I) (w. Chorus) (Or. Sabaino)								
46lai	9/2/12	88394	6265	052378	DB 180	—	79.13	LM 20150; VL 47215
70. Il Gitano Re (Alfredo Gandolfi—Anthony F. Paganucci) (I) (Or. Bourdon)								
BVE-49961-1,-2	2/15/29	—	1401	—	—	—	77.43	CL 99-63

71. GUGLIELMO TELL: *Resta immobile* (Rossini) (I) (Or. Rogers)

B-14520-1	2/26/14	—	—	—
C-14520-1	2/26/14	—	—	—

72. *El Guitarrico* (Jota de Perico) (A. Perez Soriano) (Spanish) (Or. Rogers)

B-14275-1	1/7/14	87177	820	7-62013	DA 349	76.00	CL 99-63

*73. *El Guitarrico* (Jota de Perico) (A. Perez Soriano) (Spanish) (Pf. Percy B. Kahn or Gerald Moore)

OB-5464-1,-2	11/25/33	—

HAMLET: See AMLETO

74. LAKMÉ: *Lakmé, ton doux regard se voile* (Leo Delibes) (F) (Or. Bourdon)

B-29037-1,-2	11/27/23	1070	(7-52261)	DA 703	76.00	VL 47216

75. Lolita (Serenade) (A. Buzzi-Peccia) (I) (Or. Bourdon)

B-29034-1,-2	11/27/23	87393	1019	(7-52258)	DA 687	76.00	CL 99-63

76. MALENA: *Disse il saggio* (Ettore Titta) (I) (Or. cond. by composer)

10549b	5-6/07	87142	2-52624	DA 162	80.00	AGSA 20	Rococo R16; Scala 855

77. MALENA: *Ma tu sfiorata di rugiada gentil* (Ettore Titta) (I) (Or. cond. by composer)

10548b	5-6/07	87149	2-52623	—	80.00	AGSA 20	Rococo R16; Scala 855

78. Marechiare (F. Paolo Tosti) (I) (Or. '12 Sabaino; '23 Bourdon)

465ai	9/3/12	052383	DB 404	76.00	—
B-29038-1,-2	11/27/23	995	(7-52263)	DA 748	76.00	—

79. Maria, Marì (Vincenzo Russo—Eduardo di Capua) (Neapolitan) (Or. Sabaino)

1912ah	9/3/12	932	2-52829	DA 353	80.00	CL 99-63

80. MARTA: *Chi mi dirà* (Canzone del porter) (Flotow) (I) (Or. Pasternack)

B-25951-1,-2	1/12/22	87352	876	7-52225	DA 396	77.43	VIC 1680; LM 20150; VL 47215
B-27024-1,-2,-3	10/12/22						

Discog. No. / Matrix No.	Date mo/day/yr	SF Victor Cat. No.	DF Victor Cat. No.	SF HMV Cat. No.	DF HMV Cat. No.	Special "78" Rpm Issues	Speed of Original	Transcription to EPs or LPs
*81. Mattuttino (P. Mario Costa) (I) (Pf. accompaniment by Percy B. Kahn or (Gerald Moore))								
OB-5462-1,-2	11/25/33						——	EJS 223
82. Meriggiata (Leoncavallo) (I) (Or. Sabaino)								
9224e	11/24/08	87150	——	2-52685	DA 351	——	79.13	Rococo R16;
83. Mia sposa sarà la mia bandiera (A. Rotoli) (I) (Or. Bourdon)								
B-31696-1,-2	1/21/25		1076	(7-32093)	DA 748	——	76.00	CL 99-63
84. Munasterio (Salvatore de Ciacomo—P. Mario Costa) (Neapolitan) (Or. Pasternak)								
B 24111-1	5/13/20	87323	821	(7-521G9)	DA 350	——	76.00	——
*85. NABUCCO: Che tenti? Oh trema insano!...Tremin gl'insani del mio furore (Verdi) (I) (Or Rogers)								
B-14518-1	2/26/14	87194		7-52063	DA 358	AGSA 10	76.00	Rococo R16; VIC 1680; VL 47215
86. Non penso a lei (Ferradini) (I) (Or. '08 Sabaino; '12 Rogers?)								
9229e	11/26/08	87152	——	2-52680	——	——	79.13	——
B-12623-1	11/17/12	87121	933	7-52040	DA 348	——	76.60	——
87. Novembre (Paul Bourget—Edouard Trémisot) (F) (Or. Pasternack, Pf. Bourdon)								
B-24112-1	5/13/20	87343	820	7-32039	DA 348	——	76.00	CL 99-63
88. Oh che m'importa? (Ettore Titta) (I) (Or. Rogers)								
B-14519-1	2/26/14	87195	——	7-52062	DA 356	——	76.00	——
*89. OTELLO: Credo in un Dio crudel (Verdi) (I) (Or. Rogers)								
C- 14278-1	1/8/14	88466	——	2-052090	DK 114	6267 8045	76.00	LM 20110; VL 47216 EJS 142
Sound Film Disc	3/8/29							

No. Scene 1, 381-7 (a-134) 550 ft.

90. OTELLO: E qual certezza sognate...Era la notte (Verdi) (I) (Or. Pasternack)

| C-23948-1,-2 | 4/20/20 | 88621 | 6267 | 2-052181 | DB 404 | —— | 76.00 | LM 20110; VL 47216 |

91. OTELLO: Oh! mostruosa colpa!...Sì, pel ciel marmoreo giuro! (Verdi) (w. Enrico Caruso) (I) (Or. Rogers)

| C-14272-1 | 1/8/14 | 89075 | 8045 | 2-054049 | DK 114 | —— | 76.00 | 17-0025; LCT 1001; LCT 1004; CSLP 510; SP 33-75; RB 16128; LM 6056; ORL 312; VL 47216 |

92. PAGLIACCI: Si può? (Prologo, Part I) (Leoncavallo) (I) (Or. Sabaino)

| 462ai | 9/3/12 | 88392 | 6268 | 052381 | DB 464 | —— | 76.00 | COLH 155 |

*93. PAGLIACCI: Un nido di memorie (Prologo, Part II) (Leoncavallo) (I) (Or. '07 & '12 Sabaino; '26 Bourdon)

1341c	10-11/07	92040	6405	052192	——	——	74.23	
467ai	9/3/12	88393	6268	052379	DB 464	——	76.00.	COLH 155
CVE-34918-1,-2	2/26/26	——	——					

94. PAGLIACCI: Si può?...Un nido di memorie (Prologo, Parts I & II) (Leoncavallo) (I) (Or. Pasternack)

| C-24113-1 | 5/13/20 | 88392 | 6268 | —— | —— | —— | —— |

95. PANURGE: Je suis né...Touraine est un pays (Massenet) (F) (Or. Bourdon)

| B-27749-1,-2 | 4/11/23 | —— | —— | —— | —— |
| BVE-49966-1 | 2/18/29 | —— | —— | EJS 223 | |

*96. PANURGE: Je suis né...Touraine est un pays (Massenet) (F) (Pf. Percy B. Kahn or Gerald Moore)

| OB-5467-1 | 11/25/33 | —— | —— | —— |

97. PATRIE: Pauvre martyr obscur (Emile Paladille) (F) (Or. Pasternack)

| C-24620-1,-2 | 10/11/20 | 88643 | 2-032063 | DB 401 | —— | 76.00 | —— |

Discog. No.	Matrix No.	Date mo/day/yr	SF Victor Cat. No.	DF Victor Cat. No.	SF HMV Cat. No.	DF HMV Cat. No.	Special "78" Rpm Issues	Speed of Original	Transcription to EPs or LPs
98. *Perjura!* (Miguel Lerda de Tejada) (Spanish) (Or. Pasternack)									
	B-27025-1,-2, -3,-4	10/12/22	87394	1019	7-62053	DA 347	—	77.43	—
Perjura! (Miguel Lerda de Tejada) (Spanish) (Pf. P. B. Kahn or G. Moore): See Discography No. 58									
99. I PURITANI: *Suoni la tromba e intrepido* (Bellini) (w. Andrès Perello de Segurola) (I) (Or. Sabaino)									
	10906b	10-11/07	87158 87564	—	54360	VA 16	—	73.47	RococcoR16; TAP 321
100. *Querida* (Sigmund Spaeth, trans. George Godoy—Albano Seismit-Doda) (Spanish) (Or. Pasternack)									
	B-25214-1,-2,-3	4/13/21	87331	822	(7-62031)	DA 769	—	76.00	CL 99-63
101. IL RE DI LAHORE: *Le barbare tribù...O casto fior* (Massenet) (I) (Or. Pasternack)									
	C-24623-1	10/11/20	88639	6265	2-052190	DB 401	—	76.00	VIC 1680; LM 20150; VL 47215
102. *El Relicario* (José Padilla) (Spanish) (Or. Pasternack)									
	B-25950-1,-2,-3, -4,-5	1/12/22	87341	822	7-62050	DA 349	—	77.43	CL 99-63
103. RIGOLETTO: *Pari siamo* (Verdi) (Or. '07 Sabaino; '20 Pasternack)									
	1330c	10-11/07	92041	—	052191	DB 502	—	74.23	COLH 155; ORL 217; 17-0363; LCT 1039; HER 403; LM 20110; VL 47215
	C-23946-1,-2	4/19/20	88618	6263	2-052185	DB 402	—	76.00	
104. RIGOLETTO: *Ah! Deh non parlare al misero* (Verdi) (w. Giuseppina Finzi-Magrini) (I) (Or. Sabaino)									
	02535v	10/15/12	89058	8059	054396	DB 175	—	80.00	COLH 155

105. RIGOLETTO: *Veglia o donna* (Verdi) (w. Maria Calvany) (I) (Or. Sabaino)
4727h 10/06 91500 3033 54315 DA 564 —— 73.47
ORL 217; EB 37 & 78; Scala 855; ATL 4051; COLH 155

106. RIGOLETTO: *Povero Rigoletto! La rà, la rà...Cortigiani, vil razza dannata* (Verdi) (w. La Scala Chorus) (I) (Or. Sabaino)
2735f 11/24/08 92066 8054 052251 DB 175 —— 79.13
ORL 217; COLH 155

107. RIGOLETTO: *Miei signori, perdono* (Verdi) (I) (Or. Sabaino)
4733h 10/06 87151 937 2-52555 DA 165 —— 73.47
ORL 217; EB 78; Scala 855; ATL 4051; COLH 155

108. RIGOLETTO: *Ah! Piangi, piangi fanciulla* (Verdi) (w. Maria Calvany) (I) (Or. Sabaino)
545i 10/06 92502 8059 054100 DB 177 —— 73.47
HER 403; ORL 217; Scala 855; ATL 4051; COLH 155

109. RIGOLETTO: *No, vecchio t'inganni...Sì, vendetta, tremenda vendetta!* (Verdi) (w. Maria Calvany) (I) (Or. Sabaino)
4730h 10/06 91501 3033 54316 DA 564 —— 73.47
HER 403; EB 78; COLH 155; ORL 217

110. RIGOLETTO: *Oh mia Gilda! fanciulla...a me rispondi!...Lassù in cielo* (Verdi) (w. Graziella Pareto) (I) (Or. Sabaino)
2733f 11/23/08 92506 8053 054228 DB 176 —— 79.13
HER 403; ORL 217; EB 78; Scala 855; ATL 4051; COLH 155

Le ROI DE LAHORE: See Il RE DI LAHORE

Discog. No. Matrix No.	Date mo/day/yr	SF Victor Cat. No.	DF Victor Cat. No.	SF HMV Cat. No.	DF HMV Cat. No.	Special "78" Rpm Issues	Speed of Original	Transcription to EPs or LPs
*111. Ruffo speaks: Mock conversation with Chaliapin (In Italian; Ruffo speaks both parts)								
OB-5468-1	11/24/33	—	—	—	—	—	—	EJS 223
OB-5469-1	11/24/33	—	—	—	—	—	—	—
112. Santa Lucia (Folk song) (I) (Or. Bourdon)								
B-29036-1,-2	11/27/23	87383	995	(7-52260)	DA 687	—	76.00	—
113. Sei morta nella vita mia! (Guglielmo Capitelli—P. Mario Costa) (I) (Or. '20 Pasternack; '29 Bourdon)								
B-24109-1,-2	5/13/20	87342	821	7-52168	DA 347	—	76.00	CL 99-63
BVE-24109-3	2/18/29		1460	(40-2197)	DA 1120	VA 55	77.43	—
*114. Sei morta nella vita mia! (Guglielmo Capitelli—P. Mario Costa) (I) (Pf. Percy B. Kahn or Gerald Moore)								
OB-5463-1,-2	11/25/33	—	—	—	—	HMB-51	—	—
*115. Suonno 'e fantasia (La Canzonetta) (Cenise—Capolongo) (I) (Or. '12 Rogers?; '29 Bourdon)								
B-12658-1	11/27/12	87123	823	7-52029	DA 162	—	76.60	CL 99-63
BVE-12658-2,-3	2/15/29	†	1388	(7-52429)	DA 1049	—	77.43	—
*116. Suonno 'e fantasia (La Canzonetta) (Genise—Capolongo) (I) (Pf. Percy B. Kahn or Gerald Moore)								
OB-5466-1	11/25/33	—	—	—	—	—	—	—
117. TANNHÄUSER: Forier di morte, già il crepusco cade...Oh! tu bell'astro incantator (Wagner) (I) (Or. Pasternack)								
C-25216-1,-2,-3	4/15/21	—	—	—	—	—	—	—
118. THAÏS: No, il cuore tieni amarezza...Abimè! fanciullo ancora di rugiada gentil (Massenet) (I) (Or. Rogers)								
B-14267-1	1/5/14	87137	934	7-52048	DA 354	—	76.00	VL 47216
119. THAÏS: Ecco dunque l'orribil città (Massenet) (I) (Or. Rogers)								
B-14268-1	1/5/14	87143	934	7-52050	DA 354	—	76.00	VL47216

120. TIZIANELLO: *E canta il grillo* (Pastorale) (V. Billi—E. Bicci) (I) (Or. '08 Sabaino; '29 Bourdon)

9215e	1/23/08	87145		2-52679	DA 169		79.13	CL 99-63
BVE-49960-1	2/15/29		1460	(40-2196)	DA 1120	VA 55	77.43	

*121. TIZIANELLO: *E canta il grillo* (Pastorale) (V. Billi—E. Bicci) (I) (Pf. Percy B. Kahn or Cerald Moore)

OB-5459-1	11/25/33	——

122. *Torna a Surriento* (Ernesto de Curtis) (Neapolitan) (Or. '13 Sabaino; '29 Bourdon)

1911ah	9/3/12	87139	932	2-52828	DA 353	80.00
BVE-50959-1,-2	3/20/29		1401			77.43

123. TOSCA: *Già, mi dicon venal* (Puccini) (I) (Or. Rogers)

B-15891-1	4/14/15	87220	938	7-52143	DA 163	77.43

124. La TRAVIATA: *Dite alla giovine* (Verdi) (w. Maria Calvany) (I) (Or. Sabaino)

546i	10/06	92503	8055	054101	DB 176	73.47	HER 408; Scala 855; ATL 4053

125. La TRAVIATA: *Di Provenza il mar* (Verdi) (I) (Or. Sabaino)

9060b	10/06	87141	936	2-52529	DA 165	78.26	Rococo R16

*126. II TROVATORE: *Di geloso amor sprezzato* (Verdi) (w. Fosca Titta & Emanuele Ischierdo) (I) (Or. Sabaino)

10900½b	10-11/07	87157	54359	DA 462	73.47	OPS 401

127. II TROVATORE: *Il balen del suo sorriso* (Verdi) (I) (Or. Sabaino)

9059b	10/06	87148	936	2-52528	——	78.26	Rococo R16
B-12661-1	11/27/12					

128. II TROVATORE: *Per me ora fatale* (Verdi) (w. La Scala Chortis) (I) (Or. Sabaino; Chor. dir. Venturi)

9216e	11/24/08	87156	2-52687	——	79.13	Scala 855
9217e	11/24/08				HRS 2015	

Discog. No. / Matrix No.	Date mo/day/yr	SF Victor Cat. No.	DF Victor Cat. No.	SF HMV Cat. No.	DF HMV Cat. No.	Special "78" Rpm Issues	Speed of Original	Transcription to EPs or LPs
*129. Until (Edward Teschemacher—Wilfrid Sanderson) (E) (Pf. Percy B. Kahn or Gerald Moore)								
OB 5465-1	11/25/33							—
*130. Visione Veneziana (Barcarola) (Angiolo Orvieto — Renalo Brogi) (I) (Or. '12 Rogers?; '29 Bourdon)								
B-12659-1	11/27/12	87133	823	7-52030	DA 350			—
BVE-12659-2,-3	3/22/26						76.60	—
BVE-12659-4	2/15/29		1388	(7-52428)	DA 1049		77.43	—
*131. Visione Veneziana (Barcarola) (Angiolo Orvieto — Renato Brogi) (I) (Pf. Percy B. Kahn or Gerald Moore)								
OB-5461-1	11/25/33					HMB-51		—
Visiting Card to Chaliapin: recitation by Ruffo: See Discography No. 111								
132. ZAZÀ: Buona Zazà, del mio buon tempo (Leoncavallo) (I) (Or. Rogers?)								
B-12621-1	11/17/12	87114	824	7-52035	DA 355		76.60	VL 47215
133. ZAZÀ: Zazà, piccola zingara (Leoncavallo) (I) (Or. Rogers?)								
B-12660-1	11/27/12	87125	824	7-52031	DA 355		76.60	VL 47215

Notes to the Recordings

19. The 1933 recording was made at "His Master's Voice" Abbey Road studios, London.

23. The 1907 recording is with chorus. In the 1920 recording the orchestra includes harp, played by Lapitino, and piano, played by Bourdon.

27. In the New York recording (take 3) the orchestra consists of 4 first violin, 2 second violin, 2 viola, 2 violoncello, 2 clarinet, harp, bassoon, oboe, trombone, 2 cornet, bass, trumpet, tuba; including Schmidt, Lennartz, Keneke, Reitz, Barone, and Lapitino.

30. Ruffo made three sound film shorts called "Metro Movietone Acts" for MGM. Titles were "Titta Ruffo [Sings] Figaro," "Titta Ruffo Singing Iago's Credo from Verdi's Opera Otello," and "Titta Ruffo as Nelusko, the Slave, in Meyerbeer's L'africaine." The sound was recorded on 16" discs at 33.33 rpm, probably in New York. The first showing of the Barbiere excerpt seems to have been at the Sam H. Harris Theater, New York, on April 24, 1929. This date would not be in conflict with the date on the disc which is given as Feb. 28, 1929. The Otello disc is dated March 8, 1929. The dates of copyright appear to have been about a year later. The sound from these two film discs has been transferred to an LP disc, listed here (nos. 30 and 89), while that from the Africaine has apparently not yet made its way to disc.

32. Take 3 was issued on a 45 rpm disc only as a special Christmas gift edition in 1950.

33. The 1908 Milan version contains the second verse only. The 1923 Victor recordings were sung in French, without a chorus, and the orchestra was conducted by Rosario Bourdon.

34. The role of Chatterton was originally written for a tenor. The aria has been transposed down.

39. This recording is known to exist in private pressings.

40. The composer, Ettore Titta, was Ruffo's brother.

41. Sung half tone low to score.

55. Take 3 shown in error on some copies of 933.

58. Recorded at "His Master's Voice" Abbey Road studios, London. The recording books show that both Percy B. Kahn and Gerald Moore took part in the session of Nov. 25, 1933, but do not indicate which artist played for which recording! The recording books show the title *Perjura* but indicate the composer as "Seismit-Doda" who was the composer of another Ruffo favorite, *Querida*. It is presumed that the title listing is correct. One verse of *Perjura* could stand alone as a companion piece to the short FALSTAFF excerpt.

64. Sung one whole tone low to score, in E; a standard transposition approved by Verdi. Unpublished, except as a special Club issue. (Ruffo makes some errors in notation near the middle of the aria.)

73. Recorded at "His Master's Voice" Abbey Road studios, London. Both Kahn and Moore were present at the session; the books do not show which played for this recording.

81. Same comments as Note 73.

85. Ruffo opens the record in the role of the High Priest, Zaccaria, sings an exchange of lines between Nabucco and Zaccaria, and concludes with Nabucco's aria, Tremin gl'insani.

89. See note to Discography No. 30. Numbers given are as shown on the disc.

93. Late copies of 88393 (those bearing the "Victrola" label) and all copies of 6268-B are mechanical dubbings, bearing the mark S/8, and are inferior to earlier pressings.

96. Same comments as Note 73.

111. Listed in the recording books as "Visiting Card to Chaliapin" which has been released on LP disc, the first part is a delightful bit of fantasy in which Ruffo imitates the speaking voice of Chaliapin in a mock conversation. The language used is Italian. The second disc is reported as "Chaliapin's Monologue on Mythology." The next matrix number was assigned to "Hamlet: Soliloquy (Shakespeare)" but no details as to the exact title or the language are known.

114. Same comments as Note 73.

115. The 1929 recording is sung one half tone lower than the 1912 recording.

116. Same comments as Note 73.

121. Same comments as Note 73.

126. Fosca Titta, the soprano in the trio, was Titta Ruffo's sister. Her name, like Ruffo's own, is found occasionally reversed in professional references.

129. Same comments as Note 73.

130. Same comment as Note 115.

131. Same comments as Note 73.

Bibliography

RUFFO TITTA, JR. and
ANDREW FARKAS

BOOKS AND ARTICLES

Aldrich, Richard. *Concert Life in New York, 1902-1923.* New York: G. P. Putnam's Sons, 1941.

Arnosi, Eduardo. *Titta Ruffo, el titán de los baritonos.* Buenos Aires: Ayer y Hoy de la Opera, 1977.

Barrenchea, Mariano Antonio. *Historia estética de la música con dos estudios más sobre consideraciones históricas y téchnicas acerca del arte del canto y la obra maestra del teatro melodramático.* 3rd ed. Buenos Aires: Claridad, 1941.

Biografia y juicio critico de Titta Ruffo. Madrid: Pérez de Velasco, 1912.

Blyth, Alan. *Opera on Record.* London: Hutchinson, 1979.

Carretero, José Maria. *Galeria: Más de cien vidas extraordinarias contadas por sus protagonistas y comentadas por el Caballero audaz* (pseud.) Madrid: Caballero audaz, 1943.

Castellan, Joëlle. *Spécial Monte-Carlo centenaire de la Salle Garnier, 1879-1979.* Paris: Opéra International, 1979.

Castro Cerquera, Paulo de Oliveira. *Um Século de Opera em Sao Paulo.* Sao Paulo, 1954.

Celletti, Rodolfo. "Titta Ruffo." In *Enciclopedia dello spettacolo.* 9 Vols. Rome: Le Maschere, 1954.

———. "Titta Ruffo." In *Le grandi voci.* Rome: Istituto per la collaborazione culturale, 1964.

———. "Titta Ruffo." *La Scala.* Milan, October 1958.

Celli, Teodoro. "Ricordo di Titta Ruffo il Caruso dei baritoni." *Epoca.* Milan, March 4, 1973.

———. "Voce di bronzo per personaggi terribili." *Carriere Lombardo.* Milan, July 8-9, 1953.

I Cento anni dei Teatro di Pisa (1867-1967). Pisa: Giardini, 1967.

Chiadò, Michele. "Titta Ruffo, 1877-1977." *Musica.* Milan, October 1977.

Confalonieri, Giulio. "Il figlio del fabbro 'teneva' una note per quaranta secondi." *Epoca.* Milan, August 6, 1963.

Contreras, Vicente. *Titta Ruffo y su arte: Biografia y estudio critico en dos idiomas del eminente barítono.* Madrid, 1910.

Cunelli, Georges. *Voice no Mystery.* London: Stainer & Bell, 1973.

D., R. "Titta Ruffo." *Musical Courier,* March 11, 1920.

Davis, Ronald. *Opera in Chicago.* New York: Appleton-Century, 1966.

Della Corte, Andrea: "È morto Titta Ruffo." *La Stampa.* Torino, July 7, 1953.

Duval, John E. *Svengali's Secrets and Memoirs of the Golden Age.* New York: J. T. White, 1958.

Ewen, David. *Musicians since 1900: Performers in Concert and Opera.* New York: H. W. Wilson, 1978.

Favia-Artsay, Aida. "Titta Ruffo." *Hobbies,* Chicago, October 1953.

———. "Titta Ruffo." *The Record Collector.* Ipswich, June 1951.

Farkas, Andew. "Titta Ruffo." *Opera*, London, August 1983.

Farkas, Andrew. *Titta Ruffo: An Anthology.* Westport: Greenwood Press, 1984.

Fitzgerald, Gerald. *Annals of the Metropolitan Opera: Chronology 1883-1985.* Boston: The Metropolitan Opera Guild/G. K. Hall, 1989. 2 vols.

Gaisberg, Frederick W. *The Music Goes Round.* New York: Macmillan, 1943.

———. *Music on Record.* London: Hale, 1946. (Same as his *The Music Goes Round.*)

Gara, Eugenio. *Cantarono alla Scala.* Milan: Electa, 1975.

———. "Il nome di Titta Ruffo non fu scritto sull'acqua." *L'Europeo.* Milan, July 14, 1963.

———. "Ritrattino di Titta Ruffo." *Le vie d'Italia.* Milan: TCI, December 12, 1963.

———. "Titta Ruffo, fratello di Amleto." *Corriere della sera.* Milan, July 3, 1955.

Gentili, Alfredo. Cinquant'anni dopo... (*Il Regio teatro Verdi nei suoi ricordi*). Pisa, 1915.

Giuntini, Renato. "Sentì una sola volta Turiddu e si scoperse una voce di rara bellezza." *Historia.* Milan, August 1974.

Gobbi, Tito. *My Life.* London: Macdonald and Jane's, 1979; Garden City, N.Y.: Doubleday, 1980.

Gunsbourg, Raoul. *Cent ans de souvenirs... ou presque.* Monte Carlo: Rocher, 1959.

Jellinek, George. "Ruffo and Rigoletto." *Metropolitan Opera House Program.* New York, October 1964.

———. "Ruffo in Retrospect." *The Saturday Review,* New York, August 29, 1953.

Kesting, Jürgen. *Die grossen Sänger.* Düsseldorf: claassen, 1986, 3 vols.

Kolodin, Irving. *The Metropolitan Opera 1883-1966.* New York: A. A. Knopf, 1966.

Lancelotti, Arturo. *Le voci d'oro.* Rome: Fratelli Palombi, 1942, 1953.

Lauri-Volpi, Giacomo: *A viso aperto.* Rome: "Corbaccio," 1954.

———. *Incontri e scontri.* Rome: Bonavita, 1971.

———. *Voci parallele.* Milan: Garzanti, 1955, 1960. (3rd ed., Bologna: Bongiovanni, 1977.)

Legge, Walter. "Titta Ruffo." Part I, *The Gramophone.* London, October 1928. Part II, *The Gramophone.* London, November 1928.

Less, Aleksandr. "Immortal Recordings of Titta Ruffo." *For Record Lovers.* Moscow, February 8, 1972 (in Russian).

———. "Razgovor s Titta Ruffo." In *Vtoroia stikhiia: Rasskazy.* Moscow, 1969.

Liburdi, Daniela. *Titta Ruffo: I costumi teatrali.* Pisa: Teatro di Pisa, 1993.

Maggiorotti, Aldo. "Opera Stars on the Screen." *Record News.* Toronto, September 1956.

Marchetti, Romeo. *Mezzo secolo: Ricordi di un giornalista caricaturista.* Rome: Vittorio Ferri, 1940.

Mathews, Emerys G. *Titta Ruffo, a Centenary Discography.* Penybanc, Llandeilo: by the author, 1977, 1981.

Meltzer, Charles Henry. "The Real and the Unreal Titta Ruffo." *The Independent and the Weekly Review,* October 8, 1921.

Monaldi, Gino, *Cantanti celebri.* Rome: Tiber, 1929.

Montale, Eugenio. *Prime alla Scala.* Milan: Mondadori, 1981. (Contains his "Un ricordo di Titta Ruffo.")

———. "Un ricordo di Titta Ruffo." *Corriere d'informazioni.* Milan: July 5, 1958.

Moore, Edward C. *Forty Years of Opera in Chicago.* New York: Horace Liveright, 1930.

Moore, Grace. *You Are Only Human Once.* New York: Doubleday, Doran, 1944.

Mouchon, Jean-Pierre. *Les Enregistrements du Baryton Titta Ruffo: Guide Analytique.* Préface du Dr. Ruffo Titta, Jr. Marseille: Académie Régionale de Chant Lyrique, 1990.

Mouchon, Jean-Pierre. *Les Enregistrements du Baryton Titta Ruffo: Guide Analytique.* Préface et Chronologie du Dr. Ruffo Titta, Jr. Marseille: Académie Régionale de Chant Lyrique, 1991. 3rd edition.

Natan, Alex. *Primo uomo: Grosse Sänger der Oper.* Basel: Basilius, 1963.

Núñez y Dominguez, Roberto. *Descorriendo el telón; cuarenta años de teatro en Mexico.* Madrid: Graficas Editorial Rollán, 1956.

Pahlen, Kurt. *Great Singers from the Seventeenth Century to the Present Day.* Translated by Oliver Coburn. London: W. H. Allen, 1973; New York: Stein and Day, 1974.

Patrón Marchand, Miguel. *100 grandes cantantes del pasado.* Santiago: Andrés Bello, 1990.

Peeler, Clare P. "Ruffo Titta—His Personality." *Musical America,* December 27, 1913.

Perez Lugin, Alejandro. *De Titta Ruffo á la fons Pasando por Machaquito.* Madrid: Tovar, 1912.

Pleasants, Henry. *The Great Singers.* New York: Simon & Schuster, 1966; London: Gollancz, 1974.

Ponselle, Rosa, and Drake, James A. *Ponselle: A Singer's LIfe.* Garden City: Doubleday, 1982.

Roeseler, Albrecht. *Eine kleine Lachmusick: Musikeranekdoten aus unserer Zeit.* Munich: Piper, 1971.

Rosenthal, Harold D. *Two Centuries of Opera at Covent Garden.* London: Putnam, 1958.

Ruffo, Titta. *La mia parabolda: Memorie.* Milan: Fratelli Treves, 1937.

———. *La mia parabola: Memorie.* Rome: Staderini, 1977.

———. *Parabola moei zhizni: Vospominaniia.* Translated by A. D. Bushen. Leningrad: Muzyka, 1968.

Saltzman, Leopold. "The Victor Café." *Opera News,* February 19, 1966.

Santi, Piero. "Dieci anni fa moriva Titta Ruffo grandissimo artista e sincero democratico." *Avanti!* Rome, July 6, 1963.

Sassone, Felipe. *La rueda de mi fortuna: Memorias.* Madrid: Aguilar, 1958.

Schauensee, Max de. "The Lion of Pisa." *Opera News.* New York, April 8, 1967.

Schwarzkopf, Elisabeth. *On and off the Record.* New York: Charles Scribner's Sons, 1982. (Contains Part I of Walter Legge's 1928 article—q.v.)

Scott, Michael. *The Record of Singing to 1914.* London: Duckworth, 1977; New York: Scribner's Sons, 1977.

———. *The Record of Singing, Volume Two: 1914-1925.* London: Duckworth, 1979; New York: Holmes & Meier, 1979.

Seltsam, William H. *Metropolitan Opera Annals: A Chronicle of Artists and Performances.* New York: H. W. Wilson, 1947.

Steane, John. *The Grand Tradition: Seventy Years of Singing on Record.* London: Duckworth, 1974; New York: Charles Scribner's Sons, 1974.

Tartoni, Guido. "Titta Ruffo, un leone che non belò nemmeno per un milione di dollari." *Musica e dischi.* Milan, January 1967.

Tegani, Ulderico. *Cantanti di una volta.* Milan: Valsecchi, 1945.

Titta, Ruffo. See Ruffo, Titta.

Titta, Ruffo, Jr. "Titta Ruffo in Privato." *The Record Collector,* Longshots Close, Broomfield, 1990.

Tuggle, Robert. *The Golden Age of Opera.* New York: Holt, Rinehart and Winston, 1983.

Valenti Ferro, Enzo. *Las voces: Teatro Colón, 1908-1982.* Buenos Aires: Arte Gaglianone, 1983.

Vehanen, Kosti. *Efter applåderna.* Göteborg: Aktiebolaget Bokförmedlingen, 1946.

———. *Rapsodia elämastä.* Porvoo: W. Söderstrom, 1956.

Walsh, T. J. *Monte Carlo Opera 1879-1909.* Dublin: Gill & Macmillan, 1975.

Wayner, Robert J. *What Did They Sing at the Met?* 3rd ed. New York: Wayner, 1981.

Wolf, Albert. "Titta Ruffo." *The Record Collector.* Ipswich, May 1947.

COMMEMORATIVE LECTURES

Alisedo Gonzales, Horacio; Costa Valenti, Pedro; Serra Lima, Ivan. Buenos Aires, Teatro Colón, November 7, 1953.

Dell'Ira, Gino. Pisa, Teatro Verdi, July 5, 1973.

Gara, Eugenio. Florence, Teatro Comunale, July 5, 1963 (published in *Discoteca*, no. 34, 1963).

Gualerzi, Giorgio. Pisa, Teatro Verdi, December 16, 1963.

Mariani, Renato. Pisa, Teatro Verdi, July 5, 1954.

Novotny, Antonin. Prague, January 24 and March 30, 1954.

RECORD NOTES
(with LP record numbers)

Caputo, Pietro (RCA VL 47216), in Italian.

Celletti, Rodolfo. Titta Ruffo, a Biographical and Critical Memoir (COLH 155).

————. (RCA Victor LM 20110).

Favia-Artsay, Aida (Rococo R 16).

Höslinger, Clemens (Court Opera Classics CO 321-323), in German.

Jellinek, George (RCA VIC 1680).

Lebow, Bernard (Scala 855).

Salwitz, Bruno (EMI 3C 065-00749), in Italian.

Smith, Edward (Top Artist Platerrs T 309).

Soprano, Franco (RCA LM 20150), in Italian

Tassart, Maurice (EMI Falp 500039), in French.

UNPUBLISHED BOOKS

Less, Aleksandr. "Prisoner of perfection." (In Russian.) Detailed illustrated biography of Titta Ruffo. Unpublished due to the death of the author in 1972, at the time he was about to deliver the manuscript to the printer. The whereabouts of the manuscript is unknown.

Ruffo, Titta. *La mia parabola: Memorie.* English translation completed by George L. Nyklicek (1965). Second English translation completed by Emerys G. Mathews (1982).

WORKS BASED ON THE LIFE OF TITTA RUFFO

Brocchi, Virgilio. *Il posto nel mondo.* Rome and Milan: Mondadori, 1921.

————. "La razza." In *Gioia di raccontare: Due romanzi.* Milan: Mondadori, 1935.

Kuprin, Aleksandr Ivanovich. "Solovei." In *Sobranie sochinenii.* Vol. 6 *Proizvendeniia 1899-1937.* Moscow: Gos. Izd. Khudozhestvennoi Literatury, 1958.

Index

Photo Sources

Enio Vitali (5), Matzene Studio (26, 31, 32, 43, 44, 48, 49), Carlo Edwards (33), Vaudamm Studio (35), Ermini (38), Frans van Riel (39), H. A. Atwell (45), Manrique & Company - Caracus (50), Vasquese (60), Langfier, Ltd. - London (61), Metropolitan Opera Association (62), Zuretti & Fiorini (68).

All photographs are from the private collections of Ruffo Titta, Jr., Kurt Binar, Andrew Farkas, and Horacio Sanguinetti.

GREAT VOICES

Volumes published in this series:

Ruffo: My Parabola
Tebaldi: The Voice of an Angel